Shell Connections 2005

NEW PLAYS
FOR YOUNG PEOPLE

00208659

D1635621

Connections Series

Shell Connections 2005

**NEW PLAYS
FOR YOUNG PEOPLE**

A copy of
Shell Connections 2003, Shell Connections 2004
and
Shell Connections 2005
*has been placed in every secondary school
in the UK through the generous support of
The Foyle Foundation*

faber and faber

First published in 2005
by Faber and Faber Limited
3 Queen Square London WC1N 3AU

Typeset by Country Setting, Kingsdown, Kent CT14 8ES
Printed in England by Mackays of Chatham plc, Chatham, Kent

Information regarding applications for performance
will be found preceding the individual plays

A CIP record for this book is available from the British Library

0-571-22882-8

2 4 6 8 10 9 7 5 3 1

Contents

Introduction

This year's *Connections* anthology is as imaginative and thought-provoking as ever. Settings include a spooky Venetian piazza, a suicide chatroom, an ancient city in Japan and a Young Offenders' Insitution . There are strange and surreal tales of justice and of madness, a bold stand for teenage rebellion, flights of fancy and heroic fights against insuperable odds. This seventh volume aims, as before, to provide the best scripts by the best writers for and about teenagers.

We hope you'll dip into them all, and better still stage productions of the works that grab you. You'll see you have a lot of choice among the ten plays. The first, Isabel Wright's *Blooded*, is the story of a group of girls facing adulthood and leaving adolescence behind over the period of one long summer. They struggle between themselves and find childhood fracturing against the backdrop of the murder of a local girl

In *Burn* by Deborah Gearing Birdman is a reluctant loner in foster care. His attempts to befriend local kids lead him to take a girl on a date in a stolen car. One day, on the river bank, the group of friends he so wanted to be part of tell the story of his last day on earth.

The possibility of danger, torment and even death continues with *Chatroom* by Enda Welsh. This is about three fifteen-year-old boys and three fifteen-year-old girls who gather in various internet chatrooms to talk nonsense to each other. Boredom and frustration lead to two of them turning on the quieter one. They decide to talk him into killing himself.

Citizenship by Mark Ravenhill is a bittersweet comedy about growing up. A teenage boy has a recurring dream in which he is kissing a shadowy figure. The trouble is, he can't tell if it's male or female. Help in sorting out this crisis is unforthcoming, even from the most obvious of sources.

Ali Smith's play, *Just,* is about a girl called Victoria who has been accused of a very British crime: there's a body onstage stabbed in the back with a pointed umbrella. The townspeople accuse her of writing on the leaves of their pot plant. Here is a fast and spooky satire on contemporary justice.

Just as mysterious is *Lunch in Venice* by Nick Dear. It tells of a perfectly lovely cultural trip by a group of sixth-formers that isn't everything it seems. Something is decidedly weird on the Rialto. Venice, possibly the most sad, beautiful and macabre city in Europe, is as much a character in this play as the teenagers and the acrobats who appear to them.

Andrew Payne's *Mugged* is about a group of schoolkids who every day hesitate to cross the park because of a thuggish group of older boys. Marky, in a foolhardy act of gallantry, offers to retrieve Soph's mobile from them and ends up stabbed to death. Dig wrestles with his conscience. To save his dead friend's reputation, he must tell the truth about the killing. But he needs to consider the risk he'll be taking.

Samurai by Geoffrey Case is an epic adventure story. Yuki saves the ancient city of Utagowa from famine by bringing the citizens a magical sword which will give them exactly what they ask for. The trouble is, it's only on loan. The story tells how he and the young empress fight to return it to the god-like golden army of samurai in the northern forests.

Seventeen, the title of Michael Gow's play, is the age his central character, Ella, is about to turn in one week.

A few days before her birthday, a strange group of people appears on the street, then at her door. It turns out they're relatives coming to prepare her for her birthday – alarmingly, in her family people sometimes go mad at seventeen.

Catherine Johnson's *Through the Wire*, is a musical by the writer of *Mama Mia*. Here various levels of criminal and anti-social behaviour have seen Dan, Rashid, Max, Scott, Ant and Philip wind up in Stoke Leigh Young Offenders' Institution. Their only contact with family and friends is the weekly visit. Today is the visiting hour none will forget. Here is a musical with fun and irreverent lyrics set to existing songs by Frankee, the Spice Girls and many more.

All ten plays have been workshopped and performed extensively by the schools, colleges and youth theatres listed at the back of this book. In the autumn of 2004 each group was asked to choose one of the works. They workshopped the piece at a retreat hosted by Bath Theatre Royal over a long, riotous and creative weekend. Each session has been recorded and the notes and exercises are here in this anthology for you to read and try out for yourselves. We are grateful to the fabulous list of facilitating directors, the note-takers and the participants whose observations and ideas they have generously allowed us to pilfer. We're also grateful to Jim Mulligan for providing insightful interviews with all ten authors.

As I write, in spring 2005, some three hundred premieres of the work are due to take place, and each show will be visited by one of the *Connections* team and receive a detailed report. Most shows will become part of the ongoing festival to be launched in March by Everyman Palace Theatre, Cork, and Plymouth Theatre Royal, continuing through April with The Castle, Welling-borough, The Garage and Playhouse, Norwich, Brewery Arts Centre, Kendal and, in May, Greenwich Theatre,

Watford Palace, Theatre Royal Newcastle, the Stephen Joseph Theatre Scarborough, Clwyd Theatr Cymru, Nottingham Playhouse, and Bath Theatre Royal, moving into June with the Old Vic, Royal Lyceum Edinburgh, Brighton Dome and the Lowry Manchester, before culminating here at the National in July, when all ten works will be presented.

The 2006 portfolio is already in development. If you would like to be a part of the programme, please visit our website at shellconnections.org.uk. In the meantime, I hope you enjoy this sparkling collection of some of the most exciting contemporary writing for teenagers.

SUZY GRAHAM-ADRIANI

National Theatre
March 2005

BLOODED

Isabel Wright

Characters

Amy

Lou

Donna

Fat B

Tess

The Dead Girl

SCENE ONE

The Dead Girl appears. She is sixteen, slim, pretty, with long blonde hair. She is dripping wet, covered in seaweed and strips of plastic and rubbish from the beach. She looks both grotesque and beautiful at the same time.

A girl, Fat B, appears. She is sixteen.

Fat B She's under the curve of the prom. A tattoo of sand gritted to her skin. She's blue and green and silver like a fish. I stop.

Fat B and the Dead Girl look at each other.

All the blood in me freezes.

The Dead Girl smiles.

She's perfect so she is. A mermaid. I want to hold her till she's warm. It's not real. It's not happening. It's a film. It's *Taggart*. I want it to stop.

The Dead Girl disappears.

SCENE TWO

Amy, Donna and Lou appear. They pace around the space in their own pattern of movement. Then, all together, they stop.

Amy We were all there that summer.
Lou Was a good summer.
Donna Was a shite summer.
Lou No, it wasn't!

5

Amy Ay, it was.
Lou So we were there that summer.
Amy Was an alright summer.
Donna Bit of booze 'n messin about.
Amy Waiting for something to happen.
Lou Something to happen.
Donna Anything to happen.

> *The lights flash on, blinding white. Amy, Lou, Donna and Fat B break suddenly into a dance routine, like the slick routines in videos. They do this with various degrees of panache, but without self-consciousness.*
>
> *The lights flash on again, blinding white, they freeze, then –*

SCENE THREE

Amy has a can of beer. She chases about the space, keeping it out of reach of Donna, who crashes after her. Fat B sits on the floor. Lou watches Amy and Donna helplessly. Amy opens the can of beer and lets it fizz out of the can, all over Donna. Donna screams and retaliates, grabbing a huge bag of crisps and stuffing them down Amy's neck, and grinding them in her hair. They struggle with each other, then Amy gets bored with it suddenly and breaks away.

Donna Ye bitch.
Amy Askin fur it.
Donna No get a shag smellin like a tuckshop, will I?
Amy No get a shag anyway.
Donna You can talk.
Amy Dinny have to fling it about, do I?
Donna Shut yer face, ye wee boy-girl. Ye wee scruffter –
Amy Shut yer own.
Donna You 'n whose army?

6

Amy Take you any day, Donna Delaney.

Donna I eat ye fur breakfast, Amy Matheson, and ye ken it. An I spit ye out for break 'n all.

Fat B Ye've wasted the beer, then?

Amy and Donna look sheepish.

Donna Was fun, but, Bernie. Was fun.

Fat B Ay, always is.

Amy and Donna look at each other and laugh, then tickle each other mercilessly until Fat B and Lou are forced to drag them apart. Then Amy and Donna turn on Fat B and Lou till all are helpless on the ground, exhausted with laughter.

Donna Where we going, then?

Fat B I'm skint.

Donna There's a surprise –

Fat B Canny help it!

Lou Somewhere good this time.

Donna You think of it, then.

Amy Go watch the game?

Donna Ay, get tae fuck!

Lou A film or something?

Fat B I'm skint!

Donna Youse are fuckin useless, you know that? A film? We're no wee lassies! Something good!

Fat B Something that's a laugh . . . 'n cheap.

Donna Ach, you're fuckin cheap.

Lou We do loads of good stuff!

Donna Like what?

Lou That's why folk always want to hang with us, eh? Cos of the stuff we do.

Donna I'd never hang about with any of that shower.

Lou We're the best, eh?

Fat B The best!

Amy Know what we'll do?

7

Donna What?

Amy Chum us to the hospital?

Donna Boring!

Amy Chum us up the top the scaffoldin then?

Donna You fuckin wouldnae!

Lou You can't!

Amy Can't stop me.

Donna You'll no do it. You'll be peeing your pants at the sight of it.

Lou You can't, Amy!

Amy Dare you then.

Donna Dare you back.

Amy Dare you what?

Donna Fuckin name it.

Amy You fuckin name it!

Donna Awright. Bet ye ma Gucci jeans you canny.

Amy Don't fuckin want them!

Donna They're quality!

Amy Nah, I'll do it for nothing.

Amy races off.

SCENE FOUR

Amy is climbing the scaffolding. The others watch her climb.

Donna See us at the corner.

Fat B See us coming at you.

Donna 'N you see them take care.

Fat B 'N you see them take cover.

Lou Cos we're something.

Donna Gonna be something.

Fat B Safe in the grip 'n the lock of what we've got.

Donna Safe in the smile and the shock of what they havnae.

8

Lou Safe in the same old.
Donna Same old.
Fat B Mad.
Donna Crashing.
Fat B Days of.
Lou Amy, Lou.
Donna Donna.
Fat B Bernie.
Lou See us at the corner.
Donna See us coming at you.
Fat B An you see them take care.
Donna An you see them take cover.
Fat B Cos they canny quite make it.
Lou Cos they canny quite break us.
Donna Cos they'll never fuckin be us!
Fat B Hard as they try!
Lou See us at the corner.
Donna There, looking skywards.
Lou Watching Amy, Amy, Amy, reaching for the stars.
Donna Watching the mad bitch clinging to the bars.
Fat B Watching her climb for all of us, carry us on her back.
Lou 'N she's there.
Fat B 'N she's made it!
Lou 'N we breathe.
Donna Took yer time.
Fat B 'N she's there!
Lou Tiny against the sky.
Donna Proving us wrong.
Lou Makin it alright.
Donna Showing off.
Fat B Takin us.
Lou Up, somewhere.
Donna On somewhere.
Fat B Wondering where we want to be.
Lou Amy in the sky wi diamonds.

Donna Cocky cow.

Fat B Amy at the top. 'N us wi her.

Amy is on the top of the scaffolding by the hospital. She climbs onto the roof.

Amy Into the world burst Amy followed by Lou, crashing an smashing at life and the world no a patch on us, into the world burst Amy, reaching up at the stars and almost almost takin them wi both hands. Into the heavens burst Amy, a mad girl and an eejit and a nippy wee bitch wi too much to say fur herself, but fighting fur Lou, and fighting fur the girls, and takin us all on whatever they say about us, cos we're made of steel, us, an the bullets just bounce off us, and we're out stalking the town and the way folk smile and talk means nothing to us, cos we've been there always, ever since Lou first opened her gob to say 'You're my bestest pal in the world', ever since Amy first opened her gob and took on all comers, ever since Amy took her first steps and hit the world running. Cos you can see the whole world fae here, and there's no bedroom ceiling crushing down on you, an there's no disappointed faces at every turn, you're a queen here, girl, and if you took off a step, the world'd catch you, the world'd fuckin catch ye and set you on its way! Cos if there is Amy, and there is Lou, and there is Donna and there is Fat B! If there is all that! If there is – us! Us! Then fuck! The world'll stop and let us pass when we're coming at it, and one day you'll be heading out of this pokey wee mess o' a town into something like a life, and there'll be no stopping you then, Amy! There'll be no fucking stopping you then! Hey! Hey Lou! Step out over the edge! And the world'll catch us, Lou! The world'll fucking catch us!

The sound of Lou screaming 'Amy!' echoes round the space. Lou, Donna and Fat B are staring up at Amy.

*The Dead Girl appears. She passes alongside Fat B,
who turns and sees her. Fat B freezes. They look at
each other. The Dead Girl disappears.*

SCENE FIVE

*Donna, Fat B, Lou and Amy are together. Donna is
staring at her face in a mirror looking for spots. Amy is
kicking at things.*

Amy You know what sums the whole thing up?

Lou What?

Amy *The Little Mermaid.*

Lou What?

Amy That book we read when we were wee. I hate that
fucking book – it used to give me nightmares.

Donna I don't know it.

Amy You do!

Donna I fucking don't!

Amy Disney did it. With singing fish.

Donna Oh, that thing.

Amy You've got this mermaid girl, right? An she cuts
about the water cool as fuck. An then she meets this
loser guy – he's a prince or something – isn't he a
prince?

Lou Probably.

Amy An then cuttin about wi the seahorses isnae enough
for her any more. An she starts on and on and she's
getting on the other mermaids' tits with her carryin on.

Donna I know the feelin –

Amy An then the only way to be with him is to cut off
her tail! An it's really fuckin sore to walk about on her
new legs but she does it cos she loves him, an it's like
the way my mum hobbles about on crap high heels!

Fat B How is it?

Donna Don't knock heels!

Lou Get old Imelda Marcos here –

Donna Who?

Lou She had a lot of shoes.

Amy All I'm sayin is –

Donna What the fuck are you saying?

Amy – the story sucks! An they shouldn't give it to kids!

Fat B The Disney one was alright –

Amy The point is – what the fuck's it meant to teach us? To cut ourselves up for love? Marry a prince?

Donna What the fuck's she on about?

Fat B Fuck knows.

Lou It's just a story, Amy, what's it matter?

Amy My point exactly!

Donna Eh? (*Beat.*) Hey, Fat B! Tell us how you found her on the beach again!

Lou You're a sicko, Donna.

Donna I know, but tell us!

Fat B No.

Amy I think I saw him.

Donna When?!

Amy I did! I walked home that night!

Lou Amy!

Amy Why not?

Donna You're such a fucking mum, Lou.

Amy Boysey was pissing me off trying to cop a feel, an I hate feelin you have to stay with some arse rather than go where you want! An I wanted a walk! The night was magic!

Donna You never saw him!

Amy I saw the car. White Mazda.

Donna You're no sure, though.

Amy Doin all this weird driving. Had to be him.

Donna You gonna tell the cops?

Amy Tell em what? An nobody calls them cops, Donna, fuck sake.

Donna My dad calls em fashies.

Amy You what?

Lou Like fascists.

Amy Oh.

Lou It could've been you, Amy!

Amy Why can't I walk home if I want to? If I'm with some bore or some plukey wee boy tryin to stick his tongue in?

Donna Don't get stuck wi plukey boys, then.

Amy Why shouldn't I walk?

Lou Cos you might end up dead.

Donna What were you doing on the beach that morning anyway?

Fat B Walkin Rizla.

Donna That fat wee pug!

Fat B He's not fat!

Donna His skin's three sizes too big for him!

Fat B Leave Rizla out of it!

Donna Calm yoursel.

Pause.

Fat B It's her funeral soon.

Lou It's a shame.

Fat B I'm gonna go.

Donna An I get called sick!

Lou You never knew her, B.

Fat B I found her! I sat with her! Called on my mobile and sat with her till they came!

Lou What did you do?

Fat B When?

Lou While you were waitin for them.

Fat B Nothin. Didn't touch her. Remembered that from the telly. Didn't cover her up or nothing. I wanted to! I wanted to cover her up!

Donna You just sat and looked at her!

Fat B She needed company. After everything.

Donna She's hardly gonna know you're there, is she?

Fat B How do you know? If that was me, and some bastard'd done that to me, and someone had found me lyin there, and they couldn't even look at me, and they left me all alone again . . .!

Lou What if he'd come back?

Fat B He wouldn't have.

Lou How d'you know?

Fat B They always crawl back into the woodwork.

Donna No gonna hang about to get caught.

Fat B Naw.

Amy Naw.

Donna Naw.

Lights change.

Amy See us at the corner.

Donna See us coming at them.

Lou An you see them stand back.

Amy An you see them take cover.

Lou Cos we're strong.

Donna Cos we're something.

Amy An they don't know what we've got.

Donna But they want it.

Lou See us coming at them.

Fat B Scared of what we might do!

Donna Scared of what we might become!

Fat B See us!

Amy An fear us!

Donna We can buy the world!

Amy Crush it underfoot!

Lou Take hold of anything.

Amy Take on the world and win.

Lou An they know it!

Donna They can see it.

Fat B An you see them looking at each other.

Amy You see em stop an wonder.
Donna When it happened.
Lou Cos we were wee lassies.
Amy 'They were such nice wee lassies.'
Donna And now we wipe em out with a look.
Amy Slice through em.
Donna With a sneer or something.
Fat B We can be whatever the hell we want and they
    know it!
Amy And they don't quite cut it.
Lou They see us coming at them.
Amy An they move out the way!

SCENE SIX

The light focuses in on Amy and Lou.

Lou I've known Amy since for ever, see?
Amy Into the world burst Amy, closely followed by Lou!
Lou Since . . . for ever . . . since . . . first day of nursery.
    Me and Amy met in the sandpit.
Amy Doctor Lou. Our baby genius.
Lou She was so cool.
Amy A double act.
Lou She had good bunches.
Amy Dangerous.
Lou Funky dungarees.
Amy Flyin down the prom on a shared pair o' skates.
Lou And this wee boy comes up and tries to muscle in.
    He's got a whiny wee voice, and no one's ever said no
    to him his whole four years of life.
Amy Sling an arm round Lou.
Lou Cos I'm hers and she's mine. She lets fly a look.
    Like . . .
Amy This sandpit aint big enough for the two of us.

Lou Wee gnaff doesn't get the hint. So she gives him the biggest shove, and he goes reelin back, his arms flyin, and the look on his face! Then I knew what she was! Magic! And that was us.

Amy Stuck together.

Lou Like glue. Like cement. Like for ever. Nothing gettin past us, eh, Amy? Nothin in this world.

There is a flash of white light and Lou and Amy freeze, stuck in a pose for a photo-booth photo, then –

SCENE SEVEN

Amy is moving about, she has condoms blown up like balloons, is hitting them into the air. She grabs Lou round the neck and blows a raspberry into her ear, then hits a condom balloon to her.

Lou Did you buy them?

Amy Don't be daft! Old hackitface gave us them.

Lou In class?

Amy Told her I'd been shaggin away since I was ten. Could've been too, Donna has been . . . pretty much.

Lou No, she hasn't!

Amy Well, whatever. Told her I was too skint to buy them and I'd go right home and get pregnant just to show her. Told her she shouldnae sit there with that moralising face on her. Told her she should just fuckin give us what we need to keep safe and say nothin. I said fuck 'n all!

Lou You didn't!

Amy I did!

Lou But you don't even need them, Amy!

Amy She doesn't know that! I'm your fear, I says! My great ambition is to have a baby and beat the council-flat queue! They'll get the joke, I figured. They'll say,

you're sharp, Amy, ironic. You can be a brain surgeon,
a physicist, a UN ambassador like Geri Spice (you're
fuckin jokin, man). But she thought I meant it. She
says, 'You're capable of anything,' An I says, 'Ay,
I am!' Just fuckin wait 'n see!

Lou What'll they do to you?

Amy Dunno. Big chat about 'my language and attitude
in the classroom situation', I expect.

Lou You're a nutter, Amy!

Amy Ay, ay, tell me something I don't know.

Amy starts to roll herself a cigarette.

Lou Don't!

Amy What?

Lou What about your dad?

Amy Ach, he had a good old time before he went.

Lou snatches away the fag and crushes it with her shoe.

Hey, what're you doing?

Lou I'm not watching you die!

Amy Lou!

Lou Let's get some chips.

Amy Come on then.

SCENE EIGHT

*Light comes up on Donna. She is lifted onto someone's
shoulders. The others gather around her, crushed together
and laughing, pushed by the crowd and moving as if in
slow motion.*

Donna The summer of Tea in the Park! An we get a tent
and it's muddy as fuck! An you wake up in the
morning with inch-thick mud on your face! An just
when you think you've got through the day all clean

some wee eejit comes and splashes your best white
jeans or hugs you when he's muddy, just to be funny.
An the food's alright, but it's dead expensive, man!
Fuck me so it is! But when you're right there in the
middle of it! An there's so many, many people and
you've never seen that many people in your life all
together! An the sun's going down and it's rainin like
fuck down on you likes! But you don't care cos it's the
best thing ever! An there's a big man on your right
who's like a big fuckin wall! An there's a big man on
your left who's like seven foot tall, and then there's a
big wave when everyone gets swept right along and
you're in the middle of it! And Amy canny stand up
any more so you're draggin her to her feet. And some
wee gnaff's tryin to snog you so you're fightin him off
likes! An you've lost your sister long ago cos she had
to stand up the back by the kebab van cos of the baby.
But you can still see! And everyone's jumpin, jumpin,
and you're jumpin, jumpin, and everyone carries you
with them, and there's some big guy puts you on his
shoulders and you're high above everyone reachin
for the skies! An you're wavin at the camera an you
might get on the telly! An it's the best – the best – and
one day it'll be you up there onstage with millions and
millions of folk standin and wavin and thinkin you're
it! An that'll be you made, Donna Delaney! That'll be
you made!

*White lights come up bright like a stadium, and there
is the sound of a huge crowd roaring. Donna basks in
the glory.*

Fat B Don't even think of tellin her!

Donna slides down from their shoulders with a bump.

Donna Tell us what he said!
Lou Nothing.

Donna Tell us! You can't be feart! If Darren says something I want to hear it! To my face and not behind my back!

Lou (*mumbles*) He says you were his friend.

Donna What?!

Lou He was chatting up some girl and he says he's not had a girlfriend for a whole year and you were just his best friend.

Donna You're lyin to me!

Lou I'm not! I'd never!

Donna I'll kill him!

Lou He was all over her by the Slam tent.

Donna I'll tear him apart! An I'll tear her apart! Fuck! I loved him, Lou! I loved him! An it's all a lie, so it is! He's betrayed me! He's a fuckin Judas!

SCENE NINE

Lou We were all there that summer.

Fat B Scraping by.

Amy An scrappin with each other.

Fat B Feelin like the world was closin in on us.

Donna Feelin like no one really heard what you were sayin.

Lou Just this endless stream of words.

Fat B Like we were mad-mouthin underwater.

Amy Banging your fists against windows.

Donna Of the places you'd never get into.

Amy Smashing a fist.

Donna Through the glass that stops you.

Lou Trying.

Fat B Trying.

Lou Trying to be what they need you to be.

Amy Pulled in all directions.

Fat B House too small.

Amy An you too big.

Fat B Legs an arms sprawlin out through windows an doors. Stuck in a poky wee room, dreamin huge dreams.

Lou We were all there that summer. Amy and Lou.

Donna Fat B and Donna.

Fat B An Tess.

Donna An Tess.

Amy An Tess.

Tess appears. She is a fourteen-year-old Goth with braces, funny hair, DM boots and a tassle skirt.

Tess I don't want to be fuckin Barbie or Buffy or Dawson or Lara Croft! I don't want to be Kylie or Geri or Kate fuckin twinset Winslet! Or Kate skinnyhips Moss! Or Zoe chirpy Ball! Or Skeleton Beckham! Or whatever fake girlpower riot girl they're shovin at us next! Not fuckin Steps! Or Weepy Gwynneth! Or Britney sparkly-tits Spears! Or fuckin Louise!

SCENE TEN

Amy, Lou, Fat B and Donna. They are sprawled on the floor, arms round each other, playing with each others' hair, casual and comfortable in their physicality.

Fat B My auntie's put me on another diet.

Donna Yeah?

Amy Guess who I saw today?

Lou Who?

Fat B I'll do it this time I reckon.

Amy Scotya!

Donna What d'you get to eat?

Lou Who the hell's that?

Amy Primary Seven! You fancied him!

Fat B No carbohydrates. Just protein.

Donna You what?

Lou No I never!

Fat B It's what Jennifer Aniston does.

Donna Are you sure?

Amy You fuckin did!

Fat B It's true! You can have like – chicken – or fish – or –

Donna No bread?

Fat B Nup.

Lou Why would I have fancied him?

Donna No pasta?

Fat B Nup.

Amy He had a cool wee gold ring –

Donna No –

Amy An his hair was all cute and curly at his neck!

Fat B You can have like . . . bacon . . . but no toast,
    I guess. Or fish –

Donna But no chips?

Amy An he was dead mouthy.

Fat B I s'pose.

Lou You know a lot about it.

Donna Sounds like hell.

Amy Maybe I fancied him.

Fat B It's a bit confusing.

Amy Can't remember.

Donna Water's the way to do it.

Lou Thats more like it!

Donna Drink like twenty glasses a day.

Fat B I hate water.

Donna You don't hate it.

Fat B I do! I can't drink it!

Amy It's awful, that! You're so in love 'n that! You'd do
    anythin for them. Flunk something cos you're starin at
    them. Let em kiss you. Then six years later – you can't
    remember their name or nothin!

Donna Cucumber. Grapes. Lettuce. They've got nothin in them.

Lou You remember his name.

Fat B 'N they taste of nothing, 'n all.

Amy Yeah, Scotya.

Lou What kind of name is that?

Amy He took stuff! Scotya purse! Scotya bag!

Donna It's just hard, B.

Lou That's really lame.

Donna Face that it's hard.

Amy I never made it up!

Fat B Thing is, right? I don't eat much.

Donna No?

Lou Why's Spud called Spud?

Amy Cos he looks like one?

Lou That can't be it!

Fat B I eat less than Amy!

Donna She's always jumpin about.

Amy He's got a spuddy kind of face.

Fat B I eat less than Lou!

Donna It's how things are, I guess.

Fat B It pisses me off.

Lou He gets old and one day he runs into one of us and we're like, 'Spud! How're you doin, man!' And then his wife and kids look at him and go, 'He does look like a spud!' And then it's all fucked.

Donna Maybe we're just meant to be like this.

Fat B You think I'm stuck being fat?

Lou His kids are like, 'Fuck, Dad, they called you Spud at school! An you said you were cool!'

Donna I never said you were fat.

Fat B You call me Fat B!

Donna That's just a laugh!

Lou Fat B was dead funny last night. Dunny said something dead shan and she came right at him – she said – she said –

Fat B My dad used to say I was big-boned.

Donna Yeah?

Amy Never mind.

Lou No – I'll – It was –

Fat B I don't think about it mostly. It's other people make you think about it. An you just feel sick.

Donna Don't think about it, then. Maybe it's like boys . . . My mum says it's when you're not trying to fall in love that it happens.

Amy You never remember!

Lou It was dead funny anyway. Fuck. I hate that.

Fat B What about if you're thinking about it but you're pretending not to be thinking about it?

Amy I thought she fancied him.

Lou Fat B?

Donna I don't think that works.

Fat B Oh.

Amy Why not?

Lou Well . . . she's a laugh . . . she doesn't fancy anyone, does she?

SCENE ELEVEN

The Dead Girl appears, dripping in water.

Fat B I can't sleep for seeing you. Mermaid girl. Everyone's got stories for what happened to you. What did he do to you?

The Dead Girl shakes her head.

What did he do?

The Dead Girl starts to circle Fat B.

Did you see him coming at you? Did you know there was no way out?

The Dead Girl starts to look scared.

You had it all, didn't you? Perfect. Skinny. Bet you were clever. Bet you were rich. Saw your mum and dad on the news. Looked like they had money. They looked terrible. Cried for you. Think people would cry for me?

The Dead Girl smiles and shrugs, then disappears. Lou, Donna and Amy appear.

Everyone keeps askin who'll be next.

Lou We should be careful.

Amy Fuck careful.

Lou I clutch my keys when I walk home late from school.

Donna For what? So you can stab him with them?

Lou Maybe.

Amy Gives you a metal punch, eh, Lou? Get him in the balls.

Donna Stupid.

Fat B Dunny's brother's in the army. Took three guys out with a kebab!

Donna Shut up!

Fat B Three guys come at him and he just stays cool. Splits the kebab – pow-pow – blinds two of them. While they're stumblin round with kebab sauce in their eyes he takes out the middle one. Then he knocks their heads together, the two kebab boys. Three down, done and dusted.

Amy starts dancing round them as a boxer. The others are still laughing at Fat B, who is still acting out the kebab encounter.

Amy I'm sick of bein afraid! I can outrun anyone! Stand ready! Maximum offence. Maximum defence. Punch like you mean it, Mr Bailey says! Punch, punch-punch!

Boys get in fights, cause trouble. We're the ones who get locked up. Get the flak. It's like – your mum always goin on about us not hangin round the amusements.

Lou She doesn't like us hangin about there.

Donna Why not?

Lou Cos that wee lassie –

Amy Cos a wee lassie went missing there when we were six. But now why don't we hang about there?

Lou People have long memories.

Amy But we're old now!

Lou Ghosts maybe.

Donna Why d'you want to go there, anyway?

Amy I don't.

Donna So what's yer fuckin point?

Amy Youse never fight nothing! Youse just accept. You – (*to Lou*) letting all the teachers call you by your sister's name by mistake, and push you to do as well as her!

Lou What's that got to do with –

Amy Everything! Everything's got to do with everything!

Donna I don't get it.

Amy Naw, you never do!

Lou, Donna and Fat B leave Amy on her own, sit down in the corner. Donna pulls out a magazine.
The Dead Girl appears to Amy. They face each other. Then Amy starts to get scared. She tries to move away from the Dead Girl. The Dead Girl follows her, then disappears.
Light focuses on Lou.

Lou The thing with Amy is – her head goes racing on without you. And just when you think you've got what she's thinking or who she likes, she's off again. You can't catch her. Ever. And it's always been.

Voice Amy's wild!

Voice 2 And Lou's quiet.

Voice Lou's a good girl.

Voice 2 Keep her on the straight and narrow.

Lou But I don't want the straight and narrow! I want to go crashing off the track like Amy! I want the wild path off the edge of the computer screen!

Voice Lou'll do us proud.

Lou But you should see Amy run! Flinging herself out to catch some ball! Saying all the wrong loud things that are somehow the right loud things! You love her! She's . . . your hero! She's all you can believe in sometimes!

Amy appears in a pool of golden light. Then she gives a scream of frustration.

Amy Fuckhead comes – tries to squash me – to make me small. Fuckhead comes, with his baldy head and hair combed over. The world's so big and I want to tell him, 'The world's so full of things I want to do!' 'What is it you want to achieve in life?' he says. I want to climb mountains, be a fighter, run races, charge down streets with bulls, bungee-jump off the side of the world! I want to learn a million languages and make all the fuckheads in the world understand me. I want to put them all together and smash a big brick into their fathead faces, make them do something with the world! I want to be more than a mouthy cow! More than –

Voice Amy has a degree of intelligence –

Amy I want to take on the world and leave it shaking behind me! But I don't say all this! And fuckhead comes with his sad wee vest showing through his shirt and says 'You'll have nothing, my girl, unless you 'BUCKLE DOWN! BUCKLE DOWN,' he says, 'BUCKLE DOWN!'

The words 'buckle down' echo round the space as does Amy's laugh as she jumps down to join Lou. Donna is reading a magazine. Fat B joins her.

Lou Why'd you do it?

Amy Had no choice.

Lou You can choose what you say.

Fat B What are you reading?

Amy No, I can't!

Donna The way you shave your legs and how it reveals your personality.

Fat B You what?

Amy He was being a fuckhead and I couldn't stop myself!

Donna That's what it says!

Lou Amy . . .

Fat B How many ways are there?

Amy He needs to know! If I was a crumbly old fuckhead I'd want to be told!

Donna Loads.

Lou He knows what you think of him.

Amy He should!

Donna How often you do it?

Amy He should know that someone he's supposed to teach thinks he's a loser.

Donna Whether you start at the shins.

Lou Sometimes you have to learn to live with fuckheads.

Amy He doesn't know what he is!

Donna Whether you only go up to your knees.

Amy I mean, psychos don't think they're bad, do they?

Donna Bikini-line.

Amy As far as they're concerned, it's cool killing people, an just a wee matter between them and the victim and the rest of the world shouldn't get involved.

Donna Brazilian – what's that?

Lou Amy –

Fat B Please stop –

Amy And Hitler never knew he was wrong!

Lou What are you –?

Amy I know it's different! I'm just saying, fuckheads
should be told! Even if they're just little fuckheads, not
Hitler or anything. I mean, if no one tells them, then –

Donna Apparently I'm . . .

Lou He probably knows he's a fuckhead, Amy. That's
the thing.

Donna Vivacious and ambitious with a strong feminine
side.

Lou Fuckhead must be, what, forty? If someone's that
old it's too late to change. They don't need you
rubbing their face in it.

Donna D'you think I am?

Amy You always have to stick up for everyone.

Lou No, I don't!

Donna Here. Numerology.

Amy You do! You can't just hate someone, can you? You
have to find some way of letting them off the hook!
You can't sit on the fence your whole life, Lou!

Donna You have to add up your birthday, then add other
stuff – and I'm a nine!

Amy Nothing gets done! I sorted him out, alright? And
all the veins in his neck are standing out and I think
he'll have a heart attack or something!

Donna That's intuitive and romantic, see!

Amy Cos he knows he's a dinosaur and the future's me!

Donna You add up like a five and a three and a one and
a nine.

Amy We'll not grind them in the dust or nothing, the
dinosaurs.

Donna And eight and three and that's two.

Amy But they'll not be patting us on the head like
children any more!

Donna And then you add six –

Amy Cos we'll be taking control.

Donna And that's – oh, that's eight.

Amy Stealing it piece by piece!

Fat B It helps with your maths, anyway.
Donna Is that your phone?
Amy What?
Donna It's your phone.
Amy It's not – it's your phone.
Donna Is it your phone?
Fat B No.
Lou Don't look at me!
Fat B It's not my phone!
Donna It's somebody's phone!
Amy There's no fucking phone ringing, Donna!
Donna There is!
Amy/Lou There's not!

*A beat's silence while they listen for the imaginary
mobile phone sound, then stalk away from each other
in a sulk.*
*The Dead Girl appears. She is sobbing. She is
bruised. She stumbles through the space.*

SCENE TWELVE

*Donna is in her shoe-shop workshirt. She is applying
lipstick.*

Fat B You shouldn't be working all the time, it's not
    good for you.
Donna You can talk!
Fat B That's different. That's family.
Donna I'm good at it.
Fat B I know.
Donna I'm shite at school.
Fat B You're not!
Donna It's okay. I know how things are. I know how
    to make the guys want me and the women want
    what I sell.

29

Fat B Is that what you do?

Donna Course, I could make it to the top, maybe. If that – that –,

Fat B Arse?

Donna Yeah, if he'd move on.

Fat B Maybe we could like . . . tell his wife what he's like.

Donna She knows.

Fat B You reckon?

Donna She's divorcing him. He asked if I'd ever had 'a relationship crumble around me'.

Fat B You what?

Donna So I says, ay, I suppose I have.

Fat B Meaning Darren?

Donna Yeah, and he says, 'That is a baby grief compared to mine.'

Fat B What the fuck's that mean?

Donna He's always sliding up against me when he can behind the desk.

Fat B Eurgghh!

Donna Makes me run over to catch the bank before it closes and watches my tits bounce up and down like they do.

Fat B I hate that.

Donna His skin's all shiny like a cheese sandwich on a hot bus.

Fat B What a minger!

Donna He wears the best stuff in the shop and makes it look sad.

Fat B I know. It sort of hangs funny off him.

Donna An he thinks I want him. Thinks I sit at that cash desk dreaming of rubbing against him – fondling his Disney ties.

Fat B You're making me sick!

Donna I'll end up his boss. That's what he knows.

Fat B Couple of years and you can sack him!

Donna I know how to play him. I know how to play all
of them. It's how you get on, B, it's what you have to do.

Fat B I'm rubbish at all that.

Donna I'll sort you out, you'll see. A bit of hair-putty
and some attitude and you'll be fine. Get that job at
H and M. Anything.

Fat B You reckon?

Donna Just leave it to me. I'm your pal and I can get
discounts.

Fat B You're brilliant, Donna.

Donna You just need to say fuck off to your da and
sister is all.

Fat B Why?

Donna They hold you back, family.

Fat B Well . . .

Donna That's the answer, B, you know it is.

SCENE THIRTEEN

Tess One day it'll come up on the screen, the answer
you've been looking for. The reason why nothing
seems real. And till it comes all you can do is bang
your head against some majorvector AI wall and
scream for help. Cos it ain't coming in the shape of
Amy, and it ain't coming in the shape of Lou. It's
gonna be bigger than Bernie could handle. Amy says
she's free but she knows jackshit.com about freedom.
It's gonna be bigger than they can imagine. Bigger than
some kid finding out how to make bombs on the net.
It'll be minds falling down web-rings, sliding down
links into stuff they could hardly imagine. It's calling
into the darkness to find a whole colony of mutants
just like you. A whole new Zion calling you to it. And
there's nothing they can do to stop us. Nothing.

SCENE FOURTEEN

Amy, Lou, Donna and Fat B. Donna is absent-mindedly
walking through a dance routine she is making up,
humming a tune away to herself. Amy is hanging from a
part of the set. She jumps down and picks up Lou, slings
her over her shoulder and swings her round, Lou giggles
and Amy lets her down. Fat B is daydreaming. Amy goes
to Donna and starts to get in the way of her dance steps,
standing in front of her, trying to hook her legs out from
under her, and tickle her waist. Donna refuses to rise to
the bait this time and calmly gets out of her way.

Amy They're so fucking scared. Like we're some kind of
sponges or something. Like any old bullshit folk tell us
we're gonna take for the word of God. So it's like, give
a girl a c-card and make her a slag. Naw. Give Spud a
condom and he'd never know what to do.

Donna There'd be no one *for* him to do.

Fat B You hear about Spud in Maths today?

Donna What did he do this time?

Fat B They all dared him to ask Sweetface McKenzie
what masturbate meant.

Donna Did he do it?

Fat B You bet.

Donna Sad wee Spud.

Amy What did McKenzie say?

Fat B Sweetface tells him in his ear and Spud gets a
massive beamer and Sweetface turns to the class and
says, 'It's people like you that got *Captain Pugwash*
banned.'

Donna (*losing her rag finally and shoving Amy out of*
her way) What the fuck's that supposed to mean?

Fat B Fuck knows.

Donna I've gone off Sweetface. He's not that cute.

Fat B He is!

Donna And he says loads of weird stuff. That makes you think he just looks young and he's really dead old.

Fat B Like what?

Lou Like going on about TV programmes that were on in the Ark.

Fat B He can't help that, can he? It's better than pretending he likes something just to impress us.

Donna You lurrve him! You lurrvve him!

Amy It's a fucking mess, this world.

Lou What do you mean?

Amy Sometimes I get this fear, right? That one day we'll wake up all old and just as bad as the losers we slag off now. And we'll know there were all these times we could have done something to change things and we never. An we'll spend our days moaning about sex being boring, and not finding the right blinds for our windows, and we'll spend our nights shagging in front of 'Who Wants to Be a Millionaire?' answering questions as we come, saying, 'We love Carrie Bradshaw,' she knows how we feel!

Donna Let's never get old!

Amy Let's never get brain dead!

Lou Let's never have dinner parties!

Donna Or spend our Saturdays in Ikea!

Amy Let's never say, we should have changed the world, but there was never enough time!

Tess appears.

Fat B Hey, Tess, you alright?

Tess I guess.

Donna What're you creeping about for? Gave me a heart attack.

Tess What're you talking about?

Donna Nothing.

Amy Getting old.

Tess What's wrong with getting old?

Amy We're going to do something with our lives.

Tess I guess everyone says that at our age.

Pause.

What's for tea, B?

Donna (*mimicking her*) What's for tea, B?

Fat B Don't know yet. You hungry?

Tess Starving.

Donna stands behind Tess and impersonates her. Fat B almost laughs despite herself. The others laugh also. The mood is ugly.

Fat B Can I . . .? I'll just be . . . Give me twenty minutes, eh?

Tess Whatever.

Tess leaves.

Amy Headcase! We'll be different, you'll see! We'll say we'll do stuff and then we'll do it!

Lou It's okay, Amy.

Amy Fuckin weirdo.

Lou She's alright.

Amy You think it too! At least I say it out loud!

Lou How did it go today?

Amy shrugs.

What happened? What're they going to do to you?

Amy They want me out.

Lou They never said that.

Amy They don't have to.

Lou They can't kick you out.

Amy They said I'm not going to pass anythin the way I'm goin so what's the point? It's my decision, they said. But I've been warned.

Lou You have to stay.

Amy What's the point? Once they've started 'persuading' you out. Stamp failure on your forehead.

Lou You'll do it.

Amy What do you know? You never fail nothing! I can be smart sometimes, I guess. At least I tell myself . . . I'm a different kind of smart, a kind they don't get. But I go in they exams an I panic. All goes to goo inside my head.

Lou They brand me too. Keep on and on about what I should do.

Amy It's not the same.

Lou It is!

Amy It's not! We're different now! I'm nothing! We do all this talkin – like all we need is you an me an fuck the rest! But you know what the world's sayin to me? We want nothin from you's what. From you, Amy, we want nothing!

Pause. Lou gets something from her pocket.

Lou Here. It's for you.

Amy What is it?

Lou A friendship band. Look, I've got one.

Amy Cool! Tie it on me.

Lou ties it on, they put their wrists together.

Blood brothers!

Lou We'll be alright, Amy, I promise.

Amy Yeah.

SCENE FIFTEEN

Fat B I'm the last one standing. Get folk home. I'm the one they know is there when they're fucking out of their tree. Fat B'll be there. Big boobs B. Fat Momma. She'll get you up the road. Carry you to your door.

Carrying this fatsuit round all day. I'm just a dog or something. A wee fat pet they keep around. If I wasn't funny I'd be nothing. 'Hey, fat pet', I hear them.

Voice Hey, B! Hey!

Fat B It's all around.

Voice Rolly-polly-big-jobby-rollo –

Voice 2 Hey, fat girl!

Fat B It's what I am.

Voice Fat girl!

Fat B No face. No brain.

Voice 2 Fat B!

Fat B Just fat. And my auntie says –

Voice Your face is quite pretty.

Fat B An my auntie says –

Voice If you'd use a bit of slap.

Fat B An my dad used to say –

Voice 2 Don't start her caking it on! Mutton dressed as lamb –

Voice Fat pig dressed as –

Fat B There's always another girl following me. Skinny. Pretty. I see her in my head.

The Dead Girl appears.

She fits in. Could've been me. Daughter they should have had. Pretty big sister they should have had. Pretty wee pal they should have had. Can't be me now. I ate and ate an killed her.

The Dead Girl exits.

An my auntie says –

Voice People warm to her.

Fat B Like I'm a funny fat hot-water bottle. An my da used to say –

Voice 2 She's always got a joke in her.

Fat B Food keeps chasing you all day. It's all you can think of. An I never eat the way they do.

36

SCENE SIXTEEN

Lou appears. She is starting to dress the way Amy dresses.

Lou All I want is for Amy to see me . . . really see me . . . notice I'm there. When she hurts, I feel it. When she laughs, I'm on top of the world. But she's so busy taking on all comers. She hardly knows you're alive.

Amy comes flying into the space.

Amy Always had this thing like I should've been a boy. Let my dad down. Used to play footie with him, in my white patent-leather t-bar shoes.

Lou She just goes flying past you –

Amy I have a big mouth in class and my mum says –

Voice Watch they don't call you bossy –

Voice 2 Or strident –

Voice Or Thatcher –

Amy Or something.

Lou Everything she does – the way she flicks her hair, or blows smoke rings, the way she sits in a chair –

Amy And I think of the boy I should've been.

Lou – is just cool.

Amy And those rugby boys we grew up next to. We wait patiently in class for them to spit some half-baked sentence out! And everyone listens to them!

Lou She knows her place in the world!

Amy They never get called mouthy.

Lou Her voice low – like too many late nights and fags –

Amy An my mum says –

Voice Feminist.

Amy – is a dirty word that'll –

Voice 2 – get you nowhere but sent to Coventry.

Lou She was born knowing where she fits, I guess.

Amy And my mum says to wear heels cos it's –
Voice – playing their game.
Lou She always fits whatever she does.
Amy But I only like being quick and sleek on the footie pitch, and screaming at the top of my lungs, and running like a maniac, that's when I know who I am.
Lou She always just fits.
Amy That's when I feel at home.
Lou She's always just . . . perfect.
Amy I can shoot pool and shoot the breeze! Talk shit with the best of them! All these stupit girls around me – wee Britney types at school – silly wee skirts and wonderbras pushed up to here! Line them up against the dinner hall and (*Makes a machine-gun noise. Beat.*) But sometimes you feel you're getting it wrong – the battle. You talk like a guy, and run like a guy, but sometimes, inside you, you wonder if you're missing something.

Light changes.

Lou Here, Amy, here!
Amy What's up?
Lou I got something for you! (*Pulls out a locket.*)
Amy Why? It's not my birthday or nothing.
Lou Put it on! Look, it opens! You can put a photo in it.
Amy Oh . . . thanks.

Lou gives her the locket.

Lou It's just for . . . it was you, that's all.
Amy I can't, Lou.
Lou You have to! Please!
Amy You shouldn't give me stuff.
Lou I want to.
Amy Well . . . thanks . . . It's pretty.

Amy hugs Lou.

SCENE SEVENTEEN

Donna and Fat B rush into the space.

Fat B Where did you do it, then?
Donna Where d'you think?
Fat B At his house? Were his parents in?

Donna laughs.

Donna Imagine them walking in on you!
Fat B So . . . was it any good?
Donna Takes years to get good.
Fat B Yeah?
Donna Unless you're a natural . . . like me!
Fat B So? Tell me!
Donna Tell you what?
Fat B Tell me all about it!
Donna Nothing to tell.
Fat B He won't put it like that. He'll tell everyone.
Donna You think?
Fat B Everyone'll say they knew.
Donna Everyone'll say they did it with me too!
Fat B So you're glad? You don't regret it?
Donna I don't regret anything I do!
Fat B Course.
Donna Chocolate is better. My mum was right.
Fat B No!
Donna It's so hit-and-miss. A good cream egg you can depend on.
Fat B Think he will tell everyone?
Donna Who cares? Who cares what they think! You're a slag or you're quiet, that's what they all say. You're a girl to have tea with their mum, or you're a girl for sex. An havin tea's boring! Who cares? What are boys anyway? Load of bighead bufties!

Fat B Ratpack o' hassle!
Donna One-track mind!
Fat B Getting your tights down!
Donna Can't live with them!
Fat B Can't live without them!
Donna Bunch of knobs!

SCENE EIGHTEEN

Donna They start on at you again.

Voice How old were you?

Voice 2 When did you lose it?

Donna On and on at you. And the whole world's had sex. And the whole world did it years ago. And you're the last one in the world, so you are. And they did it. In a car or . . .

Voice 2 In the square.

Voice On the cold hard gravel.

Voice 2 Under coats at a party.

Voice In my mum and dad's bed.

Donna An some days you figure you're too square to show your face. So you talk the talk, like you've done it all too. An before you know it you've got a name.

Voice Slag.

Donna But who gives a fuck? It's better than being a –

Voice 2 Virgin!

Donna Every time I open my mouth I'm sure they'll find out.

Voice Virgin!

Donna And they all believe me, Fat B, Amy, Lou, all of them. And they're jealous.

Voice 2 Virgin!

Donna Sometimes I want some different kind of story.

Voice A car!

Voice 2 A bush!

Voice My mum and dad's bed!

Donna An I'll go so far with some boy, and then I'll
know I don't love him enough. He's just a wee boy
fumbling around. You're worth more than some crap
wee lie. He's not the one to be all open and scared
with. He's not the one to go there with. He never is.

*The Dead Girl appears silently behind Donna as she
nears the end of her speech. Donna looks her in the
eye and tries to take her on. The Dead Girl isn't
frightened of Donna. It is Donna in the end who backs
off.*

    *The Dead Girl exits. Donna is alone. She starts to
go through her dance-routine steps, starting slowly,
then getting faster and more frenetic, trying to work
out her feelings through the steps. Then she stops. Fat
B, Lou and Amy appear.*

Fat B They found her clothes, you know that? He
dumped them in a skip.

Lou Do we have to talk about this again?

Amy You afraid?

Lou It gives me the creeps.

Amy I'd have fought him off.

Fat B How can you say that? You think she never tried?

Amy The police did a drawing of what they think he
looked like.

Fat B He looked like a monster.

Donna Eyes like . . . holes . . .

Lou He probably doesn't look like that.

Donna What d'you mean?

Lou He probably looks normal. We probably know him!

Donna Shut up!

Fat B They've got everyone out looking for clues.

Donna What're they gonna find?

Fat B They can do stuff with tiny bits of fabric now, with
hair, or skin or –

Donna You watch too much fuckin *Cracker*.

Fat B It's what I want to do when I'm older.

Lou Thought you wanted to be a marine biologist?

Donna That was last week.

Fat B Stop taking the piss!

Amy They interviewed my uncle.

Donna What?

Amy He's got the right kind of car.

Donna What happened?

Amy He was with my auntie and half the bowling club that night.

Donna Oh. (*Beat.*) Imagine if it had been your uncle!

Amy What?

Donna Well . . . it'd be mad . . . exciting!

Amy Fuck off, Donna!

Donna It'd be crap for you, I know.

Amy You're unreal.

Fat B They have to find him. They have to.

Lou I'm scared.

Amy Why? There's always a rapist on the loose. What're we gonna do? Never go out? Never live our lives? It's a load of balls.

Lights change.

There's a moment where you know.

Lou Where you can feel –

Amy – yourself get old.

Donna There's a moment where you can feel –

Fat B – you've passed a line.

Lou And you can be one of them, one of the adults, one of the living –

Amy And you know you'll be one of them, one of the adults, one of the brain dead –

Fat B And you're scared.

Lou And you smile.

Donna And you want to run back.

Amy And you want to chase on.

Fat B There's a moment where you know –

Donna You're not a kid any more.

Amy And they'll keep trying to push you about.

Donna Mess you about.

Amy Fuck you about.

Fat B But they'll see it in your eyes.

Lou You know the score.

Fat B You're older.

Amy And you won't take any more of their shit.

SCENE NINETEEN

Donna and Fat B are together. Donna is putting on her make-up for work.

Donna See, Bernie, what the world wants is people who can sell.

Fat B You could sell me anything.

Donna I know. See, it doesn't matter if you're good at school any more. You can still make it if you're smart in a real way. In a money way.

Fat B Like you are?

Donna Like me. See, everyone in our year wants what I've got.

Fat B What's that?

Donna I'm cool!

Fat B Oh yeah.

Donna An that's what makes it these days. Not history, or writing reports on books. I'm getting it all ready, and then I'll get the hell out of here and down to London.

Fat B London? You can't!

Donna Why not? I'll take it by storm. I'll be bigger than Victoria Beckham.

Fat B You could be, you know. I can see it.

Donna See, I head straight down to their offices and
walk in the door. An I go, 'I can't sing, I can't dance, I
can't do anything. But I look like this. And I know
what sells.' And they'll see a look in my eyes like I'd
kill to make it. And that'll be me made.

Fat B That'd be so magic, Donna.

Donna I won't forget you or nothing. You can be my PA.

Fat B What's that?

Donna You look after me. Get all the stuff I need.

Fat B Oh.

Donna We'll get to travel the world! Imagine!

Fat B The whole world!

Donna Ay, the whole fuckin world cryin out for us!
That's what we'll have. What was that?

Fat B What?

Donna Is it your phone?

Fat B No, is it yours?

Donna Naw, mine plays Fat Boy Slim now.

Fat B There's no phone ringing.

Donna Yes there is!

They listen.

Fuck, I'm going senile.

SCENE TWENTY

Tess enters. She is reading The Divine Invasion *by Philip
K. Dick.*

  *Fat B goes to her. She tries to look her in the eye. She
tries to read the cover of her book. Tess moves away.*

Fat B Talk to me.

Tess What about?

Fat B About . . . stuff. Boys . . . homework . . . whatever.

Tess Don't start, Bernie. Don't start.

Fat B What?

Tess Don't give me that bonding shit.

Fat B Fuck sake, Tess.

Tess There's no point.

Fat B Tell me what you're reading.

Tess You wouldn't get it.

Fat B Tell me how today was.

Tess You'd just smile and pretend to know what I'm talking about and we'd both feel like shit. We just get on with our lives. What's it matter?

Fat B Don't talk like that.

Tess Why not? What's wrong with the truth? Eh?

Fat B Did something happen today?

Tess What d'you mean?

Fat B At school . . . I heard someone –

Tess Stop talking about me behind my back.

Fat B I'm on your side here.

Tess It was just . . . girls . . .

Fat B From your year?

Tess From yours.

Fat B Go on.

Tess Doesn't matter.

Fat B Tell me.

Tess Doesn't matter.

Fat B Tell me.

Tess I see them coming at me down the street. And right together – like they planned it – they burst out with this laugh, and it's like no laugh you've ever heard. It's like . . . animals or something. And they look at me so I know it's me they're after.

Fat B And then what did they do?

Tess They . . . walked on.

Fat B Maybe they were laughing at something else.

Tess Forget it.

Fat B Wait! I know it's horrible when . . .

Tess You know nothing about it.

Fat B Tess, wait –

Tess What do you know about not fitting in?

Fat B Plenty.

Tess You've got pals. All I've got is this stupid body that won't do what it should! Big breasts and no periods!

Fat B (*laughing*) Oh Tess . . . love . . .

Tess Don't fucking laugh at me!

Fat B I'm not . . . it's just . . . everyone feels like that!

Tess Just leave me alone! You don't get it! You don't get it at all!

SCENE TWENTY-ONE

Donna stands in a cold blue light.

Donna I sneak into the boys' bogs after school. Write up all the stuff they say about me.

Voice Donna's a whoor!

Voice 2 Donna's a tease!

Voice Donna'll suck your dick for fifty p!

Donna Donna's easy.

Voice Donna's a slag.

Voice 2 Donna's got a saggy bucket.

Voice And a face like a duck.

Voice 2 Put a bag on her head when you do it.

Donna I scratch it into the tiles. Cos fuck them. Nobody's done it with you –

Voice But we know someone who has.

Donna I'm the sure thing.

Voice 2 Easy.

Donna The Big Man initiation for every weak wee shite with a big gob and a tiny willy. They all do it. Word spreads like infection.

Voice I did it with Donna. (*Starts repeating this over and over till end.*)

Donna And I say nothing! I say nothing! Cos fuck them!

SCENE TWENTY-TWO

Lou appears. She is now dressed exactly like Amy.

Lou It was the summer it started. I was in New Look.

Amy Lou . . .

Lou And I saw this gorgeous wee top.

Amy It's not my birthday or nothing.

Lou It's bright. Magic. But they've made it that expensive.

Amy You shouldn't have!

Lou But as I was walking round town it's nagging at my brain, a wee voice in my head all day. 'It's hers, you know it's hers.'

Amy It's gorgeous, Lou.

Lou I found myself back there. Didn't know I was doing it. Happened so fast.

Amy Why're you giving me stuff?

Lou After that it happens again.

Amy Shouldn't spend all your money.

Lou I got good, bringing stuff to get the tags off. I did it in shops where the girls at school worked.

Amy It's lovely.

Lou They gabbed away to me before I did it.

Amy Really lovely.

Lou And they didn't know. Best buzz in the world.

Amy What are you like?

Lou Next to giving it to Amy.

Amy Lou . . .

Lou Next to seeing her smile.

47

SCENE TWENTY-THREE

Tess is alone.

Tess All you have . . . all the time . . . is opening your mouth and having folk stare at you. Like you're speaking some language they'll never understand. And it's like you've lived your whole life in some alternative universe, and been eating different food, and hearing different sounds, and watching different television. All they do is look at you with –

Voice Freak.

Tess – in their eyes. And they're scared cos they can't put you in any fuckin box no matter how they try. It makes them short-circuit or something. And every day, every single day, you've got a big hole inside you and you don't know what the hell it means. And then one day in some stupid corny film or some stupid TV programme some stupid character says –

Voice I'm lonely.

Tess – and you almost fall apart right there, because that's what it is, how you feel, and you never even knew. You're alone. You're alone. You're so fucking alone and you can't bear it any more. And then one day it happens for you, some wisecracking teacher, who's trying to relate, lets you on a computer and it's all you ever wanted to see. And it all makes sense. And finally! Finally! It's something that works the way your mind works! And it's the sound of a million doors opening, and you don't have to be stuck in your pissy wee room in a pissy wee city. You can scream through the doors into space! And maybe, if you're lucky, some other freak'll call back at you. Cos everyone needs to feel at home sometimes. And not alone.

Donna, Lou and Amy together. Amy is picking up Lou and swinging her round.

Donna Hey, did you hear?

Lou What?

Donna Fat B against the hospital wall. Guess who with?

Amy Wee freaky Pete?

Donna Nup.

Amy Who, then?

Donna Nobody we know!

Lou You're kidding!

Donna I'm not!

Amy Naebody we know!

Lou You're kidding!

Donna I'm not!

Amy Naebody we know! How does she know naebody we know?

Donna I'm telling you the truth!

Amy Tongues 'n all?

Donna Tongues 'n not caring who's watching.

Lou Nice kissing or what?

Donna What d'you mean?

Lou Was it like . . . *Titanic* . . . or was it like *Trainspotting*?

Donna Dunno.

Amy Was he slobbering on her?

Donna She didn't seem to mind.

Amy Way to go, Fat B!

Lou Ay, who'd have thought it!

Amy She's no that fat, I s'pose.

Donna She is.

Amy No, she's not Britney, but she's not . . .

Donna No, she is. Well, come on! She is.

Lights focus on Fat B.

Fat B Mum always sent me to a pharmacy across town. 'Don't want folk knowing all our business,' she said. 'Don't want that lemon-faced cow round the corner knowing all our ins and outs.' Now I go all the way over there just to see him . . . Martin. In his sparkling white coat. His smile's sexy as hell. We gab away like anything. I feel like . . . I'm safe . . . like . . . I'm home. And it's not that way where your voice disappears down your throat and you squeak like Minnie Mouse or something! I'm funny. And he's funny. And we're the same kind of funny. And it's like . . . all over my body . . . every single particle of me is alive or something! All of my skin and all of my hair and all of my arms and legs and fingers and toes are just waiting for him to touch me! And if he does I might explode! I might just explode! Cos if he does touch me, if I'm too busy gabbing to notice a car and I'm about to die or something, he'll pull me back and laugh and it's the best thing in the world! The best bloody thing in the world!

SCENE TWENTY-FOUR

Fat B It was a bright summer. A brilliant summer. A never-wanting-to-head-home summer.
Amy A wondering-if-you-could-still-sulk –
Donna – still-strut –
Fat B – still-strike-a-pose summer.

Beat.

It was a sad summer.
Amy Like getting old.
Fat B There'd be laughs.
Donna Loads of laughs to come.
Amy But different.

Fat B We'd become –

Amy – something.

Lou Gone our separate ways.

Donna And strange.

Lou There was no reachin back into the past for it.

Amy No searching for something that's vanished.

Donna Over the curve of the road.

Lou Our old selves.

Amy Smashed wi the glass bottles in the wee kid's playpark.

Lou And nothing to be the same again.

Donna Whatever they say.

Lou Nothing.

For a second they burst into the pop-video dance routine of the start, but this time the sound and movement are distorted and fragmented. They cannot seem to get into stride and the music fades out.

SCENE TWENTY-FIVE

Amy appears. She is crashing round the space, climbing and kicking at things, trying to burn off the frustration inside her.

Lou Amy, wait, please . . .

Amy What is it?

Lou Tell me what happened.

Amy I just –

Lou What?

Amy – got in a fight.

Lou Amy!

Amy I knew you'd say that!

Lou How?

Amy What's your problem? So I took him out. I was tryin to run the track, and he keeps starin at me!

Lou Staring?

Amy Yes! His eyes all over me! And laughing. Couldn't block him out.

Lou But people are always laughing at us. What's it matter?

Amy Why aren't you proud of me?

Lou I don't like fighting.

Amy You can't let people walk all over you, Lou! I couldn't let them think I was weak.

Lou Never that, eh?

Amy I pushed his face first, and he's still laughing at me. So I slapped him across the face. And that gives him a fright. Looks at me and sees I mean it. An he's fighting with himself cos he's not supposed to fight girls and all. And then I piss him off and he starts fighting back. And everyone's looking and it gets my blood up and I'm not gonna be beat and I keep on and on and he keeps on and on, and we're rolling around with grit in our eyes and he can't take it! So he goes for my tits, punching hard, so I knee him in the balls and then he's finished. I leave him then, I don't keep at him when he's down.

Lou Right.

Amy An then it's like nothing else I've known. Walkin through that crowd. With them all starin. An some of them hate you. But some of them love you. An some of them can't believe what they've seen.

Lou What're they gonna do to you?

Amy Don't know yet. I told them I did it. They can't take it. Old Fife's convinced I must be innocent cos I'm a girl, and Old Green thinks I should get it worse cos I'm a girl.

Lou Why'd you do it?

Amy Cos he was laughing.

Lou But he's not worth it.

Amy You weren't there. You know nothing about it.

Lou If it was some guy slapping girls about you'd be
onto him in a shot.

Amy You weren't there!

Lou You need something to give you a story. That's what
you need.

Amy Is it? Or is it what you need?

Lou I can't watch you knocking chunks out of people –

Amy Fine.

Lou They'll be after you.

Amy At the bell I'm out the side door! They won't even
see me for dust!

Lou They'll get you eventually.

Amy What d'you want me to do, Lou? Take whatever
they throw at me lying down?

Lou Sometimes you've got to learn to walk away.

Amy Like you do?

*Amy leaves. The Dead Girl appears. She looks Lou in
the eye. Lou tries to reach out and touch her. The Dead
Girl remains cold, impassive. The Dead Girl leaves.*

SCENE TWENTY-SIX

*Donna is alone. There is a cold white light on her, an
unforgiving spotlight this time.*

Donna The summer I gave up fighting them. You figure
you might as well be what they call you. And you just
get too tired to keep saying no. First time you do it
you feel good for a bit. But it was an awkward an a
lonely thing. An you couldnae even look each other in
the eye after. So you figure it's you, and maybe you're –

Voice 2 – tight –

Voice – frigid –

Donna – crap at it or something. I wish there was a way
of waiting without them dumping you.

Voice Once a guy's started . . .

Donna Cos I remember how it used to be, when he could
   only hold you and kiss you and that. It was kind of
   sweet. Sometimes I wonder if they want to go back
   too. Boys. I just . . . That's what I think sometimes.
   That's all.

The Dead Girl passes through.

SCENE TWENTY-SEVEN

Fat B He looks at me. Martin. My heart's fit to burst
   right out me. He says: 'I was just – Well, I thought – '

An I say: 'Yeah . . .?'

He says: 'I just – (*Laughs.*) Probably not but – '

'What?'

'Silly but – probably – thought – If you – It's a –
   Saturday. Are you –? Anything? Well, maybe you –
   probably don't but – maybe – it's a – I thought – '

Then I let him off the hook: 'So Saturday? Just – a film –
   or a – eight?'

Eight? That's thrown him.

'Or seven? Or nine? Or –'

'Eight's good.'

'Good!'

'See you,' we say.

'See you.'

'See you.'

'See you.'

SCENE TWENTY-EIGHT

Amy Standin by the scaffoldin, the old hospital wall.

Donna Darin Amy to climb it, silent, darin with our eyes.

Lou But no.
Donna But no.
Fat B She stays on the ground.
Amy Canna be arsed.
Donna 'N mebbe it's a kids' thing. Like playparks and paggers.
Amy Mebbe it's no excitin.
Lou Just stopped climbing maybe.
Amy You ken what you'll see.
Fat B You ken what the view is.
Donna You ken what the score is.
Amy Nae fuckin point.
Fat B Standin by the scaffoldin, the old hospital wall.
Lou It's gonna go any day now.
Donna Blow it up.
Amy Pull it down.
Lou They've got to keep the front of it. It's old, see? Protected.
Fat B Just the sad wee front, standin on its own.
Donna Fake front of a wall, wi nothin behind.
Amy Standin brave an cocky like, with the windows all holes.
Donna We'll be there to see it go.
Amy We'll be cheerin as they do it.
Lou We'll be there to see it go.
Fat B Come crumbling down round us.

SCENE TWENTY-NINE

Tess One day when they wake up I'll be gone. No more voices behind your back.
Voice Freak.
Voice 2 Loser.
Tess I'll show them. I'll laugh in their face. I met him online. He's called Mark. He has the mark of the

chosen one. Says I have to meet him. We'll understand each other. I read his mind down the computer. I just want to talk to someone. Without seeing –

Voice 2 Freak.

Tess In their eyes. I try. But it's so tiring . . . trying to be yourself. All this is . . . is . . .

Voice Game one.

Tess All this we think is real. There's a battle between the two worlds. I know it! There's a message in the frequency between radio stations, a picture forming in the static. It's the other world fighting to get through.

Voice 2 Freak.

Tess They're waiting for someone like me –

Voice Loser.

Tess – who's not just nose-down living. Who can look up and see the sky. It's not just who you hang with. You're getting scarred. And however they mark you, you'll keep chasing to change it your whole life. The cool ones want to be clever. The smart ones want to be liked. The freaks just want to fit in. Branded all the time – thirteen, sixteen, eighteen, for ever. It's all initiation. They just never call it that.

SCENE THIRTY

Lou and Fat B are together. Donna and Amy appear. They are shoving at each other.

Donna (*to Lou*) Just fucking admit it. (*to Amy*) You want a kickin?

Amy From you?

Donna Ay.

Amy Don't make me laugh.

Donna Don't know what you think you are these days –

Amy Get out my face, Donna –

Donna Strutting about like you think you're something –
An as fur her! (*Turns on Lou.*)

Amy You say nothing about her! You hear me?

Donna Just fuckin get out of here!

Amy Fuck you!

Lou Calm the fucks, eh?

Amy/Donna Keep out of it!

Lou Hey . . .!

Donna I saw you do it! In my shop, ya cow!

Lou Do what?

Donna I saw you take it!

Lou Don't know what you're talking about.

Amy You just leave her alone!

Donna Or what? Any fuckin shop but mine, alright?

Amy Lou'd never do it!

Donna You keep out of it!

Amy You worry about your own life – an keepin your
legs and gob shut once in a while!

Donna throws herself at Amy, who pushes her off.

I'll not touch you, alright? Just get away from me!

Donna You two better sort it. You're over the edge.

Amy Oh, fuck you.

Donna Fuck you.

Amy Fuck you.

Fat B pulls Donna away from them. They exit.

What's she on, eh?

Lou I don't know.

Pause.

Amy Guess what?

Lou What?

Amy The best thing!

Lou Tell me.

Amy Today wee Spud comes up looking shit-scared and says there's gonna be a kickabout after school! An God – they never ask us to play, right?

Lou You can't, Amy.

Amy Why not?

Lou Why d'you think they asked you?

Amy They think I can play! I don't play like a girl or nothing.

Lou You're getting to them.

Amy Don't know what you mean.

Lou They want to get you back for battering Souser.

Amy No.

Lou You think they'll let you get away with it?

Amy Stop being paranoid.

Lou I'm just saying –

Amy It's all forgotten.

Lou – you'd be stupid to go.

Amy You're so scared of the world, you know that? You've got to fuckin live!

Lou Stop swearing at me!

Amy You can't be afraid of boys. They smell the fear on you. You've got to fling yourself out across the mud with them. Get the ball before anyone!

Lou So it's to prove something?

Amy The whole school'll be watching!

Lou Not the whole school.

Amy Pretty much. You're just jealous.

Lou I'm worried about you.

Amy Don't bother.

Amy leaves and Lou follows her.

SCENE THIRTY-ONE

Fat B and Donna.

Fat B What was that about?
Donna She gets on my tits.
Fat B Amy?
Donna Both of them. Something's got to change, B, we've got to blow this open.
Fat B Blow what open?
Donna It can't go on, you ken that? Like we're lassies and what we do means nothin.
Fat B Why're you so ragin?
Donna Her. Lou. Her kind. Should keep her hands to herself.
Fat B Her kind?
Donna You ken what I mean.
Fat B What's going on, eh? This is us. Strong. The girls.
Donna What the fuck does that mean any more? All you've got is what you can grab wi both hands and hold on to. An fuckin Princess Lou's out to pull it all apart for us. Tryin to get us sacked. Choryin stuff she doesn't even want, to make out she's no as fucking dull as she seems.
Fat B What's this about?
Donna It's about everything.

Pause.

We'll just make it you an me this weekend. Fuck them.
Fat B I'm . . . busy.
Donna What?
Fat B It's always youse fuckin out your faces knowin I'll get youse home!
Donna What're you talkin about?
Fat B I've got a date's what.

Donna I've seen you with him.

Fat B What?

Donna Doesnae seem like much.

Fat B What?

Donna Forget it, B, an come out with us!

Fat B All I get is worryin. Cookin and cleanin and makin sure my da's comfy or my sister's fed. Makin sure he's taken his medicine and not thrown it up or thrown it away. An when I do go out all I get is looking after you.

Donna Nobody makes you.

Fat B If I don't do it, no one does.

Donna We're sorry about your da an all . . .

Fat B Things do have to change. You're right.

Donna Is that what your new boyfriend says?

Fat B It's what I say.

Donna Yeah. An where you gonna be without us, eh? Tell me that.

Donna leaves.

SCENE THIRTY-TWO

Amy, Lou, Fat B and Donna are together.

Amy We're all there when it goes.

Donna Blows.

Fat B Comes crashing down.

Donna We cheer as they do it.

Lou Though they're taking something from us.

Amy Old hospital wall.

Donna Scene of so many snogs with greasy-chip fingers.

Amy Scene of so many fights.

Lou Floor scattered wi condoms and battered old syringes.

Donna Scene of so many double dates.

Lou And emergency briefings.

Fat B What should I do?

Donna He loves us, loves us not, he loves us, loves us not.

Amy Scene of too many crimes, but it's done now.

Fat B Gone now.

Donna Fuck it.

Lou Old hospital wall.

Fat B An naebody asked us!

Lou They'd never ask us.

Donna No, they'd never ask us.

Amy Naw, they'd never.

SCENE THIRTY-THREE

Fat B, Lou and Amy.

Fat B Did you hear?

Amy What?

Fat B Donna.

Amy What about her?

Fat B Got herself pregnant.

Amy You what?

Fat B She has! She is! I heard!

Amy Bollocks.

Fat B It's the truth.

Lou She told you?

Fat B Well, she willnae will she?

Amy Shoots her mouth off about other folk enough.

Lou What'll we say to her?

Amy We canny say nothing to her.

Fat B Why?

Amy She's got to tell us herself.

Lou This is stupid.

Fat B She won't want folk talking about her.

Lou But we are talking about her!

Fat B We're different! We're her friends!

Amy Well . . . she had it comin maybe.

Fat B What?

Amy It's what you're thinking.

Lou Amy . . .

Fat B You just leave her alone!

Fat B leaves them.

Lou What's got into you?

Amy Nothing.

Lou You never used to be so hard on folk. An you used to talk to me. I feel like . . . I'm losing you.

Amy You know what you sound like?

Lou It's like we're not . . .

Amy Drop it.

Lou All that stuff I give you. Donna was right. I take it. So we can be close again. Don't you see?

Amy You'd never steal nothing.

Lou I do. So I can give you things.

Amy What, you think I want that junk?

Lou Don't –

Amy Never heard anythin so stupid –

Lou I went in the police station! And they looked at me like I was a nice girl, brought up right. And then I told them what I'd done. I really got them!

Amy You got no one! It's fuckin sad, that's what it is! Take what you want but don't try and blame me for it. It's not cool or flatterin or nothin, it's creepy, that's all.

Lou Don't say that, I'm warning you!

Amy Or what? . . . You'll copy me to death? (*Laughs.*)

Lou Please, Amy. It's always been you and me.

Amy You're a fuckin loser, you know that? A loser.

SCENE THIRTY-FOUR

Tess is alone. Fat B joins her.

Fat B You alright? Tess?

Tess What d'you think?

Fat B I don't know. What you been doing?

Tess Nothing you'd understand.

Fat B Try me.

Tess Just drop it, Bernie.

Fat B Why can't we talk?

Tess You tell me.

Fat B I'm tryin, Tess . . .

Tess God yeah. Mother Teresa B. Everyone knows you try . . .

Fat B It's not like that.

Tess What is it like, then? You never let me do anything in the house – like you're sure I'd mess it up. You never let me talk to him – not that there's any point – Someone should have stopped them havin us – they were too old!

Fat B They were always there for us.

Tess Mum died!

Fat B I know.

Tess An Dad hardly knows we're there.

Fat B That's not true. Come on, eh? There's you and me, that's something.

Tess Stop tryin to pretend we've got something strong. That we're family. We're nothing. A bunch of losers clinging together, a fat girl, a freak and a vegetable!

Fat B slaps Tess.

Fat B Don't you ever say that! Not till you've carried him from the bed to the loo and he gives you a look like he knows what's going on and hates the whole humiliation of it! All he wants in the world is to be himself again! D'you not remember him swinging us round and round as kids? And coming out with some stupid *Monty Python* line at the wrong moment? And playing bloody Bob Dylan! An his magic cooking! He's still all that! He is!

Tess He's dead now, Bernie. As good as. He doesn't know we're here.

Fat B Get away from me. Go. I don't want to see you.

SCENE THIRTY-FIVE

Donna I eat something funny. And I'm throwing up in the bogs. And when I come out, looking rough as fuck, I see that cow Sally Byatt looking at me. An she gives me one of her smiles, like she's ready to spit out glass at you the next minute. An I know she's thought of some way to get me. And it's not cos she's worth anythin. But to have someone stand there hatin you like that. To know you're hated . . . Anyhow. That's when it starts. And it's just a laugh at first. I mean.

Voice Slag.

Donna I reckon folk who know me'll know.

Voice 2 Slag's knocked up.

Donna They'll listen.

Voice Got what she deserves.

Donna An we'll go laugh in Byatt's face.

Voice 2 Up the fucking duff!

Donna We'll stand there tough as rock.

Voice 2 Stupit cow!

Donna And watch her crumble, I'll say nothing.

Both Voices Stupit fuckin bitch.

Donna And the true folk'll show themselves.

Voice She had it coming.

Donna They'll be there. They'll be there. They will.

SCENE THIRTY-SIX

Amy Things break up. It's how life is. People hold you
 back is all. When they talk about ties . . . I never
 wanted them. Never wanted the shitty Girl Guides.
 Never wanted to join. Lou goes on like she's lost the
 whole world. We were just a gang is all. Not like cool,
 or New York or nothing. Just girls who got stuck
 together, who hung about. Canny even remember how
 it started. People crash into each other is all. Doesn't
 make you who you are. Lou says a lot of things. But
 what does she know?

SCENE THIRTY-SEVEN

Tess How old are you?
Voice How old do you think I am?
Tess Nineteen?
Voice Age is a state of mind!
Tess Yeah. I think that too.
Voice Tell me what you like to do.
Tess What do you mean?
Voice Tell me what you wear to school.
Tess Why?
Voice You feel lonely sometimes?
Tess Do you?
Voice I guess everyone does.
Tess That's true.
Voice You know we should meet.
Tess You think?
Voice Definitely. I feel close to you.
Tess Really?
Voice Will you meet me?
Tess Is that what you want?

Voice Yes. If you're in this for real. Are you in this for real?
Tess Yes.

SCENE THIRTY-EIGHT

Fat B Talk to me, Donna.
Donna Why? What did Amy say?
Fat B We didn't know what to say.
Donna But you believed it. Don't bother. She as good as said it to my face. Count on old Amy for that.
Fat B I'll help you, Donna. It was a shock but –
Donna I don't need your help.
Fat B Please . . .
Donna I'm not pregnant.
Fat B What?
Donna Never thought of that, eh?
Fat B But you never said . . .
Donna What was the point? People believe what they want.
Fat B I'm sorry.
Donna Sorry gets you nowhere. Bernie, I thought you'd put two fingers up to the world! I thought you'd be the one who knew.
Fat B I do. I am.
Donna I slept with one guy. Once. And that was only cos of what folk called me.
Fat B You lied to me.
Donna You believed it.

SCENE THIRTY-NINE

Amy It all went to fuck that summer.
Lou A messed-up summer.

Amy A ripped-out-and-torn-up summer.

Lou A not-wanting-to-be-what-we-were summer.

Donna Looking at ourselves in the mirror.

Fat B Hating the look of your face.

Amy It was a fucked-up summer.

Donna With losers and losing.

Lou See us at the corner.

Amy See us coming at you.

Fat B And you'd see right through us.

Amy It was a gone-to-fuck summer.

Lou Pushed apart when we could have done something.

Fat B It was the summer I lost Tess. My fault. Wasn't watching.

SCENE FORTY

Donna She's this weird wee thing – admit it! Everyone thinks it but no one'll say it! She was just Bernie's weird wee sister who hung about us cos there was no one else!

Lou How can you say that now?

Donna None of us could handle her! So don't go pretending you were her best friend or nothing now!

Lou She wasn't weird.

Amy You couldn't talk to her!

Lou She was clever.

Donna She was weird!

Fat B appears.

Fat B Is that what you think?

Lou Shit.

Donna I'm just saying –!

Fat B Just shut it –

Lou We should have talked to her more –

Donna What was there to say?

Lou She'll come back, B.

Donna She might be in trouble, B.

Fat B Thanks, Donna.

Donna What do you want me to say?

Fat B You don't give a fuck about anyone, do you? Unless it's anyone you can fuck. Why is no one doing anything? It should be in every paper, it should – Tell me the last thing you said to her.

Amy I don't remember.

Fat B You do.

Amy We talked about – fighting – telling the truth.

Fat B And what do you know about truth? Tell me she's got some friend we never knew about! Feeding her and keeping her safe. Tell me she'll come back and I can just hug her and hug her and never let her go! Tell me that! Tell me! (*to Lou*) You tell me what to do! You're supposed to be so smart.

Lou I don't know.

Fat B It's not enough! She's not – skinny build – blonde hair – dark jacket – jeans – she's – she's –! You can't watch everyone all the time! You can't hold together all the cracks! It's too much! Too much! Too much!

SCENE FORTY-ONE

Amy Best game of footie. Half the school there. Lou was there, like the old Lou, screaming for me. And I'm quick and I'm sleek – I'm a star out there and everyone can see it.

Lou And then there's a moment, like it's all been planned –

Amy Someone's foot catches me – and I'm down –

Lou And when she's down, they all surround her.

Amy And the game stops.

Lou And the crowd holds its breath.

Amy And I look up at their faces, and I see they mean it.
  And the wee guy I did over is standing at the back.
Lou And I can't breathe and I can't move.
Amy And it's leather and mud – and boots and studs –
Lou And I look around and the crowd's all frozen –
Amy And the breath's knocked out of me –
Lou And there are faces that cheer it on, and faces that
  just let it happen –
Amy And they're at my ribs, my back, a million feet,
  legs, at me –
Lou And I can't hear a sound but my breathing –
Amy I can't breathe for the blood –
Lou And I'm scrabbling through air to get at her – and
  all I can do is watch –
Amy And the wee guy gets revenge.
Lou And everyone who feared her – lay right into her –
Amy And just as the world is spinning and almost turned
  black, it stops. And there's nothing.
Lou They drop me in the mud.
Amy And all I can hear is the silence of the pitch, and the
  wind, and Lou sobbing, sobbing, sobbing above me.
  They've taken the wind out of me.

SCENE FORTY-TWO

Lou They used to see us at the corner.
Amy See us coming at them.
Donna And you'd see them stand back.
Fat B And you'd see them take cover.
Amy Cos we were strong.
Donna Cos we were something. We could wipe them out
  with a look.
Amy Slice through them –
Donna – with a sneer or something.
Fat B But it was such a fucked summer –

Donna I never knew what happened.

Fat B One minute we were there –

Donna Me and Fat B.

Lou Amy and Lou.

Fat B And Tess –

Lou Tess –

Donna Tess –

Amy Tess –

Fat B And the next we'd exploded.

Lou Feels like –

Donna Feels like –

Fat B Feels like –

Amy But you just keep going –

Fat B And any minute – any minute now – Tess'll walk in the door and we'll be complete again . . . We will . . . We will . . . We will . . .

Amy You go in the ring, you've got to take a few blows.

SCENE FORTY-THREE

Amy is still beaten up and bruised.

Amy I scared them, see? So that was something. I was so good they had to take me out. One day I'll run and run so fast I'll leave you all behind. I'll be shining on the telly, a streak of lightning flashing through the Olympics, picking up all the gold. And Dunny and Johnson and all they boys who laugh at girls'll have nothing to say . . . They'll have nothing to say.

Pause. The lights focus on Lou.

Lou It was the summer we lost it. And Tess went missing. And a dead girl got dumped on the beach. And there were all these voices, calling us names, all summer. And some of the names stuck. Mouthy. Quiet. Fat.

Slag. Freak. Sometimes without your mates you think you might just spin off empty into space. They say it means nothing, who you hang with. But sometimes it's your anchor. Sometimes it's all you've got. We were all there that summer. And the next we were gone.

Without Your Mates
You Might Just Spin off into Space

Isabel Wright interviewed by Jim Mulligan

Throughout a long summer a gang of girls tear through the streets, fighting each other, uniting to take on the world and unknowingly moving towards tragedy. Their lives are haunted by a grotesque and beautiful dead girl who has been murdered and left under the pier. They feel the world is closing in on them, that they are banging their fists against windows of places they will never get into, and when Tess is abducted at the end of the play they realise that their teenage world is fractured beyond repair. This is *Blooded*.

> It's *Blooded* because that gives a sense of initiation, of being marked with blood to make you one of the gang. I'm interested in the dynamics of how groups of one gender interact. You see these girls on the street and they are quite intimidating and strong but at the same time they are young and vulnerable. There is a strength there and a weakness. It is very specific in some ways to a particular place with a specific language but I hope that their experiences and the exploration of their lives are universal.

At first sight the structure of the play seems complicated. There are soliloquies, dialogue that is antiphonal, chorus parts where the characters all speak together looking back on the summer or speak together in the present tense, moments when the characters break into dance routines, the appearance of the Dead Girl and voices that comment on the action and the characters.

The voices are surreal. They are inside the heads of the girls and they are also society. They are censorious and we ask ourselves: are they real or imagined? They could be the school commenting on the reputations the girls have gained for themselves. But it is also the girls themselves commenting on the roles they have created. There is an element of them being judged but also of them judging themselves. The voices represent other people but also the fears the girls have built up in their own heads.

There is a very dark side to *Blooded*. It starts and ends with an abduction, and the action is punctuated by the appearance of the Dead Girl. She represents something different to each character. For Fat B she is a perfect girl, slim and well off. Amy is scared and tries to get away from the vision which brings out the vulnerability she does not want to face. Once a phone rings and the dead girl appears sobbing and bruised, a powerful image that encapsulates what has happened to her, but each member of the audience must fill in the details for themselves. Donna tries to challenge the Dead Girl but in the end backs off. Lou reaches out to touch her, but she is impassive and leaves her. The story of the Little Mermaid is invoked at the start of the play and clearly links with the Dead Girl.

I wanted Amy to say things about feminism that she stumbles on without quite realising their full meaning. Her friends don't realise that what she is saying is right. Amy's teachers probably find her the most annoying person in the school. She has an attitude all the time. I wanted to make her bright, but that gets obscured by the fact that she chooses not to be academic. She challenges the assumption that a woman has to be mutilated to be successful. I hope young people who probably haven't read a lot of books on feminism will pick up on this truth. The choice is not as one young woman said to me: 'You're either allowed to be quiet or a slag.' That distilled a lot of feminist thinking in the words of a fifteen-year-old.

The roles the girls play illustrate the choices young women are forced to make. They are consciously projecting false images of themselves because they cannot see what their strengths are and that they are actually strong, attractive individuals. Fat B, who is not that fat, has accepted the sobriquet and plays her part appropriately. Amy is the aggressive girl who takes on everyone and learns that no matter how tough you are there will always be someone who will beat you. Lou has grown up in the shadow of Amy to the point where she imitates her in every way possible and loses her own identity. Donna talks herself into a reputation, but in fact is no more experienced than the other girls. And Fat B's sister, Tess, the weird, clever little girl who is overwhelmed by family difficulties, seeks refuge in an internet relationship.

The disappearance of Tess is a tragedy. She has become dislocated and, when she tentatively reaches out to the other girls, they do not help her. With the other girls it is a series of little tragedies. They each suffer loss in different ways, the strong friendships are fractured. There is a real sadness at the end that they have lost their innocence.

Blooded is about a messed-up, ripped-out and torn-up summer when the girls were pushed apart and Fat B blames herself for losing Tess. One minute they were there – Donna and Fat B, Amy and Lou and Tess – and the next minute they'd exploded. The last word goes to Lou. She recalls the names they were called, names that stuck: mouthy, quiet, fat, slag, freak. 'Sometimes, without your mates, you think you might just spin off empty into space. They say it means nothing who you hang with. But sometimes it's your anchor. Sometimes it's all you've got. We were all there that summer. And the next we were gone.'

I hope it rings true. I'd like the young people who take part to be able, as a result of their experience, to question the misconceptions or the boundaries imposed on them. I think *Blooded* is about accepting who you are rather than accepting who the school or society says you should be. I hope it helps them to resist those who are forcing them into something they are not.

Production Notes

Isabel Wright wrote *Blooded* after working closely with a specific group of fifteen-year-olds, with teenagers in a youth group, and with drama-college students aged eighteen or nineteen. She was keen to address the dynamics of friendships and the roles of individuals within friendship groups. Much of the material for the play grew out of a workshop she ran on 'perception' in which one girl said you are either 'quiet or a slag', which to some extent forms the essence of the play. Rather than presenting stereotypes, Isabel wanted to keep the gang realistic, so portrays a tough girl gang as a group but also shows each member as an individual, each with their own individual strengths. *Blooded* was written alongside a piece of forum drama called *Initiate* that addresses the same issues. The term 'blooded' comes from the use of blooding as an initiation into a group or gang, and serves as a physical manifestation marking the separation between 'us' and 'them'.

STAGING THE PRODUCTION

The play could be set on a rubbish dump, in a children's playground, a café, a bar or in a plain white space. Whatever setting you choose, it needs to be specific, consistent, and to allow for easy and smooth transition between scenes. The location is where the gang hangs out. It could be an old bandstand or bench. An unexpected setting could be effective since it can create atmosphere, contrast and mystery, and will serve to sustain audience attention. The girls are getting too big for where they have grown up. There is not enough happening in their local area. Create spaces that convey this and spaces that equally are too small for them.

The Dead Girl represents something different to each of the girls and to the audience. She was well off, attractive and was brutally murdered. Fat B sees her as the girl she should have been. Amy sees her as a victim. For Donna, she represents mortality, and therefore a weakness. She 'appears' and 'disappears'. Make her entrances and exits as simple as possible. Avoid using technology or being over-theatrical by using trap-doors etc. Tess and the Dead Girl are definitely not the same character although Isabel intended parallels to be drawn between them. It would therefore be confusing and inadvisable to cast the same actress as Tess and the Dead Girl.

The image of the Dead Girl is a very strong one and how effectively it is achieved will set the tone of the play. She is covered in seaweed and strips of plastic and rubbish from the beach, and with this image you could even explore creating a mermaid effect. She should, however, appear to the audience as obviously dead. There must also be a clear connection between what the audience sees and what Fat B is saying. The Dead Girl could start by being obviously dead but then become more real and alive as the play progresses and as she becomes more present in the minds of the girls. Equally, as she becomes more active in the minds of the girls she could become more grotesque and dead-looking.

Blooded is a complex play because it jumps between time zones and is often in two time zones at once. A solution to potential confusion could be to double-cast so that the older girls look back on their younger selves of that summer.

STRUCTURE AND MOVEMENT

The play contains forty-three scenes. Think about the architecture and structure of the piece and rehearse the play in sections so that the cast learns to see the play as a whole rather than simply a collection of separate scenes. Make sure the set is flexible enough so that scene changes only take place when absolutely necessary.

Decide who it is that Fat B is talking to and make it clear. If you decide she is addressing the audience and letting them into her world, she needs to talk to them directly, to open up and establish a relationship with them. In the first scene, Fat B could be anywhere – she could be on the prom, close to the place where the death happened, transported back to the prom in her mind, or even being interrogated about finding the girl. You decide.

In terms of movement, the second scene falls into two parts. The first is the stylised movement of the individual girls. The second is the dance routine for which they can come together. Despite dancing the same dance, they nonetheless demonstrate their own physical and expressive individuality. This section is set a few years after the summer, when the girls are about seventeen or eighteen.

Two approaches can be taken to the 'chorus'. In its traditional sense, the chorus is a group of people acting in perfect unison. Here, however, the individuals could distinguish themselves as such while in the chorus. This could encourage more humour in the play since it is a piece that has many witty moments in need of being brought out. You could make the chorus male, which would give the whole show a very different slant.

The flashing light could be directed either onto the stage or onto the audience. It could represent a photographic flash capturing the girls that summer. It could be capturing a moment in life with the knowledge that that moment is already passing. Alternatively, it could pick up on the theme of a forensic detective taking pictures of the body.

Scene Three can be seen as the beginning of the play, with the first two scenes being the prologue. There is a change in pace. The actors will need to hit each scene with great energy and focus.

Scene Four explains a lot about Amy. It shows her teasing Lou. She knows she means the world to her and tests her by joking that she may go over the edge. The whole play is very energised, and sustaining this energy will be a challenge. Seeing Amy climb onto a higher level may help raise energy. There could to be a surprise appearance of Amy, for example, on the balcony in the audience. The appearance of the Dead Girl is just a reminder of mortality at a point when Amy is feeling invincible. After the Dead Girl, an action is needed straight away. The Dead Girl's appearance has provided a moment of calm that could potentially be ruined if the mood isn't swiftly changed.

We learn about all the characters in Scene Five and it is very useful to draw up a picture of who these people are. A useful exercise to ask for each scene is:

> What do we learn that's new about the group?

> What does the audience learn that's new about your character?

It is clear that this scene shows the group's solidarity. It also explains a little about each of them individually.

There needs to be a clear differentiation between the action of the play and the chorus sections. The lights change to distinguish these sections from the rest of the action, but more could be done through the characters and the change in tempo. The chorus section could be played between the characters or straight out.

Amy and Lou are both in Scene Six: they appear to be talking to themselves and may only be mentally, rather than physically, in the same place. This could equally be directed to the audience with the two coming together at the end of the scene. Lou is testing her relationship with Amy. She is explaining it, probably to the audience, but seems slightly unconvinced, demonstrated in the final word of the first sentence: 'I've known Amy since for ever, see?' This 'see' undermines what Lou has said. Amy seems to like the fact that Lou loves her but is bored by it, like childhood friends who grow apart when they get older. The storyteller here is Lou, and Amy seems to have complied with her story despite not wholly agreeing with it. The others are on stage at this point.

Fat B's sister Tess is a problematic character – she is meant to be, and is written as such. Despite being widely read she is very vulnerable, treated badly by the others and left out of the gang. They mimic her and this mimicking needs to feel really nasty. Her appearance as a Goth shows that she wants to be different but whereas most Goths are in a gang, she hasn't yet found hers.

Tess's speech comes out of the blue and is not supposed to fit. The main challenge, however, is getting her on and off stage. Her rant is very energised so it is important to know exactly what happens before and afterwards so that Tess's moment is maximised. A question to consider when she has finished speaking: does she feel embarrassed and relieved or excited? People may laugh, but what is important is that Tess's anger and frustration – from the performer's perspective – should be real and convincing. She probably did meet the guy who abducted her. The 'An Tess' of the chorus could, therefore, have a hint of tragedy – the girls know where the story of Tess is going to lead, how her story ends.

It could work well to have Martin present in Scene Twenty-Seven or even just a male voice.

Amy is still beaten up and bruised in Scene Forty-Three but she hasn't been offstage since Scene Forty. Taking her offstage may be difficult and could break up the rhythm in the final run of scenes before the end of the play. Find a symbolic or expressionistic way of representing this, depending on what 'language' has evolved or been decided upon.

Don't use too much music in your production, because it may detract from the musicality of the script. Use it as a good way of changing the pace and drawing together a potentially fragmented play.

CHORUS SECTIONS

LOOK AT SCENE FIVE The girls are being sarcastic at this point, 'wee lassies' could therefore work outside of Scotland in the context of mocking someone with such an accent.

In keeping with the rhythm of the play's language, there is a need for emphasis on certain words:

Lou Cos we were wee lassies.
Amy They were such nice wee lassies.

In this section, there are thoughts that begin with one character and are developed by another. It will be important from the perspective of rhythm to look at where one character completes another character's sentence or introduces a new subject.

Don't let the energy drop at the end of the scene: carry it through to spur on the next.

LOOK AT SCENE EIGHTEEN   The pulse and rhythm from the main scene is carried through into the chorus section. The positioning of the characters needs to shift in order to be consistent with the change in focus. It could be a big change or a slow, blurring shift. Don't get too tragic too soon, otherwise it will be difficult to optimise the later tragedy when it comes to Tess's disappearance. The tone of this section is, 'Isn't it funny getting older?' and it forms a trailer to what is to come.

LOOK AT SCENE THIRTY-TWO   The blowing-up of the hospital wall is markedly different from the other choral scenes because, while the strong pulse is present, there is no sense of a dance routine. It would be useful for the cast to pinpoint where the top of the hospital wall is located so that they can have a focus. The hospital wall could come down at any point during the scene, experiment with it coming down at a specific moment or as a slow descent throughout the scene. Sound effects could be added by the cast to complement and enhance their onomatopoeic vocabulary – 'goes', 'blows', 'comes crashing down' – or it could all simply come from outside.

CHARACTER WORK

Have each actor create four lists pertaining to their character. The director should do the same for the cast. These lists should be:

Facts about the character, such as their age, whether they have brothers and sisters, if they work, whether they are at school, etc.

What the character says about herself.

What the character says about other people.

What others say about the character.

This method can also provide a good basis for hot-seating and improvisation work.

USEFUL VOCAL EXERCISES

Pass a football around the room and throw it on the last word so that pace can be maintained.

Change direction at a punctuation mark. Voice coaches teach that a sentence is a thought is a breath: that an inspiration (literally a breathing-in) is needed before voicing a thought. The sentence structure/punctuation is an important guide as to how a character thinks, however eccentric that structure may be (playwrights are trying to reflect a version of everyday speech).

Have the cast read some scenes with viewers snapping their fingers when there is a comma and clapping their hands when there is a full stop. This helps them to hear the energy and to really listen to what the text is saying.

Speed running can also help with drawing out the clarity and spontaneity of the text. It must, however, not be reduced to gabbling – the mouth needs to be moving fast, but so does the brain: a good speed run will get actors thinking and reacting faster.

ACCENTS AND STRONG LANGUAGE

Isabel provides below a glossary of alternative words and phrases for suggested use in place of the Scottish idiom. Use them if you need to. Placing too much emphasis on playing the characters with a Scottish accent should be avoided if it is not your own accent. This is because the emotional self might be compromised, rendering the character a caricature.

If you choose not to use Scottish accents, Isabel would be happy for appropriate translations of any local teenage language to be used instead. Although she has set the play in Portobello, it is nonetheless an imaginative and non-specific setting and as such could be transposed to other areas. It could be exciting for students to make the language uniquely their own. The author's only caution is that the rhythm could be upset unless appropriate attention and care is taken in relation to the language.

Whatever you decide, make sure the accents are consistent because the gang is close-knit and they all come from the same area. To omit the swearing completely would impact on the nature of the play, as it is an intrinsic part of the lives of the characters. Swearing could be cut down, though the rhythm of the sentences needs to be carefully considered.

Ay	Yeah
Dinny	Don't
Ye wee scruffter	You old scruffhead/You big scruff
I eat ye fur	I eat you for
Ye ken it	You know it
Canny	Can't
Get tae fuck	Get to fuck
Youse	You
Folk	People
Ach	Aw
Wee lassies	Little girls
That shower	That crowd
Chum us	Come with us
Wi	With

Eejit	Idiot
Fae	From
Isnae	Isn't
No sure	Not sure
Plukey wee boy	Zitty boy
Pair o' skates	Pair of skates
Wee gnaff	Little shit
Feart	Scared
Poky wee room	Poky old room
Dead shan	So unfair
Weak wee shite	Weak little shit
'N mebbe	And maybe
Paggers	Punch-ups
Choryin	Stealing
Willnae	Won't

The word 'wee' is used frequently to mean small. This can be omitted where the rhythm of the sentence is not compromised, or can be replaced by 'old' where the rhythm requires it.

Workshop facilitated by Edward Kemp
with notes taken by Daisy Lloyd

BURN

Deborah Gearing

All professional and amateur rights in this play
are strictly reserved and applications for permission
to perform it must be made in advance, before rehearsals begin,
to Peters, Fraser and Dunlop, Drury House, 34–43 Russell Street,
London, WC2B 5HA

Characters

Aaron
rhymes with Darren, also called Az, fifteen

Sal
Aaron's younger sister, nine

Birdman (Joey)
fifteen

Linda
fifteen

Jan
the social worker

Mel
sixteen

Marie
sixteen

Sita
sixteen

Tom
fifteen

Niall
sixteen

Rachel
sixteen

Colin
seventeen

About the stage is the debris which is washed up by the river, a fridge and some chairs, which may be used to make the car or indicate rooms as necessary.

SCENE ONE

A red glow.

Sal Where are you starting?
Aaron At the beginning.
Sita Birdman's story? It doesn't have a beginning.
It flows. It just all flows along this stretch of dirty water.
Linda Where are you starting?
Aaron On the way down river.
Birdman went marching
Down from the Manor and out towards the sea.
Rachel Where are you starting?
Aaron Early in the morning.
Birdman came to see me.
It was early in the morning
on that particular day.

> *The red glow fades to daylight.*
> *Riverbank.*
> *Aaron, Sal, loaded down with fishing rods and a*
> *plastic bag, and Birdman.*

Aaron Hear this.
Sea tang rising off the river.
I'm out of bed and down the stairs.
Birdman's waiting.
With his board.
Not boards, I say. Not today.
Smell that –
Birdman flaring his nostrils in the wind like some beast.
Wolf.
Me and Sal, we're the pack.

But today I'm leading.

It's my shout.

(How Sal come to be part of this I don't want to tell –
  tag-along, tell-tale, carry-all or I'll kick you down the
  bank.)

Come on, I say. Come on.

And we leave the Manor

Heading for that white bridge that swoops

Across the river.

Hogweed, cow parsley, rush, sedge, madder.

(Yeah, it's a girl thing, plants.

But I like the way they sound.)

I've got my stick

And a steady rhythm –

Thwack, step, thwack, step, thwack.

Heads flying. Backs broken.

Smells – rank.

But we've got a steady pace –

I don't let up – sun's moving up over the river.

Flies buzzing.

It's two miles down the river.

We're keeping step. Then.

Full stop.

Fence.

Railway line.

Sal (sniveller, snot-maker, here blow it or I'll burn you to
  a cinder).

Birdman. Me.

Birdman Leave her here.

Aaron Can't do that. C'mon, Sal.

Sal I can't do it. I can't do it. It's too dangerous. I said I
  wouldn't. I promised Mum.

Aaron C'mon, Sal. Just don't tread on the rails, that's all.

Sal I can't. I haven't got rubber shoes. I'm only wearing
  jellies.

Aaron They're rubber, Sal. They'll be okay.

Sal They're plastic, stupid. Plastic's not the same as rubber.

Aaron You don't *have* to tread on the rails. Just don't tread on them. And you'll be okay.

Sal I might touch the electric. By mistake.
And what if a train comes?

Aaron We'll hear it coming.

Sal But what if I trip, and get caught up in something? I might fall on the line. Or the train will come and chop my head off.

Aaron Just shut up and get moving. Shut up.

He pushes her.

Sal I can't. I can't do it. There was that boy.

Aaron What boy?

Sal A boy from round here. Got killed on the line. They said.

Aaron Who said?

Sal The police.

Aaron The police! When did you talk to the police?

Sal At school. They came to visit.

Aaron That's just what they say. It's a show. They make it up to scare little kids. Like you.

Sal No. It's true.

Aaron How do you know?

Pause.

How do you know?

Sal They said so. (*Beat.*) She was all right, the copper. She wouldn't make it up.

Aaron No? Well, next time – you ask who it was. She won't be able to tell you. I guarantee. She'll say she can't tell you. And that's because she made it up. You can't ask them anything. They'll always lie. Now get through this hole and follow me.

Sal shakes her head.

Birdman Leave her here.
Aaron Can't do that.
Middle of nowhere.
No.

Pause.

Okay. Yes.
Sal. You come or you wait here. Up to you.
Sal I'll stay here.
Aaron We'll be gone a long time.
Sal I'm not coming. Leave me my sandwiches.
Aaron What if a dog comes?
Sal I'll throw him my sandwiches.
Aaron Yeah?
Sal I'll tell him to go away.
Aaron Yeah.
Sal I'll scream.

Pause.

I think I'll go home. Now. Take me home.
Aaron Take you where? We've been walking for over
    half an hour. We're heading down the river. You wait
    here or you come with us. No – you come with us, or
    I'll knock your head off. I'll take you down the
    allotments and pass you round like Linda.

I shouldn't have said that.
That I shouldn't have said.
No one knows about the allotments except Linda. And
    Sal and me, 'cos we found her. And the blokes who
    took her there. She won't say who.
I shouldn't have said that.
Sal – supersonic. Really scared now.
Jelly in her jellies. Green in pink.
Pissing in her pants.
Birdman –

94

Birdman Gobshite. You gobshite. Talking to her like
that. She's your sister. You don't talk to her like that.
Not your sister.

Come on, Sal.

Sal Where are we going?

Birdman Taking you home.

Sal What, my house?

Quickest way?

Birdman Quickest way is back the way we come.

Sal What about the bus?

Birdman No money. You got any?

Sal No.

Birdman Come on then. Walk.

Aaron What about the river?

Birdman Sod the river. Get her home. Why did you bring
her anyway?

Aaron Had to.

Birdman Had to? Do everything your mum says?
Do you?

Aaron Get out of my face. (*Beat.*) You know she said
I had to stay away from you.

Birdman goes quiet.
Picks up the pace.
In front.
Way in front.
Heading back up the river, back to the Manor.
Through swarms of flies.

SCENE TWO

Linda's house. Linda, with a dress shredded into strips.

Linda Hear this.
I shred that dress. The dress I wore that night. Long
strips. Red splashed on yellow. Mother came.

Ten fingers on my face.
Left. Right.
Red on yellow.
You're sick, Mother said.
I might be.
And what's that mark on your arm?
Only half the mark I've got on my face, Mother.
Get to bed, you cheeky mare. There's something wrong
    with you. Tearing up a good dress like that. Stinking
    out the place with Dettol. What do you do with it?
You're sick.
Yeah – sad-sick.
Mouse mouse in the house, shred herself a bed, lying in
    it, waiting for the sad-sickness to swell through her
    body.
Mother – and keep that door shut. Don't think you're
    going anywhere today.
Closing the door – there's something wrong with that
    girl.

Now see this. (*hiding the strips of cloth*)
Midday. High sun.
Loud knocking at the door. Man's head in the circle of
    light.
From the top of the stairs:
Who is it?
From the foot of the stairs:
Whisper
Who is it?
Mouse mouse in the house
Eight and a half hours to dusk.
Who is it?
Boy's voice.
Boy, not man.
Open up.

Jesus Christ, Birdman. What are you doing here?

Birdman Dunno.

Linda What do you mean, you don't know?

Birdman Dunno. Just passing, I suppose. Thought I'd come round. See what you were doing.

Linda Well, you've seen and you've been.

Birdman What are you doing?

Linda Just hanging.

Birdman You coming out?

Linda What, with you?

Birdman Yeah. If you like.

Linda I'm busy. (*Beat.*) Where?

Birdman Park? I've got my board.

Linda I'm busy.

Birdman No you're not.

Linda I am.

Birdman You're just saying that.

Linda Well, that means no, doesn't it?

Birdman Later then?

Linda Listen, Birdman, you're doing my head in. I said no. N.O. You're making the place look untidy. Go play with your friends.

Birdman (*pause*) You okay, Linda?

Linda I will be when you go.

Birdman What you do to your arm?

Linda What? Knocked it.

Birdman It's burnt.

Linda Yeah. I burnt it.

Birdman Your mum in?

Linda No. She's at work. But that doesn't mean you can stay. In fact it means you've got to go. Bye, Birdman.

Birdman Linda.

Linda Bye, Birdman.

Holding open the door.
Noon sun pouring in.
He's got freckles.

Birdman.
Birdboy.
Touch his arm as he passes.
Yeah, go on, Birdman. You stick him for me.
Make his sixpack grin.

SCENE THREE

Birdman's foster home.
  The Social Worker, sorting out her papers in a
briefcase.

Social Worker Birdman. Not really my call. Two-ish.
  I can't be more exact than that. I've lost my watch. But
  it would be about two-ish, because I noticed the time
  on the clock as I paid at the toll bridge. I love the drive
  across that bridge. For five minutes you swoop across
  the river, lifted up above the water, looking down on
  all the little dolls' houses and the little doll people, and
  the children playing on the boats. Some daredevil
  hanging on to the highpoint about to dive in. Don't
  fancy his chances. But I don't get out.
As I said – I've lost my watch. Or maybe that's the kind
  way to put it. Actually they nicked it. Someone did.
  One of them. It was a long time ago. I never replaced
  it. I just got used to guessing the time, and being late
  for appointments is part of the job. They don't like
  you for it. But they don't like me anyway.

  Pause.

They've got other things to do.

  Pause.

And I'm usually a disappointment.

  Pause.

There's nothing I can do to hide these rings of sweat I get.
I know it makes them dislike me. Jesus Christ. It's not my
    fault. And my feet hurt. Jesus Christ. I don't know
    why it happens.
Don't ask me why it happens.
What do I know? Some careless god flicked a pebble up
    in space and it landed here. Jesus Christ.
Open the door and let's get going.
Smiling now –
Birdman at the door.

Ah! Birdman!
Birdman Don't call me that.
You got no right to call me that.
Social Worker Fine. (*consulting her papers*) I thought
    Karen – your regular social worker is Karen, isn't it?

Pause. Birdman doesn't reply.

Well, I thought she left a note saying that was what you
    liked to be called.
Birdman To you it's Joey.
Social Worker Fine. My mistake then. I'll get Karen to
    take that note out. (*Pause.*)
Joey. (*smiling*)
How's things?
Cool trainers.
Good haircut.
Birdman You always say that.
Social Worker I don't believe we've met before.
Birdman You're all the same. You all say the same thing.
Social Worker Fine. Well. My name's Jan, by the way.

Pause.

How's things?
Birdman You already said that.
Social Worker Just testing you.

99

Birdman Yeah, right.

Social Worker Well, Joey. Shall we have a cup of tea?

Birdman No. Just get down to it.

Social Worker Right. Well. You talked to your social worker about a new placement. Because this one isn't suitable. Right? – Well. We've been looking for a new placement.

Birdman And?

Social Worker And it's good news and bad news. It's a bit of both.

Birdman Meaning?

Social Worker Well. I've found you a new placement.

Pause.

It's a family with teenagers. They're used to taking teenagers. That's good, isn't it?

Pause.

Birdman So what's bad about it?

Social Worker It's quite a way from here. Well. Not to beat about the bush – it's in Birmingham.

Birdman Birmingham! But that's up north. It's miles away. I'm not going.

Social Worker Joey. We've talked about this – your social worker talked to you about this. You can't stay here. This isn't an appropriate placement. You need to go somewhere more suitable for you. Somewhere you can stay for longer.

Birdman I'm not going.

Social Worker You should at least visit.

Birdman I'm not going.

Social Worker I hear you're uncomfortable at the thought of going.

Birdman I'm not going.

Social Worker I hear you're uncomfortable at the thought of going. So I'll leave you to get used to the idea.

Sue needs the space for her own family. She's not kitted
    out for long-term placements with teenagers. We
    always knew this was only a temporary placement,
    didn't we? I'm sure Karen never disguised that fact.
    (*Pause.*) We need to move you in two weeks. Sue will
    help you pack your things. (*Beat.*) It's for the best,
    Joey. (*Beat.*) Isn't it hot?
Birdman I'm not going.
Social Worker Goodbye, Joey. I expect Karen will be
    back off leave soon, and you can talk to her. She'll be
    able to tell you all about it.
Birdman I'm not going.
Social Worker I'll see myself out. Goodness, it's hot.
    Goodbye.

SCENE FOUR

Riverbank.
   Sita, Mel, Marie.

Sita After three, before four.
Easy, yeah –
We're on our way to the park
On the path along the river.
Mel – hobbling –
'Cos she's wearing stupid shoes,
So we can't go that fast.
Taking for ever.
Marie, moaning 'cos it's hot.
Why's she wearing that jacket?
Just because her aunt said
It took pounds off her.
We met at ten.
Haven't had lunch.
Tide's out –

Stinking river.
That's where Marie went in one night.
Riding on a trolley.
Broke her arm.
We laughed.
Marie howling in the mud.
We had to go and get her.
After three, before four.
Birdman's coming down river.

Birdman!
Birdman going on past.

Mel Hey, Birdman, she's talking to you.

Marie Yeah, she's talking to you. You trying to be rude
or something?

Birdman No. What?

Marie Where you going, Birdbrain?

Birdman Birmingham.

Sita What, now? You got no suitcase. Where's your gear?

Mel She means *now*, where you going *now*?

Birdman Dunno really. Just walking. I suppose.

Marie Well, keep walking then. Ta-ta.

Sita We're going up the park.

Mel Sita! We don't want him tagging along.

Marie No. Doh-brain. No taggers-on. Specially not little
boys.

Sita's phone rings – it's a text message.

Mel Who's that, then?

Sita It's my mum. She wants to know where I am. She
always wants to know where I am.

Mel Tell her we're round my house.

Sita Too close.

Marie Tell her you're round Linda's.

Mel Yeah. Tell her you're round Linda's. She's not
allowed out.

Marie She's grounded.
Birdman Why?

Silence.

Mel None of yours.
Birdman Why?
Marie What's it to you? You fancy her?
Mel What, Linda? You fancy Linda?
Birdman Why's she grounded?
Marie Girls' stuff, little boy. Now run along. We've got
     things to do. Places to go. People to see. Know what I
     mean?
Mel Bye, Birdman.
Sita Birdman, bye. See you later down the park?
Marie Not if we can help it.

SCENE FIVE

The park along the riverbank.
   Niall and Tom are lying in the grass.

Niall Park.
Just hanging.
Too hot. Shade's moved. We haven't.
Pegged out in the sun.
There's a buzzing noise coming in at us from across the
     water.
Gobs of sound going drip, drip in the middle of my
     forehead.
My stomach's curling in this heat.

Pause.

Tom Niall?
Niall?
Niall What is it?

Tom What time?

Niall Is it?

Tom Yeah. What time is it?

Niall Dunno. (*Pause.*) It was two.

Tom That was hours ago. It must be at least four.

Niall At the clock, it was two.

Tom You've been asleep.

Niall Have not. Maybe.

Tom Get some chips?

Niall You got any money?

Tom No. You?

Niall No.

Tom I think I might go home.

Niall What for?

Tom Food. I'm hungry.

Niall Bring us something.

Tom Don't your mum feed you?

Niall Not if she can help it.

Tom She's dead tight, your mum.

Niall It's not her. It's her boyfriend. She's all right. He thinks if they don't feed us, we'll go and live somewhere else.

Tom He's dead tight.

Niall He's not going to last.

Tom They never do with your mum.

Niall It's not her fault. She's all right. She just can't tell a good bloke from a bad one.

Tom Maybe she should give it a rest.

Niall Maybe. You going to get us some food, then?

Tom In a minute.

Niall's phone rings. It's a text message.

Who's that from?

Niall (*pause as he reads*) I wish she wouldn't do that.

Tom Who is it? Marie?

Niall Marie? No way. It's Kirsty. She always puts loads
of kisses. I wish she wouldn't do that.

Tom You don't do it back?

Niall Nah. Well, some. I kind of think – she expects it.

Tom Well weak.

Niall That's just girls, isn't it? What they expect?

Tom You meeting her tonight?

Niall She's not allowed out down the park.

Tom She's not allowed out with you, you mean.

Niall Maybe.

Have you met her mum?

Tom No. You?

Niall jumps up and waves.

Niall She wouldn't speak to me.

She wouldn't speak to me. Standing in her doorway,
holding on to that brass knocker, puffing out her chest.
I saw it. That look. I know it. That look. It just says –
dirt. You're a piece of dirt. That's what it says. Looks
at my feet. That's enough. I know that look. Breathes
deep. Stitches her lips together. Breathes deep and
turns away. Walks deep into the house, calling Kirsty.
Hissing Ki-irssty. Jabber, jabber, jabber. Course she's
not coming out. Not with me at any rate.

Hey! Birdman! Birdman!

Birdman turns.

Tom What did you call him over for?

Niall Hey, Birdman. Az is looking for you.

Birdman So?

Niall Just telling you. That's all. You fishing tonight?
(*Pause.*) Meet you up Stonebridge later?

Pause. Birdman stands and looks.

Tom His brains are mashed.

Niall We'll be there about eight. Got stuff to do before then.

Pause.

See you, then.
Birdman Is Linda going?
Tom (*laughing*) It's too late for her.
Birdman What? What did he mean by that?
Niall She's not allowed out, is she?
Birdman I heard that. What does he mean, it's too late?
Tom Too many questions, Birdman. Too hot to talk.
(*Pause.*) Do you fancy her? Do you? Loser, you.
Niall I'm starving. Come on Tom. Let's go and get some food.

They move off and leave Birdman, who seems undecided about what to do next.

SCENE SIX

Sal is hiding in the shadows. She comes out and speaks as Birdman lingers. He kicks some rubbish around for a while, then leaves.

Sal I see them. I see them all from my hidey-hole. They don't see me. Watching them. I've got my eye on them all. And Birdman. Especially Birdman. What's up with him? There's something up with him. I know.

The Social Worker comes on. Takes a plastic bag out of her briefcase, spreads it on the ground, sits on it, takes off her shoes. Begins to smoke.

Sal You'll get muck on your skirt.
Social Worker I'm sorry?
Sal There's a bench down there. You don't have to sit in the dirt.

Social Worker That's all right. I'm prepared. (*She
indicates the plastic bag.*) Am I in your space?

Sal No.

Social Worker You don't sound too sure about that.
I won't be long. Just stopping for a breather.

Sal You shouldn't smoke. Then you won't get out of
breath.

Social Worker True. Really I just stopped because it's
hot. It just takes it out of me, this heat.

Sal You a teacher?

Social Worker No.

What makes you say that?

Sal My teacher has shoes like that.

Social Worker They don't fit me. They hurt my feet.
Maybe I should get some different shoes.

Sal So you won't look like a teacher?

Social Worker Just so I can walk without limping,
actually. It would help.

Sal I'm sure you could still be a teacher, if you like.

Social Worker What, even with the wrong shoes?
Thanks, but I don't like.

Sal What are you then?

Social Worker What am I?

Sal So what do you do?

Social Worker That's a good question. Actually. I've
been trying to answer that myself this morning.
What do I do?

I take a piece of paper. I go to see someone or they come
to see me.

I talk, they don't listen. I listen, they don't talk.

Then they ask me questions I can't answer. Then I put the
piece of paper back in the file it came from.

Sal You are a teacher.

Social Worker Do you like your teacher?

Sal Not really.

You shouldn't smoke.

Social Worker I know.

Sal Mr Hill smokes in the art cupboard.

Social Worker I like the sound of Mr Hill.

What about you? Are you here all by yourself?

Sal My brother's around.

Social Worker Does he know where you are?

Sal Why?

Social Worker This is a lonely part of the park.

Sal I'm not lonely. I've got a den.

Social Worker Well, that's all right then. You've got
somewhere to go.

I have to go now. Got another appointment.

Sal You could stay a bit longer. If you wanted.

Social Worker Thanks. I'm late already. It's all too late.
But it won't wait.

Sal You've left your plastic bag.

SCENE SEVEN

Linda's house.

Aaron My turn now.

Linda No. No. It's me.

Aaron What, you?

Linda Yes. Me.

Birdman comes round my house.

Knocks on my door.

Mel What again? What does he want from you?

Linda I don't know, do I?

Asking things I haven't got the words to answer.

See this.

There's a knock at my door.

I can see it's him.

But I'm not opening up.

Birdman one side of the door, Linda the other.

Birdman Linda. Linda.
Linda What? What you want, Birdman?
I told you to go away this morning.
What you want?
Birdman Talk to you.
Linda Yeah.
Birdman Really.
Linda What about?
Birdman What happened?
What happened, Linda?
Linda I don't know what you're talking about.
Birdman You do. What happened?
Linda None of yours. If you're here, you know what
  happened.
Birdman Open up Linda. Let me in.
Linda Go away, Birdman.
Birdman Just for a moment. Please, Linda.
Linda No.
Birdman Please. It's really important.
Linda I'm going upstairs now. You can shout all you like.
  I'm not going to let you in. (*She moves away.*) I'm not
  listening, Birdman.

  *Linda moves off and hides her head, so she can't hear
  Birdman shouting.*

Birdman Linda! Linda!

  Birdman turns on his heel and walks off.

SCENE EIGHT

Aaron with two rods.

Aaron Now it's me.
Sun still glancing from the west off the river.
So it's sevenish. Way after six.

Nettle, thistle, bramble, dock
choke that path around the Manor.
Further up the water's slimmer,
Faster, sliding through the park.
I'm heading up to Stonebridge,
It squats in the river. Sits beyond the tide-head.
It's where the fishing's better.
Round the bend – see Birdman chucking stones in the
    water.

Birdman is sitting, gazing out across the water.
Occasionally flipping stones.

All still.

Hey, Birdman.

Birdman grunts.

Not talking, then.
Birdman, hey.
Girl.
Birdman What? What is it? What do you want?
Aaron Going fishing. Stonebridge. You coming?
Birdman Why would I want to do that?
Aaron You might catch something. I've got a spare rod.

Pause.

You waiting for someone?

Pause.

I said you waiting for someone?
Birdman No.
Aaron You coming, then?

Birdman gets up.

So that's how we get there.
Me in front, Birdman behind. Silent.

Sal behind him –
I know she's there, even though she pretends not to be.
I've seen her.

*Sita, Mel, Marie, Tom, Niall are on the bank of the
river.*

Tom Hey, Aaron. Lend us that rod.
Aaron It's for Birdman.

He gives Birdman the rod. Birdman gives it to Tom.

Why did you do that?
Birdman Don't need it. Don't want it.
Aaron I thought we wanted to fish today?
Birdman You wanted to.
Aaron Yeah. Right. What you using for bait, Tom?
Tom (*shrugs*) Bread? You got maggots?
Aaron Don't need maggots.

Tom casts his line.

You're casting in the wrong place, doh-brain. You're
casting where the current runs, you've got to stay
along the bank.

*Aaron threads his line. Tom and Aaron fish. The girls
sit on the bank with Niall. Birdman sits to one side.*

Mel *Ich angele gern.*
Marie What?
Mel *Ich angele gern.*
Sita I like fishing.
Mel *Fantastisch.*
Marie Whatever.

Pause.

I'm never going to speak another word of German again.
Mel You never spoke a word of German before.

Marie Well. I'm never going to walk in that classroom again. And that woman's never going to ask me to speak another word of German.

Pause.

Hey, Birdman – they speak German in Birmingham don't they?

Birdman Shut it, Marie.

Marie Ooh. Now that's not very nice, is it? Did you hear that, Sita? That wasn't very nice, was it? You packed your case yet, Birdman? Don't hang about on our account.

Birdman moves further away.

Marie Oh, I thought you was going then, Birdman. I was just getting ready for an emotional goodbye scene. Where's my tissue? Anybody got a tissue?

Sita Leave it out, Marie.

Marie I will when I want to. Not because you say.

Mel Niall's good at German, aren't you, Niall?

Marie He's not.

Mel He is. He got the top mark for a boy.

Marie She just likes him, that's all. She likes all the boys.

Mel Niall's only got to open his mouth and he's *fantastisch.*

Marie He's what?

Sita Fantastic.

Marie Yeah, well. She's a lesbian, isn't she?

Sita So she likes boys?

Marie Covering her tracks.

Sita Oh.

Aaron has caught something – he's pulling on the line.

Mel Aaron's caught something. Az's got a bite. Hold on, Az. Hold on.

They all jump up and run to the water's edge,
commenting, encouraging Aaron as he fights with the
line – eventually he lands a fish. They all crowd round
and look.

Sita What's he going to do now? He's got to get it off the
hook. Oh, I can't look.

Niall Oh, you beauty. It's huge, Az.

Tom What is it?

Aaron Chub, I think. Not sure, really. (*He unhooks the*
fish.) Where's the bucket?

Tom Here.

Niall It needs water in it, doh-brain.

Tom (*scooping water into the bucket*) Here.

Mel It's too big for the bucket, Az. Its head's gonna stick
out.

Marie Oh my God. See it wriggle. It makes me feel sick.
Put it back.

Sita Yeah, Aaron. Put it back. Look at its eyes.

Aaron Stick its head in. It's got to breathe.

Sita What you going to do with it? You're not going to
eat it, are you?

Sal comes out from the shadows.

Sal Don't kill it yet. I'm going to get Mum. She's got to
see this. She'll never believe you if she doesn't see it.

Aaron No, don't do that.

Sal Why not? She'll want to see it. I'll tell her to bring
the camera. She can take a photo.

Aaron Don't do that. Don't bring her here.

Sal I'm going anyway.

Aaron You stay here, Sal. You're not going anywhere.

Sal You can't stop me.

Exit Sal.

Mel Can I hold it, Az?

Sita Oh no, Mel. Don't do that. It's disgusting.
Marie Go on then, Sita. You hold it. Go on. Touch it.
Sita No. I can't. I'll be sick.
Marie Go on, Sita. Touch it. Touch it, I said. Go on.

Pause.

You scared?

Sita hesitates a moment, but Marie is looking at her hard. She touches the fish.

Yeuch. Smelly. Don't come near me with your smelly fingers.
Sita Well, you didn't touch it, did you? You wouldn't do it.
Marie I will. Watch this. Give it here.

She takes the fish. The others jeer. Then they pass the fish round. Niall drops it. Tom stamps on it, then kicks it in the river.

Aaron While we're passing round the fish, Birdman goes. Doesn't say anything. Doesn't say where he's going. Just takes off. I didn't notice he'd gone until later.

SCENE NINE

Rachel's house.

Rachel It was after eight when I saw Birdman.
How I know –
It's a bit complicated – I'll start at the beginning.
Me sitting listening for Col –
He's always late –
Sitting listening to that little gold clock on the mantelshelf.
It chimes on the half-hour – just once.

Then on the full hour it does the whole works –
Me sitting listening to it chime eight times –
he's late he's late he's late he's late.
Me sitting listening on the edge of my seat –
I can't sit back because I'll put creases in my top.
At eight he's late.
Well late.
I'm beginning to think he's gone off with someone else –
Mel or Linda or Jackie or Marie – they'd all go with him –
he's only got to whistle.
That's a line from a film, but he meant it nice.
I mean – they're dogs – and they're nothing to him.
I'm beginning to think I'll chuck that little gold clock out
    the window.
I'm beginning to think I'm not feeling too good – I'm
    beginning to shrink on the inside, and my mouth's all
    dry.
Then the doorbell rings.

Doorbell.

That's him.
And in a minute we're gonna go out.
And in a minute we're gonna kiss.
And in a minute we're gonna get all loved up.

Hang on a minute, Col. I just need to get my shoes.
    Where's my handbag? Okay.

Outside – at the car.

Colin Da – da!
Rachel Where's the van?
Colin My dad's got it.
Rachel Is this his car, then?
Colin Yeah.
Rachel Borrowed it?
Colin Yeah.

Rachel Does he know?

Colin Course not.

Rachel Well, we can't go out in it, then.

Colin It doesn't matter.

Rachel It does.

Colin It doesn't. Because he thinks Phil's got it.

Rachel Oh.

Colin All right now?

Rachel Yeah. I guess. Where's Phil, then?

Colin Dropped him off round Gary's house. They've got business.

Rachel What kind of business does your brother do?

Colin (*pause*) Look, are you coming or not? I can always get someone else, if you don't want to come.

Rachel I'm coming.

Colin Get in then.

They get in the car.

Rachel It's nice.

Colin Yeah.

Rachel It's really nice. Nice colour.

Colin Persian silver.

Rachel Does the CD work?

Colin Course it does.

Rachel Really nice. Where are we going, then?

Colin Up Spike Hill.

Rachel Not the pub?

Colin We'll do Spike Hill, then the pub.

Rachel How fast does it go?

Colin Faster than you'd want to know.

Rachel Go on, then. Show me.

Colin Just shout if it gets too fast. Shall we have the roof down?

Rachel Yeah.

Colin That fast enough?

Rachel It doesn't go any faster, does it?

Colin Course it does.

Rachel Slow down now, Col. We're coming up to
   Miller's Bend. Colin. Slow down. What are you doing?
   Put your hands on the wheel, Colin. I said on the
   wheel.

Colin You scared, Rachel?

Rachel Course I'm bloody scared. You're going too fast.

Colin Ah. Chicken.

Rachel Stop the car. Stop the car, Colin. Let me out.

Colin All right. All right. I'll slow down. I'm slowing
   down now, see?

Rachel Slower. Go slower.

Colin Like this?

Rachel Both hands. Drive with both hands. And both
   feet.

Colin Like this?

Rachel Both feet at once, both hands at once.

Colin Like this?

Rachel Don't look at me, look at the road.
Okay. Stop the car. Stop the car now.

   She gets out.

Colin Where are you going? It's miles to the pub.

Rachel I'll walk.

   He's driving along beside her.

Colin Get back in the car, Rachel. Come on, get back in
   the car.

Rachel No.

Colin Last chance?

Rachel No.

So he goes off, burning rubber.
I'm in a huff –
these shoes aren't meant for walking
and my top's all creased.

Then I hear it –
it's somebody screaming.
Sounds like murder
and she won't last much longer.

*She stops. Listens all about her. She is rooted to the
spot. Birdman comes.*

Rachel (*whispers*) Birdman. Birdman.
Birdman Fox. It's a fox. Calling for its mate.
Rachel Oh. Oh. I thought. (*She laughs.*)
I thought it was –
Birdman It's a fox.

Pause.

Rachel What you doing round here?
Birdman Been to see my sister.
Rachel Natalie? I thought she moved away.
Birdman Not Natalie. Gloria – she's my big sister.
Rachel I didn't know you had a big sister.

Pause.

Birdman She wasn't in.
Walking home now. You?
Rachel I was out with Colin.

Pause.

He's gone now.
Birdman You walking, then?
Rachel I guess.
Birdman Why do you go with him?
Rachel What? Why do you want to know?
Birdman Why?
Rachel You wouldn't understand.
Birdman When you know you're not the only one?
You do know you're not the only one, don't you?
Rachel I know.

118

But – it doesn't stop him kissing me the way he kisses me.
It doesn't stop me from liking it.

Pause.

Besides. It's none of yours. You ask too many questions.
Birdman Cut through the track to the park?
Rachel I don't really like it. It'll be dark soon.
Birdman Go on. It'll save us ten minutes. I'll hold your
hand if you're scared.
Rachel Shove off. I'm not scared.
Birdman Come on then.

Rachel So we cut through the track.
I really don't like it.
It's full of nettles. And old mattresses. A fridge.
Things that don't rot.
You could fill a house with all this junk.
Then.
We see her.
She's lying in the last patch of sun.

Birdman Vixen.

Rachel I swear to you she sees us.
She turns and looks right at us.
But it doesn't make her move.
She's not moving.
She's not a scabby fox at all.
She's rich and glossy.
I'm thinking it's like one of those books you read at the
dentist's.
I'm thinking it's almost a good thing I got out of the car.
I'm thinking it's a good thing we came down the track.

*Birdman grabs Rachel and tries to kiss her. Rachel
struggles and pulls away. She looks at him.*

Get off, Birdman, what do you think you're doing? Get
your paws off me.

Birdman says nothing.
Just turns and walks off quickly.
I have to follow him. Not staying here on my own.
Then, at the road, he disappears.

SCENE TEN

At the Stonebridge – dusk.

Aaron It's not dark yet. But it's getting there. Things are
  coming to a head.
Sita I don't see that. I didn't see that.
Tom I didn't see it coming, did you?
Aaron We're all gathered at the water. Standing in the
  grey light at the water's edge. Same as yesterday and
  the day before.
We're all tied to this ribbon of dirty water.
Sita Aaron's mum didn't come. It's better that way.
Tom We chucked that fish back in.
It floated a bit.
Mel Drifted downstream. Then disappeared.
Aaron What would she have done? Nothing much.
Sal Taken a photo. She could have brought the camera
  and taken a photo. For the family album.
Aaron In your dreams, Sal. But you don't give up, do
  you?
Sita But there's still that boy.
Tell the story of that boy.
Sal Why do you call him that? He's still got a name.
Niall But later on,
After it's all drifted down the river
He'll be just another boy who . . .
Sal What do you mean?
Niall You know what I mean.
People will say, 'There was that boy,'

Marie 'What boy?'
Niall 'That boy from round here who . . .'
Sal Birdman. You mean Birdman.
Mel For the moment, yeah . . .
Sita Then tell the story.
Sal No. You. I don't like the next bit.
Tom What's to like or dislike about it?
It's just a story about a boy from round here who
Kept coming back to the river.
Niall What? No, that's not it. He asked too many
   questions.
Tom What? No. Did he?
Niall I said: he kept asking questions.
Aaron It's true. He's right.
He kept asking questions.
Sita So there was this boy who kept asking questions.
Mel Then what happened?
Sal I don't like this bit.
Aaron Shut up and tell it. Just tell it.

*Everyone is standing and sitting around on the bank of
the river, some with cans they share around.*
   *Music is coming from the car. Aaron and Niall are
fishing. Tom and Col are sitting with Mel and Sita and
Marie.*
   Sal sits a little apart.

Birdman arrives.

Sal Birdman.
Birdman You should be at home.
Sal Says who?
Birdman Go home.
Sal Why?
Birdman It's too late for you.
Sal Mum's not in.
Birdman (*to Aaron*) Take her home.

Aaron I'm fishing.

Birdman She shouldn't be here. What's she drinking? What's that you're drinking, Sal?

Aaron What's the matter with you? She likes it here. And I'm fishing.

Birdman What's she doing here?

Aaron She's not doing anything. Now shut up. I'm fishing.

Rachel arrives. Colin sees her. She sees him.

Mel Rachel. Hi.

Nice top.

Rachel Thanks.

Mel Looks special.

Rachel It's new, yeah.

Sita Az caught a fish. It was gross.

Rachel Where is it?

Sita Swam off. No, it didn't. Kind of floated off, then sank. I think. It was kind of sad, wasn't it, Marie?

Marie No. Not half as sad as that cat we found.

Mel Yeah. That was sad. It still had its bell. It almost lived.

Tom I tell you, cats can't swim. I guarantee. You wouldn't believe me.

Marie That was sad. It tried, though, didn't it? You shouldn't have thrown it in.

Tom You should have believed me.

Sita Someone might have missed that cat. Wondered what happened to it.

Perhaps they put food out, and then they went to call it. And it never came back.

Mel It was funny, though, the way it skated in the air.

Marie Yeah. That was funny.

Rachel takes off her shoes, dangles her feet in the water.

Mel What you doing, Rachel? The fish'll get your toes.
That one Az caught had teeth.
Rachel My feet hurt.
Marie You walked from home?
Rachel Might have.
Marie You walking home after?
Rachel Might be.

Pause.

Marie Hey, Col. You taking us all home later?
Colin No room tonight.

Colin gets up.

Marie Where you going, Col?
Colin None of yours.

*Colin walks off to go and sit in the car. Rachel gets up
and goes to join him.*

Rachel You got room for me later?
Colin Dunno. Got some things to do.
Rachel What things?
Colin Just things.
You took your time getting here.
Rachel It's a long way from Miller's Bend.
Colin You didn't have to get out.
Rachel I was scared.
Colin You didn't have to get out.
Rachel Col. (*She puts her hand on his arm.*)
Colin What?

*Colin clucks quietly, like a chicken. Rachel turns and
walks off. Puts on her shoes.*

Colin Where are you going?
Rachel Home.
Colin Don't expect a lift.
Rachel Don't want one.

Colin Hey, Mel, Marie – do you want a lift?
Mel We're walking.
Colin Sita – I'm going round Linda's, do you want a lift?
Sita I'm walking.

Birdman looks up.

Rachel Shove off, Colin.

Colin laughs. Then goes over to Niall and Tom.

Colin Hey, Rachel, come here. Come on. Come over here.
Rachel I'm going home.
Colin It was only a joke, Rachel. Come back.

He goes and puts his arm around Rachel. She shakes him off. He grabs her again. She winds out of his embrace.

Come on.
Birdman Leave her alone.
Colin What?
Birdman Leave her alone.
Colin Stop twittering, Birdman.

Birdman faces up to Colin.

Rachel Keep out of this, Birdman.
Birdman Why do you do that? Why are you sticking up for him?
Rachel What is it to you?
Birdman Why do you let him do that to you?
Colin Hang on a minute. What's going on? What is she to you?
Rachel Nothing. It's nothing, Col. Shut up, Birdman. Just keep out of this.
Birdman No, I won't. I won't shut up.
Why don't you ask him what happened to Linda?
Go on. Ask him.

You won't, will you? You afraid of what he'll say?
Or maybe you know. You know, but you don't want to know.
If it's not him it's someone else.
Don't you ever ask your friends what happens to them at night?
You never ask, do you?
You just don't want to know, do you?
Don't you ever wonder about it? Why it's them and not you? What they've done to deserve it?
Why it's them and not someone else?
Why don't you ever ask why it happens?

*Birdman runs and gets in the car. Locks the door.
Colin runs and bangs on the outside. Shouting at
Birdman.*

Colin Get out the car, Birdman. You bloody madman.
Get out. I'll tear your head off. Get out.

*Col carries on shouting. The others watch from a
distance. Birdman turns up the music.*
 *Birdman stares straight ahead, drives off – Col is
flung back.*

SCENE ELEVEN

Linda in the house.

Linda I hear him.
I hear him moving around outside the house.
Round the doors, round the windows.
Trying to get in.

I can hear you, Birdman.
What you want now?
Birdman I just want to hang around with you for a while.

Linda Who sent you?

Birdman No one.

Linda What you want?

Birdman I'm just here to hang around, OK?

Linda Hang around. Hang around. What does that mean?

Birdman I'll just be here while the clock ticks, OK? It's just the clock ticking, and I'm here.

Linda I can't let you in the house.

Birdman Then I'll hang around outside. I'll sit here, so you know where I am. You can be inside where the clock ticks, and I'll sit here.

Birdman sits down. Linda is on the inside, listening.

Linda Listen, Birdman, I can hear the clock tick but I can't hear you. Can't you breathe more loudly or something?

Pause.

Birdman? You still there?

Birdman I'm still here. How much time has gone?

Linda I don't know. I didn't look at the clock, did I?

Birdman I think it goes slowly. Time passes slowly when you're hanging around.

Linda Yeah, well. When you're having fun. It's a daft idea anyway. Passing the time like this. It's a stupid idea.

Birdman Then let me in.

Linda I already told you, I can't do that.

Birdman Well, come outside. Come on. Come outside and sit in the car.

Linda You got a car?

Birdman Yeah. Come for a spin.

Linda We're just passing time in the car?

Birdman Yeah.

Linda Till when?

Birdman Whenever you like.
Linda Then you'll take me home?
Birdman Wherever you like.

Linda comes out of the house, smiles when she sees the car. Birdman holds open the door for her. She gets in.

Linda No questions.
Birdman No questions.
Linda No touching.
Birdman None of that.
Linda Where shall we go?
Birdman You want to see some foxes?

SCENE TWELVE

At the track.
  Birdman and Linda get out of the car. Linda stumbles.

Linda Ouch. I've twisted my ankle. I can't see a thing.
  Shine the torch this way a bit more.

They pick their way across the track, move amongst the rubbish.

You're sure there are foxes here?
Birdman Yeah. I saw the vixen earlier on. Look, sit up
  here.
Linda What about you?
Birdman I'll sit over here.
Linda Give me the torch, though.
Birdman All right. You can have the torch.

Linda sits on top of the fridge, takes the torch. She shines it on Birdman.

What you doing that for?
Linda Just looking.

Birdman Just don't shine it in my eyes, that's all.

She shines it in his eyes, moves it over his face, shines it in his eyes again. He puts his hands over his face. They wait. Linda tires after a while, and gets down and begins to look through the rubbish. She opens the fridge door, shuts it again. Moves on.

Linda Birdman.

Birdman That's me.

Linda What's your real name?

Birdman No questions. We said no questions. We're just passing the time.

Linda Hm. Birdman.

Birdman Yeah? Is it a question?

Linda Kind of. Not about you though. Can I ask it?

Birdman You can ask it. What if I don't know the answer?

Linda You make it up.

Birdman And then you guess if it's right?

Linda Could do. Yeah.

Birdman Okay then.

Linda Birdman. How many bones in a body?

Birdman What?

Linda If you break all the bones in your body, how many do you break?

Birdman I dunno. Fifty? A hundred? Do you think that's right?

Linda More I reckon. Must be more. If you look at your fingers, think about your toes. And there must be loads of other ones all over the place. If you think about it. You're wrong, I reckon.

Birdman I don't get the prize, then.

Linda You don't get the prize. Have another go?

Birdman Not so hard this time.

Linda Just keep your eye on the prize, Birdman.

Birdman I keep my eye on the prize. What is the prize?

Linda You find out when you win. You have to win first.

Birdman What's the question, then?

Linda sits back up on the fridge, thinks for a minute.

Linda How long can a human being be without air?
Birdman Linda. Can't you ask a proper question?
Linda It is a proper question.
Birdman A different question, then.
Linda How long before you faint if you don't get any air?
Birdman Hell, I don't know. Two minutes?
Linda Two minutes.
Birdman You think I'm right?
Linda I think you're right.
Birdman Yes!! So I get the prize! And the prize is?
Linda (*picks up an old crash-helmet from the fridge and gives it to Birdman*) Here, the champion's crown.
Birdman Really? I really get to wear the champion's crown? Great. Fantastic. (*He puts it on.*)
Linda (*slides off the fridge and stands beside it*) Now shut me in.
Birdman What?
Linda You shut me in.
Birdman No.
Linda Shut me in, Birdman.
Birdman No. I won't do it.
Linda You can let me out again.
Birdman How long?
Linda Two minutes.
Birdman That's too long.
Linda Just hang around. You do two minutes there. I'm two minutes here.

Linda gets in the fridge.

Birdman It's dangerous.
Linda Two minutes. It's not. That's a fact. There's air in there.

Birdman Why?

Linda I just need you to shut me up. That's all.

Birdman Only two minutes, then. That's all. No more. After two minutes I'm opening up.

Linda Not before. Have you got a watch?

Birdman No.

Linda You can have mine. It's got a second-hand here. Look.

Birdman I don't want to do this.

Linda Close the door, Birdman.

Birdman takes the torch and closes the door to the fridge. He stands beside it. Walks away from it. Comes back and puts his arms around it. For two minutes he hugs the fridge, tapping his fingers gently on the outside.

Birdman Linda. Linda.

He checks the watch. At two minutes he tears open the fridge door, and Linda falls out. Birdman grabs her. Then she opens her eyes and laughs. She gets up quickly.

Linda I said no touching, Birdman.

Birdman Sod you, Linda. Don't do that again.

Linda smiles.

Linda We could stay here. Got a fridge. Got some chairs.

Birdman We could live here.

Linda We could make a roof.

Birdman We don't need a roof.

Linda We will need a roof when it rains. I'm not getting wet. I haven't got my big coat.

Birdman starts to pull bits of junk into place to create a makeshift roof.

Birdman That's our roof.

Linda brings over a mattress or some rags.

Linda That's my bed. Where are you going to sleep? You can sleep on a chair. Two chairs.

Birdman I'm on guard. I'll sleep outside, look at the stars.

Linda Well, if it rains, you can come in. That'll be your space there. You'll always sit there. And sometimes I'll come out and look at the stars.

Linda sits down on a chair, looking out.

What you going to do with that car, Birdman? It can't stay there.

It's all over the garden. It's spoiling the view.

Birdman Dunno. Take it back, I suppose. Better do it tonight.

Take it for a ride first?

Linda Where to?

Birdman Wherever you like.

Linda The sea?

Birdman If you want.

Linda Come on then.

They get in the car – Birdman turns on the CD player.

Aaron So that's Birdman heading down the river,
Heading for the white bridge and out towards the sea.
If we'd been listening we might have heard him coming.
If we'd been looking we might have seen him smile.

Rachel So he scattered his questions over the water.
Who and what and why and why and why
and if we knew we couldn't say.

Sita But it wasn't our fault.

Colin He's not any kind of a hero. So don't think he was going to help. Or that we're going to help him.

Mel And don't go thinking that's an end to it all. It's all just water under the bridge. Things stay the same. If it's not him, it's someone else. In a while we won't even remember his name.

Sal He's just another boy from round here.

Aaron Too late we look and now we see it –

Freeze-frame.

The silver arrow in the air.

All those questions hanging in the air.

Joey Hawk.

Birdman.

Flies.

> *The music becomes much louder, there is the sound of a crash. Blackout. Then the sky lights up red.*

A Silver Arrow in the Air

Deborah Gearing interviewed by Jim Mulligan

Burn is Birdman's story, flowing like a river, meandering without a beginning throughout the events of the day to its tragic end that is signalled in the oblique reference to Birdman marching out towards the sea. The opening sets the structure and tone of the play. Aaron is the narrator of a story that is a ritual and a memorial. The listeners are a group of friends who know the story because they were part of it and who will play their parts when the time comes, even though they do not all know all the parts of the story at the start.

> I'm very interested in language. It intrigues me. I knew I wanted to do something rhythmic. I wanted somebody to be telling a story and as soon as I found Aaron and that first speech I knew it was going to be rhythm that shaped the play. I wanted to give these young people some dignity. We have such preconceptions about young people, and sometimes our fears are fulfilled, but I wanted us to see beyond the events, to give them something that, if not exactly heroic, at least lifts them out of everyday things.

There is a restlessness about all the characters and a mundane cruelty. They are rude and dismissive of each other but they are all capable of moments of connection: all, in their own ways, finding out how to 'be'. But Birdman is more perceptive and sensitive than most of them. He is appalled at what Aaron says to Sal when she is too scared to cross the railway line. 'You gobshite. Talking to her like that. She's your sister. You don't talk to her like that.' And he takes Sal home.

I've worked a lot with children who have problems
and issues in their lives, looked-after children, and I've
only recently learned that if there isn't a space near
you when you have to be moved on you can be sent a
long way from where you live. I was shocked by that.
It's one thing to make a choice and go somewhere but
to be taken away from your friends and everything
you know is really a huge thing. Joey Hawk's character
grew from the groups I worked with. The young
people were very needy, as Birdman is, but they took
care of each other, and were tender to each other even
though from time to time things could kick off in
unexpected and frightening ways.

The river and the spaces around it are Birdman's territory.
He mooches around on the fringes of things, pops up
everywhere and accepts the scorn of the others as if it
did not matter. Inside, however, he is trying to deal with
the disastrous news that he is going to be moved to
Birmingham within two weeks. He says, 'I'm not going.'
But he knows it is hopeless. Despite this, he can still care
for others. When he encounters Rachel he questions her
about what she sees in Colin, and he takes her through
the detritus dumped beside the track by feckless adults
who will no doubt moan about 'bloody teenagers', where
they see the vixen. Rachel sees that the vixen is rich and
glossy and she thinks it's a good thing they came down
the track and then Birdman has to spoil it all by trying to
kiss her. She pulls away and says, 'Get your paws off me.'
But he says nothing and walks quickly away.

The sadness is that Birdman loves Linda. Throughout
the day you are not sure who he is going to meet next,
but whoever it is he can't make contact. It's like water
going round rocks. He goes to see Linda because he
fears something terrible has happened to her and there

is this tenderness in him and a great concern that grows during the day. I know what happened to Linda but I deliberately left it open. It might have something to do with Colin's brother but it is certainly someone from outside their group. There's an undercurrent (water image again) where everybody except the adults knows what's going on.

Burn is a tragedy. For Deborah Gearing, Birdman's death is an accident. He is not a very good driver and as a result he crashes the car through the bridge parapet. It is just one of those things that happen. An alternative reading, however, could be that Birdman is so burdened by the news he has had that day and so hurt by the careless rejections he has received that he deliberately crashes the car. Either way, accident or suicide, 'It's just a story about a boy who kept coming back to the river' and 'who kept asking questions'. The question we are left with is: if he hadn't died, what kind of a life would he have had? For the friends who are telling the story it's all just water under the bridge. He scattered his questions over the water but it wasn't their fault. He isn't any kind of hero. He is just a boy who is almost nameless and soon will be. There is not even a photograph of him so that they can remember him.

I see it as a very simple play. It relies on the acting. Birdman is a very strong part, but it is an ensemble piece and the actors will have to work together onstage. They might not be saying anything but they must be aware. They will all have to dig deep and be sympathetic. That's what acting is all about, after all. It's about finding the part of you that corresponds to the part that is written, emphasising those parts of you that fit with the play and finding out about yourself in the process.

In the final freeze-frame, Joey Hawk, Birdman, is a silver arrow in the air. He flies. A heroic, tragic death if ever there was one. The boy who asked questions leaves a few for us to answer.

Production Notes

Deborah Gearing's background involves working with abused children through drama youth groups. One thing that profoundly shocked her about the way these children lived was that they existed with the knowledge that at any point they could potentially be uprooted and moved to an environment that was alien to them. She was drawn to capturing the way in which they seemed overloaded and overwhelmed with anxieties, and how they developed and expressed defence mechanisms in order to deal with these feelings. Clearly these are very different from an adult's way of dealing with such feelings. Within the language patterns of the groups she worked with, the language of the children was governed by quite unpredictable waves – at one moment there might be a sudden consensus which meant that the group began swearing, but much of the time they found other ways to express their frustrations. This could be why the play shifts in an intricate, and subtly dynamic way between its poetic and naturalistic elements and in the tempo of its dialogue and situations.

SCENE ANALYSIS

SCENE ONE

Birdman is killed in the final accident, and Linda survives. Don't be concerned about there being ambiguity at the final image itself, but these facts should be clear. The play's final scene in the camp should feel like an 'opening up' rather than conveying a sense that events are spiralling out of control. Consequently the feeling at the beginning of the play is that there is a sense of undefined urgency being processed by the group, which stems from the events conveyed at the play's climax. But there is also a sense that these events are happening in the present.

You need to communicate the importance of where the story begins. Sal's line, 'Where are you starting?' emerges from the opening 'red glow', and its delivery is important since it sets the trajectory for the rhythm of the scene, with characters who are full of the sense that they need to tell a story. The characters are grasping towards making some sort of sense out of the tension and disorientation of the events which end the story and which also provide its starting point.

Make specific linguistic moments resonate in the sense that the characters need to capture moments with an almost forensic relish. Aaron's 'Hear this . . .' is a moment where we need to sense that Aaron is making an effort to own the story, perhaps by standing up and making eye contact with the audience. The 'Hogweed' speech where the opening characters track their way through the undergrowth, is one where it's important that no detail is thrown away. We should get a sense that every detail encountered in the scene has the potential to be important. The lines written in brackets have a separate, distinct rhythm.

Aaron's treatment of Sal not only serves as a mask for his own nervousness, but also demonstrates that he is aware of the charismatic power of Birdman, who attracts attention through stillness rather than being dogmatic or resorting to overt intimidation like Aaron.

We should sense that Aaron is reviewing his actions in lines like 'That I shouldn't have said' and 'You know she said I should stay away from you.' Such moments should hang in the air, so that we can understand that Aaron has been affected by self-questioning. But Aaron is also the least neurotic of the characters in the play – his presence bookends the action. While we get the sense that he has to work hard to gain the kind of presence that belongs to Birdman, he has a kind of stability, especially in the opening scene, where we see signs of his pride at being Birdman's friend.

Birdman's angry reaction to Aaron's treatment of Sal and his mention of Linda being taken to the allotments come from a sense of affinity with Linda's traumatised state. Although she does not appear in this first scene and her rape is mentioned quite allusively, we should gain an early insight into the depth of Birdman and Linda's connection. Aaron and Sal's reaction to Linda's situation is also one of shock – it should give us the sense that what has happened to her is exceptional.

SCENE TWO

In this scene, Linda's image of her red-and-yellow dress sustains the sense of anxiety smouldering beneath the surface of the action.

Linda is speaking only the day after her rape. It is important that when she tears up the strips of her dress, she is not seen to be revisiting past sexual experiences. Linda should not be identified as being either overtly tarty or overly virtuous: rather we should get the impression that this experience is exceptional for her. She is not someone who is intended to be portrayed as significantly more weak or different from the other girls – but in her specific situation she is finding a way to work through her anxieties. Phrases like 'sad-sickness', and the shredding of the dress illustrate her powerful feelings. In a simple way, they magnify the sense that her concerns are multiple and overwhelming and not completely assimilated into something understandable for her.

The mother should not be demonised. She and Linda certainly don't have a good relationship, but the mother is angry about the dress and is unaware of the real purpose of the Dettol. Though lines such as 'You're sick' are intended to refer to Linda's mental state, it is also possible to see an element of inevitability in the mother's reaction – though without her necessarily being portrayed as sympathetic.

Birdman's reaction to Linda is similar to someone recognising their own mirror-image in someone else – there is an instinctive understanding between them that comes closer to a kind of love than indicative of simple attraction. In the rhythm of their dialogue we should get a sense of two friends who might be able to finish off one another's sentences, so close is their connection. Birdman's 'Dunno' may be slightly defensive, since it should be obvious that he has come to see Linda because he likes her.

At this point we sense that Birdman knows about Linda's predicament, but understands her enough to take a step back and doesn't force her to refer to it. On Linda's part, we feel that when she talks of Birdman as 'boy not man', she is sensing that his presence makes her feel better, but is not sure how or why. His status as outsider here is beginning to represent something more attractive.

Attention should be paid to how significant reactions and details can be etched by 'frozen moments'. Linda opening the door is a potential opportunity to explore this idea. Here the action can be suspended for a moment as the audience absorbs her verse-like speech in which she recounts her experiences and her reaction to Birdman.

At the line 'Open up,' there should be a complete break from Linda's sensitive introspection. Here she reverts to the feisty persona that has more in common with the social fronts presented by some of the other female characters like Mel and Marie. It is also important that Birdman doesn't hear her encouragement to 'make his six-pack grin'.

It is possible that the mark on Linda's arm is the result of self-harm, and that Birdman perhaps notices this.

SCENE THREE

This scene centres around the presence of Jan, Birdman's Social Worker. The character of Jan should not be satirised. Our first impression is of a character isolating five minutes of pleasure in a dismal day. In her interview with Birdman it is important we realise that she isn't insensitive and that she is aware of her own inadequacy at only being able to 'go through the motions' with him. Jan does not lead the kind of life that will allow her to meet someone, and she probably started out with a very strong belief in her job.

Don't present Birdman too sentimentally. His background is one of being moved from place to place – there is a volatile element in his character that makes the Social Worker aware that he has the potential to become violent. Consequently she has a nervousness stemming from the knowledge that he can be hostile.

Jan's monosyllables 'Fine. Well . . .' convey complicated feelings. Don't let these words get lost in performance but treat these small moments as 'a shot in a film', or as 'a cut'.

SCENE FOUR

In this scene the gang of Mel, Marie and Sita encounter Birdman. While they allude to Linda being 'grounded', it is clear from the story that only Aaron and Sal know about what has actually happened to Linda, so Mel's 'None of yours' indicates less knowledge than she suggests.

Marie is the protagonist who keeps the other two in line. Sita has a naivety and we feel a stronger sense of parental hold on her. We see her attraction for Birdman more easily than we can read any affection in the other two. Marie and Mel have a feisty bravado that makes it impossible to tell how they really feel about him.

There is also a comic contrast between the stance of coolness that Sita evokes in her opening speech and her description of what has happened to Marie. In Sita's speech we should feel an engagement with the graphic detail of her surroundings.

SCENE FIVE

Introducing the characters of Niall and Tom, this scene represents a shift in rhythm from what's gone before. The atmosphere should convey a very hot day – the feeling is 'half doped-up', and directors should try to communicate this through the non-sequiturs present in the characters' speech at the beginning of the scene.

The identity of the boys is less obvious than Niall's statement, 'She wouldn't speak to me,' might indicate – he and Tom are quite sensitive boys and in terms of their status in the group they are closer to being outsiders rather than yobbish.

These protagonists are meant to be neither rich nor poor 'trendies' – either way, it's certain neither would be palatable to Kirsty.

Tom's allusion to Linda – 'It's too late for her' – again brings up the question of how much the protagonists know about her situation. The way Birdman reacts makes for another telling moment where we sense his feelings towards Linda.

Niall and Tom might have been on the periphery of rumours about Linda, but certainly would not have talked about whether or not they were true. This is quite an innocent statement on the part of Tom. Niall's first 'She wouldn't speak to me' should be communicated to Tom, and the second to both himself and the audience.

SCENE SIX

Sal is at the centre of this scene – we should gain a sense that she is curious, older than her years, and that she is someone who has a determination to work things out. She is written as a little girl but she doesn't need to be played as such. It is more important to play the spark and tenacity that her lines imply. She is aware that there is something troubling Birdman, though she doesn't quite have the maturity to work out exactly what. As self-sufficient as Sal seems, her line 'I'm not lonely' raises the question of whether or not this is said with some defensiveness.

The Social Worker appears again, and here we see a slightly more relaxed, even humorous figure.

SCENE SEVEN

The presence of Mel in this scene to some extent provides a mouthpiece for the audience's curiosity. Like them, she is not completely sure of what's happened in the story, but is becoming consumed by the desire to know more. There is a sense that everything is fragmentary in the play, and that no single character is aware of the whole story.

We experience the feeling of disorientation affecting Linda in an unsettling way. This has the effect of pulling us into a frightened, paranoid atmosphere as Linda denies Birdman entry to her house.

In their dialogue held through the closed door, there is a very simple, precise image of close proximity. There is also division between Birdman and Linda, until Linda moves away.

SCENE EIGHT

The atmosphere in this scene should be full 'middle of summer' – that of an endlessly hot day. There is a volatile, perhaps slightly dangerous sense that these are children creating their own moral universe. There are also echoes in the scene of the play's starting point.

The passing round of the fish is not a symbolic moment. Instead consider how central the scene is to the play as a whole and how the protagonists' reactions to the fish tell us something unique about their characters. The play is very dense and intricate at a human level.

This could be a golden opportunity to be exploring props, and be imaginative. Nothing cumbersome enough to break the flow of the play should be used to represent the fish. The handling of the fish could represent a point of relief that provides a counterpoint to the play's intense pleasure in its words and rhythms. The moment could become something that is akin to a dance.

SCENE NINE

The appearance of Rachel is another embodiment of the play's theme of anxiety. Perhaps she is from a more socially aspiring, if not wealthier, background than some of the other characters, especially in her preoccupation with the 'little gold clock' ticking. The characters Deborah saw were not specifically from any kind of background. She envisioned quite a mixed group who might potentially live on the same street. This scene is a kind of odyssey in itself. It builds to the point where there is an incident in a car that represents a breach in Rachel and Colin's relationship. The fact that Colin is older than Rachel is significant in that his undeniable swagger can be seen as being merely an aspect of his seniority – it's possible that his charisma is an illusion created by this.

We should feel Birdman's need for a greater under-standing quite strongly. In his quite intimate moments with Rachel, his need to understand his situation is motivated by questioning about why his family has left him, and why Linda doesn't want to be with him.

In the moment where Birdman and Rachel walk down the path, we sense Birdman's need to connect with someone. There is the feeling that he realises Rachel's low self-esteem and is trying to understand it. He has encountered a variety of social situations, and has had to learn to adapt accordingly. He has always had a questioning, introspective side to his character, but the unusual events of the day are bringing things to a head.

It's important that the moment where they see the vixen should be sustained until Birdman breaks the atmosphere.

It is Rachel who actually breaks away from Birdman – this is perhaps to do with her innate sense of social embarrassment (Birdman is younger than her). The protagonists are all piecing together their movements through the day. There is always an element of feeling that they are trying to understand how they played a part in Birdman's downfall.

SCENE TEN

The action here should build with a frightening sense that things are coming to a head. Birdman's need for a confrontation, and to have questions answered, becomes the impulse that leads him to the scene – a place where he instinctively senses the others will have gathered.

In Birdman's anguish, there is the implicit protest against the feeling that dreadful things have happened to him in his life, but that no one has taken the trouble to ask him about it. His anger at Colin begins as being specifically directed towards that character, but then becomes more universal. His reaction to Colin is perhaps motivated by the fact that Colin is almost synonymous with the type of character who he thinks has attacked Linda – it's not because he actually suspects Colin of doing so.

SCENE ELEVEN

There is a steadiness and impulsiveness in Birdman which dictates the rhythm of this scene. At first he is allowing Linda responsibility, but gradually we sense that he is reeling her in as he persuades her to come for a 'spin'. Birdman's impulse is not a calculated attempt at revenge, but we should certainly feel an escalating sense that he wants to get into the car and put his foot down. His reaction to Colin is the only moment where he breaks from rationality. At the same time, this feeling is in conflict with a kind of tenderness between Birdman and Linda –

think about how the implied rhythm of the clock affects the atmosphere of the scene.

There is a further moment of anxiety that deserves to be isolated and drawn out, as should the earlier moment with the vixen. This occurs at the point where 'Birdman sits down'.

SCENE TWELVE

This climactic scene occurs geographically at the same spot that Birdman brought Rachel. Even more than at that moment, this scene represents either a respite or an adrenaline rush that culminates in Linda tumbling from the fridge.

Her actions in climbing into the fridge represent her need to create a sense of catharsis for herself. Without articulating what has happened to them, Linda and Birdman both have to find other ways to work through their emotions.

Linda has been the victim of an environment that has proved unreliable. With Birdman, she is testing this environment. This is quite a big moment for Birdman to hold his nerve. But it will work if you hold the suspense for the full two minutes that Linda remains in the fridge.

STAGING THE PLAY

It is important to think about how the play moves forward from a visual perspective in terms of time. How does the progression of the day show itself through shifts into different atmospheres and lighting effects? It might be possible to listen to the play itself to determine this. Ultimately you will find that a stripped-down approach will work best visually. Deborah has indicated where and what there is sound- and rhythm-wise. This is important as much for suggesting what isn't there as what is. As an example: when sound enters with the car, this is a rhythm change that is indicated in the text. No other sound is needed except where indicated. Similarly in terms of set and props – even moments involving the car will benefit from a pared-down approach.

The note at the start of the script indicates that chairs might be used. A lot can be done with sparing use of these chairs – but too much busy-ness can seriously impede the course of the action. One definite item on stage is the fridge. A fridge can be obtained with a licence and the back removed for safety reasons. This should be a peripheral object through much of the performance – its significance should only be brought out in Scene Eleven. Linda wearing the crash helmet at the end of Scene Eleven might help overcome any ambiguity about whether or not she survived the crash.

Many directorial decisions are involved in determining how the breaks in verse and speech indicate change in tempo; similarly in how the characters connect, and how and when their attention transfers from one another to include the audience or to indicate the simultaneous tension between retrospection and living in the moment.

Lighting might enhance these changes, but nothing too elaborate that would potentially interrupt the flow of the action. The concluding line, which is closely followed by the red glow emerging, represents a definite rhythm change. Think about how the atmosphere effected by this change can be brought into play at other important moments.

Finally, remember that these young characters are not caricatures – don't succumb to the temptation to make them coarser-grained than they really are. Rather, while there is still a sense that they have distinct characters, think about how each individual is a 'presence'. Each presence is dealing with varying impulses presented by the situations and pressures brought up in the circumstances presented in the play, some of which come from their social backgrounds.

Workshop facilitated by Paul Miller
with notes taken by Paul Williams

CHATROOM

Enda Walsh

Characters

Jim

Laura

William

Jack

Eva

Emily

All the characters are about fifteen years old.

There are six identical orange plastic seats in a row at the very front of the stage. There's a two-metre gap between each seat. Beside each seat on the ground is some sort of bag from which the characters take out their various small props, e.g., bags of crisps, nail varnish, cups of tea, make-up, hair brushes . . .

The song 'Oompa Loompa', sung by the Oompa Loompas from the film Willy Wonka and the Chocolate Factory, *is heard.*

Oompa Loompa, doompadee doo
We have a perfect puzzle for you.
Oompa Loompa, doompadee dee
If you are wise you will listen to me.

What do you get when you guzzle down sweets?
Eating as much as an elephant eats?
What are you at getting terribly fat?
What do you think will come of that?
I don't like the look of it.

Oompa Loompa, doompadee dah
If you're not greedy you will go far.
You will live in happiness too
Like the Oompa Loompa doompadee do
Doompadee do.

Three actors appear from one side of the stage and the other three appear from the other side. They walk casually towards each other in a line, stop, turn and face the audience. From left to right they are: William,

*Jack, Eva, Emily, Jim and Laura. They are all about
fifteen years of age. They stand there for a while and
look at the audience. They then look at each other.
They seem to be sizing each other up in that passive-
aggressive teenage way. In unison they walk towards
their seats and sit down.*

   *This should all last one and half minutes. As they
sit, the Oompa Loompas' song comes to an end.*

William What's there to like about it?

Jack It's a classic.

William What, a single bloke lives in a castle in the
middle of . . . where is it set again?

Jack Film or book?

William There's a difference?

Jack The film changed some details. It doesn't matter.

William Well, it's set wherever it's set . . . and this bloke
lives in his big gaff in the middle of the town. He lives
with dwarfs. Nothing wrong with that. Fair whack.
But they're orange. Orange dwarfs with green hair.

Jack And there's only around twenty of them making the
world's supply of chocolate . . . none of this is meant
to be realistic.

William But why make them dwarfs . . .? Why make
them orange in the first place? What's wrong with the
ordinary?

Jack It's for children. Ordinary's boring.

William Exactly! Which is my original point about these
children's writers! As if a little boy who shares a giant
bed with his grandparents . . . *four* of them . . . as if
he'd ever . . . in the *real* world . . . win this chocolate
factory!

Jack (*groans*) Jesus.

William You know, in the real world it would have been
that fat German boy who falls into the chocolate lake
at the beginning of the tour. In the real world he's the

winner. This is how it ends, right . . . He falls in. His father gets these big-time lawyers to sue the shit out of Willy Wonka. They look into his shady past and his dodgy personal life with those orange midgets! He's dragged through the tabloids and they make shit out of him! He's done! The Germans win, 'cause let's face it, the Germans always win. The fat German kiddy –

Jack His name is Augustus.

William Right, Augustus . . . well, he inherits everything as part of the settlement. He gets it all. And because he's a glutton he can't stop eating all this chocolate. The more the Oompa Loompas make, the more Augustus eats. He's eighteen years old and forty stone. One day he wakes up, stretches for the television remote and dies of a massive heart attack. The end. *That* is the real world.

Jack It's only a children's story.

William It's a lie! What's the point? What are they telling us?

Jack What are *who* telling us?

William The writers! Our parents! Harry *bloody* Potter? In the real world he's still under the stairs. He's a thirty-year-old retard who's developed his own under-the-stairs language!

Jack The point is . . . is that children don't want to read the true stories. What child wants to read the news? It's just escape. Isn't it alright to dream of other things?

William Why? Life's too short. If the world is going to develop in any way . . . we should be told what's really happening.

Jack Well, a lot of these children's stories are metaphors anyway. They're talking about important issues in creative ways!

William Oh please! Do you think any eight-year-old finishing watching *Willy Wonka* thinks anything other than, 'I'd love an Everlasting Gob Stopper'? Listen to me, John . . .

Jack It's Jack.

William They're trying to keep us young! They don't want us thinking for ourselves. They see us as a threat. They want to keep everything 'fantasy'. All these children's writers . . . and this J. K. Rowling woman! *She* is the enemy. She should be taken out?

Jack So that's what you're doing in a Harry Potter Chatroom? Trying to drum up some interest in an assassination attempt on J. K. Rowling?

William Well, are you interested?

A slight pause.

Jack I can't. I have to do my homework.

Music. The King's of Leon's 'Red Morning Light' is heard. We hear the first verse and chorus until it cuts abruptly.

Eva But I was younger then and she just came on the scene, remember?

Emily Yeah.

Eva And the video with her in school in her school uniform and pigtails . . .

Emily She looked lovely.

Eva You wanted to be her, didn't ya?

Emily She didn't have her tits done then?

Eva That was much later.

Emily But even then they were a decent size.

Eva But wasn't it a bit creepy . . . in hindsight . . . but that thing she was doing with her tongue. It was very sexual.

Emily We didn't notice.

Eva Well, we were young and it wasn't for the kids.

Emily It was for the older boys . . . and the dads.

Eva She's sticking out her tongue, but it's subtle. Flicking it in and out like a little parrot.

Emily It was a bit seedy.

Eva I remember seeing that only last year after not seeing it for a while . . . and I have to say I felt betrayed by Britney. You know how her songs and videos were all about that journey from girl to woman . . .

Emily Yeah.

Eva And it sort of felt good, didn't it? Like Britney was a part of your puberty.

Emily I remember having my first period and listening to 'I'm Not a Girl, Not Yet a Woman' and thinking, 'Thanks, Britney. My sentiments exactly!'

Eva She felt like a spokeswoman.

Emily Oh, definitely.

Eva But when I saw the video to 'Hit Me Baby One More Time' last year and all that sexual stuff with her tongue and just how cropped that crop-top was . . .

Emily Was her belly button pierced back then?

Eva Probably.

Emily Sorry, go on.

Eva Well, I got really angry over that betrayal. It's no longer Britney who's talking to us but some pervert record producer. He's got this vision, this plan of turning every eight-year-old in the Western world into a tongue flicking, crop-topped belly-button-pierced temptress.

Emily Have you got your belly-button pierced?

Eva Well, yeah, of course.

Emily Did it hurt?

Eva It's not as bad as you hear. But anyway, Britney . . . Don't you think a lot of young girls began to feel that way about her?

Emily Well, both of us did.

Eva And maybe that's why her career's dying a slow death. She lied to us.

Emily You don't think it has to do with her music being crap?

Eva A little bit . . . but I really would like to think that girls realised that they were being manipulated . . . that they made a stand against that pervert record producer. But do you know what the sad thing is?

Emily Britney got burnt.

Eva She was thick.

Emily She made her money, I suppose.

Eva But she doesn't have our respect any more. She's got a few houses, nice clothes, new breasts . . . but if I met her tomorrow . . .

Emily Like on the bus?

Eva Or in Tesco.

Emily Or Argos.

Eva If I met Britney Spears tomorrow, I would gently pull her to one side, place my arms around her shoulders like I'm going to hug her, move my face towards her like I'm going to kiss her . . . and whisper in her ear, 'Britney Spears, you sold my childhood soul.'

Emily Oh, that's cruel.

Eva 'You sold my childhood soul.' Then I'd smash her in the face.

Emily And what would Britney say?

Eva 'Hit me baby one more time'?

Emily Nice one.

Eva Her day of judgement will come when some teenager will stop her outside Prada and say, 'You sold my childhood soul, bitch.'

Emily laughs but Eva doesn't. She's serious. Pause.

Emily I better go. It's been nice talking to you, whoever you are.

Eva Can we not just talk for another little bit? I had an argument with my bitch-mother and I'm feeling terrible.

Emily What do you want to talk about?

Pause. Eva thinks and decides.

Eva Murder.

Emily laughs but Eva doesn't. Music. The Jam sing 'That's Entertainment'. We hear the first verse and chorus before it cuts abruptly.

Jim Are you sure you don't mind listening to this?

Laura That's what the room's all about. If you have a problem just get it out.

Jim Maybe I shouldn't even be in this place. I don't know whether it's that serious yet.

Laura It doesn't matter. There isn't a scale of depression here. I'm here at the other end and I'm here to listen to you, Jim.

Jim Right.

Laura Don't be nervous.

Jim I'll start, then.

Laura Okay.

A pause.

Jim Well, it's Easter time and every year our church does a big Passion play. My mother's very active in the church. She's the Virgin Mary.

Laura Which would make you Jesus Christ.

Jim In the Passion, she's Mary.

Laura Right.

Jim And my whole family get involved. I've got three other older brothers and they're Roman soldiers. They're very big . . . not like me . . . and they look the part. One year my brother Derek went too heavy on Jesus and actually popped his knee right open. It was a mess. But anyway, this year my mother comes into my bedroom with her 'good news'. She's building it up like she's going to tell me that I'm going to get a stab at playing a centurion . . . until she tells me . . . they want me to play John.

Laura Well, John's a great part.

Jim Yeah, but he's a bit gay.

Laura How do you mean?

Jim I've got nothing against gay people.

Laura St John was gay?

Jim Historically speaking, probably not. But in our parish it's always the slightly effeminate boys who get to play John.

Laura Okay.

Jim Like I say . . . I've got nothing against gays. I respect them. They're tough, they know their own mind, they stand out and they don't care, you know. I respect them. But I'm not like that at all. I'm just a sap with no bottle who knows nothing. I'm not interesting enough to play the gay icon that is St John. In a million years I could never get away with those purple robes.

Laura Purple?

Jim It's sort of an unspoken thing in the parish. It's a bit weird.

Laura Right, carry on.

Jim Well . . . we do a few rehearsals with my mother as the Virgin Mary and I've got to get emotional when Jesus is dying on the cross and he says to Mary, 'Woman behold your son,' while looking over at me. And I'm supposed to break down at that point because I know that Jesus is just about to croak it but I'm getting very nervous because basically I'm a terrible actor and I'm all blocked up.

Laura Emotionally?

Jim Exactly.

Laura Right.

Jim So I tell my mother I want to drop out. I say it quiet so the others can't hear but she starts screaming at me and saying how typical it was . . . and did I have a back-bone . . . and why was I such a coward . . . and why wasn't I like my older brothers . . . and all this shit. And then she says I'm like my dad. But what would I know? I haven't seen my dad since I was six . . . but she starts shouting, 'You're just like your dad, Jim!' . . . 'Just like your dad, walking out on things! Walking out on me! Gutless!' I mean, I hated her just then. Why did she have to bring up my dad in front of all of those people like that? Why?! So the following night is the Passion proper and I'm kneeling and looking up at Jesus. He's doing a great job dying on the cross, this guy called Barry Doyle. He's into amateur dramatics in a big way. I actually saw him in a production of *Babes in the Wood* playing the Widow Twankey and he was hilarious . . . but as Jesus Christ he was even better . . . obviously not in a hilarious way, but . . .

Laura I understand.

Jim Right. So Barry's line to me and my mam is coming up and I'm still really furious with her from the night before. 'Woman behold your son,' cries Barry. (*Slight pause.*) At the start I didn't know whether it was his great delivery or just thinking about my mother being *my* mother . . . but I started to cry. I'm crying really hard. People are thinking that this is great. I completely upstage Barry's crucifixion and the night's suddenly about St John and whether he's going to be alright and if he'll have the strength to carry on and start and finish his gospel. But anyway! Anyway! Afterwards, and my mam is having a lemonade in the sacristy at the back of the church and I'm out of my purple robes and looking over at her. And I realise why I was crying back then. (*Pause.*) I was crying because I know my mother doesn't like me. (*Pause.*) If I really remind her of the man she hates, the man who left us when I was six . . . then maybe I should walk away too. But where to? Where do I go to?

A pause.

Laura The rule in the room is we don't give advice. We just listen.

Jim Fine.

A pause.

So what about you? Do you have anything you want to share?

Laura Nah. I just listen.

Jim No problems?

Laura Of course . . . but I prefer to listen to other people's.

Jim What do you get out of that?

Laura I'm not too sure.

Jim Does knowing that there's others struggling make you feel better about your own problems?

Laura No.

A pause.

Jim These are strange places, aren't they? Like I said, I don't know whether I should really be here. Whether it's that serious yet. What do you think?

Laura As I said . . .

Jim 'The rule in the room is we don't give advice.' Fine. (*He sighs. Pause.*) Have you been to many suicide rooms?

Laura Yes.

Jim And do they help you?

Laura Who said I needed to be helped?

A pause.

Jim Can I know your real name?

Laura You can call me Laura.

Jim But is that your real name?

Laura Maybe.

Jim Where do you live?

Laura It doesn't matter. None of that really matters. You just need to know that there's someone listening to you. That's enough, isn't it?

Jim (*unsure*) I suppose.

A pause.

Jim Will we talk about something else, Laura?

Laura I don't talk, I listen. You talk.

Jim Talk about what?

A pause.

Laura Tell me about the day your father went missing.

Music. Stiff Little Fingers blast out a verse and chorus of 'Suspect Device' before being cut abruptly.

William Well, we need to set some rules.

Emily Why?

Eva We don't use our real names. We don't say what schools we're from . . .

William We know we're from the same city and that's enough to tie us together. Just leave out the details. It gives us more freedom.

Eva Keeps it impersonal.

William I'll use William.

Eva I'll be Eva.

Jack I always use Jack.

Emily Emily.

Eva How do we know you're not middle-aged men trying to get off chatting up two teenage girls?

William How do we know you're not frustrated housewives trying to take advantage of two innocent altar boys?

Emily Are you altar boys?

Jack Are you desperate mammys?

Emily *and* **Eva** No.

William Okay.

Jack I was an altar boy.

William Oh God.

Jack No, I quite liked it.

Eva How?

Jack Well, when you're eight you've got a very simple idea of life and for a while I really thought I was some sort of angel. I called myself 'an angel-waiter'.

Emily Angel-waiter?

Jack You see back then I believed in Adam and Eve and that God created everything in six days and that he had a rest on the Sunday and all that shit. And I had this image of the church being like a restaurant/café for God to rest in . . .

Eva Or a McDonald's?

Jack Yeah, exactly. And it was my job as an angel-waiter to serve him on his day off.

Emily So what does God eat?

William Chicken nuggets.

They laugh.

Jack I *was* only eight.

Emily That's very cute.

William How long did you think this?

Jack A few months.

Emily And the whole altar-boy thing?

Jack Four years.

Eva Christ!

Emily Are you religious now?

William Do you know, I'd rather not talk about religion? You either do or you don't believe. End of discussion.

Eva Who made you – Big Brother?

William We're all around fifteen years old. We're all middle-class kids, probably. I think we know each other's views on *boring* issues like religion.

Emily Oh right. So what's mine?

William You're disillusioned with the official church and yet you remain spiritual and have defined your own personal religion based upon the simple idea . . . that people should be nice to each other.

Slight pause.

Emily Bastard.

William It's a cliché. We're all clichés . . .

Emily Yeah, all people can be placed in little boxes like that.

William They can.

Eva So what are you?

William A pain in the arse.

Eva Apart from that.

William I'm a cynic. I'm an angry cynic.

Eva Very attractive.

William I'm not interested in being attractive. Why should I be?

Eva Because attractive people go further . . .

William Yeah, I think I read that article in one of my sister's magazines . . .

Eva What I'm saying is that people see a cynic as a black hole. They're nothing. While a person who might be attractive or charming . . . well, they're at the very centre of things . . . changing things . . . manipulating events. What are you but a bad smell?

William Thanks very much.

Eva You know what I mean.

William You think I'm heavy-handed?

Emily You certainly sound that way.

Jack You're bloody opinionated.

William Well, that's the name of this room, isn't it! 'Cork's Bloody Opinionated'!

Emily Jesus.

William I'm at the age . . . we're *all* at the age when we have to stand for something, right? To me it's not about making friends and going bowling and sitting in McDonald's bumming cigarettes and talking about the latest Busted LP . . . that's a waste of fucking time! Now's the time to be a pain in the arse and step away from other people. We're *teenagers*! That used to mean something. It was about revolution, wasn't it? Apart from the punks, what have teenagers done in the last thirty years? Nothing.

Jack And punks didn't even last that long, did they?

William They made their mark! They were angry and they showed it.

Emily My mother was a punk. We've got this photograph from 1976 and she's got a coldsore on her face the size of a tennis ball.

Eva It was dirty work being a punk.

William Nowadays teenagers wouldn't go that far before cracking open their cleansers.

Emily Definitely.

Jack Oh, I don't know. I cultivated a boil on my neck last year for a few weeks. My mother brought me to the doctor and I was gutted when he said he wouldn't lance it . . .

Eva God.

Jack But he gave me this black plaster with this tiny hole in the middle. It sort of draws the pus out towards the little hole.

Eva Do we have . . .

Jack So I'm watching television with my dad and my baby brother and above the telly I hear this noise, right. (*Makes a quiet splurting noise.*) I swear to God it hit the wall behind me.

Emily That's disgusting.

Jack But it was a revolution!

Eva How?

Jack My body was revolting.

Emily Ha ha.

William But does anyone know what I mean?

Eva Yeah, I do. I went on an anti-war march and for an hour or so I felt really good and I felt empowered, you know. But it was just so small. In the great big scheme of my life it was just one hour of saying that I believed in something. I suppose the rest of the time we're just sort of sleepwalking and just waiting for something to happen instead of *making* something happen. It would be so great to accomplish something important. To have a cause.

Jack William wants to assassinate J. K. Rowling.

Emily and Eva laugh.

William I was only joking.

Jack You talked about it for an hour last week in the Harry Potter Chat Room.

William It's not her personally . . . it's the idea of her . . . what she stands for.

Emily And what's that?

Jack William reckons children's writers simplify everything to keep children simple.

William They see us as a threat.

Eva Who do?

William Adults.

Jack It's a conspiracy theory.

William It's like the adults support these writers to write these pointless stories of fantasy so that children have this cutesy warped idea of what life is about.

Eva So J. K. Rowling is the high priestess?

William She's the enemy. Not her, but the idea of her. If I could kill the idea of her without getting her hurt, I'd do it tomorrow.

Emily You're a lunatic.

William I just want to do something important. It's frustrating.

Emily Would you ever really kill anything?

William No. Any idiot can kill something. Where's the glory in that?

Jack Aren't you meant to say that each life is sacred?

Emily Exactly.

William Well, that's crap. There are some people and life is just wasted on them. Terrorists, dictators, racists . . .

Jack PE teachers.

Emily laughs.

William They don't do anything. They suck all the goodness out of living.

Jack Like William.

William Shut up.

Eva I think William just wants a cause. He wants to see that cause through. He wants to make a big statement.

William Exactly. I want to make a big statement. Who doesn't? (*Slight pause.*) Thanks, Eve.

Eva It's Eva.

William Right. Eva.

A long pause where the four of them do very little. Then –

Jim Is there anyone there?

A pause.

Are people still awake? Is this room really called 'Cork's Bloody Opinionated'?

William We don't use our real names, names of schools, any details. It's enough that we know that we come from the same city.

Jim Right. I'll be Jim, then.

Eva Hello, Jim, I'm Eva.

Emily Emily.

Jack Jack.

William I'm William.

Jim So what happens here? I don't know this place. What goes on?

William Heated discussion. Chit-chat. Bullshit.

Eva We're looking for a cause. William wants to make a statement.

Jack We're all a bit frustrated.

Emily If you have any causes handy, feel free.

A pause.

Jim Can we talk about our problems here?

Eva Oh God.

A pause. William laughs a little. Then:

William Have you got problems, Jim?

Jim Yeah, I do.

William Are they *big* problems?

Jim Well, I think so. Big to me, anyway.

Emily And you want us to listen to them and give you some advice?

Jack Jesus, William . . .!

A pause.

Jim Are you still there? Look I'll go to another room if you want.

William starts laughing to himself. He sits back down and faces Jim.

William Jim?

A pause.

Jim Yes?

William We're here to help you.

Music. The Undertones' 'Teenage Kicks' plays. They rearrange their seats so Jim is between Eva and William. The music cuts. During the following,

William eats a bag of crisps below while Eva paints her toenails as they half-listen to Jim.

Jim So I've been bullied all the way through primary and now in secondary school. I'm small and a bit skinny so it goes with the territory. You expect it. But I have bigger worries . . . deeper worries that I can't really explain. And that's tricky. And very recently I've started to feel, 'What's the point? What's the point in everything!' But not in a moaning, teenagey way . . .

William Your depression isn't put on . . .

Jim No way! I'm not someone who keeps an altar to Kurt Cobain or anything like that. I actually can't stand Nirvana. I don't need their music to feed my depression. I can happily do it all by myself . . .

Eva Obviously not happily.

Jim Yeah! Yeah, 'happily' is the wrong word . . . but you know what I mean.

Jack What does depression feel like?

William It feels great, what do you think!

Jack No, I know it's crap . . . I just want to know what it feels like to Jim.

A pause. A look of exasperation on William's face.

William Well, Jim?

A pause.

Jim It's like the whole world has turned into soup. Everything has the consistency of soup. And your insides and your heart . . . well, they just sort of ache . . . and it's like you're clogged up with about five sliced pans of bread. It's exactly like that.

A slight pause.

Jack Depression's like bread and soup?

Eva Shut up, Jack!

Jack I'm only repeating . . .

Jim The food comparison probably doesn't work.

William Schizophrenics often say they feel like a mixed salad.

Eva, Jack and William laugh. Jim smiles.

Emily You sound sweet. Do you have a girlfriend?

William Ohh, wait a second! We're here to give Jim some advice . . .

Jim I did have a girlfriend. And I don't now.

Emily I just wanted to know if you had anyone close to you. You don't have anyone in your family to talk to. so I thought maybe an understanding girlfriend would help you to . . .

William Jesus, Emily, if you'd been listening to Jim for the last hour you wouldn't ask that. Jim doesn't have our normal teenagey problems. It's not a problem that can be solved by a quick feel outside the chip shop!

Eva He's different.

William Of course he'd love a girlfriend! But that can't happen 'cause he's dealing with just getting up in the morning and facing into another one of his shitty days!

Jim I'm not *that* bad . . .

Eva Maybe think before you speak, Emily!

Emily Piss off!

Eva No, it's just bullshit! I expected more from you! You didn't strike me as some head-in-the-sand princess.

Emily I'm not like that!

William Selfish cow!

Emily Jesus, all I said was . . .

William Jim has the courage to come into this room and open up and tell us all this pathetic crap. All you're asked to do is imagine that others can be different from you.

Emily You have no idea what I'm like . . .

Eva Well, by a comment like that . . . like Jim could be cured by the heart of a good girl . . .

Emily I didn't mean . . .

William Sorry about this, Jim . . .

Jim No really, it's . . .

Eva I think we've all got a good impression of the type of girl you are, Emily!

Emily Fuck. Off!

Eva Living in a little suburban bubble. Small group of girlfriends who hang around after music lessons sniggering over copies of *Bliss*.

William They're all called Sarah, right. Sarah-Jane, Sarah-Marie, Sarah-Louise, Sarah-Anne . . .

Eva The hairband brigade in your deck shoes and pink-and-yellow Lacrosse shirts.

William What's the worst that's happened to you?

Jack Easy now.

William Scuffed your Chinos in the park? That night daddy didn't pick you up from Pizza Hut and you had to get the *bus* home?

Eva Or maybe when your pony had to be put down 'cause your big fat preppy arse was buckling its back . . .

Jack Hoy!

William Shut up, Jack!

Emily I had anorexia, you know!

Eva So what!

William Weekend anorexia was it? Bursting out of those Chinos? Had to lose a few pounds?

Emily Shithead!

Eva Anorexia's a status symbol for your type of girl. You wear your six months' anorexia like a badge of honour. You think it gives you an edge? It makes you a cliché! That's why when someone talks to you about depression you can bat it aside with that shit about 'If only you had a girlfriend you'd be feeling a lot better.' Christ, if we let you drone on you'd be singing that song, 'Cheer up, Charlie'.

Jack *Willy Wonka's Chocolate Factory*!

William I *hate* that fucking film! Get out of here, Emily!

Eva We want people who are here for Jim.

Emily I'm here for Jim!

William Someone who understands his problem. Who gets the cause.

Jim What cause?

Emily What, Jim, is your cause now?

William We're here one hundred per cent and on twenty-four-hour call. Jim's feeling cut up over something and we're here to listen and advise him, understood?!

Eva That's right.

William We don't need any chaff! Jim doesn't need some ex-anorexic pony-rider whining little *TV Digest* sound bites!

Eva Put simply . . .

William Piss off!

A pause. William and Eva are laughing. Emily looks very upset.

Eva Is she gone?

William I think so.

Jack That was a bit harsh.

Eva Silly cow.

Jim Maybe she didn't mean what you think.

William There's no need to defend her, Jim. She's not needed.

Jack Anorexia's terrible. You shouldn't mock it like that.

Eva Forget about her . . . she's debris. We're here for Jim. What about you, Jack?

Jack *(unsure)* Yeah, I suppose.

Eva A wonderful vote of confidence there . . . maybe a bit more conviction?

Jack Well, no offence, Jim . . . but we're your age . . . shouldn't you be taking advice from a doctor, maybe?

Jim Well, I was actually thinking . . .

Eva Christ, Jack, that's so fucking cruel. Don't you get it? He doesn't have *anyone*. We're it!

Jack All I'm saying . . .

William Jack!

A pause.

Can we step out? I want to talk to you in private.

A pause.

Jack Okay.

Jack and William take their seats to one side to talk. Emily takes her seat and sits away from the others. Eva is left with Jim in the room.

Jim That was all a bit weird.

Eva Well, you don't have to worry about that now.

Jim Okay then.

Eva So tell me about the day your father went missing.

Jim Well, it's sort of important . . . Shouldn't I wait for the two boys to come back?

Eva looks exasperated.

Eva (*sweetly*) I'll get them my notes.

Jim Alright then.

A pause.

Jim Right, well, I'm six years old and my three brothers are going away with my mother for the weekend . . . a treat for something or other. My dad's staying behind and my mother says that he's to look after me. That it would be a chance for us to bond. So they're gone and me and my dad are sat at the kitchen table looking at each other. Like we're looking at each other for the first time, you know. He asks me what I want to do, and straight away I say I want to go and see the penguins in the zoo. When I was six I was going through some mad penguin obsession. I used to dress up as a penguin at dinner times and always ask for fish fingers . . . stuff like that. If it wasn't penguins it was cowboys. Cowboys were cool. A penguin dressed as a cowboy was always a step too far, funnily enough!

Eva (*groans to herself*) Oh God.

Jim So we go to the zoo and I wear my cowboy outfit . . . get my gun and holster, my hat and all that. We get the bus and it's sort of funny to see my dad on the bus and away from the house. We start to have this chat about when I was born and what a really fat baby I was . . . but how after a day or so I stopped eating any food and everyone was dead worried. That *he* was very worried. That he was so happy when I got better and they could take me home. (*Slight pause.*) We're in the zoo, and I go straight to the penguins. Standing in my cowboy gear . . . looking at the penguins . . . having such a great chat to my dad on the bus . . . it was a perfect childhood day. (*Slight pause.*) He lets go of my hand and says he'll be back with my choc-ice. And he goes. (*Pause.*) He's gone. (*Pause.*) I'm happy looking at the penguins, but it's an hour since he's left and I go to look for him. I'm walkin' about the zoo, and I'm not worried yet. And I don't talk to anyone. I leave the zoo and I go to the bus stop we got off at earlier. I get on the bus. I tell the driver my address. He asks where my parents are and I say they're at home waiting for me. I stay on the bus in the seat nearest the driver. After a while we end up at the end of our street and the driver says, 'So long, cowboy.' (*Laughs a little.*) He was nice. (*Pause.*) I get the key from under the mat and open the door and go inside the house. And I'm alone there and I suppose I still think my dad will be coming back soon. I take off my cowboy clothes and hang up my hat and holster. It being Saturday night I have a bath and get into my pyjamas because my dad would have liked that. I have a glass of milk and some biscuits and watch *Stars in Their Eyes* 'cause that was his favourite programme on the telly. (*Slight pause.*) It's getting dark outside and I start to worry. The house is feeling too big so I get my quilt and take it into the bathroom and lock the bathroom door and it feels safer with the door locked so I stay in there. And he's not coming back. (*Pause.*) He's never coming back. (*Pause.*) I stay there for two days.

Eva looks bored. William talks in private to Jack.

William It will be a laugh. Right now we're all he has. We're there for him 24-7 . . . it will be a blast! Eva gets it, why can't you? He's our cause. Let's let him talk. Mess him up a bit. See how far he'll go.

Jack gets up and walks away from his seat.

Are you there, Jack? Are you with the cause, Jack? (*Calls in a 'mammy' voice.*) Ohh, Jack?!

A pause. Jack returns to his seat.

Jack What next?

William smiles.

Music. Green Day's 'St Jimmy' belts out. Eva and William sit on either side of Jim. They each have a small notebook and take notes as we see Jim talking non-stop. Jack sits just away from them. After one and half minutes of Green Day the music cuts, and Eva and William read out their notes.

Eva So a lower-middle-class family with your mother having notions above her status. Hence the extra-curricular activities. The rugby, the horse-riding, the sailing classes . . .

178

William Et cetera, et cetera, et cetera.

Eva At the age of four and your first realisation that the children on your estate laugh at your brothers for their aggressive social climbing.

William And the people in the sailing club laugh at them for wearing the shittiest clothes.

Eva Your first feelings of anxiety when you understand that you are living in a family hated by everyone and that *you* are one of them.

William You decide to stay indoors. But being the youngest brother to brothers built on the rugby field they adopt you as their plaything and later their punchbag.

Eva So at the age of five you go back outside to play with the other children only to see that bonds of friendship have already been formed and there is little room for a small tubby toddler who has an unhealthy obsession with penguins.

William You are alone but you *do* find a friend in . . . ahhh?

A slight pause.

Jim Timmy.

Eva Little Timmy Timmons?

Jim Yeah.

Eva A tiny six-year-old with severe bronchial problems who has to drag a small oxygen canister behind him. When the other children play road-football . . .

William . . . you are watching Timmy's mother slap phlegm out of Timmy's chronic lungs and into a Tesco bag.

Eva Watching this at the age of six you have your first thoughts on your own mortality.

William One momentous day, your father leaves you in the zoo leaving the family in the shit.

Eva You're mother is forced into getting her very first job. She finds work in a petrol station, ending all her dreams of the posh life and throwing her into a depression eased only by . . .

William . . . gin and tonic . . . the tonic being . . .

Eva . . . Valium.

William Your best friend Timmy dies, not from the tragic weakening of his lungs in the middle of the night . . .

Eva . . . but a speeding Ford Mondeo which flattens his trailing oxygen canister and leaves Timmy walking zombie-like through the estate as the other children shout . . .

William . . . 'Spa-Boy!'

Eva The day of Timmy's funeral you take your first Valium. You are aged eight.

Jim Eight and a half.

Eva (*correcting her notes*) Eight and a half!

William You try to make contact with your dad by placing leaflets on lamp posts but to no avail.

Eva You try to make friends with anyone you meet by ingratiating yourself to whatever they want you to be . . .

William . . . but to no avail. You decide to retreat back into the indoors and your Neanderthal brothers' daily beatings.

Eva You hide yourself in books of the occult, which leads to a period of bed-wetting.

Jim (*embarrassed*) Is that important?

Eva Oh, definitely!

William You briefly turn to religion and take part in a Passion play, where you realise that you hate Jesus Christ only slightly less than you hate your mother, the Virgin Mary.

Eva At thirteen you read your first porn, which only creates more of a distance between you and those girls you will *never* get to touch.

William You hate yourself and decide to stop communicating with other people entirely. Your life is directionless.

Eva The next two years is a sad cocktail of home-made beer, the odd Valium and the odd shot of whisky.

William Nights begin to take on a pattern of aggressive self-analysis and blame until one night you're talking to an American bloke on the internet who's planning to kill himself. His unfortunate name is *Chad*.

Eva Like Chad and the others in the suicide club . . . you reach a moment of recognition. You are searching for a purpose.

William A purpose. (*Closes his notebook.*) Right.

A pause.

Jim (*sighs*) A purpose. Fuck. Fifteen years. It's depressing . . . and a little embarrassing.

Eva If it wasn't such a tragic life it would be a very funny story.

William I don't think you've ever been given a chance. For some reason you're the one who always gets burnt.

Jim But why me?

William You can't take responsibility for what people have done to you or what people think of you, Jim.

Eva The reasons why people have done those things to you isn't something you have control over. 'Why me?' is a pointless question. Stupid even.

Jim Right. Sorry.

William What you are feeling *right now*, that's all that matters. Concentrate on that.

Jack But try and think more positive . . .

Eva Oh shut up, Jack!

Jack But all this . . .

William Jack!

Jack gets out of his seat and snaps:

Jack Shit!

William (*soft, to Jim*) You have to focus on your anger and channel it into something that will get these bastards back.

Jim How do you mean?

A pause.

Eva How do you think you would hurt your mother for all those years of neglect? All those years she treated you like nothing.

Jim Well, I've been fighting her for so long now . . .

William But she doesn't listen, does she?

Jim No. She doesn't. And it doesn't make me feel any better.

Eva So?

A pause.

Jim I've been thinking about if she came into my room in the morning and if I had done something – (*Pause.*) – like maybe I've cut my wrists or taken pills or something . . . I can imagine her face.

Eva Bitch.

William She'd be crushed. The guilt would kill her.

Jim Yeah, it would.

A pause.

But I don't know if I'm ready to do that.

William and Eva look really irritated. A pause. William settles himself.

William Jim?

Jim Yes.

William Me and Eva can't imagine what your life's been really like. It just sounds so . . . so sad. Without hope, probably.

Eva laughs a bit.

But we've been giving up our time and listening to you
for the past few nights, haven't we?

Jim Yeah. And thanks, lads, really.

William Well, I just want you to do *one* thing for me,
alright?

Jim Yeah sure, William.

William I want you to ask yourself two questions before
you go to sleep tonight. Do you have a pen to write
the questions down?

Jim Yeah, go on.

William Why is it people treat me like I'm nothing? If no
one cares about my life why should I care?

Jack (*to himself*) Bastard.

*William smiles. A pause. Jim writes them down and
then silently reads them back to himself. Suddenly
something's got his attention. He looks sharply to his
left. He sighs.*

Jim It's two o' clock in the morning and my mother's
outside hoovering the stairs and landing. Tonight my
three idiot brothers called me a freak for not wanting
brown sauce on my chips. (*Slight pause.*) I better go.
Thanks, guys.

William Sweet dreams.

Jim stands up and away from his seat.

Eva He's ours.

*Music. The Prodigy's 'Smack My Bitch Up' screams
along. William and Eva burst out laughing. Jack hangs
his head. He then stands, as does Emily. The two walk
over and sit on either side of Laura. The music ends
abruptly.*

Laura The rule in the room is we don't give advice.

Jack He spoke about you. He spoke about this place and we just thought . . .

Laura I can't help him! So if you're not here for anything else . . .

Emily But he might listen to you.

Laura If he's suicidal the last thing he needs is someone else giving their half-arsed opinions. It doesn't help, believe me.

Jack Well, it's not like that. He's being talked into doing something . . .

Laura I can't get involved! Look, what I do is sit here and listen to people my age who have these urges to hurt themselves. Most of the time they don't do anything. A lot of the time they just need to know that someone is listening to them, because they either feel they don't have anyone or they actually don't have anyone. That's all I do!

Emily But right now the only people he has are two strangers who want to see him do something to himself.

A pause.

Laura I don't go into other rooms any more. There's too much shit that goes on. People get hurt.

Emily Exactly.

Laura stands away from her seat. She's agitated. A pause.

Jack Are you still there?

Laura sits.

Laura If you want to pass on my e-mail to him, it's laura15%@aol . . .

Emily Please come with us!

Jack You don't have to talk if you don't want to. Just come and listen in and you'll see.

A pause.

Emily If it gets too much, you can get out. We'll be there.

A pause.

Laura But who are you? How do I know I can trust you?

*Music and The Prodigy's 'Smack My Bitch Up'
resumes from where it was cut. William and Eva place
their seats to face Emily and Jack. Jim places his seat
between the two groups. Lastly Laura places her seat
next to Jim's. All six stand and look at each other like
they're sizing each other up for the big showdown.
Jack is the first to sit, then Emily, Laura, Jim, Eva and
finally William. As William sits, the music cuts out.*

Eva Well, as little babies you can't do any wrong, can
you? You're bloody perfect! All you do is eat and shit
and laugh and cry and sleep and don't sleep, but
you're loved. And I suppose you're loved because your
parents have this blank page, don't they? And all their
hopes and dreams can be projected onto this beautiful
little blob.

William And the blob can't disappoint because it's just a
beautiful little blob.

Eva Exactly! But that only lasts a few months until
BANG!

William Suddenly the blob's a little too hungry, a little
too loud, a little less beautiful.

Eva And then it's a little toddler and its character is
forming and it's only right to be a bit more critical
now that it's a little toddler. It's too quiet, too shy, too
aggressive, can't stop eating, a little too cranky, blah
blah blah blah blah blah . . .

William Before you know it, the toddler's ten years old
and let's say that another baby is born.

Eva Oh, typical.

William The ten-year-old is this big mouth to feed. This ever-growing child who disappoints, causes worry and sucks your money. Your parents' hopes and dreams are already on the next blob because at ten years of age a person is made, a character's developed.

Eva The damage is done.

William Well, it was with me.

Eva Now just imagine what the teenager means to its parents if a ten-year-old means that?

William Well, we're not a child, not an adult.

Eva Not a girl. Not yet a woman.

William Oh Jesus!

Eva Britney speaks the truth!

William A teenager is a sub-person.

Eva Not that Britney said that . . .

William This hormonal mess. A boy-man, a girl-woman. We're like a bad experiment.

Eva True.

William If God had really thought things through . . . we'd be babies born on the Monday and fully grown adults on the Tuesday, 'cause everything else in between is this long list of fumblings, mistakes and bad skin.

Eva Ohh the bad skin!

William The teenage years.

Eva And the voice we have.

William What voice!?

Eva Well, any voice that hasn't been shaped by some shit children's writer or some draining pop star. If we do have an original thought . . . well, it's just seen as a joke, isn't it? It's a joke 'cause those adults who have lived through these years remember them with complete and utter embarrassment.

William It's not that we're misunderstood or not understood at all. They understand us *completely* because they've lived through these years and see it as their right –

Eva As their adult duty!

William – to patronise us with the words, 'Whatever you're going through, you'll get through it, love.'

Eva 'Now clean that bloody bedroom!'

William That's when you understand, at the age of fifteen, that life is just like that. Life is all about passing through phases.

Eva By fifteen you've realised that the individual doesn't mean shit and the average teenager is seen as the big embarrassing joke.

William We're all just folded up neatly and placed into a box marked 'The Awkward Years'. We're trapped in the cliché by those who have already lived through the cliché.

Eva But you know, when you allow yourself to be summed up *that* simply . . . from fifteen onwards you will live the rest of your life through these different phases. You will be summed up into little boxes until they stick you in your final box and shove you in the ground. Guaranteed. Only a few teenagers make a stand. Only a few brave souls make a statement. Teenagers like you, Jim.

Jim Like me?

William I was thinking that Jim's depression allows him to see things clearer than us. He's been neglected by his family and friends so that maybe his isolation represents perfectly the average teenager's plight. It's like a metaphor.

Eva Oh brilliant, Will!

William But you know, Jim, maybe the more public you make it the more of a statement you'd be making.

Eva Excellent idea!

Jim How do you mean?

William Imagine all those forgotten teenagers you'd be speaking for if you killed yourself *publicly*. Maybe that's your statement. You'd be a hero. A legend.

Eva Very brave. Very romantic. Sexy, even.
Jim Do it in public?

A pause.

I'm not too sure about that.
William Maybe show it over the internet, then. Would it be easier in your bedroom?
Jim Yeah, I suppose.
Eva It sort of seems right that he remains alone. That people see him die like that.
William Well, it's stronger, isn't it?
Eva Definitely.

A pause.

Jim Well, I'm usually alone anyway so . . . And lately I don't like being out in public places so much. Seems easier if I do it here.
Eva Can you get a little webcam to broadcast it?
Jim My brother Derek has one.
William Perfect.

A slight pause.

Jim Of course he'd kill me if he found me using it.
William Well, we wouldn't want that to happen, would we?
Eva It sort of steals your thunder.
Jim Yeah.

William and Eva laugh.

Laura Jim, this is Laura.

A pause.

Eva Who are you?
Emily She's come in with us.
Laura I've spoken with Jim before. We know each other.
William You're a friend of his?

Laura Why exactly are you harassing him like that?

William We're here for Jim. Do you know what state he's in?

Laura I know he's not feeling well.

Eva (*incredulous*) What!?

Laura He hasn't been feeling good about himself. He's lonely. He feels detached.

Eva He's suicidal! He's ready to take his life.

Jack That's what you want!

Laura Why is it you're doing this?

William We're his friends.

Emily No you're not.

William Well, we didn't abandon him like you two. He came to us looking for advice and we've been making things clear for him.

Laura Are you serious?

Eva Why don't you piss off!

Laura You're talking to him like there's no options. You're making him believe that there's nothing else. That suicide is some romantic gesture. Like one fifteen-year-old's death will be held up by other fifteen-year-olds and celebrated for something. Will make a big statement for all those 'trapped' average teenagers! Trapped by who, trapped in what?

William Trapped by adults . . . to them we're faceless.

Laura It's not about what others think about you.

Eva We're powerless.

Laura The power is knowing what you are . . . what you want to be! If you think of yourself as some blob who's moulded into this empty child and sent on a set pattern through life . . . if you think that . . . it will happen.

William It *will* happen! Choices are made and choices *will* be made where you have no control. Your life is set!

Laura That's shit! Every single moment in life there's possibilities.

William gets up from his seat and snaps.

William Bitch!

Laura The statement being made is yours. But what are you saying, William? That you've got power? That you're smart enough to take advantage of someone vulnerable and talk them into the corner where they might kill themselves? And this is some joke to you two, right? Some big comedy. Because you can't see him, it's easier. It's easier when you don't have to see a dead boy and just imagine it like you read it in a book or something. It's easier than murder, 'cause Jim's faceless to you? . . . But it's just like murder. In these rooms words are power and you and that bitch have all the right words, haven't you?

William You've tried to kill yourself but chickened out, haven't you?!

Jack Oh shut up, William!

William You think I'm going to allow Jim to be lectured by some whinging coward like you? Some New Age happy-clappy princess! Jim has *real* problems.

Laura This isn't some competition about who's the most sad here! And if you need to know, you dick, I have tried to kill myself! I did slit my wrists. It did come from a very *real* place! But I'm happy I'm alive. And some days are better than others and the future scares me but I'm ready for the struggle! And I *like* the struggle! I like it a lot more than being dead and stuck in the ground and watching over my family and friends who I've ripped apart. Stay alive and they can help me! There are always possibilities! There's always a life!

William You're one of those sad girls who hangs out in suicide chat rooms. Who just sits there like some black hole. All silent and dumb and soaking up the sad stories. Wallowing in other people's pain. What

statement are you making, bitch!? You talk about a life
of possibilities, choice, love, happiness . . . but I bet
you'd like nothing more than a world of sad, morose
fifteen-year-olds droning on about their pathetic lives.
Well, why not support those who want to kill
themselves? Why not allow them do it?! They're like
the front line, aren't they? The public face of our
gloom, printed in the papers and shown on the telly!
They need our support to do the brave thing . . . do
the decent thing. To get rid of the chaff and make a
true revolutionary teenager! So do the decent thing, you
worthless cow! Next time don't cry out to Mammy
and Daddy! Just do it!

Jim (*quietly*) Stop.

A pause. Laura is visibly upset.

Five of us are from the same city. Tomorrow at one
o'clock I want you to be at McDonald's in Winthorpe
Street. I want you to be there because I can't be in my
bedroom any more. Maybe I'll be quiet but I want you
to see me do it. Will you be there then?

A pause.

Laura I'm still here to talk to.

A pause.

Jim You know I don't think I can listen to me talk any
more. I only have a few words left that I want to say
now, Laura.

Laura (*soft*) Don't.

Jim Let's finish this.

*The beautiful 'Dawn' by the Cinematic Orchestra
('Man with a Movie Camera' album), is heard
underneath all of Jim's final speech.*

William, Eva, Laura, Emily and Jack all leave the stage with their seats. Jim talks to the audience. As he does he wheels out three television sets from the wings and places them in the downstage position.

It's funny, but I slept well. Probably the best sleep I've had in months. I left the house with my bag full of stuff and there was no one there. My mother was working her shift in the petrol station and my brothers were at this American wrestling thing that was happening in the city. I got the bus and there was this man with his young son, which got me thinking about me and Dad and the zoo and the cowboy outfit . . . and all that. Seemed appropriate that I would see them. Typical. In the bus I started to think about all those thousands of teenagers who kill themselves every year. Somebody would be killing themselves right now, maybe . . . while a number of others would have it all planned out. And a lot of them are doing it because . . . they really are very sick. And some are doing it because they're alone . . . or maybe they're sad because someone hurt them somehow. There are so many reasons to do it. And I started thinking about all the families and friends who are left behind and the regret that must eat them up. It's all so quiet and violent. (*Pause.*) I got off the bus and walked through the city and imagined all the ghosts of the dead teenagers looking at me. And what were they thinking? And what would they say to me? It's like they all follow me down Whinthrope Street and into McDonald's. And they watch me buy some chicken nuggets and a Coke and find a table. And the angels see me taking out my camera.

The televisions turn on and we see a digital camera image of the inside of the McDonald's. We see William, Eva, Jack and Emily dotted around the restaurant, just faces in the crowd.

In this room those angels waiting for me. And I don't see myself as anything other than me. I don't imagine what I'm about to do is making a big statement or speaking out for millions of teenagers. I'm alone.

The camera finally rests on Jim sitting alone at his table.

I give the camera to this little ten-year-old boy to hold. I tell him to point it at me and the table.

During the following we see Jim take his cowboy hat, sheriff's badge, gun and holster. People around him start to look at him as he gets into the outfit.

There's no question but I've been very sad about things. And I'm probably like thousands of teenagers who get depressed. It's almost enough for me to know that someone is there for me and someone is listening. But I had to do something for me. I had to grow up fast when my father left and it's as simple as that. And I really miss him and I can't understand why he's gone. Something *that* simple can mess you up for a long time. When you're six and wearing a cowboy outfit and looking at penguins you shouldn't be made to grow up so fast. But I was. And I tore myself up over it for years and tried to find answers but honestly . . . what can a child do?

He has taken an iPod out of his bag with two little speakers.

I want my childhood back. So this is the place where the smart talking stops. It's just something for me . . . and maybe a little something for those angels to smile at. (*Slight pause.*) Maybe.

He is now standing on the table dressed in his small cowboy hat, sheriff's badge, gun and holster. He presses the iPod and the song 'Rawhide' is heard through the speakers. He closes his eyes and just stays still. People around him are smiling and laughing. We watch him for some time until a security guard asks him to get down.

The televisions cut to the lyrics of 'Rawhide' as they come up on the screen and the song is pumped loudly into the auditorium.

Lyrics: 'Rollin', Rollin', Rollin' '

Rollin', rollin', rollin'
Rollin', rollin', rollin'
Rollin', rollin', rollin'
Rawhide!

Rollin', rollin', rollin'
Though the streams are swollen
Keep them dogies rollin'
Rawhide!
Rain and wind and weather
Hell-bent for leather
Wishin' my gal was by my side.
All the things I'm missin',
Good vittles, love, and kissin',
Are waiting at the end of my ride.

Chorus

Move 'em on, head 'em up
Head 'em up, move 'em on
Move 'em on, head 'em up
Rawhide!
Count 'em out, ride 'em in,
Ride 'em in, count 'em out,
Count 'em out, ride 'em in
Rawhide!

Jim sits down on his seat for the remainder of the song. When he looks towards Laura's seat she walks onstage and sits down in her seat. She smiles.

Lyrics: 'Keep Movin', Movin', Movin''

Though they're disapprovin'
Keep them dogies movin'
Rawhide!
Don't try to understand 'em
Just rope, throw, and brand 'em
Soon we'll be living high and wide.
My heart's calculatin'
My true love will be waitin',
Be waitin' at the end of my ride.
Rawhide!
Rawhide!

A final crack of the whip and 'Rawhide' ends and the televisions cut out.

A pause as we watch Jim and Laura sitting in their seats looking at each other. Then –

Laura Everything alright now?
Jim Yeah. (*Slight pause.*) You?
Laura Yeah. (*Slight pause. A little hesitant*) Thanks for the film, Jim. It was good.
Jim It's alright.

A pause.

Will we talk about something?
Laura (*smiling*) What will we talk about?

A pause. Jim thinks really hard and his mind finally settles on –

Jim Bunny rabbits.

They both smile. Music. Wheatus are heard singing

'A Little Respect'. We hear the first verse as Jim and Laura do nothing.

As the chorus pumps in we cut to –

Blackout.

Music continues through the curtain call.

Lord of the Flies in a Chatroom

Enda Walsh interviewed by Jim Mulligan

It is an unusual idea to place on a stage six fifteen-year-olds who constantly talk and clearly can see each other but, because the drama takes place in chatrooms, the actors must convince the audience that they cannot see each other and do not talk to each other face to face. Five of the characters live in the same town. This is essential for the dramatic climax of this black comedy.

The problem facing the actors is that with scarcely any physical action and using only a bag of simple props they have to make the audience believe that they have locked themselves away in their bedrooms. They are freed from all adult supervision and are not connected emotionally to the actors sitting next to them. They are editing the role they want the others to believe in and there is no guarantee that what they say is the truth. As the play develops, it becomes apparent that William and Eva, apparently spontaneously but then with callous planning, try to convince Jim that he should kill himself.

These two are sophisticated and dangerous. *Lord of the Flies* had a massive influence on me. That story tells me we are only moral because of the strictures of society. Take them away and we revert to something primitive. I wanted the play to have that edge to it. We have a group of young people learning from each other and they end up speaking with the same voice. As a writer I have to believe that we all have the potential for evil and we are all capable of doing anything.

Music is an essential part of the play. It creates the framework for each scene and gives the audience a break

197

from the words, allowing them to reflect on the progress of the play. Enda Walsh expects directors to select their own tracks but they must be in keeping with the raw aggressive tracks he himself has suggested.

It might seem that the language of William in particular is stylised and artificial. What fifteen-year-old is going to say, 'I was thinking that maybe your depression allows you to see things clearer than us. You've been neglected by your family and friends so that maybe your isolation represents perfectly the average teenager's plight. It's like a metaphor.'

> I'm not so sure the language is stylised. William is just very clever. And really smart fifteen-year-olds do exist. In *Chatroom* I try to avoid lengthy monologues – there are only two for Jim – and I have kept the dialogue short and rhythmic. I decided I would allow them all, but particularly William to be über-smart. Jim, the only normal one, is caught in this maelstrom of really clever young people who attempt to undermine him.

Enda Walsh is not interested in William's history. The play lasts for an hour and we only know his character in that time. He allows William to say, 'By the age of ten the damage is done. Well, it was to me,' but he has not speculated on the nature of that damage although, after visiting chatrooms to research this play, he probably could.

> I found the experience revealing and depressing. You hear kids talking about wanting to commit suicide and some are apparently about to. Some chatrooms suggest the best ways of doing it, what tablets to take, and in some there are people trying to counsel these seriously depressed young people. It's devastating. Some of them are really ill and there are some who will undoubtedly kill themselves but there is nothing you can do.

Jim is the only character who has a past history. He gives an extraordinary account of how he was abandoned at the age of six in the zoo. His father went to get an ice cream and is never seen again. There is no explanation. There is a horrific magic, a fairy-tale quality to the disappearance, and we can speculate all we want on what happened, but the simple truth is that Jim never saw his father again. Jim also tells of a hilarious scene in the parish Passion play. He is playing the part of a gay John, the Beloved Disciple, and steals the show by weeping real tears not because he is distressed by the plight of the Virgin Mary but because his mother is playing the part and he realises he has no relationship with her. We are also told of his mother's bizarre behaviour and how she takes her frustration out on Jim because she has come down in the world and has to work as a petrol-pump attendant.

Jim takes decisive action to bring *Chatroom* to a close that should have the audience oscillating between tears and laughter. After being goaded to kill himself, he commits social suicide, by standing on a table in McDonald's dressed in ridiculous cowboy gear that doesn't even fit him, playing 'Rawhide', and having the whole thing videoed. In so doing he reclaims himself and also Laura, the one person who is really in danger of killing herself. Jim sends the film to Laura, and this act allows her to connect with him.

I see this as a very positive play. Jim has decided that he will not take his life and he leaves us with hope. I just hope the performances are real. It is up to the actors to make the audience believe in them. It will be great for teenagers to see people who are like them and for adults to see what some teenagers are really getting up to. A lot of times we don't look at teenagers, but the theatre gives us the chance to do this. I would direct it with a few days to talk about the play, the background and the arc of the characters and then just get them to do it. No lights, no nothing. Just do it. You don't have to tell untrained actors to speak louder or be more angry or be clearer. Just let them get on with it and they are brave enough to do that.

Production Notes

WARM-UP

As a warm-up do the 'Chatroom Bounce'.

> *Everybody stands behind one another in lines across the room.*
>
> *The front line then bounces up and down to music from the show for a count of eight, turning around on eight – in perfect harmony.*
>
> *The people behind them then take on the bounce for a count of eight.*
>
> *This passes right across the room until the last line. They do a count of eight and then turn back with a count of six.*
>
> *Then four.*
>
> *Then two.*
>
> *Then one.*

It is a wonder to behold.

MUSIC

The music suggested in the script is there because it reflects the teenage attitude in the play. The eclectic selection offers more ways into the piece than an entirely contemporary choice. Enda doesn't mind what music you use in the show, just be aware of its tempo and energy when changing it. 'Oompa Lumpa' and 'Rawhide' are key tracks, though. Whatever you do. make sure they stay.

THE TEXT

The play has ten sections or units, which run between pieces of music. The following are among the questions answered by Enda at the Bath retreat.

UNIT ONE – WILLY WONKA

Why is Jack in a Harry Potter chatroom?

No idea! He might like Harry Potter. Perhaps it indicates he is slightly softer, he is there for the chat.

Why are any of them in a chatroom?

Boredom? Coincidence? Avoiding work?

How firm are the stage directions and orange chairs at the top of the show?

They're quite funny, simple, direct. Orange connects to the Oompah Lumpas, a non-flashy start that comes from nowhere. Not a big number, but theatrically hints at it. It's also to show that they are not in their bedrooms and at keyboards.

William in this scene – is it revelatory or slightly down? With undertones?

William begins the piece very full-on and is a bit hyper. Think Red Bull. He is quite masculine with his opinions, and very honest. The opinions about the discussion topic have been thought through. This is the first time they have all met.

Do you want any physical interaction of eye contact?

The actors explored the answer to this question by reading a section of the scene playing with direct eye-contact between the characters and the lack of eye-contact true of a real chatroom. They decided there is no definitive answer. Try this out in rehearsal for yourself.

What do you see the other four doing?

Mundane, slight reflections of the characters, quite independent of each other. Whatever people do when they are surfing.

Is William like this all the time or just in chatrooms?

He makes an effort to remain anonymous, so he perhaps is very different. What William is on the internet is what he aspires to be. He is maybe low status outside of the chatroom because he always toys with power. The suicide fascination – he may have tried to kill himself.

Why does Jack keep talking to him?

Possibly taken in a bit by the danger and drama of him – also he is funny. They will probably never meet – so it is safe.

UNIT TWO – BRITNEY CHAT

What chatroom are they in and why is Eva there?

Britney chatroom? Any reason you like. Maybe to preach her message, nothing better to do, looking for someone to toy with? Eva is a kind of mirror of William.

What are the key differences between Eva and William?

Male anger and female anger have very different energies. Their manipulation tactics differ through their gender as well.

Why and who 'Murder'?

This could be mother or Britney or just the extreme act of violence for a reaction. She is exposed to the audience as vulnerable by moments like this very early on. There is always the pressure of mother on the other side of the door. The girls' conversation is quite confessional.

What sort of argument was it with mother? Is it ongoing trouble?

Yes, persistent pressure – she was forced to Irish dance in an early draft!. There is also a definite class difference between the two. Emily has a real sense of innocence – Bus, Tesco, Argos are all clues. Eva discovers things about her she uses later when she takes her to pieces.

The two scenes move chronologically through the dialogue from childhood to the beginning of adolescence.

UNIT THREE – JIM AND LAURA

Why did the father leave?

His hate seems to be for his mother not his dad, who left in a romantic way. There is a lot of strength in the father just leaving without a clear reason. The storytelling is very calm.

If he doesn't think his problems are that serious, why is he in the suicide chatroom?

It seems these feelings recur – this is exploitable. The scale of depression has different levels, sometimes he's low, sometimes not. He is trying on a different lifestyle for size – even within his depression.

You discover Laura's staleness and the element of sadism – she is never giving advice. She is inactive. She is also quite scary. She wears suicide like a badge. You discover her volume of issues. She is closer to suicide than anyone else.

Key question for the Director – how much attention does she pay? She is the only one who doesn't get up or move for the whole play. She needs power in this scene when we first meet her. By listening to Jim's problems, it works through her own – later she discovers that she is needed. She has to live with her own failure to kill herself.

Why is this conversation not enough for Jim? What takes him on this downward spiral?

Chad gives him nothing, Laura gives him nothing, the first advice he gets is bad advice. Again the teenage search for purpose. Just because he's in a suicide chatroom doesn't mean he definitely wants to kill himself.

Why doesn't Laura give advice? Why is she there?

She may have a phobia of words, previous advice may have pushed her too far. She's back there to discover what pushed her, maybe.

How long ago was Laura's suicide attempt?

Not long, and it's still possible that it could happen again.

UNIT FOUR

Is this William's chatroom?

Yes.

Why, 'Who made you – Big Brother?', not 'God?'

It's more teenage and more recent and God has just been rejected.

Do they believe they are clichés or is this just William's perspective?

'Cliché' is his new word and another teenage rebellion subject.

Why does Jim come in?

Geography. It's his town – that's the title of the chatroom – he wants advice and through this to offer his opinion.

There is an interesting difference between what is typed in a chatroom and what is delivered. Therefore lines can be received in a very different way from their delivery. This makes the class difference slightly less apparent to each other.

Can you regionally adjust the stereotype dress that relates to the class comments from William?

Yes, please do. Change the address of McDonald's if you like.

What would make William assume their class?

His own. The language they use. William and Emily are probably middle class, the others aren't.

How aware is Will of the sexual tension between him and Eva?

They are aware of the power relationship between them. Let the actors find out where the sexual tension lies. Laura is distant. She is away from the others. This could be made clearer with an accent.

What is Jack doing here?

He has been invited by William. William is sparky and interesting, maybe a bit lonely and naive. Jack is a joker who rarely offers a genuine opinion.

Enda, how much of your personal experiences are in the play?

Lots! I'm mostly Jack.

UNIT FIVE

'Cheer up Charlie' is a song from *Willy Wonka*.

How can you stage the private chatroom scene?

That depends on the whole style of the show. The lighting could indicate it. Wheely chairs maybe. Move away from the others. The life of the play continues whether a character is the focus or not. The interruptions are poetic licence – you can't interrupt on the web.

Why does Jack return?

It is an important moment for him. He's not quite strong enough to leave. His inactivity doesn't take him anywhere.

Does Emily actually leave?

No, she listens. Cut the stage directions that hint that she does. It is up to you to decide, though.

Why does she stay for so long?

Eva and William have had a taste of blood from bullying easily. 'See how far he'll go' – it's a very dark line.

Does William see the others as real people?

Great question for the actor to answer. It is like a game. You don't have to see their faces, so you can hide behind a screen. William's understanding of depression seems to be clearer than anyone else.

Is Eva actually listening to Jim?

She's still online, but barely there. Ignoring is too strong but if she is listening too much and reacts like that, she becomes too much of a bitch.

UNIT SIX

What does 'Spa-Boy' mean?

Spastic – as a light insult. You can change it regionally.

To what extent are we free to move the chairs around to create scene?

Whatever you like, but it needs to be clean and not fussy.

Why have you not used 'LOL' and language like that? Can we use projections to indicate it?

Because it's theatre. Be careful setting up too much expectation of a real chatroom. The strength is silence.

At what point does Eva decide to take it further?

Eva and Will have already talked about Jim. They kind of morph into one voice. It's a gradual raising of the stakes. The reaction to Jim is very cold and direct and adult. There is a definite shift of level and intensity.

You need to develop a staging vocabulary that allows private chat, etc., and puts the audience at ease. The locations are interesting – chatrooms. They are given titles and themes but are virtual spaces, accessed from safety.

UNITS SEVEN AND EIGHT

Once the set-up of the narrative is clear it unravels quite easily. People's real colours start to come through.

Why does Jim take control?

He snaps in this scene and finds his voice. He is on the edge and you need to push it as he takes control. He is hanging on.

Why is the confrontation not between Eva and Laura?

She has got everything she wants. She has had control and moved on – perhaps reading a magazine!

Why McDonald's?

Because of the story about a guy who was involved in a chatroom and attacked someone in a McDonald's.

Why 'Bunny rabbit'

Opposite of suicide.

Where is Jim giving the speech, is it part of the film?

No. It's theatrical. A moment of clarity. Confessional to the audience. He eats the burger onstage as well. We see the other characters in the film – remember Jim doesn't know who they are.

Why are the lyrics on the screen?

It's jokey and light. A grotesque theatrical image.

Is Jim grateful to Eva and Will?

Yes, in some way, but it is unplayable.

Workshop facilitated by John Tiffany
with notes taken by Steve Marmion

CITIZENSHIP

Mark Ravenhill

Characters

Amy

Tom

Gary

Ray

Stephen

Kerry

Chantal

Alicia

de Clerk

Melissa

Tarot Reader

Tarot Reader's Daughter

Baby

Martin

ONE

Amy, Tom.

Amy You got the Nurofen?
Tom Yeah.
Amy Take four.
Tom It says two.
Amy Yeah, but if you're gonna really numb yourself you gotta do four.
Tom I dunno.
Amy Do you want it to hurt?
Tom No.
Amy Then take four. Here.

Amy passes Tom vodka He uses it to wash down four Nurofen.

Now put the ice cube on your ear.

Tom does this.

Now you gotta hold it there till you can't feel nothing.
Tom Thanks for helping.
Amy It's gonna look good.
Tom Yeah?
Amy Yeah, really suit you.
Tom Thass good.
Amy You got a nice face.
Tom I don't like my face.
Amy I think it's nice.
Tom Sometimes I look in the mirror and I wish I was dead.
Amy I got rid of mirrors.

Tom Yeah?

Amy Mum read this Feng Shui thing and it said I wasn't supposed to have them. You numb now?

Tom Almost. You got a nice face.

Amy You don't have to lie.

Tom I'm not. You're fit.

Amy I know I'm plain. But that's okay. I talked to my therapist.

Tom What did she say?

Amy That I have to love myself in case nobody else does.

Tom Your mum loves you.

Amy I suppose. You ready now?

Tom I reckon.

Amy produces a needle.

Is that clean?

Amy I put it in Dettol.

Tom Alright.

Amy Let's start.

Amy starts to push the needle into Tom's ear but he pulls away.

I can't do it if you do that.

Tom I know.

Amy You gotta sit still.

Tom Maybe we should leave it. Maybe not today.

Amy I thought you wanted an earring.

Tom I know.

Amy Thass what you been saying for weeks: I wanna earring, I wanna earring.

Tom I know, only –

Amy I'll go careful. Come here. You're a baby.

Tom No.

Amy I'll treat you nice and soft. Like a baby.

Tom Alright.

Tom comes back.

Amy Bit more vodka.

Tom drinks.

Bit more.

Tom drinks.

Bit more.

Tom drinks. Amy pushes the needle into his ear.

Tom Aaagghh.
Amy Thass it.
Tom It hurts.
Amy Nearly there.
Tom Do it quickly. Do it. Aaagghh.
Amy Soon be finished.
Tom Right. Right. Is there blood?
Amy What?
Tom Is there blood?
Amy I dunno.
Tom I can feel blood.
Amy Maybe a bit.
Tom Shit. Shit. Shit.
Amy It's not much. You're gonna be alright.
Tom Yeah. Yeah. Yeah. Yeah. Yeah. Yeah. Yeah.

Tom faints.

Amy Tom? Tom? Shit. Shit.

Amy drinks a lot of vodka.

Tom – please.

Amy's mobile rings.

(*on phone*) Kez? No. I'm fucking – I'm having a panic attack. Like I used to, yeah. Tom's dead. He died. Just

now. Shit. I killed him. I've killed Tom. I wanna kill
myself. Shit.

Tom groans.

(*on phone*) He made a noise. Yeah, well. He came back
to life. I gotta go. Kez – I'm going now.

Tom Whass going on?

Amy You sort of went.

Tom Who's on the phone?

Amy Thass Kerry. She's getting stressed out 'cos she's
gotta give the baby back tomorrow.

Tom Baby?

Amy Life Skills.

Tom Oh yeah.

Amy You remember Life Skills? Each of the girls has
gotta take it in turns to look after this baby – plastic
baby. It puts you off having a real one. You could have
memory loss.

Tom No.

Amy Like Shareen after the overdose. Her mum and dad
went to see her in the hospital and she didn't know
who they were.

Tom I haven't got memory loss, alright?

Amy Alright.

Tom Fucking stupid idea letting you do that. I should
have gone to a fucking professional. Fucking go to
somebody who knows what they're fucking doing
'stead of letting you fucking fuck the whole thing up.

Amy I was trying to help.

Tom Yeah, well, you're no help – you're rubbish. You're
total rubbish.

Amy Don't give me negative messages.

Tom Trying to kill me with your stupid needle.

Amy I can't be around people who give me negative
messages.

Tom I fucking hate you.

Amy No. I'm sorry. I'm sorry. I'm sorry.

Amy cries.

Tom Come on. Don't. No. No.
Amy I can't do anything right. I'm useless.
Tom No.
Amy I am. Thass why I cut myself. 'Cos I'm totally
useless. Ughhh.
Tom Hey hey hey.

Tom holds Amy.

Come on. Alright. Alright. Alright. You better?
Amy I dunno.
Tom You're alright. You're a good person. I like you.
Amy Yeah?
Tom I really like you.
Amy Thass good.
Tom You got a nice face.

Amy kisses Tom.

Oh.
Amy Was that wrong?
Tom I didn't mean you to do that.
Amy Oh. Right. Right.
Tom I didn't wanna kiss you. Only –
Amy Yeah?
Tom I'm not ready for –
Amy You're fifteen.
Tom I know.
Amy You gotta have done.
Tom No.
Amy Why?
Tom It doesn't matter.
Amy Tell me.
Tom I have this dream. And in this dream I'm kissing
someone. Real kissing. Tongues and that. But I can't

see who I'm kissing. I don't know if it's a woman. Or a man. I try to see the face. But I can't.

Amy Are you gay?

Tom I don't know.

Amy There's bisexuals.

Tom You won't tell anyone?

Amy No. Are you going to decide?

Tom What?

Amy What you are?

Tom I don't know.

Amy Or find out?

Tom I don't know.

Amy Don't waste yourself, Tom. You've got a nice face.

Tom Yeah.

Amy gets a text message.

Amy It's Kerry. She says the baby's gone to sleep.

Tom It's not real.

Amy It is to her.

Tom I'm gonna go.

Amy Finish off the vodka.

Tom No. Thanks. Forget what I told you.

Amy You're still bleeding. There's still some –

Tom I got coursework.

Exit Tom. Amy drinks.

TWO

Gary, Tom. They are smoking a joint.

Tom Good draw.

Gary I got it off my mum's boyfriend for my birthday. Ten big fat ones for my fifteenth.

Tom Thass cool.

Gary Thass the last. He had a fight with his dealer last night. Dealer come round the house and they had a big barney. An' me mum's Ragga CDs got smashed in the ruck.

Tom Shit.

Gary Yeah. She is well gutted.

Enter Ray and Stephen.

Ray Wass 'appening?

Gary Chilling.

Ray You shag Amy last night? We wanna know. You get jiggy?

Stephen Jiggy-jiggy.

Ray Is she your bitch? You ride her like your bitch?

Tom Fuck's sake.

Gary You got problems.

Ray What?

Gary I'm saying: you got problems.

Ray What you saying? I got problems.

Gary Yeah, you got problems. No respec'.

Ray I respec'.

Gary No respec' for woman.

Ray I respec' woman.

Gary Ride her like a bitch? Didn't he say?

Tom Yeah.

Ray That's what I said.

Stephen He said it.

Ray That's what I said. I ride her *and* respec' woman.

Stephen Yeah. Ride and respec'.

Gary You chat shit. What are you? What is he?

Stephen He is gay.

Gary All I'm saying –

Ray So gay. You are so totally gay, Gary.

Gary Just sayin' –

Ray You are like the most totally gay person anyone knows.

Gary I'm not.

Ray Gay, Gary. Thass what you are. Respec'? What you chattin'? You're chattin' gay. You are fucking wrong, man. Wrong in your head. Wrong in your, your, your . . . hormones man. Totally, totally wrong.

Gary Thass not right.

Ray (*to Tom*) Come on, man. Say something. Tell him.

Tom I . . .

Ray You're always watching. You're never talking. Tell him.

Tom Listen. I wanna –

Ray You fucking tell him.

Stephen Tell the batty boy.

Ray You fucking tell him.

Tom . . . You're gay, Gary.

Gary Shit.

Tom Everyone says it. Everyone calls you it. Gay Gary.

Gary I know what they say.

Tom You shouldn't talk gay.

Stephen Thass right.

Tom 'Cos no one likes a person who talks gay.

Gary You chat shit, Tom.

Ray Listen, he's tellin' you –

Gary Same as them. All of you. Chattin' shit. All day long. Mouths moving but it's just: chat, chat, chat. Shit, shit, shit.

Tom No, no.

Gary Yeah, yeah.

Tom No.

Gary Yeah.

Ray Fight fight fight.

Stephen Fight fight fight.

Ray Fight fight fight.

Stephen Fight.

Tom pushes Gary.

Ray Thass it.

Stephen Do it back or you're gay.
Gary Fuck's sake.

Gary pushes Tom.

Ray Fucking insulted you, man. The gay-boy fucking
insulted you.
Stephen Batty hit yer.
Ray Get him.
Tom Listen –
Ray Use your fist.
Stephen Fist for the batty-boy.
Gary Go on.
Tom Yeah?
Gary Do what they tell you. Do what they want to.
Tom Yeah?
Gary Follow the leader.
Tom Yeah.

Tom punches Gary in the stomach.

Ray Respec', man.
Stephen Total respec'.
Gary Fuck you.

*Gary punches Tom in the stomach very hard. Tom
falls over.*

Ray Nasty.

*Enter Amy, Kerry, Alicia, Chantal. Chantal carries the
baby.*

Kerry You're not carrying her properly.
Chantal Leave it, Kez.
Kerry But you're not doing the head right.
Chantal It's my baby, Kez.
Kerry I know.
Chantal Yesterday it was yours and now it's mine.
Kerry I'm only telling you.

Chantal An' I can do whatever I want with it.

Amy She's got withdrawal symptoms.

Chantal Over plastic?

Kerry Don't say that. You're not fit.

Alicia Iss the Blazin' Squad. You mellowin'?

Ray Totally chilled, me, darlin'.

Stephen Totally.

Alicia Sweet.

Ray Hear Tom was round yours last night.

Amy Thass right.

Ray Gettin' jiggy.

Amy Do what?

Ray Jiggy-jiggy-jiggy.

Stephen Jiggy-jiggy-jiggy.

Amy You say that?

Tom No.

Ray What? You never?

Amy Thass right.

Ray What? He not fit enough for you?

Amy Iss not that.

Ray You frigid? She frigid, Tom?

Tom No.

Ray Wass wrong with 'em? Why ain't they gettin' jiggy?

Alicia I dunno.

Ray Thass gay.

Tom What?

Ray Youse two are so gay, Tom.

Amy No.

Ray Oooo – sore.

Amy Your ear's started.

Tom Yeah?

Amy You started bleeding again.

Alicia Shit. There's blood.

Kerry I don't wanna look.

Amy You wanna look after that. You got a hanky?

Tom No.

Amy Chantal?
Chantal Here.

Chantal tucks the baby under her arm to find a paper hanky.

Kerry You can't do that.
Chantal Juss for a moment.
Kerry You got to hold it properly all day long.
Chantal Juss while I'm lookin'.
Kerry Give it me. Give it me.

Kerry takes the baby from Chantal. Chantal finds the hanky, passes it to Amy. Amy holds the hanky on Tom's ear.

(*to baby*) Alright. Alright.
Amy You wanna hold that there?
Ray She bite you?
Stephen Yeah.
Ray While you was doing it?
Tom I'll be alright now.
Amy You sure?
Tom Yeah.

Tom continues to hold the handkerchief on his ear.

Chantal Give me the baby, Kerry.
Kerry Later.
Chantal Now.
Kerry Bit longer.
Chantal I gotta have it for Life Skills.
Kerry I know.
Chantal So . . ?
Alicia Give it, Kez.
Kerry Juss . . . do the head properly.
Chantal Alright.

Kerry hands Chantal the baby.

Alicia Thass it. Come on.

Exit Alicia, Kerry, Chantal.

Amy Laters.

Exit Amy.

Ray How do you do the ear? She do that ear? Was she like eatin' you?

Tom Won't stop bleeding.

Ray What do you do?

Tom It was . . . we were doing an earring.

Ray Earring? Earring? Earring? Shit, man. In that ear? You was doing an earring in that ear? Shit, man. Thass the gay side. Shit. You was doing an earring in the gay side. Shit.

Stephen Shit.

Tom No. No. She's jokin'. It was –

Ray Yeah? Yeah?

Tom It wasn't –

Ray Yeah? Yeah?

Tom It was bitin'.

Ray Yeah?

Stephen Yeah?

Tom It was like love-biting.

Ray I knew it.

Stephen Thass right.

Tom We were gettin' hot and biting and that and we –

Ray Yeah?

Tom And we got –

Stephen Jiggy.

Tom Yeah. Jiggy.

Ray I knew it.

Tom Yeah, totally jiggy. Like ridin' and ridin' and ridin'.

Ray Oh yeah.

Tom And she was wantin' it.

Stephen Yeah.

Tom And I was givin' like, like, like, like –
Ray Yeah?
Tom A big man.
Ray Thass right. Big man.
Stephen Big man.
Ray Big man.
Stephen Big man.
Ray Big man.
Stephen Big man.
Gary Hey – that's sweet.
Ray Shut it, gay boy.
Stephen The big men is talkin', batty boy.
Ray Out of ten?
Tom She's a six.
Ray So you see her again?
Tom Maybe. I'm thinkin' about it.
Stephen De Clerk.
Ray Run.
Gary Give us a hand.
Ray On your own, man.

*Exit Ray and Stephen rapidly. Tom goes to help Gary.
Enter de Clerk.*

De Clerk Tom.
Tom Sir?
De Clerk A word – now. Gary – move.
Gary Sir.
De Clerk You're a stoner, Gary.
Gary The herb is the people's weed.
De Clerk Piss off.

Exit Gary. DeClerk pulls out a piece of coursework.

What's this, Tom?
Tom My Citizenship, sir.
De Clerk Your Citizenship coursework. And what's this?
Tom Blood, sir.

De Clerk Blood on your Citizenship coursework. Blood on the work which tomorrow the inspectors are going to want to see.

Tom I know, sir.

De Clerk And it's not going to be you that's going to be bollocked, is it? No. It's going to be me. Didn't I say, didn't I say many, many – oh so many – times that your coursework should be neat?

Tom Yes, sir.

De Clerk Because I don't need the hassle from the inspectors. Because I'm very stressed out I'm not sleeping. I told you all that I wasn't sleeping. Some nights nothing. Some nights just a couple of hours.

Tom I know, sir.

De Clerk The Head gives me grief, kids give me grief. And now tomorrow the inspection team arrives and what do I find?

Tom I'm sorry, sir.

De Clerk I find that you have been bleeding all over 'What Does a Multicultural Society Mean to Me?'

Tom I didn't mean to.

De Clerk I'm not showing this to the inspectors. You can stay behind tonight and copy this out.

Tom But sir –

De Clerk You want me to copy it out? I've got lesson plans, marking. I'm going to be here till midnight. I'm not copying it out. You'll see me at the end of school and you'll copy this out.

Tom Yes, sir.

De Clerk Right then. See you tonight.

Exit de Clerk. Tom mops his ear. The bleeding has stopped. Enter Amy.

Amy Why you tell 'em you slept with me?

Tom I never.

Amy Don't lie. You told Ray and Steve. Now they told everyone.

Tom I'm sorry.

Amy But it's not true.

Tom I know.

Amy So why you –? You gotta sort out what you are, Tom. You straight? You gay?

Tom Don't say it in school.

Amy You bisexual? If you want you can see my therapist. My mum'll sort it.

Tom I don't need a therapist.

Amy I know somewhere they do Tarot. The cards might tell you.

Tom I don't believe in that.

Amy What you gonna do, Tom? You gotta stop lying. You gotta decide what you are.

Tom I know.

THREE

Tom and Mr de Clerk. Tom holds a bloody handkerchief to his ear.

Tom I'm still bleeding. sir.

De Clerk Just – copy it out.

Tom I am. I'm just . . . worried.

De Clerk Mmmmmm.

Tom You know – worried that I might copy it but then I might drip blood on the, like, copy you know.

De Clerk Well don't.

Tom I'm trying only –

De Clerk Put the paper over there, lean your head over there.

Tom Alright. (*He does so.*) It feels really weird, sir.

De Clerk Shut up.

Tom I'm not writing straight, sir.

De Clerk Do the best you can.

Tom I'm trying hard but it's not going straight, sir.

De Clerk Fuck's sake, Tom.

Tom Thought so. I just dripped. Blood on the desk.

De Clerk Haven't you got a plaster?

Tom I asked at the front office but the rules say we have to provide our own.

De Clerk Well, alright – just try not to drip any more.

Tom Doing my best.

De Clerk's mobile rings.

Tom You gonna get that, sir?

De Clerk No.

Mobile stops.

Tom Might have been important.

De Clerk Nothing else matters. Nothing else matters but your coursework and the inspectors and that we don't become a failing school, okay? There is nothing else in the whole wide world that matters apart from that.

Mobile rings again.

Tom They don't think so.

De Clerk Well fuck 'em, fuck 'em, fuck 'em.

Tom They really want to talk to you.

De Clerk Uhhh. (*Answers the mobile.*) No. Still at – I told you. I told you – because we've got the inspectors. No. No. Well put it in the fridge and I'll. . . . put it in the bin. I don't care. I don't care. I can't.

De Clerk ends the call.

Tom Are you married, sir?

De Clerk I'm not talking any more.

Tom I was just wondering.

De Clerk Well, don't.

Tom Other teachers say: my wife this or my girlfriend that. But you never do.

De Clerk Well, that's up to them.

Tom It makes you wonder. We all wonder.

De Clerk Listen, I'm here from eight in the morning until eight in the evening, midnight the last few weeks – maybe I don't have a personal life.

Tom Yeah.

De Clerk Maybe I'm not a person at all. Maybe I'm just lesson plans and marking.

Tom Yeah. Maybe.

De Clerk Oh. My head. Have you got a Nurofen?

Tom Sorry, sir?

De Clerk Have you got a Nurofen or something?

Tom No, sir. I had some but I took them all.

De Clerk Right.

Tom If you want to go home – go home to your . . . partner.

De Clerk I can't.

Tom I can do a massage, sir. I know how to do a massage.

De Clerk No.

Tom It stops headaches. I done it loads of times.

De Clerk Listen. Physical contact is –

Tom Out of lessons now.

De Clerk Difficult.

Tom Sssssssshhhh. Our secret.

Tom moves over to de Clerk and massages his shoulders and neck.

You've got to breathe too. Remember to keep breathing.

De Clerk Mmm.

Tom There's a lot of stress about, isn't there?

De Clerk It's all stress.

Tom How old are you?

De Clerk Twenty-two.

Tom Lots of teachers burn out before they're twenty-five because of all the stress.

De Clerk Mmm.

Tom You're quite developed, sir. Do you go to the gym?

De Clerk Sometimes.

Tom With your . . . partner.

De Clerk Back to your work now. That was wrong. Physical contact.

Tom Sir – I'm really sorry, but I've –

Tom wipes de Clerk's shoulder.

I've dripped on you, sir.

De Clerk What?

Tom You've got blood on your shirt.

De Clerk Oh, fuck.

Tom I'm really sorry. It's a really nice shirt.

De Clerk Shit. Shit. Shit.

De Clerk scrubs at his shoulder.

Tom If you want me to get you another one, sir –

De Clerk No no.

Tom I get a discount. My brother manages Top Man.

De Clerk Tom – get on with your work. You get on with your work and I'll get on with my work.

Tom You've got good clothes, sir. For a teacher.

De Clerk Tom.

Pause.

Tom Sir . . . I keep on having this dream and in this dream I'm being kissed.

De Clerk Don't.

Tom Only I never know whether it's a man or woman whose doing the kissing.

De Clerk This isn't Biology. I'm Citizenship.

Tom I think I dream about being kissed by a man.

De Clerk I don't want to know about that.

Tom I really want to know: do I dream about a man kissing me?

De Clerk Please. Don't do this. I'm tired. I'm exhausted. I've got the Head of Department chasing me. I've got the inspectors coming after me like wolves after blood. I've still got eight hours of paperwork and I've done a full day's teaching. Please understand the pressure I'm under and just copy the work.

Tom What do you do if you're gay, sir?

De Clerk You talk to someone.

Tom I'm trying to talk to you.

De Clerk You don't talk to me. Talk to your form tutor.

Tom He hates me.

De Clerk I don't think so.

Tom What do you do at the weekends, sir?

De Clerk Alright. Go away. Go home.

Tom What about the coursework?

De Clerk I'll explain the blood to the inspectors.

Tom Alright then.

Tom packs up his bag.

Bye then, sir.

De Clerk Bye, Tom.

Tom I want to talk to someone gay, sir. I don't know any.

De Clerk Shut up, please shut up.

Tom I really want to meet someone gay and ask them what it's like.

De Clerk Well – it's fine. It's normal. It's just fine.

Tom You reckon?

De Clerk You know the school policy: we celebrate difference. You report bullies. Everything's okay. You're okay.

Tom I don't feel okay.

De Clerk Well – you should do.

FOUR

Gary, Tom. Smoking a joint.

Gary Was it good?

Tom What?

Gary You know – when you done Amy?

Tom Well –

Gary 'Cos lovin'. There's so many types of lovin'.

Tom Yeah?

Gary Yeah. Between man and woman. There's so many
types of lovin', in't there?

Tom You reckon?

Gary Oh yeah. There's sweet lovin' and there's animal
lovin' and there's hard lovin' and there's dirty lovin'.
There's millions of ways of lovin'. You follow?

Tom I think so.

Gary You lie.

Tom No.

Gary I'm chattin' shit, aren't I?

Tom No.

Gary Yeah, I'm chattin' shit. Thass the herb. I always
chat shit when I'm blazin'. But thass the way I like it.
I like to chat shit.

Tom I like the way you talk.

Gary Yeah?

Tom You talk good. You're better than the knobheads.
Ray, Steve – they're knobheads.

Gary Then how come you –

Tom Yeah yeah.

Gary – hit me when they tell you?

Tom I'm sorry.

Gary No worries. Love and understanding. Peace to you,
brother.

Tom Yeah, peace.

Gary Yo mellow, man. Love you, brother.
Tom Yeah. Brother love.

Gary puts his arm around Tom.

Gary You like the brother love?
Tom Yeah, it's good.
Gary Peace on the planet. No war. Herb bring harmony. Blaze some more?
Tom Yeah.

Gary produces another rolled joint from a tin.

Gary So tell me 'bout your lovin'?
Tom Well –
Gary Is she your woman now?
Tom Well –
Gary Or was it like a one-night lovin' ting?
Tom Well –
Gary Don't by shy. Take a big draw and tell.

Gary hands Tom the joint. Tom draws.

Harder, man. Draw as deep as you can.

Tom draws as hard as he can.

Tom I need some water.
Gary No. Not till you tell. Tell me what it was like. Come on, man.
Tom I feel ill.
Gary I gotta know. I gotta know about the ride.

Gary pins Tom to the floor, knees over Tom's arms, sitting on Tom's chest.

What was it like when you rode the woman?
Tom Get off me – off me.
Gary Jiggy-jiggy with the honey. Ya!
Tom Off.

Tom pushes Gary off.

I never, alright? I never – ?

Gary What?

Tom I never done her. We never done anything.

Gary What? Nothing? Oral? Finger?

Tom Nothing, okay. We never done it.

Gary Shit. You lied.

Tom Yeah.

Gary That's sad, man.

Tom Yeah, it's really sad.

Gary So – you not gonna tell me 'bout no lovin'?

Tom No.

Gary Shit, broth'. That was gonna be my wank tonight.

Tom Yeah?

Gary Yeah – your booty grindin' her. That was gonna –

Tom Well, there's nothing.

Gary You wanna pretend for me? Like make it up. So – you never done it. But you can make up like a story, like a dirty story so I got summat in my head.

Tom I'm no good at stories.

Gary Just make it dirty so I got something for tonight.

Tom I'm still supposed to copy out my Citizenship for de Clerk.

Gary Okay – tell me about your dreams. You gotta have dirty dreams.

Tom Course.

Gary Then tell me –

Tom I don't know.

Gary Come, brother love. (*Sits Tom down, puts his arms around him.*) Tell your brother.

Tom . . . I have this dream. And in this dream, I'm lying in bed. Not in my room. Not like my room at home. Like a strange room.

Gary Like a dungeon?

Tom No, maybe like a Travel Lodge or something, I don't know.

Gary Right.

Tom And I'm almost asleep but then the door opens and this stranger comes into the room.

Gary Like a thief?

Tom Maybe, but this . . . person, they come over to the bed and they kiss me.

Gary Right. And – ?

Tom It's a person but I don't know, I don't know –

Gary Yeah.

Tom See, this person, are they a woman or are they . . ?

Gary Yeah?

Tom leans over and kisses Gary on the lips.

You're batty, man?

Tom I don't know.

Gary Shit blud, you're batty man. The batty man kissed me. Shit.

Gary moves away and takes several draws.

Tom I don't know. Don't know. Just wanted to see, you know – just wanted to see what it felt like. I –

Gary And did you like it?

Tom I don't know.

Gary Was my lips sweet?

Tom I don't know.

Gary No blud, thass cool, thass cool. I can handle that. Peace to all. Everybody's different. I can go with that.

Tom I'm sorry.

Gary Hey – love you still, bro'.

Gary hugs Tom.

Tom I just thought – you're Gay Gary.

Gary Thass just a name. You touch my arse, I kill you, see?

Tom Okay.

Gary No, see, I like the honeys. You should see my site. Thass where I live out what's in my head see?

Gary gets out his laptop, opens his website.

See, these are my fantasies. And I share him with the world on my message board. I got graphics, see?

Tom Is that you?

Gary Yeah.

Tom You got muscles.

Gary Yeah, well – thass me older, see. And thass my dick.

Tom (*laughs*) I thought it was a weapon.

Gary (*laughs*) Yeah. My dick's a lethal weapon. And I fight my way through the desert, see, through all the terrorists and that, see? Nuke nuke nuke. And then when I get to the city – there's all the honeys, see? And I ride 'em see. And then I kill 'em.

Tom That's sick, man. I thought you was all love and understanding.

Gary Can't help what's in my head. Gotta let it out.

Tom All that – it's . . . wrong.

Gary Stuff that's in my head. I don't fight it. I let it out. Thass your problem. What's in your head, Tom? Who do you want? The honey or the homo?

Tom I dunno yet. I want to find out. I gotta try different stuff.

Gary You wanna get on line.

Tom You reckon?

Gary Yeah. You start searchin', chattin', message boards, stuff. You can try everything.

Tom Yeah?

Gary You wanna do a search now? 'Gay sex'? 'Batty man'?

Tom No.

Gary What you want?

Tom I don't know. Maybe I'll do Amy.

Gary You reckon?

Tom I could do if I wanted to, yeah.

FIVE

Tom and Amy. Tom carries hair dye. Amy has a bandage round her wrist.

Tom See? It's baby blonde.

Amy Right.

Tom I wanna go baby blonde.

Amy Right.

Tom And I want you to do it to me.

Amy I'm supposed to be doing my affirmations.

Tom What's that?

Amy I'm supposed to write out a hundred times, 'I'm surrounded by love.'

Tom Why?

Amy 'Cos I cut myself again last night.

Tom Why?

Amy I dunno. I was bored. Or something. Or stress. I dunno.

Tom You gotta know.

Amy I don't. Mum took me down the healer and she told me I had to do the affirmations.

Tom You can do them later. Do my hair.

Amy They don't work anyway.

Tom No?

Amy I did them before and they never worked.

Tom What works?

Amy I dunno. Melissa says I need a shag.

Tom Maybe you do.

Amy You reckon?

Tom Yeah. I reckon.

Amy There's no one fancies me.

Tom That's not true.

Amy Says who?

Tom Says me.

Amy Yeah?

Tom You gonna do my hair?

Amy If you want.

Tom We need a bowl of water.

Amy Alright.

Tom And a towel.

Amy Yeah yeah.

Tom Thanks.

Amy exits. Tom removes his shirt. Folds it up.
Arranges himself on the floor. Pause. Enter Melissa.

Melissa Alright?

Tom Alright.

Melissa You seen my iPod?

Tom No.

Melissa She takes my iPod. Drives me mental. We're
always having words. There'll be a ruck soon.

Tom Right.

Melissa You shagging?

Tom Not yet.

Melissa Do us all a favour and give her one, will you?

Tom Do my best.

Melissa Where the fuck's it gone?

Exit Melissa. Tom arranges himself again on the floor
to look as alluring and yet as natural as possible for
Amy. Enter Amy with bowl of water and towel.

Amy I got it.

Tom I took my top off.

Amy Right.

Tom 'Cos I don't want to get bleach on it.

Amy Right.

Tom That alright? Me getting naked?

Amy Whatever. You got the instructions?

Tom Yeah.

Tom gives Amy the instructions.

I've been thinking about what you said.

Amy (*reading instructions*) Yeah?

Tom About sorting myself out and that. In my head. You know – about whether I wanted . . . you know.

Amy You seen a therapist?

Tom No. I just been thinking.

Amy Right.

Tom About who I wanta kiss and that.

Amy Right. You got any allergies?

Tom Why?

Amy 'Cos it says here – (*the instructions*) You got any allergies?

Tom Dust and peanuts.

Amy Dust and peanuts should be alright. You wanna get started?

Tom If you like. What if you got bleach on your top?

Amy Its a crap top.

Tom Yeah, but you'd ruin it. Bleach down the front.

Amy Mum'll recycle it.

Tom Maybe you better take your top off too.

Amy I don't think so.

Tom Go on. I took my top off. Time you took your top off too.

Amy No.

Tom Come on. Take it off. Take it off.

Tom reaches out to Amy – she pushes him away.

Amy I'm not taking my top off, alright?

Tom Alright. Do you reckon I should go down the gym?

Amy I don't know.

Tom Maybe I should go down the gym. My body's stupid.

Amy No.

Tom I've got a stupid body.

Amy No. You've got a fit body. I like your body.

Tom Yeah?

Amy It's a nice body.

Tom Do you wanna touch it?

Amy I dunno.

Tom Come on. Touch it if you like –

Amy Alright.

*Amy reaches out to touch Tom. Enter Melissa
followed by Chantal, Kerry and Alicia. Alicia carries
the baby.*

Melissa Your mates are here. They're shagging.

Exit Melissa.

Chantal/Kerry/Alicia Alright?

Tom Alright.

Amy We're not – we weren't gonna –

Chantal Thass a buff bod.

Tom Yeah?

Chantal For a kid, you're fit. He's fit, isn't he?

Kerry He's alright. I mean, I wouldn't –

Amy We weren't gonna –

Kerry But yeah, he's alright.

Amy I was gonna dye his hair.

Chantal Go on then.

Tom Forget it.

Chantal No. Go on.

Tom Another time. I don't want people watching.

Chantal It's safe. Go on. We heard you cut yourself
again. You alright?

Amy Oh yeah. I'm fine. Come on – let's wash your hair.

Amy pours water over Tom's head.

Tom Oww! Hurts! Aww! Burning, agh!

Amy Shit.

Tom What you –? You put cold in that? You never put
any cold in that.

Amy I forgot.

242

Tom You forgot. Shit – I'm gonna be scarred. Ugh.
Amy I'll get cold.

*Amy runs out with the jug. Tom paces around,
scratching at his scalp, groaning. Alicia gets out
cigarettes.*

Kerry Lish – don't.
Alicia What?
Kerry Not around the kid.
Alicia Don't be stupid.
Kerry It stunts 'em.
Alicia Thass when you're pregnant.
Kerry Not when you're mother.

Kerry takes the packet of cigarettes from Alicia.

Alicia Fuck's sake. I get stressed out without 'em.
Kerry Yeah – well.
Alicia See that, Spazz? Took my fags.
Kerry Don't call it that.
Alicia Whatever.

Enter Amy with jug of cold water.

Amy Here.

*Tom kneels in front of bowl. Amy pours cold water
over his head.*

Tom Agghhh.

Tom lies back.

Amy You better now?
Tom Is there red? Like burns?
Amy A bit.
Tom Thought so.
Chantal Are you gonna shag? 'Cos we can leave if you're
gonna shag.
Tom No. We're not gonna shag.

Chantal You sure?

Tom Yeah. I'm sure. We're not gonna shag. We're never gonna . . . no.

SIX

Tom, Tarot Reader. Nine cards spread out in a fan – three lines of three.

Tarot Reader There's the Tower. You see? That's the Tower. Now – you are facing a moment of great change. A moment of great decision. Would you like to ask me a question?

Tom I . . . no.

Tarot Reader Any moment you need to – you must ask me a question.

Tom Alright.

Tarot Reader But the Tower makes sense to you?

Tom Yes.

Tarot Reader The foundation on which – you see, here these are your emotions – the foundations on which your emotions are based is unstable. They may collapse at any time.

Tom Yes. That's how I feel.

Tarot Reader Then the cards are speaking to you?

Tom Yes, yes, they are.

Tarot Reader Good. Good. Then you're getting your money's worth.

Tom Nothing feels fixed. Everything feels as though it could fall over. I'm confused.

Tarot Reader Lots of people –

Tom I don't know who I am. I want to know –

Tarot Reader That's how lots of people – Tom, I need to know. I need to choose.

Tarot Reader Of course yes, yes, but please . . . listen . . .

244

so many people are . . . nobody knows, all the time . . .
we're told choose, decide.

Tom Yes.

Tarot Reader What colour should my hair be? Will I stay
in this relationship? Should I move to South America?
All the time, we've got these choices.

Tom I know.

Tarot Reader And we feel so unprepared, but if we
explore the choices, if we tune our hearts and our
heads to the cards. Do you see? Do you see?

Tom I think so.

Tarot Reader Good. Good.

A radio off.

Tarot Reader One moment. One – please make yourself
comfortable.

Tarot Reader exits. Tom waits. The radio is turned off.

Daughter (*off*) I was listening to that.

Tarot Reader (*off*) I thought you were out.

Daughter (*off*) Yeah, well.

Tarot Reader (*off*) I want you out, Michelle.

Daughter (*off*) I got bored.

Tarot Reader (*off*) Out. I'm doing a reading.

Daughter (*off*) Nothing to do.

Tarot Reader (*off*) Go down the shops.

Daughter (*off*) Give us some money.

Tarot Reader (*off*) I gave you money.

Daughter (*off*) I spent it.

Tarot Reader (*off*) What on?

Daughter (*off*) Piercing. See.

Tarot Reader (*off*) Well – go and pierce the other one.

Daughter (*off*) Give us some more money, then.

Tarot Reader (*off*) It's all take with you.

Daughter (*off*) That's right.

Pause. Enter the Tarot Reader.

Tarot Reader I'm sorry. Are you comfortable? It's important that you're comfortable.

Tom Yes.

Tarot Reader You didn't touch the cards?

Tom No.

Tarot Reader It's very important you didn't touch the –

Tom I didn't touch them.

Tarot Reader Let's look at the future.

Tom Yes.

Tarot Reader Now this is – the cards are very strong here.

Tom That's good.

Tarot Reader Two of the major . . . we call these the major arcana, you see? Here – the pictures. The High Priestess – here. Drawing back the veil. Drawing back the veil to let you into her world.

Tom It's a woman?

Tarot Reader She's a feminine –

Tom It's a woman letting me into her – I've got to know – that's a woman –

Tarot Reader It's more complicated than that. Yes, we used to say: the cards are men and they are women. The King. The Queen. But in this day and age – it's more complex – we prefer the masculine and feminine energies.

Tom But she's a woman.

Tarot Reader Or a man with a masculine energy.

Tom Oh.

Tarot Reader And here – the lovers. You are about to enter the gate, pass the threshold and embrace the lovers. A lover for you. Yes? You've got a question?

Tom I've really got to know. Is it? Is it a . . . a man or a woman?

246

Tarot Reader It's not so simple. Look at the cards. Really listen to the cards. You are about to pass through the gateway and meet your lover. Man or a woman? What do the cards say?

Tom I can't . . . nothing.

Tarot Reader Make yourself comfortable. Be patient. Listen.

Tom No. I really can't.

Tarot Reader We have time. You will choose a course of action. With the cards you will choose a course of action. Just watch and wait and listen. And listen. Listen. Listen to the cards.

Tom looks at the cards. Long pause.

Yes?

Tom Yes.

Tarot Reader You know what to do?

Tom I know what to do.

SEVEN

Tom, Amy. Amy carries the baby.

Tom You got the baby.

Amy She made me. Said I'd have detention for a week.

Tom That's harsh.

Amy Totally harsh. I told her – I'm not fit to be a mother, look at my arms. You can't be a mother when you've got cuts all over your arms.

Tom And what did she say?

Amy Said it would take me out of myself – think about another life.

Tom Bit of plastic.

Amy And now I have to write down all my thoughts and feelings in my baby diary.

Tom What you written?
Amy Nothing. Don't feel anything. It doesn't do anything. Just sits there. It's heavy.
Tom Let me feel.
Amy Go on then.

Amy gives Tom the baby.

Tom Yeah. Really heavy.

Tom drops the baby.

Tom Whoops.
Amy You did that on purpose.
Tom Maybe.
Amy You're trouble.
Tom That's right. Do you reckon it's damaged?
Amy Shut up.

Tom picks up the baby.

Tom No – it's fine.
Amy Don't tell Kerry – she'll go mental.
Tom (*to baby*) You're alright, aren't you? Aren't you? Yes.

Tom throws the baby up in the air, lets it fall on the floor.

Amy You're mad.
Tom I'm rubbish at catching. Catch it!

Tom throws the baby to Amy. She catches it.

Amy I'll be bollocked if it's damaged.
Tom Throw it to me. Come on.

Amy throws the baby. He lets it fall to the floor again.

Why can't I catch it?
Amy You're not trying. Give it here.

Amy goes to pick up the baby. Tom stops her.

Tom No – leave it.
Amy Why?
Tom 'Cos I'm here. You can hold the baby later.
Amy What am I gonna write in my baby diary?
Tom Make it up.

Tom takes his shirt off.

Amy What you doing?
Tom I went down the gym. See?
Amy How many times you been?
Tom Three.
Amy I don't think three's gonna make a difference.
Tom Course it is. Have a feel.
Amy Yeah?

Tom flexes a bicep.

Tom Feel that.
Amy Alright.

Amy feels his bicep.

Tom See?
Amy What?
Tom It's stronger. Harder.
Amy You reckon?
Tom Oh yeah – that's much harder.
Amy I dunno.

Amy picks up the baby.

Tom Do you wanna have sex?
Amy Maybe.
Tom I think maybe we should have sex.
Amy I've never had sex before.
Tom Neither have I. I've seen it on videos.
Amy Yeah?

Tom Round Gary's.
Amy Gay Gary?
Tom He's not gay.
Amy Right. Are you gay?
Tom Come here.

Amy goes to Tom. He takes the baby out of her arms and lays it on the floor. They kiss.

Did you like that?
Amy Yeah. Is it me?
Tom What?
Amy In your dream? Is it me you're kissing in your dream?
Tom No.
Amy Are you sure? If you can't see the face . . . ?
Tom Yeah well. But I can feel it.
Amy And it's not me?
Tom It's not you. Does that bother you?
Amy No.
Tom Good.

They kiss again.

Melissa (*off*) Amy.
Amy What?
Melissa (off) You got my camcorder?
Amy No.
Melissa (*off*) You sure? I can't find it anywhere.
Amy I'm sure.
Melissa (*off*) If you've taken it again –
Amy I haven't taken it again.
Melissa (*off*) I'm coming in to look.
Amy No.

Exit Amy. Tom waits. Enter de Clerk.

Tom How did you get in here, sir?
De Clerk Through the wall.

Tom What? You just . . . ?

De Clerk Walked through the wall.

Tom Shit.

De Clerk Just something I can do. Don't tell the Head.
We're not supposed to have special powers.

Tom Alright. Are you here – 'cos I'm still a bit gay – is
that it?

De Clerk Let's not talk about that.

Tom I sort of decided I wasn't gonna be gay any more –
now you sort of – well, it's a bit gay, isn't it, coming
through the wall like that?

De Clerk Are you going to have sex with her?

Tom Yeah, I reckon. What – don't you think I should?

De Clerk We can't tell you yes or no. That's not what we
do.

Tom Why not?

De Clerk Because you have to make your own choices.

Tom But why? Everything's so confusing. There's so
many choices. I don't feel like a person. I just feel like
all these bits floating around. And none of them match
up. Like a jigsaw that's never going to be finished. It's
doing my head in.

De Clerk And what would you prefer?

Tom Someone to tell me what to be.

De Clerk No one's going to do that.

Tom I wish they would.

De Clerk When I was growing up, everyone told you
who to be. They told you what to do. What was right
and what was wrong. What your future would be.

Tom I'd like that.

De Clerk No. It made me very unhappy.

Tom I'm unhappy – too many choices. You were
unhappy – no choices. Everyone's unhappy. Life's shit,
isn't it, sir?

De Clerk That is I would say a distinct possibility.

Tom Are you still unhappy, sir.

De Clerk If I stop – if I stop working and rushing – the inspection, the continual assessment – trying to pay the mortgage every month, trying to please the Head, trying to get home before nine every night – then, yes, I'm unhappy. But only when I stop.

Tom But you've got a boyfriend?

De Clerk I can't talk about that.

Tom You're gay, sir. I don't mean that in a bad way. I just mean – like you know who you are. And you're gay. I'm going to have sex with her.

De Clerk If that's what you want.

Tom So you better go back through the wall. I'm not having you watching us.

De Clerk I don't want to watch. Use protection.

Tom I know.

De Clerk If you're having sex, use protection.

Tom That's telling me what to do.

De Clerk It's advice.

Tom It's telling me what to do. You should tell me more of that.

De Clerk I can't. Promise me you'll use protection.

Tom I might do.

De Clerk Promise.

Tom Do all gay people walk through walls?

De Clerk Now you're being silly.

Enter Amy.

Amy She's gone now.

Tom Good. (*to de Clerk*) You going?

De Clerk Take care.

Exit de Clerk.

Tom Is everyone out?

Amy Yeah. They're all out. Got the place to ourselves.

Tom That's good.

Amy Are you scared?

252

Tom A bit. Are you?

Amy Scared and excited.

Tom Well, take it slow.

Amy Yeah. Let's take it really slow. You got anything?

Tom Like what?

Amy Like condoms and that?

Tom No.

Amy Oh –

Tom Does that bother you?

Amy No. Does that bother you?

Tom No.

Amy Do you love me?

Tom I don't know. Maybe later. Is that alright?

Amy Yeah. That's alright.

Tom After – we can do my hair. I still want blonde hair.

Amy Alright.

Tom Turn the light out.

Amy I want to see you.

Tom No.

Tom turns the light off. The Baby comes forward and speaks to the audience.

Baby And so it happened. My mummy and my daddy made me that night. Neither of them enjoyed it very much. But they did it. And that's what they wanted. And that night I started to grow in my mummy's tummy. And by the time she did her GCSEs I was almost ready to come out of her tummy. I think that night as they lay together in the dark she thought they might spend all their time together from that day on. But that didn't happen. In fact, once that night was over, they were sort of shy and embarrassed whenever they saw each other until – by the time I was born – they weren't speaking to each other at all. But Mummy says for a few moments – she's sure there were a few moments that night when he did really, really love her.

And I believe her. They did talk to each other once more after they left school – but there's one more bit of the story to show you before we get to that.

EIGHT

Tom and Martin. Tom has a hat pulled down completely covering his hair.

Tom You've got a nice place.
Martin (*off*) Thank you.
Tom Yeah, really nice. Trendy.
Martin (*off*) Thank you.
Tom What do you do?
Martin (*off*) My job?
Tom Yeah. Your job.
Martin (*off*) I'm a systems analyst.
Tom Right. Right. Is that alright?
Martin (*off*) I enjoy it.
Tom And the pay's good?
Martin (*off*) The pay is ridiculously good.
Tom Well, that's good.
Martin (*off*) And you?
Tom What?
Martin (*off*) Do you have a job?
Tom Yes.
Martin (*off*) What do you do?
Tom Well, actually I'm looking . . .
Martin (*off*) I see.

Enter Martin, with two bottles of beer. He gives one of the bottles of beer to Tom.

Cheers.
Tom Right. Cheers.
Martin If you want to take off –

Tom I'm alright.

Martin Maybe – your hat . . ?

Tom No.

Martin Alright.

Tom It's just . . . I had a disaster.

Martin Yes?

Tom With my hair.

Martin I see.

Tom Yeah, this mate tried to dye my hair but it went wrong.

Martin Right.

Tom Yeah, tried to dye my hair, but I had a bit of a reaction and it's gone really weird, like ginger bits and green bits and that. Last month. I'm waiting for it to grow out. I look weird so that's why I'm wearing –

Martin It suits you.

Tom Yeah?

Martin The hat. It's a good look.

Tom Thank you.

Martin You're a good-looking guy.

Tom Right.

Martin Was it your boyfriend?

Tom What?

Martin With the hair dye?

Tom No.

Martin Have you got a boyfriend?

Tom No. Have you?

Martin Yes. Is that alright?

Tom I suppose. How old are you?

Martin Twenty-one.

Tom Right.

Martin How old are you?

Tom Eighteen.

Martin You said nineteen in the chatroom.

Tom Did I?

Martin Yes.

Tom Well, I'm eighteen.

Martin But actually you look younger.

Tom Really?

Martin You actually look about sixteen.

Tom Everyone says I look younger. That's what they said when I was at school.

Martin Right. Do you want to come through to the bedroom?

Tom In a minute. Are you happy?

Martin What?

Tom You know, in your life and that? Does it make you happy?

Martin I suppose so.

Tom With your boyfriend and your job and that?

Martin I never really think about it.

Tom You seem happy.

Martin Then I suppose I am.

Tom That's good.

Martin And you?

Tom What?

Martin Are you happy?

Tom I reckon. Yes I am.

Martin Well, that's good. Look, we really should get into the bedroom –

Tom Right.

Martin My boyfriend's coming back at five and I don't want to –

Tom Right.

Martin Sorry to hurry you, but –

Tom That's alright.

Martin You can keep your hat on.

Tom Thanks.

Martin You're cute.

Tom Thanks. I've never done this before.

Martin Chatrooms?

Tom This. All of it.

Martin Sex?

Tom No. I've done sex. Only –

Martin Not with someone so old?

Tom Not with –

Martin Twenty-one too old for you?

Tom No. Not with . . . a bloke. I mean I did it with girls, a girl, but –

Martin Did you like it?

Tom It was alright.

Martin If you like that kind of thing.

Tom Yeah. I'm shaking. Sorry. I feel nervous. Is it gonna hurt?

Martin Not if we do it right.

Tom How will we know?

Martin I don't know. You just have to . . . er . . . suck it and see.

Tom (*laughs*) You dirty bastard.

Martin Yeah.

Tom I shouldn't have come.

Martin Alright then – another time. How are you getting back?

Tom No, no.

Tom kisses Martin.

Martin Mixed messages.

Tom You're right. I'm sixteen.

Martin I know.

Tom I'm legal.

Martin What do you want?

Tom This.

Tom kisses Martin.

Come on then. Where's the bedroom? Or do you want your boyfriend to find out?

Martin The bedroom's through here.

Tom Your boyfriend, he's not . . ?

257

Martin Yes?

Tom He's not . . . is your boyfriend a teacher?

Martin (*laughs*) God, no. He's a mortgage broker. Why?

Tom Nothing.

Martin Ready?

Tom Ready. Just – don't touch my hat, alright?

Martin Alright.

NINE

Amy, Tom.

Amy Your hair's alright.

Tom Yeah. Took a few months. But in the end it went back to normal.

Amy You should still do an earring.

Tom You reckon?

Amy Yeah. I always reckoned an earring would really suit you.

Tom Maybe one day.

Amy Yeah. One day. What you up to?

Tom Not much. I'm going to college next year.

Amy That's good.

Tom Fashion.

Amy Nice.

Tom And I'm doing coat-check.

Amy In a club?

Tom Sort of pub-club.

Amy Gay club?

Tom Just Fridays and Saturdays. You should come along. It's a laugh.

Amy You got a boyfriend?

Tom I dunno.

Amy You got to know.

Tom There's a bloke . . . we . . . meet up. A couple of times a week. But he's living with someone.

Amy His boyfriend?

Tom Yeah. He's got a boyfriend. He keeps on saying they're gonna split but they haven't. Still – we have a laugh. He's got money.

Amy Right.

Tom You seeing anyone?

Amy Yeah.

Tom Who?

Amy Nosy. I mean, I can't go out much but, you know, if I get a baby-sitter –

Tom Right.

Amy I'm gonna do college in a couple of years.

Tom That's good.

Amy Just gotta wait till she's a bit older.

Tom Of course. If you need me to baby-sit –

Amy No.

Tom I don't mind.

Amy I've got mates do that for me. Kerry loves it.

Tom Yeah, but if you ever need me to –

Amy I don't need you to.

Tom I want to.

Amy I don't want you to, alright?

Tom Alright. I still . . . think about you.

Amy Right.

Tom Like . . . fancy you and that.

Amy You told your boyfriend?

Tom Sometimes, when he kisses me, I think about you. He kisses me but I close my eyes and it's your face I see.

Amy You can't have it both ways.

Tom That's what I want.

Amy Well – you can't have it.

Enter Gary, pushing a pram.

Gary Alright, babe?

Amy Yeah. Alright.

Gary kisses Amy.

She been alright?

Gary Yeah. Fast asleep the whole time.

Amy She'll be awake all night now.

Gary You want me to wake her?

Amy No. Leave her alone.

Gary Alright, Tom?

Tom She told me she was going out with someone.

Gary You guess who?

Tom No. You gonna bring the kid up to be a stoner too?

Gary No. I give up the weed, didn't I? Can't be blazing around the kid, can I? Once you got a kid to look after – that's the time to grow up, I reckon.

Tom Yeah – suppose that's right.

Amy Tom's gone gay now.

Gary Thass cool.

Tom Can I have a look at her?

Amy We gotta go in a minute. Mum's booked us up the naturopath.

Tom I just want to have a quick look.

Amy Go on then.

Tom She's beautiful.

Amy Yeah. She's alright.

Tom Can I pick her up?

Amy No.

Tom I'll be careful.

Amy I don't want you to.

Tom Alright.

Amy Not now she's settled.

Tom Alright.

Amy Best to leave her alone.

Tom Alright.

Amy I want to keep her out of the sun.

Tom Of course.

Gary We've got to get the bus.

Amy Yeah.

Tom Will I see you again?

Amy Maybe.

Tom I wanna see you again. I'm the dad.

Amy Gary looks after her – don't you?

Gary Yeah.

Tom Yeah – but still.

Enter Martin.

Martin Sorry, I tried to get away, only –

Martin goes to kiss Tom. Tom steps away.

Tom Don't.

Amy You his boyfriend?

Martin I wouldn't . . . sort of . . .

Tom Yeah. Only sort of.

Amy Better than nothing though, isn't it?

Martin That's right.

Amy See ya.

Exit Amy and Gary, with pram.

Tom Did you tell him?

Martin I tried.

Tom You were supposed to tell him about me.

Martin Any day now.

Tom You gotta do it soon.

Martin I will. I promise. He's away tonight. What do
you want to do?

Tom I don't know. Do you love me?

Martin You know I don't like to use that word.

Tom I want you to say it.

Martin I can't.

Tom Then I don't wanna . . . Leave me alone.

Martin Ooooo . . . queeny sulk.

Tom What's the point of this?

Martin The point is sex. We have sex. And I have
money. And we have fun. That's the point. And that's
as good as it gets. So . . . let's just have fun. Let's just
spend lots of money and have lots of fun and have lots
of sex. What do you reckon?

Tom I reckon . . . l reckon . . .

Martin As good as it gets.

Tom . . . Alright.

Martin Are you alright?

Tom Me? Yeah. Yeah. I'm fine. I'm just fine.

End.

A Zig-Zag Path towards Some Idea
of Who You Are

Mark Ravenhill interviewed by Jim Mulligan

Citizenship is Mark Ravenhill's second *Shell Connections* play. He did not want to repeat the successful format of *Totally Over You*, so decided to write something that would be enjoyable and at the same time challenging. The critic Aleks Sietz has suggested that Mark Ravenhill is more of a 'work shopper than a garret writer' (see www.inyerface-theatre.com/archives.html), but for this play Ravenhill wrote a first draft in his garret, as it were, and then took it for a reading to a group of young people at the National Theatre.

> I wasn't quite sure what they would make of it, because sometimes young people can be quite conservative and prudish and I was worried they might reject it, but actually they were really animated by it and talked about it for hours. They were really fired up by it so I realised I was onto a good thing.

One of the features of *Citizenship* is the stark realism and acceptance by the young characters of things that adults either disapprove of or pretend do not happen. They take drugs as a matter of course. Amy says in a matter-of-fact way to Tom, 'Melissa says I need a shag.' And Melissa says to Tom, 'Do us all a favour and give her one.' Gary wants Tom to tell him about his jiggy-jiggy with his woman because 'That was gonna be my wank tonight.' He then shows him his website with what some adults would call pornographic images. And Chantal says to Amy without any tone of disapproval, 'We heard you cut yourself again. You alright?' This is the world of some young people today, and Mark Ravenhill presents it in a non-judgemental way. In a sense he is inviting adults to be as sympathetic as the characters are.

> In my experience, kids are very understanding of each other on the whole. They are a mixture. They can be very supportive, very liberal, very friendly. And then it can turn and a herd mentality can set in and bullying and psychological torture can start. It can oscillate very quickly.

What schools may find most difficult to handle is the openness of Tom's search to find his sexual identity.

> In some ways Tom's in a privileged position because he can decide who he is and there haven't been that many periods in history when kids could decide that. The search is bewildering and difficult. He looks to his teacher, Mr de Clerk, to give him some kind of definition of who he is, he thinks he can find out from Gay Gary, he tries a Tarot Reader, and he thinks if he has sex with Amy he will know who he is, but that does not work. Then there is this rather empty relationship with a twenty-two-year-old, so Tom is gradually moving forward on a slightly zig-zag path towards some idea of who he is, but he hasn't cracked it, and in the end he is still a bit lost.

When Tom finally tries to have sex with Amy he is interrupted, first of all by Melissa asking for her camcorder and then by Mr de Clerk, who appears through a wall. This is, after all, theatre, so we can take this bit of magic in our stride. The idea is that young people sometimes imbue teachers with an all-seeing, all-knowing power but in fact the rather cynical, world-weary de Clerk is no help. He says, 'When I was growing up everyone told you what to be. They told you what to do. What was right and what was wrong.' And Tom replies with the classic existential dilemma, 'I'm unhappy – too many choices. You were unhappy – no choices. Everyone's unhappy. Life's shit, isn't it, sir?'

And then Tom and Amy make their choice and have unprotected, fumbling, loveless sex although Amy is convinced, we are told through the baby, that, 'She's sure there were a few moments that night when he did, really, really love her.'

In the end Amy seems to be the one who is most in control. She certainly seems the most content in her world, which is narrowed by the needs of her baby (those life-skills classes were not such a waste of time after all), the availability of baby-sitters and the distant prospect of college. She firmly rejects Tom's offer to baby-sit and his discontented wish to have it both ways. 'Well – you can't have it.' Gary is content to give up the weed and take on the responsibility of bringing up a child, but all Martin can offer Tom is sex. 'The point is sex. We have sex. And I have money. And we have fun. That's the point. And that's as good as it gets.'

> I think *Citizenship* will be challenging for many schools. If the play is put on in isolation then that might be difficult, but if there is a culture where students can discuss things and discuss the issues around the play it might help the school. There's no right or wrong in this play. I don't think the play has a conclusive message. But it seems to me the kids in the play are in a shapeless, formless world where they're not being taught any kind of values at home or school and they are lost. It is a search.

Once the decision has been made to put *Citizenship* on, then the challenges will be the same as for any play:

finding who the characters are, getting the balance right so that the humour breathes and the sadness is realised. This is not a campaigning play in the sense that there is one message we are invited to take away. It does not recommend a particular course of action. But it encourages teachers and students to talk about things that are not fully acknowledged, to make things a little more public, to deal with things that teachers and students know about but seldom talk about. In this sense *Citizenship* really does break new ground.

Production Notes

ONE

Mark Ravenhill has left the background of the characters very open: there are clues that need to be found, but there is also a need to create 'back-stories' based on the few clues given in the text. Both characters are 'low status', Amy doesn't like herself (and cuts herself) and Tom doesn't like his face. Amy's background may be a little 'New Age' (Feng Shui and so on). There are certain definites in the text, but create the backgrounds while being true to the text. The action of the scene takes place in a house, possibly Amy's. The clues are that needles, Dettol, Nurofen and vodka are all available.

Look at *units* and *objectives* in the text. Break each scene into units and search for the objectives of each character in each unit. Amy's objective might be to get closer to Tom. Tom's immediate objective could be to have his ear pierced. This is a scene about friendship and trust. A stronger objective is that he wants to impress people in his peer group. He may be using Amy to test his attractiveness and sexuality.

Make scenes specific by finding the *action*. This can be summed up by using a *transitive verb* – that is, a verb which needs an object, a someone or something upon which to act. Examples of this are: to take charge of, to find, to ignore and so on. The status of each character in each unit can be considered in this way. Tom's *super-objective*, that is his overall objective throughout the play, is to find out who he is, to discover his sexuality.

Amy is in charge in the first scene as she is ordering Tom around. Get the actor playing Amy to read the first unit prefixing it with the clear announcement 'Amy wants to take charge of Tom.' Before reading the next unit, have her announce the action as: 'Amy wants to mother Tom.' These announcements really clarify the action and can help the actors with their delivery.

As the baton of status is handed from one character to another, the announcements can clarify what is going on. Examples of this are: 'Amy wants to reassure Tom,' 'Tom wants to intrigue Amy,' 'Amy tries to impress Tom,' 'Tom wants to get closer to Amy.' Each time the announcement precedes the reading of the unit, it should state the objective and action thus clarifingy the job of the actor.

Ask what the back-story is concerning Tom's desire for an earring. What is the back-story about Amy's situation, her self-harm, her therapist, her mother? Does having therapy make Amy think she is more interesting? Does it raise her status among her peers?

In order to highlight this aspect of Amy's character, show a playing card to the actress reading the part, with the instruction that the higher the card the more important her therapy is to Amy. Have the actress reflect this in her delivery. Warn her not to skip over lines that would be important to the character. There are several units which could be characterised as 'Amy wants to mother Tom.' Decide if there could be a sexual element in what Amy is doing.

Look at the telephone conversation. It is important to use improvisation to establish what is being said at the other end of the line. This not only provides the actress with the right rhythm and timing but also with an idea of what she is responding to, which will influence inflection and expression and bring the conversation to life.

The next key moment is when Amy kisses Tom. This is a very sensitive moment and reveals a great deal about both characters. It signals a complete reversal of status. Tom is comforting Amy when she kisses him. It is Amy who is now initiating the action. Tom appears really to resent this. Amy's reaction to Tom's rejection and his dream revelation is desperately to find a reason: 'Are you gay?' She goes on to try to label him, to help him in his quest, finally delivering the ambiguous line: 'Don't waste yourself, Tom. You've got a nice face.'

Amy is playing the therapist role in this short unit: she is the active one, trying to keep Tom there first by drawing him into the text message and then further mothering him and trying to make him dependent by mentioning the blood and offering help. It seems Amy is desperate for a role in Tom's life. As mother? Confidante? Lover?

TWO

Rank the characters according to status. It could go as follows (marks out of ten):

Boys		Girls	
Ray	9	Alicia	7
Stephen	6	Kerry	6
Gary	9	Chantal	6
Tom	4	Amy	5

Ask where they are: at school, outside (smoking joint), somewhere people pass by (Mr de Clerk passes)

Avoid elaborate sets. Keep them simple and allow a maximum of twenty seconds for scene changes, possibly using covering music. The action is set at the beginning of the school year.

The opening unit, Tom and Gary, is very short but very revealing, particularly about Gary and his situation. Ray is obviously high status and Stephen his follower. But close scrutiny of Gary's lines suggests he is quite high status, possibly higher than first suggested, but it could be the cannabis talking. Gary is different, a little strange. Maybe this gives him a higher status amongst his peers, because it makes him interesting. A key moment is when Gary almost 'invites' Tom to betray him. Tom does so, possibly to dissociate himself from the perceived 'gayness' of Gary and to fit in with the gang.

When the girls enter, Alicia seems to be the leader, the one making all the decisions. There is a mass of obsessions. Amy is obsessed with Tom, Kerry with the baby, Chantal and Alicia with boys, Ray with sex and Stephen, with whatever Ray is doing.

Enter de Clerk, a young, highly stressed teacher. He is driven but can't cope. He makes professional errors, thinks he is popular but isn't. Ask why Ray says 'Run' as he approaches? Are they afraid, or is this just Ray's self-dramatisation? Have the actors playing Tom and de Clerk read the scene as fast and frantically as possible, which will highlight de Clerk's manic stress levels.

When Amy re-enters close to the end of the scene, it appears her action is to sort Tom out. She certainly elicits a more positive response from Tom here than she did in Scene One, when he announces: 'I know.'

THREE

Ask what Tom's objective is in this scene. Maybe he wants to connect with someone who is gay. He may want to seduce de Clerk.

Give the two actors a playing card and have them read the scene playing their attraction to each other according to the number on the card – ten equalling very attracted, and one not attracted at all. This rehearsal device allows the cast to concentrate on a very important element of the scene. Deal with de Clerk's telephone conversation in the same way as Amy's – namely, improvise the unheard part of the conversation.

Tom tries to unsettle de Clerk with lines like, 'We all wonder,' and later tries to bind him with 'our secret'. When he wants de Clerk to clarify his sexuality for him, he does so by trying to hold his attention by talking about his dream. Tom is desperate to engage de Clerk in order to elicit a response. However, de Clerk is very stressed and is desperate to avoid it. Making the actors read this scene at a frantic pace gives the scene a sense of seriousness, particularly if the actor playing Tom makes the announcement, 'Tom wants Mr de Clerk to clarify his sexuality for him,' just before the reading commences.

FOUR

Tom elicits a lot more information about Gary. He seems to be the next port of call in Tom's quest. It seems as though he naively thinks that just by kissing everyone he will instinctively know when he kisses the right one. Mark wanted to show a dark side to Gary. Gary does seem to lead the scene for the first half, but on the line: 'Shit, broth.' That was going to be my wank tonight,' it seems that that the lead is then taken by Tom. It is possible that Tom kisses Gary because he gets a lot of verbal and physical sexual 'come-ons' from Gary.

The scene finishes with Tom having had yet another change of direction and determining to 'do it' with Amy.

FIVE

Amy fancies Tom but may still be a little angry about him telling everyone they had sex when they hadn't. Also she may be disappointed that his approach isn't as romantic as she would have liked it to be.

We should believe that, if the girls had not entered when they did, then the two of them would have had sex. By the end of the scene we have yet another very definite declaration by Tom: 'We're not gonna shag!'

SIX

The first part of the scene is given over to the creating of mystery, fishing for clues and parallels. All this is dispelled and brought back to reality by the tiff with the daughter. There are questions to be asked about this scene in order to make decisions on how it is to be played. Firstly, how much of a financial expenditure was this for Tom? This will affect how driven he is to get an answer. How long has the reading been going on before the scene begins? Maybe ten minutes with no real solution being reached – this would further increase Tom's urgency. The scene ends with yet another very strong resolution from Tom: 'I know what to do.'

SEVEN

This is a surreal scene, in complete contrast to the reality of the rest of the play: it should make the audience sit up and take notice. Thus, De Clerk is invisible to Amy. She asks if she is the one in Tom's dream. He answers no. This is not what Amy wants to hear. It is honest but not romantic, so the sex they have is on that same basis.

How best to represent the Baby? Keep it simple. The Baby's speech is delivered in long, complex sentences and sounds a little like a fairy story. Beware of delivering it at one pace. Try to highlight, vocally, the 'moments' section at the end of the speech.

EIGHT

Martin appears to be happy, but would he be doing what he is with Tom if he were *truly* happy? Tom's quest to find his sexuality doesn't appear to have been entirely successful. A useful rehearsal experiment is for the actor playing Tom, when reading the part, to kiss the back of his hand with the same intensity and feeling he thought Tom would show kissing Martin. Another technique, again using playing cards, is to have Martin and Tom choose a card: if it is red, you want sex with the other person; if black, you don't. The higher the number, the greater the need. This affects the dynamics of the scene.

NINE

The ending could be interpreted as either quite upbeat or quite bleak. Tom hasn't resolved his situation; he seems to have got close, but he's not really there yet. Amy seems reasonably happy. Gary appears to be the most mature and seems reasonably happy. Tom has found out what it is like to be an adult but it is not what he expected. It is a pragmatic ending rather than a romantic/happy ending. Martin's answer to Tom that this is 'as good as it gets' is probably the only straight and true answer Tom is given throughout the play.

It is important that the final unit is played honestly, not cynically or flippantly, but in a way that represents an accurate assessment of Martin and Tom's relationship. How long might their relationship go on for? Maybe two months – they could remain friends with Martin taking an avuncular role. As for Gary and Amy's relationship? Perhaps a couple of years, no longer.

Workshop facilitated by Max Stafford Clark
with notes taken by Stephen Downs.

JUST

Ali Smith

Characters

Corpse
Victoria
Albert
Townsperson 1
Townsperson 2
Mrs Wright
Juror 1
Juror 2
Juror 3
Girl

A body is lying on the ground face down in the middle of the stage. It's dead. It has an umbrella sticking out of its back, maybe at a jaunty angle, maybe straight up – the old-fashioned kind of big black umbrella with a curved handle. Far stage left is a big green pot plant on a stand. Far stage right is a bus stop with a pedestrian bench by it.

Victoria enters and stands at the bus stop. She's waiting for a bus. She's wearing a T-shirt with a giant apple on it. She stands there for a minute. She looks over at the pot plant, frowns. She gets out an A to Z or a map and looks at it, a bit like she's not sure where she is. Looks straight ahead again. Looks down at the bench and thinks about sitting on it, decides not to.

But then she senses something behind her, turns round, and sees the body.

Victoria: Oh my – oh my God.

She goes over to take a look. She stands at a distance first, then dares herself to go closer. She stands over the body and looks all round for what can have happened. There's no sign of any explanation, anything that could have happened. Victoria shakes her head. She examines the body from feet to head without touching it. She is disgusted. Then she is, to her surprise, a bit fascinated. Then she notices how the handle of the umbrella is almost temptingly jutting into the air.

She looks all round her, a little guiltily, as if to check no one can see, then leans forward as if to touch or take the handle, as if she can't resist. Just as she reaches forward to do this, Albert enters at the back.

He's dressed as a policeman. As Victoria gets closer and closer with her arm, her hand out, about to touch the handle –

Albert (*coming forward*) Oh my God! Oh my God, what have you done?

Victoria No, it wasn't me. I was just –

Albert What have you done here?

Victoria But that's just what I'm trying to tell you. I didn't – I was just standing at the bus stop.

Albert What happened?

Victoria Like I say, just standing at the bus stop, thinking about, well it sounds a bit surreal maybe, but I was thinking about apples. And I got this creepy feeling at the back of my neck, and I turned, and I saw this, him, just, well, lying here, like that, and I said, 'Oh my God,' exactly like you just did, and I came over.

Albert Did you have a big quarrel?

Victoria Who with?

Albert (*gestures at the body*) Was it, like, a lovers' tiff?

Victoria No, no, I just told you, I don't know him –

Albert You *don't know* him?

Victoria No.

Albert Oh my God. You didn't even know him. I mean, I could have understood it if you'd quarrelled. A crime of fashion, that's OK.

Victoria A crime of what?

Albert People get very worked up when there's fashion. And rightly so.

Victoria Eh, I think you might not mean –

Albert I'm the type of person who can forgive things done in the name of fashion.

Victoria You mean passion.

Albert That's what I said.

Victoria You said fashion.

Albert No I didn't. You're twisting my words.

Victoria No I'm not.

Albert And you killed this man in old blood.

Victoria In what?

Albert I saw you.

Victoria But you didn't. You didn't see what you think you saw. Like you didn't say what you think you said.

Albert Yes I did. I *instinctly* saw you.

Victoria You keep saying things wrong.

Albert No I don't.

Victoria You don't mean instinctly. You mean distinctly.

Albert That's what I said.

Victoria No it isn't.

Albert Don't argue with me. It was one of the most distinctly things I've ever seen in my life. You stabbed that man with that umbrella.

Victoria Well, if that's what you saw you must be totally blindly as a fuckingly batly.

Albert It makes me shiver to be anywhere near someone so old-blooded.

Victoria It's cold-blooded. Cold-blooded.

Albert It's unexpectedly quite exciting. You're under arrest.

Victoria Look. I can explain. I was just reaching forward. In that way you do. Like for *Excalibur*.

Albert The film?

Victoria No, I mean, yes, it is, but I mean it's like Excalibur the sword.

Albert There's a sword as well as a film?

Victoria looks at him like she can't believe he doesn't know the story.

I just didn't know there was both a film and a sword called Exc . . . that word. Not that I didn't know, as such. It's just that never in my life, at least not so far, have I come across both. And that's not my fault, is it? Not as if I had the chance to know and turned it down and said no, I simply don't *want* to know that it's a sword and a film. Not as if someone said to me, Albert, do you want to know about all the things that . . . that word . . . can mean, and I said, no thank you, I do not wish to know.

Victoria What are you on about?

Albert The film. And the sword. Both with that name. See, I know there's a sword now, too. I'm a quick learner.

Victoria So.

Albert So.

Victoria Where were we, again?

Albert Uh, you know. The sword.

Victoria Yes. Right. Sword in the stone.

Albert In the what?

Victoria You know. Excalibur. For fuck sake.

Albert Oh, so there's a stone now as well called it, is there?

Victoria Called what?

Albert Ex . . . cammimur.

Victoria What?

Albert You know. That word. When it's at home.

Enter Townspeople, from stage left at the front, walking across the stage. They speak their lines in chorus. Victoria and Albert turn and watch them.

Townspeople
  Here's the lovely pot plant.
  Ooh, it's looking very clean!
  Someone's done its leaves again.
  D'you think with Mr Sheen?
  Ooh they're very shiny.
  Mr Sheen brings out the green.
  D'you think a real Mr Sheen exists?
  I often wonder.
  D'you think the rain'll hold off?

Weather said thunder.
Ooh, here's the bus stop.
Let's wait for the bus.
Ooh, we're first in the queue. Great!
No one here but us!

Townspeople stand at the bus stop and wait.

Victoria Am I imagining it, or are they speaking in
rhyme?
Albert Don't try and change the subject.
Victoria Not very good rhyme either.

*Townspeople hear this and are offended. They turn to
look at Victoria accusingly.*

Townspeople
Ooh! Look! A body!
Ooh, I say!
That's not something you expect to
See every day.
Ooh! He's been stabbed!
Ooh! It's like *The Bill*!
Ooh, look at her.
She looks really evil!
Victoria I do not!
Townspeople
Ooh, look at the murder weapon!
You'd think she might have hid it.
You'd think she might've made the effort.
Look at her. Evil. She definitely did it.
Victoria I did not!
Townspeople
Ooh, that's that policeman
That gets his words wrong.
I knew his mother.

*They nod darkly at this to each other. Townsperson 1
taps his or her own forehead twice.*

Townsperson 1 D'you recognise that evil-looking one?

Townspeople
She's not from round here, is she? No.
Do you recognise that fella?
No. Me neither. Well, if it rains
We can always borrow his umbrella.

They laugh uproariously, then stop and look at their watches simultaneously.

Ooh, look at the time!
I think we've missed the bus.
Ooh well, let's walk home.
A walk'll be good for us.

Townspeople go off, stage right. Short absurd pause, while Victoria and Albert watch them go, look at the empty stage where they were, then turn back to the main business of arguing with each other.

Victoria Where were we, again?

Albert I was arresting you on suspicion of murder.

Victoria Yes. See, I thought for a minute that this, all this, this sticking up in the air like this, was like a kind of grotesque Excalibur.

Albert I know. It's a sword, and a film and a stone.

Victoria Well, it's not a stone, it's *in* the stone.

Albert I know! I know!

He clearly doesn't.

Victoria So you know the story of Excalibur, then?

Albert Oh, so it's not just a sword and a stone and a film, now it's a story too, is it?

Victoria Well, yes.

Albert Are you deliberately trying to infuse me?

Victoria (*takes deep, patient breath*) The story of Excalibur, *you* know.

Albert I know, I know – I know it really well, actually, don't go thinking I don't . . . just remind me of the beginning of it again.

Victoria You know, first it's stuck in the stone and only the rightful king can take it out, and all the strong people try and pull it out and they can't, then a little weakling comes along and because he's the rightful king it just slides out of the stone in his hand and he's King Arthur. As if the sword is waiting for him and him alone!

Albert (*nodding, echoing her just a fraction after she's spoken, as if he knows, though he doesn't*) Him and him alone. . .

Victoria And then the lake, and the hand coming out of it, and someone throws it into the lake, I can't remember who, and an arm comes out of the lake and catches it, the Lady of the Lake, and it disappears for ever under the water till the rightful king comes to claim it again.

Albert Anyway, you're still under arrest.

Victoria No, listen, because I was reaching forward, when you saw me, because I just wondered, for a moment, just a moment, what it would be like to . . . It's a very unlikely urge, I know. But the point is, I never actually held it. I never actually touched it. When your detectives look for fingerprints on it, they won't be my fingerprints.

Albert That's 'cause I saw you wiping them off.

Victoria You did *not*!

Albert I know what I saw.

Victoria But you don't. You so clearly don't.

Albert Don't you dare tell me what I know and what I don't know.

Victoria Yeah, I know. You saw me 'instinctly', apparently.

Albert Are you making fun of me?

Victoria Show me exactly what you think you saw. You came round the corner, there, and you *distinctly* saw me do *what* exactly?

Enter Mrs Wright at the back. Mrs Wright is tweedy, like Mrs Thatcher, carries a handbag, and is blindfolded.

Albert (*miming what he saw*) I *distinctally* saw you let go of the handle of the murder weapon, and you letting go of the handle was distinctally immediately after you'd distinctally run at the victim even though he was a total stranger to you, who you didn't even know enough to have had a quarrel of fashion with. And then you stabbed him in the back with it. And then you carefully wiped your fingerprints off the handle of the murder weapon.

Victoria But I *didn't*.

Mrs Wright (*coming blindly forward*) Oh my God. What have you people done?

Albert Begging your pardon, ma'am, but as usual it wasn't me.

Victoria It wasn't me either. And what do you mean, *as usual*?

Mrs Wright I saw it. I saw all of you.

Victoria But you're blindfolded.

Mrs Wright I am blindfolded to prevent me from being biased about what I see. And I heard you (*to Victoria*) with your hand raised in that ghastly, violent way. I heard you with your hand on the – the murder weapon. And (*to Albert*) I heard you watching on in a gleeful accomplice-like way.

Victoria No. I was just waiting for a bus. I was thinking about apples. I'm an apple-farmer, as it happens – well, I used to be.

Mrs Wright Objection. Irrelevance.

Victoria Up to last year I still had my own orchards, the main part of my land was actually an ancient English apple orchard, well, not ancient exactly, more medieval. Dating from the 1300s.

Mrs Wright Objection. Obfuscating information.

Albert Who'd have thought it. Medieval. And she looks so young.

Victoria Orange Pippin. Ashmead's Kernel. Discovery. Worcester. Charles Ross. Russett. Gascoyne's Scarlet. And apples from all over the world. Ida Red. Jonathan. McIntosh. Northern Spy. And those are just a few. But did you know that in medieval times there were over two thousand different species of apple growing in England?

Albert I didn't know that!

Mrs Wright (*furious*) Objection! Objectionable everything!

Victoria Over the last year or so my life has changed completely. Anyway, enough about me. The point is – I was at the bus stop and I happened to see the body, and I came over to have a look because I couldn't believe my eyes, and then, weirdly, the handle of it looked a bit like it might be Excalibur –

Albert (*to himself*) Excabilur.

Victoria – so I just put my hand out – like this, and then out of nowhere this person here accused *me* of *murder*.

Albert Because I know the truth.

Victoria I know the truth too!

Mrs Wright Neither of you knows the truth. Only I know the true truth. You are both guilty. My mind's eye sees everything. You (*pointing wildly, blindly, at nobody*) are Ida the Red. And you (*pointing wildly in the opposite direction*) are Jonathan McIntosh. You are both northern spies.

Albert Begging your pardon, ma'am, but I'm Albert, your policeman. I work for you. Just lift your blindfold.

Mrs Wright My blindfold is sacrosanct. It cannot be lifted.

Enter Townspeople again, same as before, stage left, crossing the stage, speaking, as before. Mrs Wright lifts her blindfold a little, to see them and nod hello, and to check for herself who Albert is.

Townspeople
Here's the lovely pot plant.
Ooh, see how much bigger it's got!
Look! Someone's written graffiti on a leaf.
Disgusting! Whoever did it should be shot.
Protesters are worse than hooligans.
Off with their heads!
Ooh, look at him with the umbrella stuck in him.
Still there. Still dead!
Ooh, look. It's Mrs Wright. It'll all be alright now.
And there's that policeman who gets his words wrong.
And there's that evil cow.

At this, Victoria puts her hands on her hips and stares them down. They look away.

D'you think the rain'll hold off?
Shall we get the bus?
Ooh, we're first in the queue – great!
No one here but us!

Mrs Wright Now, where were we? Oh, I know. Guilty! Guilty! Guilty!

Albert No, offence, ma'am, but as usual you've mistaken me. I'm not guilty.

Victoria How d'you mean, *as usual*?

Albert There I was, just strolling along, out on a jaunt to the supermarket to get some lunch –

Victoria Oh. Supermarket. Might have known.

Albert Yes, the supermarket, and I saw it, I saw *her*, and she was old-bloodedly finishing off this poor –

Victoria (*to Albert*) Supermarket. It's you who's the
murderer. (*furious*) Why do you think I'm not an
apple-farmer any more? Eh? Eh??

Everybody looks at her, including the Townspeople.

Townspeople
What's she saying? What's she said?
Careful, now! She's off her head!

Victoria (*furious*) And why do you think medieval
ancient apple orchards like mine all over this so-called
United Kingdom are getting chopped down, burnt
down, razed to the ground as we speak? Because
people like him go *for a jaunt* to the *supermarket*!

Albert What's me going to the supermarket got to do
with anything?

Victoria Everything!

Albert My shopping choices are nothing to do with
anything.

Victoria You're being naive.

Albert Did you just – call me – naive?

Victoria Too fucking right I did.

Townspeople
What's she saying? Quick! Arrest her!
Obviously a protester!
I can't believe my ears! I can't!
Bet she wrote on our pot plant!
Disgusting, using language. Ought
To be put a stop to. Shot.
Someone ought to really tell her.
Someone should stab her to death with an umbrella.

Mrs Wright (*having listened very carefully to the
Townspeople, turning to address Victoria*) I feel it's
only just to warn you, Ida the Red, that if you use
language like that in front of me again I will have you
removed.

Townspeople
    Ooh, how splendid. Quite right too.
    Go on – tell her what to do.
    D'you think we should bother waiting for the bus?
    A walk home might be good for us.

Off they go, same as before . . . The others watch
them, including Mrs Wright, who peeps to see them go
from under her blindfold, without letting the others
see, then resumes her fixed blindfolded stance when
Victoria turns back towards her to speak.

Victoria Look. Firstly, my name's not Ida the Red. That's
    the name of an apple. My name's Victoria. And you
    can't have me removed. This is a free country. I can say
    what I like.

Albert Yes, but you can't say I'm naive. Don't call me
    naive.

Mrs Wright Now. Objections overruled. Hold your arms
    out.

Victoria Arms?

Mrs Wright is carrying a handbag, from which she
takes something silver-looking. Feels for their arms
and clicks a pair of handcuffs on them, one on Victoria
and one on Albert, chaining them together.

Mrs Wright Do not try to run away, either of you. I have
    a photographic memory for faces. I never forget a face
    I've heard. (*She goes over to examine the body, blindly,*
    sniffing it.) I know I recognise this person from
    somewhere.

Victoria (*shaking her head*) I can't believe this. What
    kind of person carries handcuffs around with them
    and just slaps them on innocent people?

Albert Oh, like, *don't you know*?

Victoria No. I can't imagine.

Albert See? That makes *you* naive.

Victoria Are you still on about naive?

Albert Could you stand over – no, not there – this way –

Victoria Where? No – *this* way –

Albert It's just that this is a bit uncomfortable –

Victoria I don't want to stand here. I want to stand over there.

Albert Well, you can't.

Victoria (*jostling him*) Don't tell me what I can and can't do!

Albert (*jostling back*) I want to stand *here*.

Victoria No, here.

Albert Okay. How about if we stand here for some of the time and then in a minute we can go and stand over there?

Victoria Look how it would look to anyone coming along and seeing us now. They'd think, there's a good person examining the body of a dead person, and there's the two bad evil people that killed him with an umbrella. We've been made to look like criminals. Aren't you furious? Aren't you desperate to clear your name? What's your name, anyway?

Albert Albert. It'll be OK for me in the end. I'm a policeman. I'm not so sure it'll be OK for you, though.

Victoria You don't say.

Albert I do say. And . . . can I just ask you something? As a favour?

Victoria It depends. What?

Albert It's just . . . Please don't call me naive again. Really. Please. Don't.

Victoria Eh . . . OK.

Albert Thank you.

Victoria Though the weird thing is, it's really really tempting to, now, you know. Now that you've asked me not to, I mean.

Albert I . . . have this thing about thinking that people think I'm naive.

Victoria Do you?

Albert Yes. I do.

Victoria Why have you?

Albert I really don't know. I actually can't seem to remember.

Victoria You mean, you're naive about knowing why you don't like to be called naive?

Albert Ha ha. Funny.

Victoria Ha ha!

Albert Not.

Victoria Yeah, but now that you've asked me not to call you it, the only thing I really want to call you is the word n-a-i . . .

Albert You promised.

Victoria I didn't promise. I just said I'd try.

Albert Please try.

Victoria You're very sensitive.

Albert Yes. I'm a very sensitive, fashionate person. But one of the things I'm not is, I'm not naive.

Victoria OK. Don't worry. You can rely on me.

Albert I appreciate it.

Victoria Why I should be anything at all to you, never mind actually proactively nice, is beyond me.

Albert What's proactive mean, when it's at home?

Victoria (*shakes the cuffs*) Look at the mess your stupid fucking I-don't-know-what's got me into.

Albert What do you mean exactly by saying *I-don't-know-what*?

Victoria What, that you're –

Albert (*flinching*) I'm . . . what?

Victoria Weird.

Albert Oh, weird's okay. Weird's fine.

Mrs Wright (*standing up, nearly losing her balance as she does, pronouncing.*) This man is dead.

Victoria Tell us something we fucking well don't know.

Mrs Wright scowls at her language.

Albert (*aside*) Is that another dig at me being, *you know*?

Victoria Oh! No. Honest. Not at all. It just came out that way.

During this last exchange the Townspeople have entered again, as usual, stage left, and are getting ready to talk about the pot plant again, waiting their chance, keen to speak. The other characters continue regardless of them. They too tut at Victoria's language.

Mrs Wright (*pointing the wrong way*) If you use that kind of language in front of the dead again I will have you removed. It's highly disrespectful.

Victoria What's disrespectful about it? He's dead, isn't he? He can't hear us.

Albert That's true, actually.

Victoria So I can say fuck fuck fuck fuck fuck fuck fuck fuck fuck fuck fuck fuck fuck as many times as I like!

Townspeople put hands over their ears, appalled, as in Munch's The Scream. Then one of them collapses.

Townsperson 2
Stop the play! Alas! Alack!
My friend has had a heart attack!

Victoria What did she say? Stop the what?

Albert Beats me.

Victoria It sounded like 'Stop the play'. What does she mean, stop the play?

Mrs Wright Never mind what she said.

Townsperson 2
Stop the play! No more pretendin'.
Bad language has done my friend in!

Albert She denifitely said it that time.

Victoria Stop the play.

Mrs Wright No no, she meant stop play. As in 'rain stopped play'. She meant it as in 'stop playing around with such harmful language'.

Meanwhile Townsperson 1 has come round again and, although a little dazed, is more or less okay.

Townsperson 1
Oh, what happened? No, I'm fine,
Really, really. Get my breath.
Shocking language nearly killed me!
Nearly brought about my death!
Can we talk about the pot plant?
Then I'll know that I'm okay.
Can we talk about the pot plant
In our usual pot-plant way?
Townspeople (*together*)
Here's the lovely pot plant, look!
The loveliest in the universe.
Somebody should write a book
Somebody should write some verse
About this lovely pot plant
And what it means to us
As we walk past it every day
Going for the bus.
Victoria Who *are* those people, anyway?
Albert It is ugly, though, when a girl swears like that.
Victoria That is so sexist!
Albert (*pretending he knows*) Yes, it is, isn't it? Don't think I didn't know that. I knew it was as soon as I said it.
Victoria And *you're* supposed to be on *my* side.
Albert Am I? Oh. Right.
Mrs Wright Very, very ugly. One of the ugliest things in the world.
Victoria (*looking straight at Mrs Wright*) I know what *I* think one of the ugliest things in the world is.

Mrs Wright Don't think I'm not making a note of absolutely everything you say.

Victoria Good. Because I want you to make a huge note of this on your cosmic fucking notepad or whatever it is you make your notes on. Ready? WE ARE INNOCENT.

Albert Well, I am, for denifite.

Victoria It's definite, not denifite.

Townspeople touch their heads as a sign of madness.

Victoria Come on. We've got to work together on this.

Albert Do we? OK.

Victoria For instance. What gives her the right to put handcuffs on us?

Albert Yes, what gives you the right?

Victoria You're not the law.

Mrs Wright Actually, I *am* the law.

Townspeople
Hee hee hee
Haw haw haw.
They will find
She *is* the law.
They will find
It's black as night
When you challenge
Mrs Wright.

Mrs Wright bows graciously in their direction. The Townspeople wave sycophantically.

Victoria Shut up, you.

Townspeople tut, outraged.

Victoria I thought law was supposed to be about justice.

Mrs Wright Law is about justice.

Victoria I thought law was supposed to be about fairness.

Mrs Wright Law is about fairness.

Victoria I thought law was supposed to protect the innocent.

Mrs Wright The innocent will be forever protected by law – from fiends like you.

Victoria She's nuts.

Albert Is she? Oh. OK.

Victoria She's totally off her supermarket trolley.

Albert But there's something likeably – (*Scratches his head.*) – fashionate about her.

Victoria Her? What's fashionate, I mean passionate, about *her*? You *don't know* passion when you see it.

Albert Well, I know what I like.

Mrs Wright meanwhile is looking very pleased with herself at the attention.

Victoria What could you possibly see in *her*?

Albert I wonder what colour her eyes are under there.

Mrs Wright Blue.

Albert I knew they'd be blue.

Victoria (*a bit hurt; realising she quite likes Albert herself*) You don't even know the proper word for passion!

Albert I do so! I'm a dedicated follower of passion.

Victoria You wouldn't know passion if it walked right up to you and kissed you on the mouth! You wouldn't know passion if it was chained to your wrist! You wouldn't know passion if it – if it came right up to you and stabbed you in the back with an umbrella!

Intake of breath from everybody.

What? Well, *what*?

Shocked silence.

It's just a figure of speech. It doesn't mean I did it. It doesn't mean I killed anyone with an umbrella.

Mrs Wright The eyes of justice are opened. Now justice will be done.

Townspeople
  Justice always wins the day.
  Told you she was queer.
  Justice. Mrs Wright! Hurray!
  She's not from round here.
  Send her down! Send her away!
  Mrs Wright is true and brave
  And keeps our pot plant safe!

Albert Look at it from my point of view. I'm handcuffed to a murderer, here. For a minute I thought she was just a regular person.

Victoria But I *am* a regular person.

Albert A foul-mouthed regular person, but still.

Victoria So. You're all going to convict me as a murderer on nothing more than a colourful figure of speech?

Albert Yep.

Victoria You think that'll be enough to send me, an innocent person, down? Innocent until proven guilty! That's the law!

Mrs Wright Not any more.

Victoria What do you mean, not any more?

Mrs Wright That's old law. New law is different.

Victoria Different?

Mrs Wright You'll see.

Townspeople
  Mrs Wright has changed the law.
  Ha ha ha ha haw haw haw!

Victoria Shut up, you, or I'll swear at you.

Townspeople (*actually scared, to each other*) Shh!

Victoria Next you'll be telling me that new law can convict me even if I'm innocent.

Mrs Wright That's right.

Albert That's a good idea. I'm surprised nobody's thought of doing that before. So now you can just choose who to put in prison, or wherever, just in *case* they were to do something that you think they might do, like if you feel it in your gut or your dinstinct or wherever.

Victoria Not dinstinct. Instinct.

Albert Thanks.

Mrs Wright Exactly right.

Victoria (*cunning, to Albert*) Which means, you know, she can choose to incarcerate you too, if she wants.

Albert She can choose to what me? (*He clearly thinks it sounds exciting.*)

Victoria No, it's not a good thing. She can choose to have you put away.

Albert (*to Mrs Wright*) Does it mean that, really, ma'am?

Mrs Wright nods regally.

But I'm innocent. I didn't do anything. I was just walking by on my way to Waitrose.

Townspeople
Ooh, Waitrose has such lovely things,
We don't mind telling you.
We shop there ourselves, you know.
All the best people do.
You can be certain.
It's a better class of person.

Victoria That doesn't rhyme.

Townspeople
Is she criticising us?
It really is the end.
Maybe we should go for our bus
In case she swears at us again.

Victoria That doesn't rhyme properly either. (*to Albert*) And you saying Waitrose to me is like me saying naive to you. Even just hearing the word.

Albert What? Hearing the word Waitrose?

Victoria Or Sainsbury's. Or Tesco. Or Somerfield. Or any
of them. (*to Albert*) Naive. See how it feels?

Albert Don't.

Victoria See?

Albert What's wrong with saying Waitrose –?

Victoria Naive.

Albert Waitrose.

Victoria Naive.

Mrs Wright Waitrose.

Victoria Oh, now don't *you* start. Ganging up on me.

Mrs Wright Waitrose is admissible as evidence.

Victoria How is Waitrose evidence?

Mrs Wright A better class of supermarket equals a better
and much less suspicious class of person. (*to Albert –
peeking to see where he is*) You are clearly innocent.

Albert (*to Victoria*) See? She's very, very fair.

Townspeople (*applauding*)
Mrs Wright is never wrong.
The long arm of the law is long.

Victoria And *that* stupid rhyme makes no sense at all.

Townspeople
Mrs Wright, our brains are reelings,
Stop that evil girl from hurting our feelings.

Victoria Rubbish.

Albert So am I free to go, then?

Mrs Wright You may go.

Albert So if you could just give me the key to these cuffs –

*Mrs Wright feels in her pocket. Then feels in her other
pocket. No key.*

Mrs Wright Ah. (*Feels in her handbag.*) Just a moment.

Panicked, feels all through her handbag. No key.

I know it's . . . just a moment . . .

Victoria (*watching wryly*) Lost your key?

Mrs Wright, still looking, tries her pockets again, empties her bag out onto the floor and scrabbles blindly about in the contents. You can have some fun deciding what she'd have in her bag – whatever takes your imagination, small pair of scales, framed picture of Tony Blair, whatever – up to you.

Mrs Wright Just . . . a . . .

Albert (*examining the lock on the handcuffs*) I'd say it was quite a small key, ma'am, like about the size of a bike padlock key.

Townspeople (*looking too*)
    We can't see
    Any key.

Mrs Wright (*giving up, straightening up and adjusting her blindfold*) I've just received a special edict straight from head office.

Victoria You have? How?

Albert (*to Victoria*) What's an edick, when it's at home? Not that I don't know, just that I've momentarily forgotten.

Victoria You expect me to tell you anything? Naive.

Albert Waitrose.

Victoria You nasty bastard.

Townspeople
    My dears! My dears!
    Close your ears!

Mrs Wright (*blindly coming forward and taking hold of Victoria by the unchained hand and shaking it*) It gives me great pleasure to award you the position of Justice Marshall, working alongside me in the fight for justice, and taking charge of the safekeeping of this prisoner here until justice is seen publicly to be done.

Victoria Sure you mean me?

Mrs Wright, realising she's awarded the wrong person of the two, drops the hand and fumbles to find Albert's

*unchained hand – takes Victoria's other hand first, by
mistake.*

Nope. Still me.

Albert Have you been made a marshmall and I haven't?

Mrs Wright (*finally taking Albert's hand*) It gives me
great pleasure to award you the position of Justice
Marshall, working alongside me in the fight for justice,
and taking charge of the safekeeping of this prisoner
here until justice is seen publicly to be done.

Albert Aw, but that's great. We're *both* marshmalls. Even
though you're a murderer. That's so nice of her.

Victoria It's not marshmall. It's marshall.

Mrs Wright *You're* the marshall. Not *her*. She's the
prisoner.

Albert Oh. Right.

Mrs Wright And the law expects you to be responsible
for the prisoner at all times until the prisoner is here-
tofore shipped away to be incarcerated in a very small
see-through box with no shade in it in the beating sun.

Townspeople

Quite right too. Be adamant.

She wrote on the leaves of our pot plant.

She made fun of our attempts at verse.

She deserves the very worst.

Victoria (*sinking to the ground*) Oh, for fuck sake.

Townspeople slam their hands over their ears.

Mrs Wright Your language deeply displeases us.

Victoria *Your* language deeply displeases *me*.

Townspeople

Let's go home now it's all just.

D'you think there'll be a bus?

Mrs Wright Or maybe you could walk instead?

Townspeople

Yes! Walking's very good for us!

Off they go, stage right, as usual.

Victoria I can't believe it. I was only passing through this town. I stopped for half a minute at a bus stop. And look at me now.

Albert Come on. Buck up. Could be worse. Look on the bright side. It sounds alright, where you're going. It won't be a bit like being in a cell, because you'll be able to look through the glass and see the scenery. And you'll always be nice and warm.

Victoria Don't be naive.

Albert Waitrose.

Victoria No, I mean it. Don't be naive.

Albert Waitrose. Tesco. Sainsbury's.

Victoria The only reason she's made you a marshall is that she couldn't find the key for the cuffs.

Albert That's not true! (*to Mrs Wright*) Is it?

Mrs Wright (*clearly lying, and shifty*) No-o.

Victoria The law is lying.

Mrs Wright The law is incapable of lying. *Abiit excessist evasit erupit. Ab imbro pectore. Ab ovo usque as mala. Ab uno disce omnes. Abusus non tollit usum. Actum est de republica. Alea jacta est. Aliquit haeret. Alter ipse amicus. Aquila non capit muscas. A verbis ad verbera. Ars est celare artum.*

Victoria Load of rubbish.

Albert How can you say that? That was the language of *the law*.

Mrs Wright (*threatening*) Are you daring to call the law a load of rubbish?

Victoria It was the language of Latin. And I'm calling what you said a load of rubbish.

Albert Wow! Can you speak the language of the law too?

Mrs Wright (*disbelievingly, scornfully*) *You* can't understand *Latin*.

Victoria You just said: 'He's gone, he's off, he's escaped he's broken away. From the bottom of the heart. From the eggs to the apples. From one example you may judge the rest. It's all up with the state. The die is cast. Something sticks. A friend is another self. An eagle does not catch flies. From words to punches in the face. True art is to conceal art.'

Mrs Wright (*shamefaced, then barefaced lying*) No, I didn't. I didn't say any of those things. The things I just said were firmly to do with ancient and long-held statutes of law.

Victoria She probably learned them all from the first page of the pages they have at the backs of dictionaries, you know, 'Phrases and Quotations from Foreign Languages'. She just wants us to think she's clever.

Mrs Wright (*it's true*) Why, what a totally absurd thing to suggest!

Victoria It's all up with the state, alright. From one example you may judge the rest, alright. From words to punches in the face, alright. As soon as I get these cuffs off.

Albert But she can't *see*. So how could she see to read and learn phrases in a dictionary?

Victoria Well, presumably she didn't always wear a blindfold. Presumably she wasn't born wearing a blindfold.

Mrs Wright From my mother's womb I came – blindfolded.

Victoria Okay. Come on. Let's get this over with. He's innocent because he shops at Waitrose. Yes?

Mrs Wright Yes.

Albert Yes.

Victoria And I'm guilty simply because you with the blindfold on say I am. Yes?

Mrs Wright Yes.

Albert Yes.

Victoria And anyone looking at this case in the future won't hesitate to convict you *and* her for convicting me on a case more full of holes than a wormy old apple, more holes in it than there are in a tea bag. You'll become famous – for a miscarriage of justice. Because I've been judged guilty in such a way that future lawmakers will hold today up as the very evidence of the end of English law, believe me they will. Where's the jury that'd convict me? Where? Eh? Eh?

Mrs Wright (*shuffling agitatedly*) Ah.

Victoria And I warn you. I will speak so well and so articulately and so straight to the heart and so truthfully to the world that, after I've sold my story to a million broadsheets and tabloids, and after I've attended the premiere of the multi-million-pound-grossing hard-hitting bio-movie of my life in which I'm played in my youth by Chloe Sevigny and in my more mature years by Meryl Streep, no one in this ancient venerable United Kingdom, no one in all the countries the world over, no one who's naturally drawn to a good true story well told, will be able to eat an apple again without thinking of you and me and what's happening right here, right now.

Albert That's exactly what I'd like right here, right now, a nice apple.

Mrs Wright (*grudgingly*) Hm. The prisoner will naturally have a fair hearing and be tried properly and institutionally within a proper court of law.

Victoria Now we're getting somewhere.

Mrs Wright (*looking blindly out over the audience*) I call, with total randomness and fairness and no presupposition or preconception at all, upon . . . (*quietly, to Albert*) I wonder, could you just move me along so I'm right next to the pot plant?

*Albert does so, dragging Victoria along the floor
behind him to do it.*

Thank you. Am I facing out the way?
Albert Yes.
Mrs Wright I therefore now call with total randomness
and fairness and entirely impartially, upon those three
people, with whom I have nothing in common and
whom I've never met, ever, sitting on the first three
seats closest to me from here in the front row, to
assemble as jury.

*The three people on these seats get up and come on to
the stage. They line up to form the jury.*

Victoria Where did they come from?
Mrs Wright I have never met any of you before in my
life, have I?
Juror 1 No.
Juror 2 We.
Juror 3 Have.
Juror 1 Never.
Juror 2 Met.
Juror 3 Or.
Juror 1 Even.
Juror 2 Seen.
Juror 3 Each.
Juror 1 Other.
Juror 2 Or.
Juror 3 You.
Juror 1 Before.
Juror 2 In.
Juror 3 Our.
Juror 1 Lives.
Juror 2 Mummy.

Jurors 1 and 3 jostle and shush Juror 2.

Juror 1: Ha ha. Just her little.
Juror 3 Joke. She was just.
Juror 2 Joking, honest, ha ha.
Juror 1 How funny and totally ridiculous to even.
Juror 2 Suggest.
Juror 3 It.

Did they get away with it? They look a little worried.
They go and sit on the bus-stop bench.

Victoria What's out there?

She pulls at Albert's arm, to try and see out into the
audience.

Albert (*shrugs*) Sometimes I think I can see . . . faces in
the dark.
Mrs Wright (*panicking, in case the secret's out*) Justice
Marshall! Please procure the prisoner for trial.
Albert Please do *what* with her?

Mrs Wright signals exactly where she wants Victoria
brought, and makes sure she has her back to the
audience, by peeking out from below her blindfold and
giving Albert directions. Meanwhile the Townspeople
have come round again, as usual, and are standing by
the plant.

Townspeople
Here's the lovely pot plant.
Droopy, though, a bit.
Maybe the pot plant needs a drink.
Let's give it a little – SHIT!
There's a queue at the bus stop!
We'll never get on the bus!
Look at the queue at the bus stop!
What will become of us?
There's no room to sit at the bus stop!

We can't contain our fury!
Mrs Wright! Mrs Wright!
There's no room at the bus stop!
Mrs Wright Calm down, now. It's just the usual jury.
Victoria What does she mean, *usual* jury?
Townspeople
Ooh. It's the trial!
Ooh. Of that vile
Monster we hate. Mrs Double-ewe
Please can we be on the jury too?
Mrs Wright Yes.
Victoria They can't be on the jury too! They're not impartial!
Mrs Wright I decide the juries around here. They seem perfectly impartial to me.
Albert (*confidentially, to Victoria*) See? Now there'll be justice alright. Feel a bit better?
Victoria (*groans, puts her head in her hands*) Oh. Tell me when it's over, won't you, Waitrose?
Albert That's not my name. I'm Albert, remember.
Victoria That's all we have in common.
Albert What?
Victoria Naive. Waitrose.
Albert Wait. Do you go to Waitrose too?
Victoria That's not really what I meant.
Albert Because if you do, you should really tell the judge. Remember, earlier. She *knew* I was innocent because I go to Waitrose.
Victoria I thought you *knew* I was guilty? I thought you *distinctly* saw me do it?
Albert Well, I thought I did.
Victoria Tell me when it's over, my old pal Waitrose.

She has her fingers in her ears, eyes closed.

Albert But maybe I *didn't* see what I saw. Maybe I saw it *wrong*. Maybe I just *thought* I saw it.

307

Mrs Wright (*clearing her throat grandly*) Members of the
jury. You have heard the evidence.

Juror 3 Yes, we.

Juror 2 Have, Your.

Juror 3 Honour.

Townspeople
And us too. We heard too.
We know exactly what to do.

Mrs Wright Do you find the defendant guilty or not
guilty? And do you sentence her to months in a glass
box with no shade in it?

Juror 1 Yes, Your.

Juror 2 Honour, and we sentence her.

Juror 3 To exactly what you say.

Mrs Wright is pleased.

Townspeople As usual, we've a different idea, Your
Honour, for the lass.
Something much quicker and much less cruel
And over very fast.

Albert Thank goodness. Because she might not actually
be guilty. See, I might have maybe possibly got it
wrong.

Mrs Wright (*to Jury*) Members of the jury, do I understand
correctly? You'd prefer me to apply the mercifully
swift and clean and just sentence we usually apply in
similar cases?

Juror 1 Yes, Your.

Juror 2 Hon.

Juror 3 Our.

Townspeople
The sentence we apply every day.
Every time we perform this play.

Mrs Wright Good. I never liked her language. Now. Our
arrangements. Let's convene to discuss.

While this is happening, Victoria has been trying to look out at the audience, trying to edge closer to get a look at them, and in doing so, inching herself across the stage away from the trial, unnoticed. Her hand comes upon something. She picks it up. She holds it up, something small and glinting. She nudges Albert in the leg. He looks down.

Albert What is it?
Victoria A key.
Albert What key?
Victoria To our little problem of connection.

Holds up their cuffed wrists. Together they fiddle with the cuffs.

Juror 2 Em, what time's supper, Your Honour? And are we having fish fingers?
Juror 1 Speaking out of.
Juror 3 Turn!
Juror 1 Saying a whole.
Juror 3 Sentence by yourself!
Juror 1 Do.
Juror 3 N't!
Juror 2 Sorry.
Mrs Wright (*getting irritable*) Members of the jury. There will be fish fingers for tea after your duty.
Townspeople
  Everybody is invited
  To our humble house for teas.
  There will be fish fingers
  And chips and peas.

Everybody except Victoria and Albert clap their hands.

Juror 1 We.
Juror 2 First carry out.
Juror 3 The sentence, as usual?

Townspeople
>Don't you really love the way
>It happens every night?
>Don't you adore our perfect town,
>Our beloved Mrs Wright,
>Our lovely flourishing pot plant?
>Our place for the bus to stop?
>Our body with the umbrella stuck in it,
>Our amnesiac idiot cop?

They tap their heads.

>Our audience, infiltrated
>In a quite impartial way,
>Our pure routine, our perfect world,
>Our play?
>Our place apart, like nowhere else,
>Our long unending poem,
>Our theatre of here, our perfect
>Home sweet home?

Mrs Wright Places, please!

Victoria (*rubbing her wrist*)! God, that's better. Now. You. Waitrose. Come over here. Look at this.

She takes him to the front of the stage.

Victoria Can you see them?

Albert Who are they?

Victoria They're the audience. It's a relief, I can tell you. I've worked it out. We're in a play.

Albert In a what?

Victoria In a play. A bad play. Like in a bad dream. So we can just leave. Thank God. For a little while I was actually frightened it was real. But that stupid bus stop. That meaningless pot plant. That comedy corpse.

Albert Comedy corpse? You think so?

Victoria We're in a bad play, Waitrose.

Albert We're in a play?

Victoria Well, we were. You still will be, if you carry on hanging around here. But I'm off. I've other places to be. I'm not hanging around in a sub-standard play. Don't know about you.

Albert I can't. I work here.

Victoria Right. Well. (*Shakes his hand.*) Bye then. All the best.

Albert Funny.

Victoria Funny what?

Albert I'm beginning to miss you already.

Victoria Well, I don't miss you. And I won't miss any of this.

Albert Even a little bit?

Victoria Nope.

Albert Waitrose.

Victoria Naive.

Albert Didn't you think me at least, you know . . .?

Victoria What?

Albert A fash – I mean, a *pass*ionate kind of person, maybe?

Victoria Goodbye.

Albert Goodbye. I liked you.

Victoria I liked you too.

Albert You really think you're leaving, don't you?

Victoria Absolutely!

Albert Naive.

He turns his back, hunched, sad.

Victoria (*generally, to everyone else on the stage*) Well, I'm off, then. Cheerio!

The others all self-consciously ignore her.

What a day, eh? God. I tell you, that's the last time I hang about anywhere near a body with an umbrella in its back.

She bends over the corpse to take a last look, then meditates out towards the audience.

Who knows who he was? Who knows what he did? Who knows who you all are, out there? If he was still alive, you know what advice I'd give him? The same advice I'm giving to you now. Eat apples. Whatever you do, eat apples. There's something about an apple that'll see you through, if it's an apple that's been grown properly, given its proper length of time on the branch, allowed fresh air and good water, tended with the respect that every small and powerful individual fruit deserves, protected from pesticides, simply understood.

Behind her, while she is speaking, Juror 1 has sneaked up and expertly jerked the umbrella out of the back of the Corpse. Juror 2 and Juror 3, holding Mrs Wright between them with linked arms, are watching now. So are the Townspeople. Juror 1 lunges the umbrella at Victoria.

Victoria Uh – what the –?

Down she goes, exactly like the original corpse, parallel to him, dead, the umbrella sticking out of her back now.

Albert (*turning round*) Every time. Even the nice ones. Why do you – why does this –
Townspeople
You are blind.
You mustn't mind.
It really isn't in the least unkind.
She was an outsider.
She didn't belong.
She wrote on the pot plant.
She did things wrong.

Albert She didn't write on the pot plant. You did that
yourselves. I saw you.

Townspeople are in shock.

Mrs Wright You didn't see anything.
Albert I did. I saw –
Mrs Wright (*firmly*) You. Don't. Know. Anything.
Albert I do! I – I saw it. I saw everything. I saw what
just happened to her, too, the apple girl. And I'm not
going to forget it. And I don't mind telling you
something for nothing. You're nothing but a liar.
You're nothing but a –

*He squares up to Mrs Wright. But then he sees Juror 1,
Juror 2, Juror 3 and the Townspeople all ranged
against him.*

Mrs Wright I'm nothing but a what?
Albert Oh, I don't know.
Mrs Wright What *exactly* do you know?
Albert (*brokenly*) Nothing.

Visible relaxation of everyone.

Townspeople
  Knew his mother. She lost her way.
  She was like him. Didn't understand the play.
  He'll have to watch it. Watch his back.
  You never know the time of attack.

The Jurors pick up the original corpse between them.

Juror 1 It's a.
Juror 2 Lesson to.
Juror 3 Us all.

*Mrs Wright waves them offstage, peeking from under
her blindfold. Albert stands over the new corpse.*

Albert Waitrose.

Small pause. No answer. He answers himself.

Naive. Excali – something. A sword. A stone. A story.
Forgotten already. What was her name? Something
about apples. A weakling comes along and pulls it out
of the stone. As if the sword is waiting for him and him
alone. I'm turning into them. I'm beginning to rhyme.

Mrs Wright (*adjusting her blindfold so she can't see
again*) How would you like to graduate from Marshall
to Personal Assistant, with the occasional Jury Duty?

Albert (*resigned*) Does it pay well?

Mrs Wright The pay is just.

Townspeople nod.

Albert The pay is just what?

Mrs Wright Just just.

Albert What's just, again, when it's at home?

Mrs Wright The pay is fair.

Albert (*sad*) My lucky day.

Mrs Wright (*nods, satisfied*) Now. Follow me!

*She walks grandly out and nearly falls off the edge of
the stage, saved at the last moment by Albert, who
can't help but reach out and stop her, almost against
his will. He leads her off the way the Jurors left the
stage, gingerly, holding only the edge of her cardigan,
not touching her. The Townspeople do one more
round of the stage, all theirs.*

Townspeople
Here's our lovely pot plant.
Here's our lovely bench.
Here's our lovely bus stop.
There's no stench!
The air is fresh and clear, here,
It's a country you can trust,
It's a country with a history

Where everything is just!
Just perfect. Just ours.
Just about right.
Just understood. Just wonderful.
Just a delight.
Just the same as always,
Always the same.
And every time we find the perfect
Someone new to blame.
And then when we think it's over
It all begins again!
Ooh, here's the bus stop.
Let's wait for the bus.
Oohh, we're first in the queue. Great!
No one here but us!

*They stand at the bus stop. Nothing onstage but the
bus stop, the bench, the plant, the corpse, and them.
They look at the corpse. They look away. They get
uneasier and uneasier about it lying there. They give it
little uneasy looks. Finally –*

D'you think we should bother waiting for the bus?
The walk home will be good for us.

Off they go, as usual.
 *Short pause. Nothing on the stage except Victoria's
body with the umbrella stuck in her back. After the
short pause, Girl enters and stands at the bus stop.
She's waiting for a bus. She's wearing a T-shirt with a
giant picture of a baby fox on it. She stands there for a
minute. She looks over at the pot plant, frowns. She
gets out an A to Z or a map, looks at it. She's lost.
Looks straight ahead again. Looks down at the bench
and thinks about sitting on it, decides not to.*
 *But then she senses something behind her, turns
round – and sees the body.*

Girl Oh my . . . oh my God.

She goes over to take a look. She stands at a distance first, then dares herself to go closer. She stands over the body and looks all round for what can have happened. There's no sign of any explanation, anything that could have happened. Girl shakes her head. She examines the body from feet to head without touching it. She is disgusted. Then she is, to her surprise, a bit fascinated. Then she notices how the handle of the umbrella is almost temptingly jutting into the air.

She looks all round her, a little guiltily, as if to check no one can see, then leans forward as if to touch or take the handle, as if she can't resist. Just as she reaches forward to do this –

Blackout.

A Cycle of Baroque Violence

Ali Smith interviewed by Jim Mulligan

Ali Smith's play *Just* starts and ends in silence. At the start a young woman, Victoria, stands at a bus stop and gradually becomes aware of a body lying near her. There is an old-fashioned umbrella with a curved handle sticking out of the corpse's back. By the end of the play Victoria is herself the corpse, stabbed in the back because she is an outsider, she doesn't belong. Another young woman stands at the bus stop and as the lights dim we know that the terrifying cycle of injustice is starting again.

> My play probably fits in with the Theatre of the Absurd. It seems to make sense alongside things by Brecht, Ionesco, Dario Fo or Kafka. We live in a very Kafkaesque age. The play is clearly political, even though I do not want to make the issues explicit. It's clearly a play about England and the UK. It is absolutely about things like Guantanamo Bay which are happening right now. There are indirect references to all sorts of things that are happening now.

If this play is about anything it is about the perversion of justice. In all the standard depictions, Justice, always a woman, is blind-folded to show that she is impartial and unprejudiced. Here, Mrs Wright maintains she is blindfolded to prevent her from being biased and then goes on to make the absurd assertion that she *heard* Victoria's hand raised in a ghastly way and she *heard* Albert watching in a gleeful accomplice-like way. She is forever peering out from under her blindfold. The jury are members of her family, Albert the policeman is completely under her sway, the public are her sycophants.

I had no specific person in mind for Mrs Wright. In fact the character started off as a man Then she became female and you can read her as anything you like. Justice is blind but hers is a different kind of blindness. It is a chosen kind of blindness. She almost always decides which direction to look.

Just is also about words, their limitations and distortions. According to the townspeople. Victoria uses disgusting language when she is provoked by the incomprehensible injustice she is experiencing. Mrs Wright's response to the rational use of words is: objection, irrelevance, obfuscating information. When Victoria explains how she has been ruined by the supermarkets and has had to grub up her medieval orchard, Mrs Wright seizes on the names of apples and invents northern spies, Ida the Red and Jonathan McIntosh.

How simple is an apple? How simple is the word 'just'? The apple is in the first story of innocence and knowledge. The play is about words and how we use words and how words change their meaning, slip away from us. That's why the play is called *Just*. That's all it is. Just means everything and just is nothing. It's about the ripples of meaning that go between the things we think we understand and the things we don't. It's about the strength of language. People are appalled at a few swearwords and they ignore things on their doorstep that are utterly appalling. It's like a displacement of dishonour, of blame, or responsibility.

Just is a very dark comedy and the comic chorus of Townspeople is the black heart of the play. They are banal and utterly sinister. They are just people waiting for a bus. They talk about their lovely pot plant, their lovely bench, their lovely bus stop. Everything is just perfect, just about right, just understood, just wonderful. They live in a country you can trust, a country with a history. But they are the people who stood by as the Third Reich sent millions to their deaths. They are the people who shrug their shoulders at detention without trial. Albert is their uniformed factotum. His tragedy is that he cannot disconnect himself from the position that he has accepted. He knows, more clearly than anybody else, despite his difficulties with language, that he is seeing a grotesque injustice being committed to the woman he has grown fond of, but he cannot get himself out of abyss.

> It will be very difficult for Victoria and Albert. She has to come across as passionate and direct and he as trapped. They must express themselves to the audience as fully human and at the same time as delineated models with great black lines around them. They are the human centre of the play, and my belief is that the sparser you make something the better it will be and the more cut-out it seems the further it will take you into the heart of something. The sparser the action is the more clearly we can see the truth behind it.

In a Brechtian move, Ali Smith breaks the dramatic reality she has created and has her characters confiding that they know they are in a play. The Townspeople say, 'Don't you love the way it happens every night?' They refer to 'our play, our unending poem, our theatre of here'. Victoria says she has worked out they are in a bad play like a bad dream and she can just walk out of it. But she delays too long to give us some advice about eating apples and the Jurors kill her with the umbrella. And that, Ali Smith, seems to be saying, is how it is with our society. Any individual can walk out of the nightmare that is going on around us but most do not realise we have a choice.

Ultimately, of course, everyone has a choice. Some will choose to remain part of society. The few existential heroes who try to rebel may be terminated in one way or another. But I do not want to close the cycle completely. Let's leave the hope there. Despite that vision, I see things going irrecoverably wrong. There's a spread of some kind of Baroque violence which is new to us. We are experiencing it for the first time in this historic cycle. What we read in the papers is absurd but it's real. It's unthinkable but it's happening. Art helps us understand where we are.

Production Notes

Warm up the face and voice:

> *Chew sounds.*
> *Massage your cheeks.*
> *Make big raspberry faces.*
> *Rub your chest and belly.*
> *Start to articulate:*
> *Make puh-fuh sounds. Repeat. Passion it – fashion it.*
> *Repeat this exercise for all the words in the play that get mixed up pronunciation-wise. If an audience doesn't get these first pronunciation distinctions their meaning will be lost. Repeat this exercise in every warm-up you do. Keep working on the words.*

Swear-words. They must be spoken. Language can shock, that's one of the points of the play. Every word has been chosen and is to be judged as part of what is going on.

The title. Think of phrases that connect to the word *Just*. That one word encompasses everything in the play – from lightness and throwaway, bleak and dark, to how we live and engage with each other and how we all aspire to some kind of just world. This should be your starting point.

Break up the play into about fifteen sections. There are no hard-and-fast rules on how to do this, but this is how we did it in Bath:

1 Victoria and the Dead Body. Ask: where did Victoria come from? Create a background to imply that she is coming in with a *purpose*. You must ask the purpose of every scene.

2 Albert and Victoria. Just before the Townspeople enter. Ask: is there a line from this section that sums up what's going on? For example, 'You didn't see what you think . . . like you didn't say what you . . .' It is important to decide what lines are key to your understanding of both the whole piece and the situation characters are in at any given moment.

3 Townspeople's entrance. Give this a name so they can then be referred to, e.g. 'Discovering the Body' or 'Evil One is Accused'. The latter is good because it actively describes how the townspeople describe Victoria.

4 Objectives of the Characters. Ask what the characters want to get out of this scene. An example for Victoria could be, to be right and convince Albert: I want the others to know I didn't do it. Perhaps for Albert: to do my job, get a criminal and go home, i.e. to arrest her.

5 Before the Townspeople re-enter. Put together a body image of what's going on between Mrs Wright, Albert and Victoria. Decide whose body language is where in order to reflect the status in their relationships.

6 Townspeople re-enter. A question to ask of all the Townspeople sections is what changes from the beginning to the end of a scene when they come in. You could choose to play it that the main characters go back to the way they were before the Townspeople entered – or you could have the Townspeople's

presence change the dynamic of the trio. Whatever you do, make sure it's a *choice*.

7 The swearing scene, and the reaction of the Townspeople.

8 Townspeople's central piece. Introduction of the self-conscious element of the play. Mention of the audience. Question for the townspeople: how much of their speech is for Victoria? How much is for the audience directly? Where is the focus? On Victoria or on the Townspeople? Who can see them? Who is acknowledging them? Identify the various characters' relationships with the audience.

9 Before the Jury. What is going to happen? Consider the person in the box – being looked at. Mythology references: Snow White in her box. The apple reference. 'Being made an example of' because everyone can look at her. So with each movement: unravel it to see what images emerge . . . There are references to mythical/medieval origins. Have the cast research the origins of the fairy tale and mythological references. The phrase 'Am I facing out the way?' could seem Scottish within a 'terribly English' play. Because this play is universal you can choose whatever the equivalent to this 'Englishness' is in your own location, e.g. Waitrose might be something else.

10 The Jury. In terms of images and costumes the Jury should be dressed the same, even though this isn't stipulated in the script. They are very camp and over-the-top. They aren't the kind of people who would fit in with the audience, so it is okay to have them inhabiting their own little trio in the front row. They should be differentiated from the Townspeople.

11 Townspeople.

12 The section with just Victoria, Albert and the audience. With Victoria saying 'God, that's better' . . .

13 Just after the death of Victoria.

14 After the exit of the Townspeople.

15 Townspeople's final speech.

16 Off with the Townspeople. Final section.

EXERCISES

Group image: think about *Englishness* in the context of the *last hundred and fifty years*. Add music. Then, one at a time, display an image of what Englishness is. Add to the tableau one person at a time.

When the image is complete: look around at your group. See each other. Gradually bring this to life. What is this experience? Try not to speak.

Same group: new music this time (softer, slightly disturbing). Think of the last two years of Englishness. What might be the same/different for you? What has changed for you?

Think of fake morality. Civilised beings. Think of all the things that make us English. These could be – apples; names; institutions; systems, weapons of mass destruction.

Workshop facilitated by Emily Gray
with notes taken by Oonagh Kearney

LUNCH IN VENICE

Nick Dear

Characters

Harley
Ben
Bianca
Conrad
Emmy
Vivi
A Troupe of Acrobats

Venice. A square or campo. In the centre is a thirteenth-century water cistern. Circling its base are stone steps, which provide some seating.

You don't need much else, but look for ways to give the impression of the high-windowed palazzi surrounding the square. If you're feeling adventurous you might suggest a canal, but it's not essential. The mood is lazy: midday heat.

Four Students enter: Harley, Ben, Bianca and Conrad. They wear summer clothes and day-packs. They each have a piece of pizza on a cardboard tray, and bottles of drink.

Bianca That was so sweet.
Conrad Yeah, they just, like, gave it to us.
Bianca What lovely people.
Ben (*eating*) Mine's fantastic. How's yours?
Conrad Could be worse.

They settle themselves around the campo, some on the steps of the well, and eat their lunch. Harley comes forward.

Harley (*to us*) Well . . . I don't know where to start . . . I guess we're all just getting used to it, really.
Ben Yeah, that's right.
Conrad It is.
Harley We were really into the Carpaccios that morning. Well, I was. I mean, I like that kind of thing – that's why I'm here. Some of the others, they came for a laugh, they do not give a fart about art. But we're in this place, Bianca comes up to me and she says, hey

329

man, who was 'Scuola' again? 'Scuola', I say, means
'school'. Scuola di San Giorgio degli Schiavoni: the
School of Saint George of the Slavs. That's why it's
all George and the Dragon and that. 'Is it?' she says.
'I thought he was ours . . .?' I said, 'Yes, he is ours,
but he crops up all over the place.' 'With his dragon?'
I'm certain she's taking the piss but, yeah, with his
dragon. 'What, sort of like a travelling George-and-
the-Dragon act?'

Bianca He said, possibly.

Harley Could be.

Bianca I loved him from that moment on.

Harley (*to us*) What got me about the Carpaccio
paintings was the everyday quality of the world of the
monks and martyrs and that. It's all just fantasy,
obviously, biblical wish-fulfilment –

Conrad A load of crap, in other words.

Harley – and yet it was kind of real.

Ben Very real. The sort of miracles you see all the time.

Conrad laughs. Bianca goes to Harley.

Bianca I know what you mean. You're stood in this
place and you can almost reach up and touch the
pictures and he was doing them *five hundred years
ago*. And five hundred years of history is like suddenly
nothing.

Conrad It's all nothing.

Ben History is so *over*.

Harley And Bianca came close in the half-dark. And that
made it all the more special.

*Bianca puts her arm through Harley's and they gaze up
at the pictures.*

I'm just trying to explain why it got to me. Partly it was
the five hundred years, of course, anyone would be
moved by that. Paint is so magical, man, the way it

just stays there, it clings on, while we come and go.
And I've felt time pass, felt it brush my face as it goes
down the street. We're all aware of what we've lost.

Bianca I totally am.

Harley And partly it was the beauty, the sheer beauty of
the whole experience, weird shimmery feeling on my
skin, and then she says –

Bianca What are Slavs again?

Harley And I reckon I can either give her a lecture on the
local geography, or I can kiss her, so I kiss her.

He does so. They clinch.
Emmy enters. She has two slabs of pizza and a plate
of salad and a slice of melon and some prosciutto and
a glass of red wine.

Ben Hi, Emmy. Got enough to eat?

Emmy nods, sits and eats.

Bianca (*to us*) This place is so dark. This Scuola. You
push your way in through a curtain. There's a
downstairs and an upstairs. God knows what it's for.
In the downstairs there are the Carpaccios, which are
silly apart from the virgin being rescued from the
dragon. But I'm not that interested in virgins. I'm more
interested in like the overall mood.

Harley The mood in the Scuola is very noir, very
chiaroscuro.

Bianca Yeah. Absolutely.

Emmy (*to us*) I'm more interested in my lunch. (*to the*
boys) Are we going to get pizza again or are we going
to a proper restaurant?

Ben Pizza.

Conrad Pizza.

Emmy (*to us*) You see? So here we are. I had hopes of
rigatoni con sugo di pesce. Or *fegato alla veneziana.*
Or at least lasagne!

Ben That lasagne we had last night was first used as ballast in the Doge's warships.

Conrad Who told you that?

Ben Mr Peters.

Bianca He's alright, Mr Peters.

Harley Yeah. He's okay.

Ben What's the world coming to, when you start to like the staff?

Everyone finds this very funny, for some reason.

Harley (*to us*) I was already mad for Venice, and I'd only been here forty-eight hours. How fast you forget Stansted Airport! One moment you're shuffling through security like Oscar Wilde in Reading Gaol, past the pissheads on their pre-flight pint of Stella –

Ben *and* **Conrad** Cheers!

Harley – the next you're on the Adriatic where they drink *prosecco* instead of cooking lager and it's magical, man! It's art-history heaven! Disneyland for grown-ups! And Byron was here, and Shelley, Henry James, Proust.

Ben (*to us*) This guy is such a name-dropper.

Harley It feels like just by *arriving* you've already changed, you're a little more interesting, a little more vital.

Bianca (*to us*) I felt a bit sick on the ferry from the airport –

Harley Aeroporto Marco Polo! Even the names!

Bianca – because they won't let you out on deck. But when you come round the tip of the island and head towards the Grand Canal, that has to be one of the sights, one of the great sights of the world.

Conrad It is. I'll give you that. It is.

Bianca (*to us still*) And I thought, this is amazing, I'm going to fall in love in Venice.

Bianca and Harley smile at each other. Perhaps surprisingly, no one takes the piss.

332

Emmy So *someone* found out what it's like . . .

Ben Yeah.

Bianca (*to us*) Everyone thinks Harley's a show-off. But he's not. He just knows a lot. He knows like everything there is to know about the Renaissance! (*to Harley*) Which is what again?

Harley It means 'rebirth'.

Bianca Oh yeah? Cool.

She looks a bit unconvinced.

Conrad (*to us*) I'd seen the pictures of the Doge's Palace, Basilica, winged lions, course I had, back at school, I thought, what a load of baroques, but when you actually get there and you look across the water to the Salute –

Harley (*to Bianca*) Big church.

Conrad – and Giudecca in the distance, and you're like *Christ*! It's so lovely! And the people! There are so many people! From every country in creation! It's like the Tower of Babel down there, every bloody language you can think of!

Ben (*to us*) If you lived here you'd need to like people. You're jammed up against them all the time. Venice is one big crowd.

Conrad (*to us*) It's like a commercial for the after-life or something. All these people, speaking in tongues, and the sun bouncing off the lagoon, and the vaporettos, and the ice-cream, and – you know what? – everybody's happy. And I stand there and think, why am I such a miserable prick? And I want to smash everything. Smash their palazzi and their stupid lions. Smash the smiles off their faces.

Bianca (*to us*) There's a big bell-tower. We went up it. Harley said that when Goethe came to Venice he went up it, and he said that that was the first time Goethe had ever seen the sea.

333

Conrad *Who?*

Bianca Goethe! One of the great painters! Honestly, Conrad!

Emmy *(to us)* I wanted to go on a gondola. Under the Bridge of Sighs. But they all laughed at me.

Harley Emmy, you can't afford it!

Emmy *(to us)* Wish I had now.

Conrad Gondolas are for suckers!

Emmy Yeah, and all the suckers are laughing their tits off. Right.

Bianca They are at first. Then they work out how much it has actually cost.

Ben Yeah, by the time they get back to San Marco, they're *whimpering*. There are medics standing by for the suicide attempts.

Emmy They've seen Venice, though.

Ben Oh, come on, Em, they've only seen Venice through a video camera.

Emmy Does it matter how you see it?

Bianca So long as you see it.

Harley Before you die.

Emmy I mean, is the experience of looking at the screen on your camera supposed to be, like, *worse*, than looking at a building?

Ben Yes.

Emmy Why?

Ben Art is about using your eyes, surely?

Emmy But they are using their eyes. To look into the camera.

Bianca You don't look *into* a camera. You look *at* a camera.

Conrad Who says they're artists?

Harley No, don't you look *into* a building if the door is open?

Conrad Not everyone's an artist.

Emmy What's so crucial about looking *directly at the thing*?

Conrad They're *tourists*!

Ben These people aren't looking. That's the thing. They're *not looking*.

Harley You come all the way from Osaka, and you don't look at the Doge's Palace?

Bianca Maybe it's like multi-media, maybe you hear all the bells, the water splashes you, you smell the fried fish and the wine – after all you're on the Grand Canal.

Emmy Yeah. In a gondola.

Conrad They only look when they get home, Em.

Emmy So? What's wrong with that? At least they saw it.

Conrad At least they're home.

There's a silence. They turn away from each other.

I think I'll have some more pizza.

Conrad exits.

Ben (*to us*) I'll tell you something in confidence. I was going to, you know, give it a try. With Bianca. Thought about it up the bell-tower. Just let my hand fall on her arm . . . as we looked out over the lagoon . . . there was a moment . . . but my nerve failed. As usual. And the thing is, with women, there's a moment, and believe me I know what I'm talking about . . . There's a moment, and if it passes, and you haven't put your hand on her arm, you're dead. It's gone. You can be great mates. But you never get back to how it was before the moment when it might have become something else. Oh yes, I'm a past master of the missed opportunity. I've got more female friends than I can count.

Emmy (*to us*) I closed in on Ben up the bell-tower. I was seriously invading his personal space. But he never noticed. The dope.

Ben (*to us*) That pretty well sums up Venice for me. One more thing I should have done while I had the chance.

Conrad returns with some more pizza.

Emmy What did you get?
Conrad *Funghi.*
Harley (*to Bianca*) Mushrooms.
Bianca I know.
Conrad (*to us*) The pizza's the only thing worth coming for. I mean if you wanted to play football, where would you go? Or tennis? Where would you go? Never mind ride a bike! And as for the shops!
Emmy They're alright if you want a chandelier.
Conrad But I don't want a chandelier! I don't want a Bridge of Sighs paperweight! I don't want a go in a rowing boat with some twat in a hat singing operas!
And I don't want to stand in no more freezing churches being told Tintoretto is *good*! When he's *crap*!
Emmy Conrad, why are you doing art?
Conrad 'Cause I can draw.
Emmy Oh. Right.
Conrad Only thing I can do. You?
Emmy Well, I certainly can't draw.
Conrad No, nor can Tintoretto.
Emmy But I do think I understand colour. Beef Carpaccio is called Beef Carpaccio because it's that deep red he likes so much, dark and bloody, the red of the ambassadors' robes. Remember? In the Accademia yesterday?
Conrad What, Saint Ursula? And the eleven thousand virgins?
Emmy I'd serve it with roast yellow peppers.
Bianca He really had a thing about virgins.
Ben Who doesn't?
Conrad When they got massacred. I liked that.
Emmy You're sick.

Conrad There are not many painters who can give you a decent likeness of Saint Ursula, eleven thousand virgins *and* the Pope, and then slaughter the lot of 'em in a single frame. Genius! I'm going to be an artist.

Ben (*matter-of-factly*) No you're not.

Harley What were they? Goths?

Conrad They didn't have Goths in those days. These were more like hippies.

Harley No, the pagans – were they Goths, or were they Vandals?

Conrad They were totally out of order, no question. You can't butcher eleven thousand and two pilgrims and not expect to get a reputation.

Emmy They were Huns. It said on the audio-guide.

Conrad The Pope got it right in the neck! It was great!

Ben The Huns are meant to be Turks. Killing Christians again. That's how you're meant to see them.

Bianca Why do you want everything to end badly and, you know, shit on everything all the time? Why do you do that?

Conrad 'Cause it's the truth. That's how it is!

Bianca It's what you want it to be. Isn't it?

Conrad What do you want it to be?

Bianca Happy. Just a happy time. You know?

Harley (*to Bianca*) Shall I get some more pizza?

Bianca Oh, go on then.

Harley Let's try the *Quattro Stagioni*.

Bianca The what?

Harley Four Seasons.

Bianca Cool.

Harley exits.

(*to us*) We're meant to have four seasons, aren't we? Four quarters of the wheel. Four bites at life. And extra topping. Aren't we?

Ben The Pizza Theory of Existence.

Bianca Thanks, Ben.

Ben Well, they have String Theory, don't they? They have Chaos Theory? I think Pizza Theory's got a good chance.

Emmy (*sighs*) As good as anything else. I'm completely baffled by it.

Conrad Pizza?

Emmy No, existence. Pizza's easy. (*to Ben*) And according to this theory of yours, pizza's the key to the universe?

Ben The key to everything. Right.

Emmy What's going to happen to us, then?

Conrad Well, first we have lunch, then I think we do a bit of sightseeing.

Emmy That's it?

Ben That's it. Oh, maybe we go to Harry's Bar for a *bellini*.

Bianca What's a bellini?

Emmy It's like peach juice with champagne.

Bianca Yum.

Conrad (*to us*) Everybody's trying to put a brave face on it. Nobody wants to look soft.

Ben (*to us*) All quietly thinking the unthinkable.

Harley returns with a large slice of pizza in each hand.

Harley Anyone for pizza?

Everyone laughs. Harley doesn't know why. He gives Bianca her pizza. They kiss.

(*to us*) This is how it's always going to be. It's always going to be like Day One, when the girl you fancy first takes you by the hand. I'm going to have goosebumps for ever! And I'm never going to get her into bed!

Emmy takes Bianca to one side.

Emmy So what's it like, being in love?

Bianca Don't tell me you haven't . . . ?

Emmy Yes of course. Only not with . . . anyone who
knew about it.

Bianca Oh, right. Well, you have to compromise a lot.
I mean there's no room for ego, if you see what I mean.
I would have preferred seafood, but I've got these
artichokes and olives and stuff. I suppose I'll just have
to put up with it.

Emmy Is that what you call a compromise?

Bianca Why, what would you call it?

Emmy Unconditional surrender.

Bianca Well, until I fall out of love with him, that's what
it's like.

Emmy And when will that be?

Bianca Never. He's my man.

Emmy Bianca, how do you save a man from drowning?

Bianca Um, no idea, how?

Emmy Take your foot off his neck.

Bianca is confused.

(*to us*) There are no decent restaurants where I live. It
drives me wild! I'm so in love with food! I was a
vegetarian for about five minutes, but then I realised
that vegetarians don't want to change anything, they
just want to be different, the luxury of saying 'no'.
They don't want to muck in. I do. I want to feed the
whole world! Give me the loaves and the fishes and I'll
have a go. I just want to give everyone a feast.

Harley This is a feast.

Emmy It's got the makings of a feast. But you could add
another course: let's say gnocchi with asparagus and
gamberetti, and a *contorno* of grilled *radicchio* – the
grilling caramelises the sugar, right, so you get a
counterpoint to the bitter taste?

Harley And to follow?

Emmy *Baverese alla pera con crema di cachi e castagne.*

Conrad Okay, what's that?

Emmy Pear with persimmons and chestnuts.

Harley Persimmons?

Emmy You got it.

Conrad How do you know all this, Em?

Emmy I looked it up on the net. The recipes aren't hard. It's getting persimmons at the Co-op that's tricky.

Harley Well, I expect you can get them in Venice . . .

Emmy (*to us*) The produce here is incredible! Sometimes it's piled high on boats. The red *radicchio* . . . *focaccia* with rosemary . . . fish flapping on crushed ice . . . heaven.

Harley (*to us*) The tastes and the colours . . . the light always changing in the moist sea air . . . Carpaccio leads us, as if through a secret door, into Venice a hundred years before Shakespeare. There's this vivid detail of daily life, and a strange kind of slant to the perspective, as if he's got hold of some extremely weird lenses, man. Like he's the Orson Welles of the quattrocento.

Ben Will you shut up about art?

Harley No. I won't. This is what I think is important. I've got to believe there's some kind of higher achievement, you know? It can't be just beer and football.

Conrad Nothing wrong with football.

Harley But there *is* great art, and it's better than crap art, and I want to know all about it. For instance, the George and the Dragon stuff is meant to be taking place in Libya, did you know that?

Bianca That's where the dragons live, is it?

Harley Yes.

Bianca (*to us*) Isn't he sweet?

Harley But Carpaccio's never been to Libya. He's barely been out of Venice –

Conrad Barely been out of Harry's Bar.

Harley – so he takes these buildings that he knows, from round here –

Emmy Did Carpaccio drink bellinis, that's the question?

Harley – and from pictures of, like, Jerusalem and that, and lines them up in the background with a few palm trees and minarets and wow! he's created a Libya of the imagination.

Ben Which is exactly what Shakespeare did with *The Merchant of Venice*. It's no big deal. It's just people making pictures, writing words. It's not important at all.

Harley Excuse me?

Ben Not compared to all the stuff that's going on. Not when there's war and devastation everywhere you look. Not when there are cluster bombs, and babies dying of shrapnel wounds, and bandits calling themselves statesmen, and terror, and fear –

Emmy And people blowing up bridges.

Ben (*to us*) But everyone's so complacent! I go on all the marches . . . It's vital to keep on saying, keep on reminding them that where we live is a paradise, that elsewhere it *really isn't like this*!

Bianca (*to us*) Ben's always handing out leaflets.

Ben (*to us*) Palestine, right? The Sudan?

Emmy (*to us*) He's on a mission. He's cool.

Ben (*to us*) What are we going to *do*? Why don't we just die of guilt?

Bianca (*to us*) Cool? I don't think so. Has he never heard of personal grooming?

Ben (*to us*) I've always said that by the time I leave this world, I want to have made a difference.

Bianca Iron your shirt, that'll make a difference.

Ben (*to us*) But I've been weighed in the balance and found wanting. Because nothing has changed. I've had no effect. I feel impotent.

341

Emmy I'm sure you're not.

Ben I am! Being away, you think about home a lot.
About who we are, what do we do, what do we make.
And it feels like the only thing we make now is war.
We export war and we import war. It's the only thing
we're good at.

Harley Men have always made war. The Venetians made
war with the Turks for centuries! It doesn't make art
unimportant!

Ben Yes it does! Art is useless, until we have peace!

Harley Oh, that's insane, Ben!

Ben It's proven itself useless!

Conrad What's wrong with a nice war?

Ben Do you have to be completely cynical?

Conrad Yeah, I'm in touch with my inner bastard, see.

Ben This is the problem, right here, this is why nothing
ever changes!

Harley So if nothing ever changes, why can't we paint
pictures? Write songs?

Ben All your precious Venetian art glorifies war! Glorifies
suffering! That's why!

Harley Most of it glorifies God.

Conrad Or the Doge. In his palace.

Ben Which is all just a symbol for war! It's all the Battle
of this and the Siege of that! It's all let's bash the
heathen! Let's kill thirty thousand Moors at Lepanto!
Why, even George and the Dragon ends with the girl
being baptised a Christian!

Conrad But that's what they believed!

Ben But it's because of what we believe that we're in this
mess! There are like a hundred churches in this town!
And every one of them says, what we believe is better
than what you believe! And we'll fight you until you
accept it! It's time that we all *stopped believing*!

Bianca (*to us*) Boys! Always arguing! The trouble with
Ben is that he isn't Harley. Harley is kind of sensitive –

342

you know – uses loads and loads of conditioner. Ben barges around like an ox or an elk or something! He'd be alright if he didn't do that. And if he got a decent haircut. I could almost like him. Because what he says has to be true, doesn't it? If we don't give up fighting each other, this kind of thing is just going to go on and on. But then I agree with what Harley says too. I want to live in a nice place and be surrounded by loveliness and nice clean linen. Who doesn't? It's human nature. And flowers, they have loads of flower shops in Venice and you can stop and smell them all the time. I love luxurious scents. I hate war and disaster. I think I'm perfectly normal.

A Troupe of Acrobats enters, with music and exclamations. The music can be anything that street entertainers might use: guitar, accordion, whatever you've got.

The Acrobats are dressed, loosely speaking, in commedia dell'arte *costumes: a Pierrot, a Pantalone, a Columbina. (No masks, though.) There can be as many or as few of them as you like.*

The Students applaud their raucous entrance, and stand back to give them space.

Emmy Hey, look! Clowns!

The Acrobats are not scripted. They perform a routine of acrobatics, or juggling, or rope-walking, or swordplay, or unicycling, or any combination of these and anything else you can think of. It should be spectacular and loud and circus-like. If any commands are spoken, they should be in Italian.

The Students applaud each trick.

When the Acrobats have finished, they take a bow and one of them goes round with a hat, collecting small change from the Students. Then they disappear as quickly as they came, their music echoing down the alleyways.

Harley That was amazing!

Bianca Yeah.

Emmy Cool tricks!

Harley That was authentic *commedia dell'arte*!

Ben (*matter-of-factly*) No it wasn't.

Bianca (*to Harley*) Has anyone ever told you you're a bit of a snob?

Harley It's necessary to be part of an elite. Otherwise you get crushed by the herd.

Ben (*under his breath*) Jesus.

Bianca Where do you get your hair done?

Harley Angelo's.

Bianca You want to have some highlights.

Harley Do you think so?

Bianca Yes.

Emmy They were excellent, weren't they!

Conrad They were crap.

Emmy What's your problem, Conrad?

Conrad (*to us*) I've always thought life was an arse-wipe. And here's conclusive proof. If there's one thing guaranteed to show that all human endeavour is pointless, it's clowns and jugglers and bloody acrobats. About the least funny person ever is a bloody clown. And I have to watch them doing handstands. I'd rather be roasted on a spit.

Vivi enters. She is wealthy, and older than the Students. She has a couple of bulging carrier bags.

Vivi I'm lost!

The Students view her with interest.

I'm lost! This map's no good!

Harley Where are you trying to get to?

344

Vivi The Hotel Bauer! I'm overdue for drinks! On the terrace of the Bauer!

Harley Where's that?

Vivi On the Grand Canal!

Bianca Have you been shopping?

Vivi Yes, found some smashing souvenirs!

Harley Let's have a look at your map.

Vivi The Hotel Bauer is clearly marked. Look, there's a picture of it! You can almost see me mingling on the terrace, raising my glass to my lips, but I'm not there, I'm here, and where the hell is this exactly?

Ben How do we know?

Emmy We're just having lunch.

Vivi Lunch? Where are the tables? The chairs? The waiters?

Conrad You just go and get pizza. It's free.

Vivi Free pizza? I can't eat free pizza. I can't eat anything free, it would be – wrong! And I can't eat pizza if the herbs have been cooked, I'm allergic to cooked herbs! God, I can't have lunch here! I must get back to the Bauer!

Vivi exits in a cloud of dust.

Emmy . . . Anyone else thinking what I'm thinking?

Harley Yes.

Emmy Hasn't she realised?

Ben I'd say she's in denial.

Conrad So? I'm in denial. I've always been in denial. For some of us it's a way of life. You can get to quite like it. In fact I like it so much I'm in denial of being in denial.

Bianca Do you think someone should go after her?

Emmy Don't see any point. Do you?

Harley No.

Ben Let the rich bitch get lost and have a shit time.

Bianca Oh, don't start that!

Ben Start what?

Bianca All that 'the rich are to blame for everything'. There's nothing wrong with having money.

Ben Did I say there was?

Bianca What's wrong with having money? Honestly!

Conrad What's wrong with wanting it?

Bianca It's human nature, that's all.

Ben Alright, Bianca! (*to us*) When I was young, like about fifteen, I did think it was all about the rich and the poor. But now I'm a little bit wiser. Now I know that the poorest of the poor in our country are – okay, let's put it this way: the internet is going to revolutionise the way we all live, right? That's what we're told. The internet will change the world. Only problem is, two-thirds of the population of the world have never even made a phone call. Internet? Let's start with clean water.

Vivi returns by a different entrance. Still panicked.

Vivi Everywhere you go there are stupid little canals! How is one meant to get anywhere?

Ben Where do you want to go?

Vivi (*exasperated*) The Hotel Bauer!

Ben Is that on the Grand Canal?

Vivi Yes!

Conrad (*pointing*) That way.

Vivi Thanks!

Vivi exits again.

Harley (*with a smile*) Cruel, man.

Ben The beauty of Venice, isn't it? Every time you go out, you get lost.

Conrad I never got lost. I took to it easily. I was never so safe in my life.

Bianca So how did that make you feel?

Conrad Completely pissed off.

Bianca (*sighs*) Why?

Conrad It made me cross that I didn't grow up here. Instead of the wasteland I did grow up in.

Emmy That's right! There's no crime here! You can go anywhere at night.

Bianca You get pick pockets on the vaporetto.

Ben Yeah, but you don't get your head kicked in for lacing your shoes up wrong.

Harley I'd live here. I would. At the drop of a hat.

Bianca No cars. That's what's so brilliant.

Conrad Yeah, no cars. It must be the only proper functioning city in the world that doesn't have a single car in it.

Emmy Isn't that an amazing thought?

Conrad And everyone walks everywhere, meeting their friends, breathing quality air, so everyone feels –

Bianca Yeah, alive.

Emmy I love the way they all kiss each other. The men kiss the men. That's cool.

Vivi returns again. She's hot and out of breath.

Vivi I can't find it. I can't find my way.

Conrad Would you like a drink of water?

Vivi Thanks. I would.

Conrad gives her his bottle. Vivi takes it gratefully, and plonks herself down on the steps.

Conrad Want me to get you some pizza?

Vivi No, I'm lunching at the Hotel Bauer.

Conrad The thing is, I don't think you are. I don't think you're going to make it. To the Hotel Bauer. I'm Conrad. This is Emmy, and Bianca, Harley, Ben.

They all say 'Hi'.

Vivi Hello. I'm Vivi. Is it a school trip?

Emmy Yeah, we were all on the bridge, taking photos.

347

Ben We'd done Carpaccio, yawn, we were heading for the market.

Vivi On the Rialto Bridge?

Ben Yeah.

Vivi So was I . . .

Emmy I was looking for Parmesan cheese, to take home for my dad. He loves Parmigiano on his pasta. There's a great little stall over there.

Vivi That's where I was. I'd been shopping all morning. Got some gifts for my nephews and nieces. I was going across the Rialto to get the boat back to the Bauer. The number one vaporetto. It's gorgeous.

Bianca Don't you remember what happened?

Vivi No . . . not really . . .

Bianca The thing is, Vivi, I think we're going to have to get to know each other. I think we're going to be here for a while.

Vivi But why?

Harley Don't you remember the burning?

Vivi Burning?

Emmy The stuff going up in the air?

Vivi What stuff?

Emmy Well . . . arms? Legs?

Ben I've got it. I think she was borderline.

Vivi Borderline?

Ben Yeah.

Harley Could be . . .

Vivi What do you mean, borderline?

Conrad Well, you were late. Then you were lost. Then you think you're meant to be somewhere else.

Harley You're trying to get a boat . . .

Vivi And what about you?

Emmy Oh, we were all killed instantly.

Vivi Killed?

Conrad On the Rialto Bridge.

Vivi Killed?

Ben (*laughs*) Upon the Rialto. Wait till I tell my English
  teacher.

Vivi (*shocked*) Dead?

Harley (*shrugs*) You get free pizza.

Ben Yeah, could be worse.

Conrad Could be a great deal worse. I'm very surprised
  that it isn't.

Emmy They have these huge ovens. You can watch the
  dough curl in the flames.

Bianca My mum's going to be furious.

Vivi . . . I *do* remember something. A rush of air, a gale
  in my ears

Ben I think you nearly made it. Tough luck.

Conrad Yeah. Sorry.

Bianca (*to us*) It was quick. I'll say that for explosions.
  They're quick.

Emmy (*to us*) Suddenly there's no air.

Ben (*to us*) It's not like a movie.

Harley (*to us*) No slo-mo.

Ben (*to us*) If you're on top of the bomb you'll be blown
  to bits. Nearby, you'll be killed by the shockwave.

Conrad (*to us*) I was blown to bits. What a surprise.

Vivi Oh my God . . .

Conrad Well, we say 'bits', we really mean your body's
  ripped into tiny little pieces –

Emmy – like when you shred a duck to make pancakes

Conrad – and then fried to a crisp –

Bianca – in a nanosecond.

Harley Then there are chunks of bridge, masonry is
  flying through the air, man, it's been there since 1588,
  now it's going in the side of kids' heads –

Ben – through the ribcage –

Emmy – down into the canal.

Bianca It's a big one.

Conrad Lot of kids on that bridge.

Harley Lot of cameras, man.

Bianca Of course. We're in Venice, aren't we?

Harley Taking snaps to show the folks at home . . .

Vivi Did you hear screams?

Bianca No screams. That's later.

Conrad If you're hearing screams, you're not dead, are you?

Bianca You might just be smelling Ben's socks.

Ben Ha ha.

Vivi But I was only stepping onto the bridge, you know past the handbag concessions? I was on my way back to the Bauer!

Emmy There's a wave –

Harley – like a Mexican wave of death –

Emmy – called 'blast overpressure' –

Ben The bomb's gases push the air away –

Emmy – you get a huge increase in pressure –

Bianca – your lungs cave in.

Emmy Yeah, they collapse so fast that all the veins and shit connecting to your heart are just *sheared off* –

Ben – so in a flash your lungs are full of blood.

Emmy Then your sinus cavities implode.

Bianca Your nose is sucked in.

Ben And your face ruptures up through your brain.

Conrad All the bones of your face smash your brain.

Harley I liked my brain. I thought it my best feature. (*to Bianca*) Didn't you?

Bianca I love everything about you, Harley. From now till the end of time.

Conrad (*to Vivi*) I've got to tell you, the pizza really isn't bad. Try the *capricciosa*.

Vivi (*sadly*) Thanks.

Emmy And we have entertainment!

Conrad But it's totally chronic.

Bianca (*to Harley, stroking his hair*) You should get those highlights, you know?

Vivi You mean when I was lost they . . . ?

Emmy I think they were trying to revive you.
Ben Bad news on the Rialto.
Vivi Oh no . . . oh dear no . . .

Vivi comes forward.

I go to Sardinia to see the flamingos. You mightn't believe
me, but they're there. I'm an inveterate traveller. I go
to Holland for the tulips, Alaska for the snow. I can
afford it and I do love to keep on the move. I have a
past and nothing pleases me more than to see it
disappearing over the horizon. Oh, the train ride from
Interlaken to Grindelwald! The Old Quarter of
Havana. Queensland, if you can get away from the
people. And every now and then I swing by Venice –
oh dear – do a bit of shopping – oh no –
Bianca It's okay, it's peaceful here.
Vivi I love my life. I really did . . . love my life . . .
Bianca Yeah, me too.
Conrad Wish I had.
Vivi These places to me are holy places . . . I don't go to
church much . . . not at all really . . . but some places
in the world just make me catch my breath! Holy
places . . . Astonishing things that we created, or that are
just there. Things to wonder at. Church for unbelievers.
A ticket in my hand like a hymnal. Have you been to
the Guggenheim in Spain?
Emmy No.
Vivi Oh, I want to take you. How can it just be over!
I want to take you all to Bilbao! To Angkor Wat! To
Chartres! All the holy places! Salamanca on Good
Friday! Fifth Avenue in the fall!

*She weeps quietly. The Students don't know what to
say.*

Conrad Cheer up. It's not the end of the –
Bianca We'll get you some pizza.

Ben (*to us*) Lunch: the great leveller.

Vivi I'm sorry, but am I just supposed to forget it, just like that? I love these places! Beautiful places make me cry!

Bianca You *are* in Venice.

Harley And a lot of famous people have died here.

Bianca Including you.

Harley (*thrilled*) Wow, man.

Vivi (*pulling herself together*) I'm sorry. Yes, I am in Venice, aren't I? This morning I was on a vaporetto, eating a very sticky cake. It was warm and bright and the seagulls wheeled and corkscrewed. Then I had a lovely time shopping. Would you like to see what I've bought?

Emmy Oh, yes please . . .

Emmy sits, near Vivi. She looks up at Ben and smiles.
He sits down next to her.
Harley and Bianca cuddle languidly.
Conrad comes forward.

Conrad (*to us*) This lady is weird, I'm telling you. We've only just met her and already she's showing us her shopping.

Ben (*to Conrad*) Woman are unfathomable.

Emmy No more unfathomable than you.

Ben I'm entirely fathomable. You can have a go if you want.

Emmy Hey, thanks. How do I do that?

Ben You have to plumb my depths.

Emmy Yeah? That shouldn't take long.

Ben It might.

Emmy It won't take the whole of eternity. What shall we do after?

Ben and Emmy grin at each other.

Vivi Look, aren't they exquisite?

From her bags Vivi produces half a dozen Venetian carnival masks.

Some are beautiful, some alarming, some transform their wearers into Casanovas or long-beaked birds or mythic beasts.

She hands them around to the Students.

Harley They're carnival masks . . !
Vivi That's right. Try one on! Try this one!

Laughing, they all try on the masks.

Conrad (*to us*) And then this music comes from somewhere, they must have hidden speakers or something . . . .

Sure enough, we hear the following: the slow Second Movement of Vivaldi's Concerto No. 4 (Winter), from The Four Seasons.

Emmy (*to Ben*) You look absurd!
Ben (*laughing*) So do you!
Bianca (*to Harley*) You look divine!
Harley So do you.

Bianca and Harley, masked as 'lovers', do a slow, close dance around the campo.

Vivi Conrad, try one! You know, in the old days, at carnival time, the poor tried to dress as rich as they could, and the rich tried to dress as poor as they could. But that doesn't matter any more, does it? Not here. Not now.

Vivi hands Conrad a mask.

You were nice to me. Thank you.

Conrad smiles at Vivi.
She moves away and puts a mask on herself.

Conrad (*to us*) And this is how I'll always remember
  Venice. The little campo where we had lunch . . . the
  hot stone and the cool green water . . . the music! This
  will live with me for ever.

*Conrad puts on his mask. Now everyone is wearing
one.*
  Harley and Bianca dance. The others are still.
*The sad dying fall of the music (which lasts just two
minutes) accompanies a slow fade to black.*

End.

A Nanosecond of Terror in Venice

Nick Dear interviewed by Jim Mulligan

In a tranquil square in Venice five teenagers eat pizzas and talk. The weather is perfect, the food delicious and the talk engaging. But *Lunch in Venice* is a play where the realisation of what has already happened to the characters gradually creeps up on the audience and, from the point where the penny drops, they will receive an emotional jolt. Their perception will be dramatically reshaped in much the same way as the characters' perceptions have been reshaped by the dreadful moment that Nick Dear has subjected them to.

> I wanted to write a story about a group of young people on a trip to Venice. I drop a lot of clues but you would probably glide over them and only get them completely on a second reading. There is a moment midway through when you actually register that something weird is going on, that it is not a normal situation at all – and from then on the audience will be puzzling to work out what exactly is happening. Some will get it earlier than others, and one of the big decisions for the director will be how much you want to point up the clues.

The characters in the play are intelligent and articulate, unlike the stereotype of teenagers that is prevalent today. Harley is an intellectual snob in an endearing way, because his snobbishness comes from his excitement about art. Ben is the most politically aware of the five, keen on literature and involved in student politics. Bianca's main ambition in life is to be a homemaker. She is a romantic. She believes in being in love and the poignant thing is that she finds herself frozen in time with someone she has just started to love. Emmy's great passion is food. She is also a romantic and, although she is a little more restrained than Bianca, she makes a tentative move towards Ben. Conrad is the loner, a fierce cynic, but he is the one who gently explains to Vivi how she will never get to the Hotel Bauer and Nick Dear gives Conrad the final elegiac words of the play.

> The young people I know talk expressively and very articulately about the things they are interested in so I thought I would give each of the five people in the play a particular area of interest about which they would be fluent. I wanted to create a group of young people who would be really interesting to listen to because the pay-off would be that much more poignant. It is very sad, a terrible waste, a terrible shame.

The language in the play is unusual. For much of the time one or other of the characters addresses the audience with the others commenting on what they are saying or joining in with natural dialogue.

> I use the parenthesis '*to us*' rather than the conventional '*aside*' because, although I want these to be confidential moments between a character and the audience, the other characters also hear what is said, and sometimes comment on it. It's an unusual soundscape for a play but when we eventually discover the world we're in, the strangeness of the place, I think it becomes more understandable.

Nick Dear does not see the interlude with the acrobats as in any way metaphorical. It is a couple of minutes' worth of action to bring movement and colour to what might otherwise be a static play. He is, however, insistent that the acrobats should not wear masks, because he wants the masks to play a particular role at the end of the play.

> I felt I could legitimately introduce masks because they are everywhere in the shops in Venice. I wanted to create a weird, slightly surreal, bizarre final stage picture. By this time, the audience knows what has happened, that we are in some kind of strange after-life, and I wanted to bring things to a gentle dying fall.

Two themes that run through *Lunch in Venice* are the Pizza Theory of Life and the historical conflict between Christianity and Islam. The Four Seasons pizza is taken as a metaphor for the four quarters of the wheel of life. The young people have only had one slice of metaphorical pizza. They are trying to put a brave face on things, all quietly thinking the unthinkable and accepting that 'this is how it's always going to be'. They might be eating pizza for all eternity but it is no substitute for what has been denied them. The final music is 'Winter' from Vivaldi's *Four Seasons*.

There are references throughout *Lunch in Venice* to the city's warlike past. We hear of the Doge's warships, the art depicts Turks killing Christians, the George and the Dragon stuff takes place in Libya, and to make it explicit Harley says, 'The Venetians made war with the Turks for centuries.' When the war is brought to Venice in the form of a terrorist bomb we are left in no doubt about what happens to the human body: blown to bits, fried to a crisp in a nanosecond, lungs caved in, the face imploding. And all told in a matter-of-fact way by the young people because it happened in a matter-of-fact way and they did not feel a thing.

> Normally when we hear press reports of terrorist outrages the victims are perceived in a generalised way:

'Eight people killed by car bomb.' I wanted to present us with the reality of people's lives that have been lost. The way I have done that is to let us get to know a bit about the lives of these different personalities. I didn't want to make any kind of comment on the motivations of the bombers except to place the event in the context of a very ancient antipathy between Christianity and Islam. I deliberately position what I see as the great conflict of the twenty-first century in a geography where that conflict has been familiar for hundreds of years. I didn't want to say anything about political motivation. I wanted us to think about the victims.

Production Notes

With the exception of the interlude and the masks at the end, this play is technically very simple. The plot is simple and it is very much about the observations the students make about each other and Venice. It is reflective and inward-looking. The focus should be on language, its delivery and the performance energy. It is vital to be precise with the internal music. You have to find it for the play to sound right. If actors start paraphrasing you can't hear it and it doesn't feel right.

Nick Dear began with the idea of a group of students in Venice. He played around with the idea of archetypal *commedia dell'arte c*haracters – the young daughter and old father, the doctor, the young lovers, the funny servant, etc. He could not make it work, however, since it was too restrictive: it was a world that didn't feel truthful and therefore limited him telling the story he wanted to tell. The interlude, where the *commedia* troupe appears, should be a moment of physical release and one that serves to lift the play. But don't be tempted to make this a bigger moment than the playwright has intended because it will spoil the rhythm of the piece.

A central question is: just how dead are the characters? More importantly, the revelation that they are dead must surprise the audience. There should therefore be no physical indication, such as white make-up. Masks should not be used until the end, since it would spoil the killer image, one that is moving, weird and wonderful. Don't reveal too much too soon – but how you choose to portray death is up for grabs.

An act of terrorism in a beautiful place, where young, vital people are killed, is terribly shocking. The shock value of the play is that it could happen anywhere. This is one of the notions that the play throws up – and the young people take it very calmly. When we learn that they are dead, the graphic detail is intended to shock, but they also move swiftly to: 'So, more pizza?'

There are key moments where the characters become unsettled and where their after-life state is hinted at. Harley from his first line tells the audience that everything is not entirely in the realm of naturalism. You'll need to consider how to deliver the speeches to the audience. How casual is it? How formal? Do they step forward?

Harley is a very detailed character and you will need to look at his dialogue line by line. Nick sees him as the 'cool swat' – he has read up on Carpaccio, but he is not always right.

Nick didn't discover Carpaccio's work until some years ago when he went to the Scuola and found it one of those places (like Iona) where one feels some sort of religious connection. All the paintings at the Scuola had been commissioned by Guilds, formed by Slavs who were trading partners with the Venetians. Nick decided to use Carpaccio because he really liked his work and wanted the characters to have the same buzz about him. He could imagine his own teenage son finding something/ someone he really liked and feeling compelled to share his enthusiasm with those around him.

The Italian language in the play should become the young people's perceptions of how it is. It doesn't matter if it is not perfect, but it nonetheless needs to be unfaltering and fluent. They should use it without fear. To help with this we have prepared a glossary of pronunciation that is included at the end of these notes.

Nick chose the 'Winter' section of *The Four Seasons* at the end of the play because this little piece is heart-rendingly sad: the choice is therefore entirely because of how the piece sounds rather than it being anything to do with winter. His choice was also motivated by Vivaldi being a significant and well-known Venetian composer, one who interestingly established and ran an orchestra at a girls' orphanage. Although Vivaldi remains enormously popular in Venice, his music has become rather debased and diluted by being played endlessly in shops and to call-centre customers on hold.

In terms of the play, an event *has* happened – but what *is* happening as the story is told is that the characters are dealing with both this event and their own relationships. The title of the play tells us what is happening, and dramatic interest is enhanced through watching characters having lunch and engaging with them.

Look at pictures and perhaps the recent BBC series about Venice. It would also be worthwhile watching Joseph Losey's *Don Giovanni* and the films *Death in Venice* and *Don't Look Now*.

EXPLORING THE TEXT

The play could be done in the round or end on. Very little scenery is required, and clever lighting could achieve all that is needed to create necessary dramatic effects. It is useful to have something for the actors to lean against or sit on. Perhaps steps?

Think about what can be done with lighting at the top of the play to create the right atmosphere. Maybe create the effect of sunlight or a window effect. It's important that the five characters are not always on a level. Nearly every square in Venice has a circular well, and this motif should be used as an evocation of Venice as well as providing something for actors to sit on or climb up. The minimum is needed to suggest Venice, so make it right; the characters are in tourist mode, so will be especially tuned in to things Venetian. In this context you should avoid using chairs.

It's clear by looking at the dialogue that the characters need to walk on at the beginning – they have just been given pizza. If they are already sitting down it becomes unclear. It is safe to assume that they haven't been in the square before.

From this opening, find ways to establish individual characters, to differentiate them from each other, by their response to this new place for example. Maybe Harley is looking around, taking in the architecture? Maybe Conrad is dragging behind – disaffected, feeling marginalised? Think about the point at which they start to sit. Perhaps after 'what lovely people'?

Within half a page of dialogue Harley is speaking to the audience, and therefore needs to pull focus. Maybe he remains standing while the others sit, or maybe he begins to speak as he is sitting down and secures focus by so doing. While he speaks to the audience, Conrad comments on this. We should therefore assume that the others can hear what is being said to the audience, and that they *know* there is an audience.

It might be useful for them to gaze up at the pictures; Bianca could be more focused on Harley and the romance. These moments are important because they start to build up the characters' back-stories, and in addition are an important part of achieving intimacy with the audience – the sharing of intimate moments from their lives.

Actors are talking directly to the audience. If the text was confrontational, you would encourage actors to attack the audience with their energy. In this case, however, the actors need to *engage* with the audience – they need to draw the audience's energy in.

Think about the food business – pizza on a tray versus a fantastic meal. Emmy's entrance immediately identifies her as someone who loves food and establishes character even before she says anything. When Ben says, 'Hi Emmy. Got enough to eat?' decide who responds to this. Who hears? Is Bianca lost in her moment? Is she aware of Emmy, but not watching?

Look at Emmy's lines:

> (*to us*) I'm more interested in my lunch. (*to the boys*) Are we going to get pizza again or are we going to a proper restaurant?

It must be clear to audience that the first line means 'I *was* more interested in my lunch,' and that the pizza line is a flashback to when they were in the Scuola. But here, time is fluid – it moves in and out of the past and present. It's important to pin this down and be clear about it. What must also be consistent is that when characters come onto the stage they are entering the square.

The students know each other, but they are not necessarily bosom buddies. It is a forced intimacy rather than an established group. But each of them has a reputation (for Harley, art and name-dropping) and a label, which would imply that they know each other a bit.

Nick is very clear that he doesn't want leaden naturalism in the play; in other words, didn't want to *mimic* how teenagers speak. He refuses to believe that teenagers aren't interested in art. The language is deliberately dense and high-flown and the audience should be wondering why. Nick wants the play to be a headlong challenge to our expectations of what teenagers eating pizza are going to be talking about.

Conrad lightens up as he develops and grows through the play: he has the longest journey of any of the characters.

In Bianca's speech to the audience, 'We're meant to have four seasons,' she should be soliciting audience response in a way that should be quite disconcerting. Through this section there is a sense that they are in stasis – nothing else is going to happen. Yet there is a contradiction as Emmy and Ben move closer to each other. There is a sense of endless replay – a kind of *Groundhog Day* element.

Harley's speech, 'This is how it's always going to be . . .' is a sudden realisation. He's going from sublime to slightly grumpy.

In terms of the arrival of the acrobats, don't be tempted to use them elsewhere in the play, this is a moment that should only last about two minutes. They are performing solely for our group of characters and it is important that there are no other people/passers-by on the stage. It is also important that the *commedia* troupe are not seen to be performing for the audience – they must stay in the world of the play. They should therefore not invite any audience participation. Use drum and accordion here if you can, and make it lively. The acrobats could also be dead, but this is up to you. They shouldn't be stylised or spooky – indeed they are very physical and should do as much and be as raucous as possible, energising the stage with vibrancy, colour and life. Their costumes should make visual reference to *commedia*.

Think of the play as an extended argument and look at every line as part of that argument. For instance, in the long discussion between Harley and Ben about art and war, there is the danger of too much generalised emotion – get actors to stick to the argument. They need to listen and worry about the other person, and to decide what effect their dialogue is having on other characters. If you can get the level of the argument right, then the emotions will naturally emerge.

Vivi is the outsider and it is very important that we get the sense that she is considerably older than the others. Her entrance is an opportunity for the audience to hear exactly what has happened. The students are quite matter-of-fact, as if they quite enjoy the telling of events. There is no bitterness, anger or emotion, which would indicate that they have adjusted to the situation.

Vivi shouldn't be too upset – or if she is it is internalised. She therefore shouldn't be sobbing and wailing. It is important to keep these extreme moments as truthful and specific. Get the actors to recall receiving bad news and remember how it felt. Share this with the other actors.

The intention is that Vivi has had a near-death/life experience. She was close to being revived, hovering on that borderline between life and death. If she had managed to get the boat back to the Hotel Bauer she would be alive. Her running around trying to find the boat serves as an image of purgatory.

The language the students use when describing the bomb is high-flown – as before in the sections about art. Work on the principle that because they are dead they know things that they didn't when they were alive. This is the point when the audience find out what is going on, and it is important not to overwhelm them by being tempted to make this a stylised moment. Keep it clear.

With Vivi, Nick wanted to write a character in contrast to the students. He wanted to indicate that the bomb affected more people than just the group we have come to know, and to suggest, therefore, that terrorism is indiscriminate. For instance, having money is irrelevant since it won't save you. He has introduced a character who has more experience of the world than the students, one who is more acutely aware of what she/they will miss.

The actor playing this part could be older. If she is not, she needs to realise the age difference – it would help to base the character on someone outside her own social group. When not playing your own age, it is easy to caricature, but in terms of playing this role, the more real, the more moving it will be.

Don't overload the imagery at the end of the play. The masks/music/dance are already powerful. Finishing a play is always difficult. It is important to think about the emotional effect on the audience. The mood here is lyrical and poignant, and this must not undermine the potency. Use of cinematic projection, for instance, could become an ending too many. There are only about five to seven minutes between the audience finding out that the characters are dead and the end of the play. They should be reeling and in need of the musical pause.

The dance should be stylish, expressive and well worked – perhaps with a period feel to it. Think about what can be done with lighting at this point. It might be interesting to focus down from the group to the dancers to the masks before fading.

WORKING WITH THE ACTORS

This is what happened when Lindsay worked on sections of the play with young actors:

He asked them to enter and try the opening section on the floor, to think about having been given free pizza and also who might be particularly interested in their surroundings.

After a few different versions, it was clear that something was missing. The actors needed to come in talking to each other in order to give the top of the play an energy as well as a sense of having arrived from somewhere. Therefore Bianca probably needs to enter first.

He reminded the actors not to let lines trail off, to think of passing a baton that is dropped if they have no energy at the end of the line. Also do not drop cues: have the thought *on* the line rather than before the line. The audience do not want to watch the line twice, since it drags the energy down. On entrances and exits – unless there is a reason for a pause – move *on* the line. You don't want dead playing time. He asked actors to move onto the stage with performance energy and purpose – charged with thought and the reason for coming on.

Harley begins his speech to the audience by being very direct: 'Well . . . I don't know where to start . . .' The line gets the audience's attention. Lindsay normally begins the rehearsal process with a week devoted to discussing the play line by line to find out what exactly is happening. For example, the opening line is *gripping*. Later in the speech Harley is *engaging* the audience – this is a version of 'actioning'. The virtue of this is that it makes everyone absolutely specific and clear about how tone can change within a speech or even a line. Harley needs to make his speech an anecdote and must develop the stepping stones of the argument to draw the audience in.

Looking at the early section between Bianca and Harley, maybe Bianca should be physically nearer to Harley from the beginning so that their relationship becomes clear.

You need to decide on the level of closeness. Nick feels that Bianca's eyes should never leave Harley.

When Bianca says, 'I loved him from that moment on,' she should move towards Harley. This also has the effect of pulling focus for her line.

Harley needs to acknowledge her line in some (small) way without interrupting his flow. You will need to think about whether they should embrace or be touching. Lindsay suggests doing some improvisations around infatuation to help realise this relationship.

Lindsay asks the actors to obey the punctuation and go for the italics. He stresses how necessary it is for actors to play *through* the line – otherwise the audience get ahead of you!

Looking at how to manage the pizza-eating: it rarely works for an actor to speak with their mouth full, so these sections need to be worked out technically/phrased. Rehearse with food – perhaps toast – to help with this. The audience obviously have to be able to hear.

Listening is very conspicuous in this play. The actors need to be very aware of each other. It's really important that they don't *act* listening – to signal or demonstrate this to the audience. Stress that listening is very interesting to watch and that the young actors need to have the courage to *really* listen.

Being 'in the moment' is also vital. The actors must summon up their imagination to make us believe that things are happening for the first time in order to keep the stakes high. If the actors are instead anticipating what is going to happen/be said, then the play becomes automatic and lifeless. Get the actors to swap parts. Have them tell a story, then tell it back. Then do this with the dialogue

The debate about art and war is the most heated part of the play. What is the argument? Art is vital. Art is useless. Two extremes. It is a row about ideas, and it is very important that the actors really understand what they are fighting for. Both have positions that they can defend. It is also important to remember that the audience *don't know* that this argument is inflamed and coloured by the fact that they have been blown up.

Throughout this section, Ben needs to be strong and passionate – challenging the audience to remember. All the actors need to pick up their cues to keep the energy of the argument.

Emmy's line 'I'm sure you're not,' in response to Ben's 'I feel impotent,' is supportive of Ben in a way that marks a new beat in their relationship. Although there is a *double entendre* in her response it may not be helpful to play it. In Ben's response – 'I am' – what are the actions? Squashing her? Dismissive? Silencing her? If this line is played strongly enough, it can hang in the air. Then a beat and a new strand to the argument.

'And it feels like the only thing we make now is war. We export war and we import war.' Persuading? Educating? Enlisting? Reminding? 'It's the only thing we are good at.' Lambasting? Embittering? Enraging? Harley's response: 'Men have always made war. The Venetians made war with the Turks for centuries! It doesn't make art unimportant!' Countering/withstanding? Topping/beating? Deriding?

'Oh, that's insane, Ben!' Needling/puncturing. Harley really believes this and feels Ben is being utopian. War is in human nature and art is the only meaningful thing.

Conrad: 'What's wrong with a nice war?' Stirring? He is trying to wind them up, illustrating the position of ingrained cynicism in society about challenging or changing the status quo.

Harley: 'So if nothing ever changes, why can't we paint pictures? Write songs?' Harley is a fatalist and a realist, as opposed to utopian or cynical. He believes that it is pointless to make judgements on art of five hundred years ago based on what we believe today.

Ben: 'All your precious Venetian art glorifies war! Glorifies suffering!' This is the introduction of a new concept and awakens Harley but he remains logical: 'Most of it glorifies God.' But Ben is more fluent – he is running this argument. Think of Ben as serving and Harley returning. Conrad's 'Or the Doge. In his palace,' marks him out as someone who has really looked at the pictures.

At the end of the argument Ben needs physically to take his energy away somewhere. The ideas in this speech are based on the pictures that they have been looking at. They have all been exposed to these and to the new ideas that they have brought up. Action this whole section to help with the clarity of the argument.

Nick was asked if Ben is a reluctant art student. He feels Ben is passionate about seeing, and thinks he may be the one with the real brain, seeing him as someone who reads a lot. He is interested, but at the same time feels that too much of the art we put on a pedestal was about encouraging people to fight the Turks. In seven hundred years of Venetian history, where Christianity is bound up with warfare, there are very few paintings without Christian symbolism. It is also worth considering whether his stance has changed because they have been blown up. What he also leaves unsaid is that he doesn't want to use art to change the world.

Encourage the actors to have a go at anything. It is important to keep working/changing – in this section (as with the rest of the play) what felt right in week one may not be right by week three of rehearsal. Also encourage actors to commit one hundred per cent to what they are doing – i.e. *turn* if they are going to turn, etc. A useful exercise would be to take the argument over the top – by allowing actors to insert swear words and improvise. This would help to create the personal element, make it feel real and raise the stakes. It is always important to discuss with the other actors what they are doing or thinking. For instance, would Conrad try to enlist the girls or does he just keep dropping in jokes? Does Bianca find Conrad funny? Is she interested in him? That said, Conrad would probably adopt a position that is non-threatening and uninvolved.

When rehearsing this section – focus initially on the argument and before Ben and Harley. This is the bedrock. When the rhythm of the argument is established, the inner music of the play emerges. Then look at the rest of the stage picture. Give the scene its backbone, and then put on the flesh. In order to put detail in, ask actors to observe people listening to an argument. It is important that they avoid *reacting* acting.

During the argument section you could use diagonals. Make eye contact – draw in energy from other actors and convey it to the audience. Physically, you should always avoid straight lines – backs are interesting, and sometimes in emotional scenes it is more interesting when we cannot see the actors' faces. Young untrained voices aren't always strong enough to be heard when facing away from the audience, so build voice work into the rehearsal period.

When young actors sit down on the floor it can easily become static as they need a big impetus to get them back off the floor and moving. Don't feel the need to keep it moving. Use moments of displacement activity. For instance – who has the water? Go and get it from them. Get something from a bag. Someone has the sun in their eyes, move into the shade.

It's worth emphasising that the play does not need a lot of movement, otherwise we will lose the image of people having their lunch. Economy and stillness are, by and large, a great thing.

THE EXPLOSION SEQUENCE

The language in this section shifts the play into a different key. It is deliberately nasty, brutal and shocking and should make the audience react.

When Vivi enters she should be dehydrated and faint. But don't demonstrate or signal this to the audience. Get the actor playing Vivi to observe this process and concentrate on what the person is trying to *stop* themselves from doing. When Vivi says that she is lunching at the Hotel Bauer, it is a difficult moment since they all know she is dead. Who is going to tell her?

It is interesting that it is Conrad who is brave enough to take control here: 'The thing is, I don't think you are.' He is levelling with her and trying to be sensitive. He wants to befriend her before he tells her everything in detail. This illustrates that Conrad's defensive attitude may not really reveal who he is underneath. It's important to play the delicacy of the situation, but don't lose the energy – he is still leading her through the story.

Ben's line 'I've got it. I think she was borderline,' is challenged by Vivi. She is trying not to panic. Conrad has to talk her through what it means. In order to prepare for this, the actor playing Vivi needs to imagine what she can remember and what she is trying to block out. It might help to create a dream for Vivi and work out what encroaches. Then have an image to draw on.

After Vivi says, 'And what about you?' there needs to be a beat as Emmy realises what she is asking. Vivi's 'Dead?' needs to be the top of this exchange.

There is a gear change when Bianca talks to the audience: 'It was quick. I'll say that for explosions. They're quick.' She is giving the audience a tough lesson. It is immediately less casual and should be unsettling and disturbing for the audience. We have arrived at what the play is about. This is the key for the audience – remember that they don't know what has happened.

After Vivi says, 'Oh my God . . .' she stops hearing what the others are saying. And the others take what they are saying out to the audience. Then back to Vivi when she asks, 'Did you hear screams?'

From 'There's a wave' the focus should be on informing Vivi. The language is so harsh here it is necessary to push it: it does need a sharper energy and faster rhythm.

THE ENDING

Vivi's speeches lead to her weeping.

It's tricky when a stage direction indicates that a character should weep, and important for the director to create the physical circumstances/conditions under which an actor can feel upset. Be aware that this often happens late in the rehearsal process, when the play has found the right emotional pitch. Would Vivi release her emotion easily? It might be in spite of herself, and she might be trying to keep it as private as possible. It might be most helpful for the actor to think of trying to stop herself from crying.

Vivi should have a large number of bags, and should have to hunt through them to find the masks. Then they could be wrapped in tissue paper. It is important that we do not see them too early. She should certainly be specific about choosing one for Harley. Use half-masks (otherwise we will not be able to hear what the actors are saying).

Once the masks are on, perhaps everything should take on a formality that is neither modern nor naturalistic.

When we come to the dance, we need to remember that Bianca and Harley will be in love for eternity. They should be looking at each other and the dance should be both intimate and elegant. Look at the dancing in Joseph Losey's *Don Giovanni*.

Bianca's line to Harley 'You look divine' is elevating and adoring. Harley responds and joins her on that pedestal. Ben and Emmy need to move away to watch the dance and Conrad with Vivi. The physical activity needs to be phased so that each part of the story is told in a focused way. After Conrad's last speech, he should move away and watch. Then perhaps a lighting change such as a spot on the dancers that focuses down while the music swells. This is a lyrical moment, and after the horror of what has happened it is a bittersweet image.

Think carefully about which mask to use for each character. Conrad at this point becomes a spokesperson for the play. He is the last one left after they have all gone somewhere else. He must be the last one to get a mask.

Vivi's line, 'Not here. Not now,' needs to be planted and filled with a sense of what has happened. Conrad is moved by what she says to him.

GLOSSARY

Palazzi (puh-LAHTZ-ee) – palaces

Campo (CAMP-o) – open area; square

Carpaccio (car-PACH-ee-o) – Italian painter from Venice, active in the late fifteenth to early sixteenth century

Scuola di San Giorgio degli Schiavoni (SKWO-la dee san GEORGE-ee-o dell-ee ski-ah-VO-nee] the building in Venice that housed the brotherhood of Dalmatia

Chiaroscuro (kee-AR-o SKOO-ro) – a style of art that focuses on the contrasts between light and dark

Rigatoni con sugo (rig-a-TONE-y con SUE-go) – rigatoni pasta with sauce

Fegato alla veneziana (FAYG-uh-toe alla ven-etz-ee-AH-na) – calf's liver with onions, often served with polenta

Doge (DOH-juh) – duke; the ruler of Venice when it was a republic (during medieval/Renaissance times)

Prosecco (pro-SECK-o) – a sparkling wine originally from the Venice region

Aeroporto Marco Polo (air-o-PORT-o MARK-o PO-lo) – airport serving Venice

Basilica (bah-SILL-uh-kah) – ref. to Basilica di San Marco, probably the most famous church in Venice

Salute (suh-LOO-tay) – ref. to Santa Maria della Salute, a large church in Venice

Giudecca (ju-DECK-uh) – one of the islands in the Venetian lagoons

Lido (LEE-doh) – one of the islands in the Venetian lagoons

Funghi (FOON-ghee) – mushrooms

Tintoretto (teen-tuh-RET-toe) – an Italian painter from Venice active in the mid-sixteenth century

Quattro Stagioni (KWA-tro sta-JOE-nee) – literally 'four seasons'; a type of pizza in which each quarter slice contains a different set of toppings

Bellini (bell-LEE-nee) – cocktail involving peaches and *prosecco*; invented at Harry's bar in Venice

Gnochetti (nyo-KEH-tee) – a type of dry pasta that resembles gnocchi

Gamberetti (gam-buh-RET-tee) – shrimp

Contorno (con-TOR-no) – vegetable side-dish

Radicchio (ra-DEEK-ee-o) – red cabbage

Baverese alla pera con crema di cachi e castagne (bav-uh-RAY-zay alla PAY-rah con CRAYM-uh dee KAH-ki ay cas-TAN-yay) – pear with persimmons and chestnuts; a dish particular to Venice

La Serenissima (la sair-uh-NEE-see-muh) – another name for Venice

Quattrocento (KWA-tro CHEN-to) – literally 'four hundred', but most often used to refer to the 1400s (the beginnings of the Renaissance)

Lepanto (lay-PAHN-toe) – a gulf in Greece where a major battle was fought during the Crusades, in which the Christians defeated the Moors

Vaporetto (va-po-RAY-toe) – a kind of 'bus boat' that transports people in Venice

Parmigiano (par-me-JAH-no) – parmesan cheese

Capricciosa (cap-ree-CHO-suh) – type of pizza (ingredients vary depending on restaurant, but may include olives, mushrooms, artichoke hearts, and ham)

Rialto (ree-ALL-toe) – the Rialto Bridge, the most famous and recognisable bridge in Venice

> *Workshop facilitated by Lindsay Posner*
> *with notes taken by Paula Hamilton*

MUGGED

Andrew Payne

Characters

Dig
Marky
Mel
Soph
Leon
Taylor
Newsreaders
TV Reporter
Gawpers
Police Officer
Vicar

ONE

Two park benches facing the audience, as far apart as the stage allows. Between the benches, a beaten-up rubbish bin with more rubbish lying around it than in it, and a sign: ALBION PARK. PART OF THE ALBION COUNCIL GREEN SPACE INITIATIVE. NO BALL GAMES, NO CYCLING, *though little of this may be legible as the sign is heavily marked with graffiti.*

Off, a police siren comes and goes.

Enter Dig, a scruffy kid carrying a bag or backpack. Eating from a giant bag of crisps almost as big as he is. Jumps on the left-hand bench. (Left and right are from the audience's point of view throughout.)

Dig stands on tiptoe, peers over the heads of the audience for a moment or two, then jumps down, sits. Eats crisps.

Enter Marky, spectacularly scruffy, also carrying a bag. Drinking a giant milkshake.

All the characters attend the same school. Whatever else they're wearing, they all have white shirts and school ties, the ties knotted in various bizarre ways.

Dig Alright?
Marky Alright?

Marky jumps on the left-hand bench, goes through the same routine as Dig, peering over the audience.

Dig Are they there?
Marky No.

Marky jumps down, sits next to Dig. A beat while Marky drinks milkshake through the straw and Dig eats crisps.

Breakfast, the most important meal of the day.

They swap. Marky eats crisps, Dig sucks on the straw – and gets a surprise.

Dig (*appalled*) Oh man!

Marky Good, or what?

Dig That is disgusting! What is it?

Marky You get a chocolate milkshake, drink half of it, top it up with Coke.

Dig Oh man! It went up my nose!

Marky I haven't decided what to call it yet.

Dig How about 'Puke'? How about 'Puke Up Your Nose'?

Marky You love it really.

Dig has another drink.

Dig Actually, that is wicked.

Marky Told you.

They swap back. Eat, drink.

Dig This is bad, what we're eating. We're going to be a health statistic.

Marky No, this is good. Protein, carbohydrates, vitamin C.

Dig Chemicals. Preservatives.

Marky I've got a theory about preservatives.

Dig What?

Marky They put preservatives in food to make it last longer, right.

Dig So?

Marky So why shouldn't they make *us* last longer?

Dig Brilliant.

Marky All the crap we eat, we'll probably live for ever.

Dig Brilliant, Marky.

Marky I rest my case.

Dig checks his watch.

Dig It's ten past. We ought to go if we're going round.
Marky Are they there?

Dig gets up on the bench, peers into the distance.

Dig No.
Marky We'll go across, then. Plenty of time.

Dig sits back down.

Dig We ought to go round the park, Marky, just in case.
If you're late again, you're going to get suspended.
Marky There's plenty of time if we go across.

Beat.

Dig The last time I got mugged, my mum didn't believe
me. She thought I made it up to get more money off
her. And I've only got two quid today.
Marky Alright, alright, we'll go *round*, okay?
Dig We ought to go then, it takes longer.
Marky Dig, man, relax, there's loads of time. (*Beat.*) You
get anything?
Dig Yeah.

*Dig rummages in his backback. Takes out a small box,
hands it to Marky.*

From the art shop.
Marky Cool. What is it?
Dig It's like a special art knife. For cutting stuff. You
know, art stuff.
Marky Cool.

Marky hands the box back.

Dig I thought there were felt-tips in it but I didn't have
time to look. The bloke in there, he's really suspicious.
What about you?

Marky rummages in his backpack, produces a pack of fags.

Marky Twenty Marlboro.

Dig Swap you.

Marky You don't smoke, Dig.

Dig Neither do you!

Marky That's not the point!

Dig Twenty Marlboro for a special art knife! It's a brilliant deal!

Marky Dig, man, I don't do art! And you don't smoke!

Dig Well, maybe I'm going to start!

Marky Why would you want to do that?

Dig Because I'm stressed!

Marky (*bewildered*) What are you stressed about?

Dig Everything. School, home – and *them*!

Dig points into the distance, over the audience.

Marky The muggers aren't there today.

Dig So they'll be there tomorrow! Or the day after! Come on, Marky! A special art knife for twenty fags! What's your problem?

Marky What do you want them for?

Dig I told you, I'll probably smoke them.

Marky No you won't, you want to give them to Soph.

Dig (*embarrassed*) Shut up, Marky.

Marky Admit you want to give them to Soph, then I'll swap.

Dig Alright. Give us them, then.

Marky You got to say it, man!

Dig I want to give them to Soph, alright?

Marky Well, I don't want to stand in the way of your future happiness.

They swap.

Though frankly, Dig, speaking as your friend, I don't think twenty Marlboro is going to do it. Of all the doomed relationships in the world, you and Soph are *so* doomed.

Dig I know.

Off, the sound of girls singing, laughing. And a boy's voice. Loud, assertive.

Shit, it's Taylor.

They hurriedly hide the knife and fags in their bags.
   Taylor enters, followed by Mel and Soph. Mel and Soph arm in arm, singing something current. Doesn't matter if they're any good. Both carrying phones, Soph texting as she sings.
   Taylor could be older than Dig and Marky, could be the same age. Whatever, he's bigger. Better dressed, full of himself.
   Soph and Mel also seem older than Marky and Dig.
   Taylor jumps on the right-hand bench, has a quick look into the distance, then jumps down, goes over to Dig and Marky on the left-hand bench.

Taylor Oi, off my bench, knobheads.

Dig I thought *that* was your bench.

Taylor It was, yesterday. Today, *this* is my bench.

Dig reluctantly gets to his feet, clutching his crisps and his bag. Marky doesn't move.

Marky Actually, Tayl, these benches are the property of the local council, therefore legally belonging to all of us –

Taylor grabs Marky and drags him roughly off the bench.

Taylor Off, you little dosser. I'm not in the mood for you this morning.

Marky Alright, alright. Watch the jacket, would you, it's Gucci.

Taylor slumps on the left-hand bench. Marky and Dig
shuffle over to the right-hand bench, passing Mel and
Soph, who are making their way to join Taylor.

Marky Alright, Mel?
Mel Alright, Marky?
Dig Alright, Soph?
Soph (*as she texts*) Looking good, Dig.
Dig Thanks.
Soph I'm lying.
Dig I know.
Marky Devastating repartee, Dig.
Dig I know.

Mel sits down next to Taylor, who flings a
proprietorial arm round her.
Marky and Dig sit on the right-hand bench. Soph,
still texting, sits on the left-hand bench. Mel shoves
Taylor off, climbs onto the bench, peers into the
distance.

Dig (*to Mel*) Anyone there?
Mel No.

Mel gets down, sits. Checks her watch.

Mel (*to Soph*) We ought to go.
Soph (*still texting*) There's loads of time.
Marky (*to Mel*) Hey, Mel. We're going across the park.
Want to come with us?
Dig (*worried*) No we're not, we're going round!
Marky (*ignoring him*) Hey, Soph, we're going across this
morning. If you want to come, me and Dig will look
after you.

Soph, Mel and Taylor laugh.

Taylor That's funny, man.
Dig (*worried*) We're not going across, we're going round!

Soph (*to Mel, holding up her phone*) The wanker won't
answer me.

Mel Wanker.

Dig (*to Taylor*) Hey, Tayl. You going across?

*Taylor gets up, struts over to Marky and Dig on the
right-hand bench.*

Taylor Why, want me to protect you from the *gangsters*?

Dig No.

Taylor Want me to hold your girlie hands?

Marky No thanks, Tayl, you're not my type.

Dig (*to Taylor*) Seriously, Tayl, are you going across?
'Cos we're going to be late.

Taylor I'm not going anywhere, man, I've got a free
lesson.

Marky No you haven't, you've got Mr Gillespie.

Taylor Same thing.

Marky How come Mr Gillespie never suspends *you*?

Taylor 'Cos I turn up *enough*. You *never* turn up. That's
the difference. It's politics, man. See what I'm saying?
That's why I'm going to be rich and you're going to be
a dosser.

Taylor does a pathetic wino shuffle across the stage.

Big Ishoo! *Big Ishoo*!

Marky (*to Dig*) He's hilarious, isn't he?

The refrain is taken up by Soph and Mel.

Taylor *Big Ishoo*! Help the poor dosser! *Big Ishoo*!

*During this, Dig stands on the right-hand bench, peers
into the distance.*

Dig They're there!

*This shuts everyone up and has them standing on the
benches immediately.*

Mel Where?
Dig There. By the playground.
Soph That's not them.
Taylor That's some old geezer.
Dig No, not him. Over *there*.
Mel Where?
Marky There's no one there, Dig.

They all get down except Dig, who's still looking.

Dig I'm sure I saw them.

Enter Leon. Big as Taylor. A bully. Struts to left-hand bench and Taylor, Mel and Soph.

Taylor Alright, Leon?
Leon Alright, Tayl?
Soph Hey, Leon . . .

Soph gets up and confronts Leon.

I was texting you all last night!
Leon So?
Soph Where were you?
Leon I was busy.
Soph Busy? Busy doing what?
Leon Stuff.
Soph What stuff?
Leon Just stuff, alright, girl?
Marky (*to Dig*) Hasn't he got a way with words?
Dig Yeah, it's poetry.
Marky You can't compete with poetry, Dig.
Dig No way.

Leon walks over to the right-hand bench, looms threateningly over Marky and Dig.

Leon What?

Leon looms threateningly over Dig and Marky.

388

Dig/Marky Nothing, Leon.
Leon Give us a crisp, then.

Leon grabs Dig's big bag of crisps, now about half full, and takes a big handful. Dig gets off the bench, tries to get them back.

Dig Give 'em back, Leon.

Leon backs away, ducking and dodging, as Dig makes half-hearted attempts to grab the crisps. Leon stuffing his mouth to overflowing as he taunts Dig.

Leon Umm, delicious!
Dig You're wasting them –
Leon (*spraying crisps*) Umm, my favourite!

Dig makes a last attempt to grab the bag. Leon crumples it in his hands, crushing the remaining crisps, chucks the bag away.
    Taylor, Mel and Soph laugh.
    Dig retrieves the bag, peers inside. Crestfallen.

Dig Thanks, Leon –
Soph Hey, got any fags, Tayl?
Taylor No.

Leon grabs Dig.

Leon (*searching him*) Got any fags?
Dig No –
Leon You sure?
Marky He doesn't smoke, Leon.
Leon (*to Marky*) Keep your dosser nose out of it.
Marky You shouldn't either, it'll restrict your growth, it'll restrict the growth of your knob which in your case will be a disaster, 'cos you already need a high-power microscope to find it –

Leon drops Dig and grabs Marky, throws him on the ground.

389

Leon You'd better show some respect, you pikey little knobhead –

Leon jumps on top of Marky, hits him. Marky yells in pain. Dig hovers nervously.

Dig Leave him alone, Leon.
Mel/Soph Yeah, leave him alone.

Leon goes through Marky's pockets.

Leon Fifty p? That all you got, you loser?

Leon gives Marky one last thump and gets off him. Marky lies on the ground. Leon turns on Dig.

Leon Got any money?
Dig No.
Leon Liar.

He grabs Dig.

Mel Leave him alone, Leon. Tell him to leave him alone, Soph.
Soph It's nothing to do with me . . .

Soph gets up, goes over to shout in Leon's face.

I DON'T CARE WHAT HE DOES ANY MORE!

Leon ignores her. Soph flounces over to the right-hand bench and sits. Leon shakes Dig.

Leon How much?
Dig Two quid.
Leon Gimme.

Dig reluctantly gropes in his pocket, Leon holding on to him, and takes out some coins. Hands them to Leon.
 Marky, on the ground, sits up.

Marky You should do something about this violent behaviour, Leon. You should discuss it with your therapist.

Leon (*puzzled*) Therapist? I haven't got a therapist.

Marky I rest my case.

Leon raises his fist.

Leon Want some more?

Marky No thank you, Leon, thanks very much for the kind offer – aaah!

As Leon hits him anyway, then turns to Soph, who's still sitting on the right-hand bench.

Leon Come here.

Soph I'm not talking to you! Hey, Mel, let's go, we're going to be late.

Leon Come here, bitch!

Soph/Mel (*furious*) Don't call me that!/Don't call her that!

Leon I'm sorry, my love, my dearest darling, please come and sit down with me on the other bench . . .

Leon extends his hand. Soph reluctantly takes it, stands.

Bitch!

Taylor laughs. Soph tries to hit Leon.

Soph Dickhead!

But Soph still allows herself to be led to the left-hand bench, where Mel tussles angrily with Taylor. Soph and Leon sit next to them, Soph pushing and and pulling angrily at Leon. The tussling between the two couples becomes more flirtatious.

Marky and Dig watch this from the right-hand bench, sharing the last of Marky's milkshake.

Dig I don't get it. Why do they like those arseholes?

Marky I've got a theory about that.

Dig What?

Marky It's their dads.

Dig What do you mean?

Marky Girls, right, if their dad treats them like shit, they think that's normal. So if you're nice to them, they think you're weird.

Dig You mean Mel likes Tayl because he's like her dad?

Marky That's my theory.

Dig And Soph likes Leon because *he's* like *her* dad? You're joking!

Marky Not *exactly* like him, knobhead. Just bits. Certain aspects of behaviour. Mind you, I've never met Soph's dad. Or Mel's, for that matter. Thank fuck.

Dig What about us?

Marky Same thing. Down to our mums.

Dig That is so total bollocks! I like Soph and she isn't like my mum!

Marky On the contrary, there are many similarities.

A spat flares up on the left-hand bench between Soph and Leon. Soph gets to her feet, hurling abuse at Leon: 'Dickhead!' etc.

Dig My mum ignores me. When she's not ignoring me, she shouts at me.

Soph looks over, sees Marky and Dig watching her.

Soph (*to Marky and Dig, shouting*) What are you looking at, dickheads?

Marky I *so* rest my case.

Dig You're wrong, man. Watch.

Dig gets the cigarettes out of his backpack, goes over to the left-hand bench.

Hey, Soph. Do you want some fags?

Soph (*suspicious*) You what?

Dig offers her the Marlboro.

Dig Do you want these? I don't need them.
Soph You sure?
Dig Go on.
Soph (*shrugs*) Alright.

Soph takes the cigarettes.

Taylor You got to give him something in return, Soph.
Soph Get lost, Tayl.
Taylor Twenty Marlboro, got to be worth a handjob.

Leon laughs, high-fives Taylor.

Soph Pig! (*to Dig*) Thanks, Dig –

*Impulsively, Soph kisses Dig, much to Dig's surprise.
Laughs, jeers etc. from Mel and Taylor. Leon is pissed
off.*

Taylor Aah. How sweet is that?
Mel Yeuch, she kissed a dosser!

*Leon aims a kick at Dig as he walks back to the right-
hand bench.*

Leon Get out of here!

Dig sits down next to Marky.

Dig (*to Marky*) See? I was nice to her and she didn't
think it was weird.
Marky Trust me, she did.

Leon gets up, goes over to the right-hand bench.

Leon You told me you didn't have any fags.
Dig I forgot.
Leon Where d'you get them from?
Dig Bought them.

Leon Lying little dosser. You've been thieving again, haven't you?

Dig No!

Leon What else you got?

Dig Nothing.

Soph Leave him alone, Leon.

Leon (*to Marky*) What about you, *Big Ishoo*. You been nicking stuff too? (*pointing at his bag*) Got any goodies in there?

Marky No, nothing.

Leon Let's have a look then.

Leon grabs Marky's bag. They wrestle with it for a beat or two.

Soph (*looking at her watch*) Ohmygod, ohmygod!

Leon What?

Distracted, Leon lets go of Marky's bag.

Soph The time! Shit! I've got to go! I'm supposed to get in early to help Miss Ransom! She'll kill me! Mel, you coming?

Mel Yeah, I'm coming.

Marky You going across, Soph?

Soph Course we are.

Marky We'll come with you.

Dig We're going round, Marky!

Marky It's too late now, we'll have to go across. It's alright, we'll go with Soph and Mel.

Dig *They'll* be alright, 'cos the muggers don't pick on *them*, they only pick on *us*!

Taylor Yeah, 'cos you're *kids*, man. Little kids.

Marky has climbed onto the right-hand bench.

Leon Time you grew up, losers.

Marky Anyway, they're not there today.

394

*Dig joins Marky up on the bench, peers. Mel and Soph
are gearing themselves up to leave.*

Marky Hey, Soph! Can we go with you?
Soph Yeah, I suppose.

Marky jumps down, grabs his bag.

Marky Come on, Dig!

Dig stays on the bench, peers a bit longer.

Dig I dunno . . . Leon, are you going across?

Leon and Taylor are lounging on left-hand bench.

Leon Me? I'm not going anywhere.
Taylor We got Gillespie, haven't we?
Marky Let's go, Dig.

*Dig gets down from the bench, picks up his bag.
Dragging his heels.*
    *Mel and Soph are about to leave. Mel realises they
are setting off with Marky and Dig in tow.*

Mel Hey, I'm not walking across the park with you two!
Soph It's alright, Mel.
Mel No way! Walk across the park with those losers!
    You're joking me!
Soph (*to Marky and Dig*) You'd better go round the
    park, then you'll be alright.

Mel and Soph exit.

Leon Yeah, go round the kids' way.
Marky If I go round, I'll be late, I'll be suspended –
Taylor/Leon *Big Ishoo! Big Ishoo!*
Marky Fuck it, I'm going across.
Dig We can still go round and get there in time if we run!
Marky Run? No way.
Dig Marky –

Marky It's alright, the muggers aren't there. You coming, Dig?

Dig *(in an agony of indecision)* No.

Taylor and Leon make chicken noises.

Marky Okay. Laters.

Marky exits. Dig gets on the right-hand bench, stands on tiptoe, peers. Taylor and Leon gambol round Dig, making chicken noises. Dig ignores them until:

Dig They're there! The muggers are there!

Taylor jumps onto the bench. Leon slumps on the other bench, unimpressed.

Leon They're always there.

Taylor Where?

Dig *(pointing)* There! Coming out of the playground!

Leon The girls'll be alright. They won't stop the girls.

Dig *(shouting)* Marky!

Taylor He hasn't seen them, the dickhead.

Dig There's *three* of them!

Leon *Three?*

Leon jumps onto the bench.

Taylor Who the fuck is that?

Dig It's the old geezer I saw, he's with the muggers. *(shouting)* Marky!

Taylor He is *big*, man!

Leon He ain't that big.

Dig *(shouting)* Marky, come back!

Taylor Who the fuck *is* he?

Dig Marky's seen them, he's coming back! Run, Marky!

Taylor The girls haven't seen them, silly bitches. *(shouting)* Oi, Mel! Soph! Come back!

Dig They're stopping the girls!

Marky enters on the run, gasping for breath. Hurls his bag to the ground, climbs on the bench.

Marky There's three of them!
Dig The big bloke's got Soph.
Marky They've got her phone!
Taylor Shit, man!

Leon jumps off the bench, runs downstage.

Leon (*shouting*) You touch her, you're dead, man!
Taylor Run, Mel!
Leon (*shouting*) I'll kill you, you thieving slag!
Dig The girls are coming back!

Mel enters on the run.

Mel They got her phone!

She is followed by Soph, who is in tears.

Soph They got my phone!

Leon tries to put his arms round Soph. Taylor jumps down off the bench.

Leon You alright, babe?
Soph (*shoving him off*) Of course I'm not alright, they got my phone!
Mel Who was that other one? I never seen him before, he was like *twenty*!
Taylor (*to Mel*) You okay?
Mel Yeah, no thanks to you!
Taylor What was I supposed to do?
Mel You could've done something!
Taylor How? We were over here!

Dig and Marky are still on the bench, peering.

Dig They're walking back to the playground.
Marky They might at least have the decency to run.

Leon (*shouting*) You're dead, dickhead!

Marky (*wind-up*) He heard you, Leon! He's coming over!

Leon (*alarmed, takes a step back*) What?

Marky (*nudging Dig*) No, he's not, my mistake.

Soph (*distraught*) It was my mum's phone!

Leon What?

Mel It was her *mum's* phone!

Soph I took it this morning, there was no money on mine 'cos I was texting *you* all night!

Soph hurls herself at Leon, punching him on the chest.

Leon It's not *my* fault, stupid bitch!

Soph (*crying*) My mum'll kill me! She'll chuck me out! She said the next time I do anything, I have to go and live with my dad!

Mel (*to Taylor*) Tayl, you've got to do something.

Taylor What? What can I do?

Mel Get her phone back!

Soph (*to Leon*) You've got to get my mum's phone back!

Leon Where are they?

Marky and Dig are still on the bench, peering.

Dig They're in the playground.

Marky Sitting on the swings.

Taylor That geezer, he's a big bastard.

Soph The other two are only *kids*!

Mel (*to Taylor*) Go with Leon, it's two against one!

Taylor He must be like *twenty-five* or something!

Leon (*to Soph*) What's the point? Me and Tayl go over, they'll just run away.

Marky You wish.

Leon What?

Taylor Who is that big geezer, anyway? I've never seen him before!

Mel Me neither.

Soph I don't think he's from round here.

Taylor I've never seen him before. (*to Leon*) You seen him before, Leon?

Leon No, I haven't seen him before.

Marky I have.

This gets everyone's attention. Marky jumps down from the bench.

Leon Who is he then?

Marky I think his name's Carl. Or Kyle. Something like that. His mum lives next door to mine. I've seen him round the flats.

Taylor You *know* him?

Marky No, I don't *know* him, Tayl, we're not *mates*, I've just seen him round the flats!

Leon You ever talk to him?

Marky No, but my mum talks to his mum.

Dig We could tell the police –

Huge derision at this.

Leon They're not going to get Soph's phone back, are they?

Taylor He'll know we grassed him up, he'll come straight back here looking for us, you knob.

Leon And what if he recognised Marky? Did he recognise you, Marky?

Marky Dunno.

They start talking over each other:

Mel He knows where Marky lives –

Soph (*crying*) My mum's going to throw me out –

Taylor Over a poxy phone? You're joking me –

Mel She will, too –

Soph You don't know what she's like –

Leon She's a nutter, man –

Taylor Get over it, girl, you ain't going to get it back now –

Mel (*shoves Taylor*) *You* get over it, dickhead –
Taylor Hey –
Soph (*to Leon, crying, hitting him*) She is *not* a nutter –
Marky I'll talk to him, Soph, alright?

This shuts them up.

Dig What?
Marky I'll go and talk to him.
Soph You will?
Marky Yeah, I'll explain.
Leon Explain what?
Marky About her mum's phone, what do you think?
Leon Yeah, but what good will that do?
Taylor Yeah, what good will that do?
Marky His mum knows my mum, alright? Maybe he'll
give it back. As a favour.
Mel Yeah, he might, mightn't he?
Soph Yeah, if you're like a mate of his?
Dig He just said, he's not a *mate*.
Mel Yeah, but you know him.
Marky Sort of.
Soph Thanks, Marky.
Dig What if they mug you, man?
Marky I haven't got anything, have I? No money, no
phone, nothing.
Soph Maybe Leon and Tayl should go with you.
Marky No, they'll think we're looking for a ruck.
Taylor Yeah, they'd do a runner, man.
Leon Soon as they saw us.
Marky (*to Dig*) Where are they?
Dig Still in the playground.

Marky picks up his bag.

Marky (*to Soph*) I'll see you back at school, alright?

Dig gets down off the bench.

Dig Marky, you want me to come with you?

Marky No, stay here, Dig.

Dig Marky man, you sure?

Marky It's alright, I know the geezer. Anyway, I've got a theory.

Dig What?

Marky Tell you later.

Marky exits. The others all climb on the benches to watch.

Taylor Where are they? I can't see them.

Dig In the playground. They've gone round by the climbing frame.

Mel Someone should've gone with him.

Leon Yeah, but he didn't want us to, did he?

Taylor We offered.

Soph No you didn't, Dig did.

Leon We would too have gone!

Taylor (*laughing*) Look at him. Little dosser with his shirt out.

Soph Why's he stopped?

Leon Oi, *Big Ishoo*, get on with it!

Dig He's waiting to see if they come out of the playground.

Soph He's going nearer.

Dig He's calling them. He doesn't want to go in the playground, it's harder to run away if you're in the playground.

Mel They're coming.

Dig No, they've stopped. They're staying by the fence.

Taylor Scumbags don't want to come out of the playground.

Leon They're shouting at him.

Soph He's going nearer.

Dig (*shouts*) Don't go in the playground, Marky!

Taylor He's stopped again.

Leon Man, they ain't going to come out.

Soph Dig, tell him not to go in the playground.

Dig (*shouts*) Marky! Don't go in the playground!

Soph I don't like this, this is bad. Dig, tell him it doesn't matter, tell him not to bother.

Dig Marky, come back!

Soph jumps down from the bench, comes downstage.

Soph (*shouts*) Marky, it's alright! Don't bother!

Leon He's by the fence now. He's talking to them.

Dig Yeah, they're just talking.

Taylor *Big Ishoo*, he'll talk 'em to death.

Mel It's okay, it's going to be alright –

Leon He's going in the playground –

Dig (*quiet*) Shit.

Soph jumps back on the bench.

Taylor Stay near the gate – (*Shouts.*) Stay near the gate!

Dig (*shouts*) Stay near the gate!

Taylor Shit!

Leon The big geezer's got him!

Taylor Fuck!

Consternation on the benches.

Leon That big geezer's got him!

Dig Marky's fighting him – !

Taylor Give him one, Marky!

Dig He's got away – !

Taylor He's out the gate – !

Mel Run, Marky!

Taylor The geezer's chasing him!

Mel/Soph (*clinging to each other, shouting*) Run, run!

Leon Behind you, Marky!

Mel and Soph scream.

Dig Oh shit!

A beat or two of complete silence.

Leon He's down –
Dig He's – he's –
Leon The big geezer hit him!
Dig No –
Taylor Get up, Marky!
Dig No.
Leon He hit him!
Soph No – he stabbed him!
Dig No.
Mel He stabbed him up!
Dig No.
Leon They're coming! They're coming after us!

*Everybody runs off in different directions except Dig.
Still on the bench, peering into the distance.*

Dig Marky! Marky, get up!
Soph (*off, screaming*) Dig!

Dig jumps off the bench and runs.
Blackout.
Off, a police siren comes and goes.

TWO

*Dig sits on the right-hand bench, slumped forward,
staring at the ground between his feet. He will remain
there throughout this scene, isolated from – and oblivious
to – the action.*
*A Police Officer in fluorescent yellow jacket stretches
police tape across the stage. Passers-by line up behind the
tape and gawp at the audience.*
*Two Newsreaders sit at either end of the left-hand
bench. They fiddle with their hair, adjust ties, whatever.*
A TV Reporter with a mike stands by the police tape.

Newsreader 1 Here is the news. Reports are coming in of an assault on a teenager in Albion Park.

Newsreader 2 Here is the news. A fourteen-year-old youth was murdered in Albion Park this morning. Early reports indicate that the killing took place during a fight between rival gangs.

Newsreader 1 The fourteen-year-old youth murdered in Albion Park has been named as Mark Bennett. He was a pupil at Albion Park School.

Newsreader 2 Reports suggest that Mark Bennett, the murdered teenager, belonged to one of the gangs that have been terrorising Albion Park School.

Newsreader 2 Albion Park School, the school attended by Mark Bennett, has been criticised recently by government inspectors for its poor disciplinary record.

Newsreader 1 Parents say police were called to the school on a regular basis. They say a yob culture prevailed at the troubled secondary school.

TV Reporter I'm in Albion Park, scene of the brutal murder of Mark Bennett, the fourteen-year-old pupil at nearby Albion Park School. Local residents say they are terrorised by the gangs which roam the park.

The TV Reporter sticks the mike in the face of a Gawper.

Gawper 1 There's always trouble. Every day. Fights, muggings. You daren't go out the house.

The TV Reporter sticks the mike in the face of another Gawper.

Gawper 2 It's the kids from the school. They hang around the benches and the playground, they never go to school, do they? They just hang around causing trouble.

Gawper 2 is pushed out of the way by Gawper 3.

Gawper 3 They attract undesirables. Druggies, winos. This used to be a nice area.

Gawper 2 I mean, don't get me wrong, I'm sorry for what happened to the poor kid, but what can you expect? There's just no discipline, is there?

Gawper 3 It was an accident waiting to happen. Somebody should've done something.

Gawper 1 Nobody cares any more, do they? People used to look after each other, now they just can't be bothered.

TV Reporter Police are asking for witnesses to come forward.

The yellow-jacketed Police Officer approaches Gawper 1 with a notebook.

Police Officer Did you see anything?

Gawper 1 Me? *I* didn't see anything!

Gawper 1 hurries off. The Police Officer approaches Gawper 2.

Police Officer Did *you* see anything?

Gawper 2 Me? You're joking! I got better things to do than hang around here all day, haven't I?

Gawper 2 hurries off. The Police Officer approaches Gawper 3.

Police Officer Did *you* see anything?

Gawper 3 Look at the time! Sorry, I got to go to work!

Gawper 3 hurries off.
Exit everyone except Dig, still sitting on the bench. Blackout.
Off, a police siren comes and goes.

THREE

The benches.
The police tape across the stage.
Dig still sitting on the right-hand bench. Hunched over,
staring at the ground in front of him.
Soph and Mel enter, walking slowly, supporting each
other. Both holding bunches of flowers. They sit on the
left-hand bench, put the flowers down on the bench
beside them. Both have been crying. They huddle
together, holding hands, clutching soggy tissues.
After a bit, Soph notices Dig. She gets up, goes over to
him.

Soph Dig?

> *Dig doesn't look up, doesn't answer.*

You alright, Dig?

> *Dig nods without looking up. Soph lingers, maybe*
> *reaches out a hand as if to touch him on the shoulder,*
> *then changes her mind and goes back to the left-hand*
> *bench, sits down next to Mel.*
> > *A beat.*

You see what they said on the news?
Mel What?
Soph They said Marky was in a gang.
Mel No!
Soph Can you believe it?
Mel Marky in a gang? You're joking!
Soph I told him to come back! I told him not to bother!
Didn't I, Mel?
Mel Yeah, you did.
Soph (*crying*) Everyone's going to think it was my fault.
Mel It wasn't your fault. Tell her, Dig!

No reply from Dig.

Oi, Dig! It wasn't her fault, was it?

No reply from Dig.

Soph Leave him.

Taylor enters, walks over to the left-hand bench to join Mel and Soph.

Taylor School's closed.
Mel We know.
Taylor And tomorrow, probably.

Taylor sees the flowers on the bench.

What's this?
Mel We were going to put them over there, where Marky was – you know.
Taylor Best leave them on the bench. They'll get trashed over by the playground.
Mel Yeah, they're better here, aren't they? He was always sat here, wasn't he?
Soph He was always on the benches, every morning.
Mel Yeah, he was.
Taylor And this was his favourite bench, right?

Nobody answers. Taylor looks over at Dig.

You alright, Dig?

Dig doesn't answer.

Mel Leave him.

Soph starts crying.

Taylor Hey, Soph.

Taylor tries to sit down on the bench but Mel pushes him away.

Mel Leave us alone.

Mel puts her arms round Soph. Taylor goes and sits down next to Dig.

Taylor I still can't believe it! (*Beat, then to Dig.*) I still can't fucking believe it. Can you, Dig?

Dig doesn't answer.

It's like a dream or something. Know what I mean?

Dig doesn't respond.
Leon enters. Goes over to Soph and Mel, who are still clutching each other. Looks at them for a moment or two.
Leon goes to the right-hand bench, climbs up, looks out over the park.

Leon (*shouts*) Fucking scumbags!

Leon jumps down, goes to the police tape, looks over it.

They show their faces round here again, they're dead meat!

Taylor There's no one there, Leon. Just police.

Leon Yeah, cops everywhere, man. I was stopped twice on the way here. (*Beat.*) Never see 'em for weeks then they're harassing you every five minutes.

Taylor I was up at the school. I was talking to Mr Gillespie. He's well sick.

Mel We all are, Tayl.

Taylor He's well sick about what they said on the news about the school, and Marky being in a gang.

Leon Worried about his job, that's what he's worried about.

Soph You didn't say anything about my mum's phone!

Taylor Course not.

Mel What were you doing at school anyway, if you knew it was closed?

Taylor Just wanted to see what was going on, that's all.

Leon Arse-licking, that's what he was doing. 'Good morning, Mr Gillespie, anything I can do to help?'

Taylor Fuck off, Leon.

Soph (*to Leon*) You can talk.

Leon Oh, right, now you're going to have a go at me, right?

Soph Yeah, 'cos you didn't help him! You let Marky go on his own!

Taylor Marky didn't want us to go with him, remember? He said they'd run away if we all went.

Soph No, Tayl, *you* said that. (*to Leon*) And you.

Leon No way!

Mel He's right, Soph. Marky didn't want them to help.

Soph (*to Mel*) What is your problem? Always sticking up for these dickheads.

Taylor (*to Soph*) Hey, you'd better be careful what you say, girl!

Soph Or what, Tayl? You going to sort me out like you did the muggers?

Taylor No, I'm just saying, that's all.

Soph You're always just saying, Tayl, that's your problem, your big mouth never stops flapping for one second!

Taylor I'm just saying you've got to be careful when you talk to the police.

Mel What do you mean?

Taylor Mr Gillespie says we have to make statements to the police, at the police station.

Leon Shit.

Taylor You have to have a parent with you –

Leon No way!

Taylor There'll be counsellors, social workers, the lot. So what I'm saying is, you've got to be careful what you say.

Soph Don't say anything about my mum's phone!

Mel Why not? Marky was trying to get it back, he was trying to help –

Soph (*tearful*) I haven't told her I took it. She thinks she left it in Tesco's. What if she finds out I took it, then got mugged, then Marky got stabbed up trying to get it back! I can't tell them that! My mum would go totally apeshit! Leon, you know what she's like, I can't tell her that, can I?

Leon Well, we don't have to tell them about the phone, do we?

Taylor That's what I'm saying. We've got to be careful. If they think Marky was in a gang, they'll think we're in a gang.

Mel Joking!

Taylor They were the gang, not us! That's what we tell them! There was a whole gang of them, right?

Dig stands. Agitated.

Dig SHUT UP! Just – shut – up.

Silence.

We tell them what happened, that's what we do.

Taylor Tell them what, Dig?

Dig Tell them what happened! Tell them who did it! Tell them who stabbed Marky up!

Silence from the others.

Taylor Yeah, but the thing is, Dig, we don't really know, do we?

Dig Marky recognised him! He recognised the big geezer! His mum lives next to Marky's mum. Marky said so. That's what we tell the police!

Taylor *We* don't know who he was, do we?

Dig Marky said his name was Carl.

Leon Carl? You sure? I thought it was Kyle.

Taylor Clive, was it? I dunno.

Mel I can't remember.

Dig It was Carl! Soph, you remember!

Soph Marky wasn't sure, Dig. He said he wasn't sure.

Dig Marky recognised him!

Leon What if he was wrong?

Dig He knew the geezer!

Taylor Mel, if you saw the big geezer again, would you recognise him?

Mel No way! All I saw was this big geezer in a hoodie.

Leon What about you, Soph?

Soph I don't know, do I? He was grabbing me, he was grabbing my phone, I didn't have time to notice what he looked like!

Leon We're not even sure what his name is, right?

Dig It's Carl!

Taylor Or Kyle.

Mel Or Clive.

Leon He knows where Marky's mum lives. His mum lives next to Marky's mum.

Mel Yeah, that's true.

Leon Think about that for one second, alright? We grass him up, he'll be straight over there, him and his mates. Then he'll be straight over here.

Taylor What if we're wrong, what if we say something about this big geezer and we're wrong, it wasn't him, and they come over here and stab us up?

Leon Stab you up, Dig, if you say something!

Taylor Yeah, and none of us can identify him anyway, so they'll have to let him go and he'll come straight here looking for us.

Mel (*tearful*) I don't want to talk to the police, I'm too upset!

Leon Well, we're all upset, aren't we? He was our mate too, wasn't he?

Taylor Yeah, he was our mate too.

*And Dig, wailing, launches himself at Taylor in a
frenzied attack. Knocks Taylor to the floor. Leon
manages to wrestle Dig off Taylor and restrain him,
twisting his arm.*

What's your problem?
Dig He wasn't your mate!
Taylor Course he was!
Dig (*in pain*) Let me go!
Leon You going to behave yourself?

Dig struggles but Leon is too strong for him.

Dig (*in pain, mumbling*) Yeah.

Leon shakes him.

Leon Are you?
Dig (*louder*) Yes!
Leon And when you talk to the cops?
Dig Yes!
Soph Don't tell them about the phone, Dig, alright?
Dig Alright!
Soph Promise?
Dig (*miserable*)Yeah, I promise!

Leon lets him go. Dig runs off.
  Blackout.
  Off, a police siren comes and goes.

FOUR

The police tape still across the stage.
  There are more flowers on the left-hand bench now.
  *Members of the public and schoolkids file past, placing
flowers and cards on the bench. Some pause to read the
cards and messages. Some take photos with their mobile
phones, some stop and hug each other.*

Meanwhile, Newsreaders 1 and 2 have settled at either end of the right-hand bench. They fiddle with their hair, adjust ties and so on.

Newsreader 1 Here is the news. Police say that Mark Bennett, the schoolboy who was stabbed to death in Albion Park, may have been killed during an argument over a mobile phone.

Newsreader 2 Here is the news. Witnesses say that Mark Bennett was seen trying to grab a youth's mobile phone moments before he was stabbed to death.

Newsreader 1 Reports are emerging that Mark Bennett was carrying a knife at the time of his death.

Newsreader 2 Police emphasise that the knife found on Mark Bennett's body was not the murder weapon.

Newsreader 1 Mark Bennett had been suspended from school on a number of occasions for poor attendance and disruptive behaviour.

Newsreader 2 Police say they are having trouble getting pupils at Albion Park School to make statements because of the widespread fear of retribution.

Newsreader 1 In a recent survey one in four children aged between eleven and sixteen claim to have carried knives.

The Newsreaders get up and leave. The last of the passers-by files out.

Dig enters, walks over to the left-hand bench, checks out the flowers. He looks around to make sure nobody is watching, then takes a small, scruffy bunch of flowers from inside his coat.

Soph enters from the other side. Dig sees her, shoves the flowers back inside his coat.

Soph sits at one end of the right-hand bench. Dig hesitates, then goes to sit at the other end.

Beat.

Dig I didn't tell them about your mum's phone.
Soph Thanks, Dig.

Beat.

Did you tell them about the big geezer?
Dig No.
Soph Me neither. I said I couldn't see anything, it was
   too far away.
Dig Me too.

Beat.

Soph We couldn't see who it was, could we?
Dig No.
Soph Even Marky wasn't sure, was he?

*Dig doesn't answer. Then Mel, Leon and Taylor enter,
all outrage and indignation, talking over each other.*

Taylor Can you believe it –
Mel They want to make out it was his fault he got
   killed –
Leon They're having a laugh, right –
Mel It's all lies –
Taylor It's a joke –
Mel They lie all the time –
Taylor Specially the telly –
Mel Never mind the telly, did you see the paper?
Leon It's that scumbag Gillespie –
Mel They lie to make themselves look better –
Taylor They lie, 'cos people want them to –
Leon If I find out it was Gillespie, I'm going to have him!
Taylor (*to Soph and Dig*) Here, you see the news?
Soph/Dig No.
Leon They're only saying Marky had a knife on him!
Soph A knife?
Mel First they say he was in a gang, now they say he had
   a knife!

Soph Marky had a knife? You're joking!

Leon That's what they said on the news.

Soph Who said?

Leon That toerag teacher –

Taylor Mr Gillespie wouldn't say that –

Leon (*scornful*) 'Mr Gillespie'. Yeah, your little mate –

Taylor Mr Gillespie wouldn't say that because it makes the school look bad! It's politics, you twat!

Mel They said it to make us look bad.

Soph Who? Who said it?

Taylor The police, the telly, everyone. The media, right? We're all bad, aren't we – all the kids at the school, all the kids in the park, it's easier for them if they make out we're all bad –

Soph A knife? You sure, Leon?

Leon Yeah, it was in his bag.

Taylor (*to Dig*) You're very quiet.

During the above, Dig has remained motionless, staring at the ground between his feet.

Dig So?

Taylor Know anything about Marky having a knife?

Dig No.

Soph Marky never had a knife, Tayl!

Taylor (*looking at Dig*) Maybe he did.

Mel No way!

Taylor Maybe he nicked it.

Leon Yeah, Marky nicked stuff, didn't he, Dig?

Taylor Him and Dig were always nicking stuff. Eh, Dig?

Dig No!

Taylor (*to Dig*) I've seen you two, sitting on the benches, showing each other stuff you've nicked.

Dig Fuck off, Tayl!

Mel Marky only nicked fags and sweets.

Leon and Taylor are now standing over Dig, menacing him.

Taylor Yeah, right! So where'd you get the fags you gave Soph?

Dig I bought them.

Taylor Joking!

Leon He got the fags off Marky, didn't he?

Taylor You nicked the knife, didn't you, Dig? You nicked the knife and swapped it for fags!

Dig No, I didn't!

Leon If you did, man, you'd better tell the cops.

Dig Well, I didn't!

Soph Come on, Leon, Dig wouldn't steal a knife –

Leon What would you know about it? Stupid bitch, if you hadn't nicked your mum's phone this wouldn't have happened –

Soph jumps to her feet.

Soph Don't say that!

Leon Sit down –

Leon shoves Soph back down onto the bench. Dig stands, confronts Leon.

Dig Don't touch her!

Leon (*laughing*) Or what?

Taylor You going to tell them about the knife, you thieving little dosser?

Dig Just stop it, Tayl, alright?

Taylor What? Stop what?

Dig Stop making stuff up!

Taylor (*to Leon*) What's he on about?

Leon No idea.

Dig Making stuff up about Marky, just to make yourself feel better! Stuff about being his mate! Stuff about his favourite bench. It's a joke! Whatever bench we sat on, you chucked us off it! Maybe I'll tell them about that.

Taylor What, you'll tell the cops about me chucking you off the benches? I'm sure they'll be fascinated.

Dig I'll tell them how you called Marky *Big Ishoo* and
dosser and I'll them how Leon beat us up and took our
money and I'll tell them about that time me and
Marky got mugged and the muggers beat us up, 'cos
we didn't have any money 'cos you two mugged us
first –

*And Leon hits Dig hard in the face. Soph screams. Dig
collapses back on the bench. Leon straddles him, hits
him again.*

Leon Don't even think about it!

Soph starts trying to drag Leon off.

Soph *Get off him, Leon!*

*Leon allows himself to be pulled off Dig. Dig lies in a
heap on the bench. Taylor leans over him.*

Taylor Nobody cares about any of that, Dig. Don't you
get it? That's not on the agenda right now.

Mel Is he alright?

Taylor Yeah, he's alright.

Leon He won't be if he tells the cops any of that crap.

Soph *(examining Dig)* You pig, you really hurt him!

Leon Good.

Soph Dig, you okay?

*Dig struggles upright, a hand over his nose. Maybe
some blood. Nods.*

Taylor Yeah, he's alright. Come on, let's go. Mel, you
coming?

Mel Yeah, I s'pose.

Leon *(to Dig)* Keep it buttoned, dosser.

Taylor Come on Leon, let's go.

Leon Come on, Soph. We're going.

Soph I'm staying here.

Taylor He's alright, Soph.

Leon Come on, girl! Now!

Soph I said I'm staying here.

Beat. Leon looks menacing.

What're you going to do? Hit me as well, you pig?

Leon (*suddenly unsure of himself*) So I'll see you later, alright?

Soph I don't think so.

Leon I said, I'll see you later, alright?

Soph I said, I don't think so!

Beat.

Leon Alright, stay with the loser if that's what you want.

Leon, Mel and Taylor exit, Leon pausing for a final look back at Soph. She ignores him. Soph and Dig sit side by side on the left-hand bench. Soph fumbles in her pocket.

Soph You want a tissue?

Dig I'm not crying. My eyes are watering 'cos he hit my nose.

Soph I know.

Soph finds a tissue in her bag, hands it to Dig.

Dig Ta.

Dig mops his nose.

Marky had a theory about Leon.

Soph What was that?

Dig Marky said Leon beat us up because he was scared.

Soph Yeah?

Dig I didn't get it. I still don't.

Soph Marky's right. Leon's scared of everything.

Dig Joking!

Soph He was scared of the big geezer, wasn't he?

Dig considers this.

Dig Yeah, he was, wasn't he? He wouldn't go with
  Marky, would he?

Soph No.

Dig He made excuses. You could tell he was scared.

Soph Yeah, he was scared. We all were.

Dig Yes.

Beat.

Soph.

Soph What?

Dig About the knife.

Soph What about it?

Beat.

Dig I nicked it.

Soph I know.

Dig You know?

Soph Well, I guessed. I got here before the others that
  morning. I was down there, texting Leon. I saw you
  and Marky shoving stuff back in your bags. Then Mel
  and Tayl turned up.

Beat.

Dig I got it from the art shop. I was after felt-tips but
  the bloke in there, he's such a suspicious bastard,
  always looking at you like you're going to do something,
  but he had to answer the phone so I just grabbed the
  box and ran. I wasn't after a knife at all, I was after
  felt-tips.

Beat.

I made Marky swap it for fags so I could give them to you.

Beat.

Why didn't you tell the others?

Soph You didn't tell the police about my mum's phone.

Beat.

Dig How do you tell the truth? About what actually
happened? You know, tell the actual truth. It's all so
complicated.

Soph I bet Marky had a theory about it.

Dig Yeah, probably.

*Dig remembers something. Stands, takes the
bedraggled flowers out from inside his coat. Even
more bedraggled now. He goes over to the left-hand
bench, looks at the flowers on the bench, then at the
pathetic offering he's holding in his hand. Chucks them
in the bin.*

I'm going to tell them about the knife, Soph.

Soph Are you, Dig?

Dig Yeah. And the big geezer.

Soph I think that's great.

Dig You do?

Soph Yeah, I do. I think that's really great, Dig.

Beat.

Soph I'll come with you.

Dig Really?

Soph Yeah. You can tell them about the knife and I'll tell
them about my mum's phone.

Blackout.

FIVE

The police tape still in place.
*More flowers on the left-hand bench. Gawpers,
including Gawpers 1, 2, and 3, stand around peering at
the flowers, trying to read the cards.*

Newsreaders 1 and 2 sit on the right-hand bench. The usual hair adjustments and so on. The TV Reporter stands to one side with Taylor, Leon and Mel. Also fiddling with their hair, straightening ties etc.

Newsreader 1 Here is the news. Police investigating the murder of Albion Park schoolboy Mark Bennett say they have uncovered important new evidence.

Newsreader 2 Here is the news. Police say a witness has come forward who may be able to identify the killer of Mark Bennett.

Newsreader 1 New evidence suggests that Mark was trying to retrieve a mobile phone which had been stolen from a friend.

Newsreader 2 Witnesses also say that the knife found in Mark Bennett's bag belonged to another friend.

Newsreader 1 Mark, who feared the knife might get his school friend into trouble, had persuaded the friend to give it to him for safe keeping.

Newsreader 2 Earlier reports that Mark Bennett's murder was gang-related may have been inaccurate.

TV Reporter I'm in Albion Park, scene of the tragic murder of Mark Bennett, where I'm talking to some of his friends. Can you tell me what your feelings are at this moment?

TV Reporter holds a mike for Taylor, Leon and Mel.

Taylor Devastated. The whole school is in shock.
Leon We're gutted.
TV Reporter You were friends of Mark, weren't you?
Mel/Taylor/Leon Yeah. Yeah, he was a really good friend. A great mate. Mark was brilliant. Everybody liked Mark.
TV Reporter It seems that Mark may have been trying to help the victim of a mugging. Was that typical of Mark, would you say?

Taylor Yeah, I'd say that was very typical of Mark. He was very concerned about the situation here in the park, with young kids getting mugged every day –

Mel They're afraid to go across the park, right, 'cos that's where the muggers are –

Taylor In fact, sometimes kids are too scared to go to school at all. They come to the park and if the muggers are here, they just go home again, which is a totally unacceptable situation, right?

Leon Totally unacceptable.

Taylor Mark used to talk about this a lot, he used to talk about organising something, right, to help the little kids. He could've done it too, he was really clever.

Leon Mark was brilliant, he was going to get A's in all his GCSEs, definitely –

Taylor Anyway, we're going to talk to Mr Gillespie the headmaster and the parents about setting up a trust, the Mark Bennett Trust, right, to help the victims of muggings, like young kids –

Leon There's going to be a hotline –

Mel – for young kids to phone up if they're scared.

Taylor So something good may come out of this terrible tragedy. Something that will make everyone remember Mark.

Blackout.

SIX

Taylor, Leon and Mel have exited. The Newsreaders, TV Reporter and Gawpers remain.

Newsreader 1 Here is the news. Police have arrested a twenty-year-old man in connection with the murder of Mark Bennett, star pupil of Albion Park School.

Newsreader 2 Friends of Mark Bennett say that Mark frequently voiced his concern about violent crime in the Albion Park area.

Newsreader 1 Mark Bennett's headmaster, David Gillespie, said that Mark's attitude showed great social awareness for his age. This was something that he and his colleagues at Albion Park school always encouraged.

Newsreader 2 Mr Gillespie said that he had already picked Mark out as a potential university entrant.

The TV Reporter has joined the Gawpers by the left-hand bench.

TV Reporter I'm in Albion Park, scene of the brutal murder of Mark Bennett, the brilliant young pupil at Albion Park School. As you can see, people are still coming here in droves to pay their respects. Excuse me, did you know Mark Bennett?

The TV Reporter shoves the mike at the Gawpers.

Gawper 1 Oh yes, he was a lovely young lad.

Gawper 2 He was always full of fun –

Gawper 3 Like they said on the news, he was always trying to help –

Gawper 1 Nothing was too much trouble for him –

Gawper 2 Course, I didn't know him myself, but I know people who did –

Gawper 3 I'd see him around the park, he'd always say hello –

Gawper 1 Always smiling –

Gawper 3 He was a lovely boy –

Gawper 2 And clever with it, you know.

Gawper 1 He could've done anything –

Gawper 3 He had his whole life ahead of him.

Everyone exits except Newsreader 1.

Newsreader 1 There will be a memorial service for Mark Bennett at St Mary's Church on Thursday.

And Newsreader 1 exits.
Blackout.

SEVEN

The police tape has gone.
The left-hand bench is still covered in flowers.
Dig enters. He pauses to check out the flowers.
Dig looks different. The changes are slight – his hair maybe, the way he wears his clothes – but he looks older, more self-assured.
Dig goes over to the right-hand bench and sits.
Taylor, Leon and Mel enter.

Taylor Alright, Dig?
Dig Alright?

They go over to join Dig on the right-hand bench.

Taylor They arrested that big geezer then. Carl.
Dig Yeah, they did.
Leon Scumbag.
Taylor You told the police, did you, Dig?
Dig I just told them what Marky said. So they arrested the geezer, then Soph went and identified him. She said it was easy, she recognised him straight away.
Mel I was going to go, right, and say something but they already arrested him, so there wasn't much point.
Leon You need a bit of time, right, after seeing something like that.
Taylor It's the shock, you can't remember every little detail straight away, can you?

Beat.

Dig I s'pose not.

Beat.

Taylor You see what they're saying about Marky on the telly?

Dig About him being a brilliant student?

Taylor That was Leon's fault, saying he was going to get A's.

Leon I was trying to be nice, wasn't I?

Dig Marky's 'social awareness', what's that about?

Mel Well, he worried about getting mugged, didn't he?

Dig Oh, that's what it means.

Taylor Mr Gillespie was well pleased. He said, 'Thank God someone's saying something positive about the school for once.'

Dig (*mild*) Pity none of it's true.

Taylor Dig, man, it's better than what they were saying before, isn't it? About Marky being in a gang and crap like that?

Dig It's politics, right, Tayl?

Taylor Exactly. And there's going to be the Mark Bennett Trust –

Mel And a hotline –

Taylor And the council are going to put a new bench there –

Taylor points at the left-hand bench.

Leon – with Marky's name on it.

Dig (*amused rather than angry*) His favourite bench, right, Tayl?

Taylor We can't put his name on a bit of mud in the middle of the park, can we?

Dig I s'pose not.

Taylor Anyway, Mr Gillespie was looking for you. He was asking, did you want to say something at the Memorial Service?

Dig Me?
Leon You were his mate, weren't you?

Dig ponders.

Dig No, I don't think I could do that.
Taylor Okay, but you're going to come.
Dig Course I am.
Taylor Okay, then, we'll see you there.

Taylor, Mel and Leon exit. Leon stops.

Leon Hey, Dig.
Dig Yeah?
Leon You seen Soph?
Dig I'm meeting her later.
Leon She alright, then?
Dig Yeah, she's alright.
Leon Right. So she's alright then.
Dig Yeah.
Leon Dig, man. I was going to say . . .
Dig What?
Leon About some of the stuff that happened before . . .
(*He tails off.*)
Dig Don't worry about it, Leon.
Leon Right. Okay. Later, yeah?
Dig Yeah, later.

Leon, relieved, exits.

Dazzling repartee.

Blackout.

EIGHT

Flowers still piled on the left-hand bench.
A blow-up of a fuzzy colour snap of Marky hangs over the stage.

Everyone, including Dig, Soph, Taylor, Leon and Mel, is onstage, backs to the audience, facing the right-hand bench.

A Vicar climbs on the right-hand bench to address them. Perhaps some organ music or a suggestion of light through stained glass.

Vicar Friends, we are here today to celebrate the life of Mark Bennett, who was so tragically taken from us. I'm sure there is no one here whose life was not touched in some way by this remarkable young man, this young man of such exceptional gifts and talents. Some of you, particularly the younger ones, might be asking: 'What are we doing here, in this church? Our friend Mark, our "best mate", has been taken from us. How is coming here going to help us in this dark hour?' Well, let me tell you: God, and his son Jesus, can be a great help at times like this, they can help 'big time', if you'll only let them . . .

Dig turns to face the audience. He's holding a giant milkshake. The straw and container are plain white – no colours, no logo. The Vicar continues to address the congregation (silently) as Dig talks.

Dig I suppose God had to get in on the act sooner or later. Well, why not? Everybody else has. It's funny, Marky had this theory, right, that if you really wanted something, you only got it when you stopped wanting it. He got this theory because of his dad. Marky's dad was supposed to come and take him out every Saturday and but he was always late or he'd never turn up, and Marky used to lie awake all Friday night worrying about whether his dad was going to turn up or not, and one night Marky thought, 'Fuck it, I don't care any more,' and went to sleep and the next day his dad turned up, bang on time, with a wicked present.

427

So that's that where that theory came from, and I didn't really get it, but I think I do now. Marky always wanted to do well at school – without having to do any work, right – and suddenly he's this brilliant student who was going to get an A in everything and go to university. And Marky always wanted to be famous, and now he's famous. And he wanted lots of friends – 'It's important to have a social life, Dig,' he used to say –

A beat while Dig composes himself.

– and now he's got all these new friends, people who ignored him or treated him like shit or didn't even know him in the first place, but it isn't much good to him now, is it? So maybe that theory is bollocks.

Beat.

Or maybe that's the whole point of it.
Vicar Let us pray.

The Congregation lower their heads.

Dear Father in heaven . . .

The Vicar leads them in prayer (silently) as Dig continues.

Dig Anyway. All the things that have been said about Marky, the good things, the bad things, they're all about someone else, this person called 'Mark Bennett', they're not about Marky. Nobody seems to mind that, but I do, 'cos I want to remember him properly.

Beat.

What I want to remember is that Marky was my best friend. He was funny. He invented weird drinks. He never did any work. He was brilliant at nicking sweets. He once wore the same shirt for two weeks. He had a theory about everything. He told the truth, not all the time, but more than anybody else I know. And he was very brave. That's what Marky was really like. And I'll never forget him.

Everyone Amen.

The Vicar makes the sign of the cross over the congregation and everyone except Soph and Dig files off silently.

    Dig goes over to the left-hand bench and carefully places the milkshake among the flowers. Soph joins him.

    They stand side by side looking at flowers for a beat or two.

Soph We'd better go.
Dig Okay.
Soph Do you want to go round or across?
Dig Let's go across.

They join hands and walk off.
    Fade out to black, leaving the milkshake till last.

End.

The Mugging of Truth

Andrew Payne interviewed by Jim Mulligan

Andrew Payne spent some years after studying at
Hornsey College of Art trying to paint, but he says, 'It
was a terrific relief when I finally owned up to myself that
I was no good.' By that time he had written a few scripts
and had a radio play broadcast. In 1979 he was
commissioned to write an episode of *Minder*, the TV
series which went on to become a huge hit, and Andrew
became one of the show's regular contributors. Since then
he has been writing TV and film scripts as well as plays.

> Television is about what happens next. It's about story
> and narrative, sometimes to the detriment of
> everything else. But I do like stories with a strong
> narrative line. That's what I tried to provide with
> *Mugged*.

In *Mugged* a group of schoolchildren hang out in the
park on their way to school. The two smaller boys,
Marky and Dig, are pushed around and bullied by Taylor
and Leon, the bigger, more assertive boys in the group.
This group is in turn terrorised by the hard-core muggers
who control the park. Marky and Dig, while they are
routinely pushed around by Taylor and Leon, also look
to them for protection.

> Taylor is a politician, a pragmatist. He is a complete
> conformist. He will end up in middle management,
> perhaps even the police. Leon is more hard-core and
> could end up inside. Leon is scared and insecure,
> which makes him more dangerous.

430

Taylor manipulates the system, being absent from lessons but attending just enough to avoid exclusion. As he explains to Marky, 'It's politics, man. See what I'm saying? That's why I'm going to be rich and you're going to be a dosser.' But Soph, Leon's girlfriend, sees through him: 'Your big mouth never stops flapping for one second.' Marky's theory on bullying is that, 'Leon beat us up because he was scared . . . scared of everything.' And Dig and Soph realise that, for all his bravado, Leon was scared of the 'big geezer' and let Marky face him because he was too scared to do so himself.

Andrew Payne does not think that bullying is confined to schools: 'It's something that goes on throughout life.' Bullying, however, wasn't Andrew's prime concern when writing *Mugged*. What interested him was the way in which the truth can become so easily distorted. This is the real mugging in the play, the mugging of the truth.

When the mugging and subsequent murder of Marky occurs, a seemingly straightforward crime becomes shrouded in ambiguity and confusion. Soph's phone, the theft of which triggers the tragic chain of events, was actually 'borrowed' from her mother. Police find a knife in Marky's bag which was actually stolen from a shop by Dig. Taylor, Leon, Mel, Soph and Dig all find themselves having to deal with their feelings of guilt, and as a result the truth becomes harder to pin down.

Once the media get hold of the story, the truth becomes even more distorted and we see lazy, cynical TV reporters presenting Marky's murder as the result of gang warfare at a hopeless, yob-dominated school. The general public gladly add their voices: the schoolkids have ruined the park; they never go to school; there's just no discipline. It was an accident waiting to happen; nobody cares any more. Inevitably the lies and insinuations escalate: Marky is represented as a knife-carrying gang member who was killed while trying to steal a mobile phone from another thug. In the face of this calumny, Dig and Soph decide to tell the truth to the police and restore Marky's reputation, only to see the media take the story to the other extreme.

> I think some journalists are incredibly lazy. The actuality is ruthlessly trimmed to fit their prejudices and the prejudices of their readers. Once they have decided their line on a story, they don't want to hear an alternative unless they really have to, as they do in *Mugged*, and then they go to the other extreme. Marky is first depicted as a knife-wielding yob, then as a paragon, a star student. Dig doesn't recognise either of these versions of Marky, and will not allow himself to be mugged of the memory of his best friend. He insists on hanging on to the memory of the Marky he knew.

Of the girls, Soph is the one who, like Dig, comes to a greater understanding of herself by the end of the play. Soph is an interesting character: spirited and independent, she has attached herself to Leon, the dominant boy in the group, and found him seriously wanting. The events of the play bring this dissatisfaction to a head and she is able to reject him in the end. In Marky's view, Dig does not stand a chance with Soph: 'Of all the doomed relationships in the world, you and Soph are *so* doomed.' But never mind, it is Leon who slouches off telling Soph to 'stay with the loser if that's what you want,' and Soph and Dig who walk off hand in hand.

One of the challenges of *Mugged* is to get the delicate balance right between humour and tragedy.

> You have to pace it so that in the end you are left with the right emotional temperature. If you get it wrong

early on – too comedic or too sombre – it is very hard to recover. I think kids understand this better than adults. When you're that age, life is volatile, a roller-coaster. Full of farcical comedy one minute, loaded with despair the next.

Dig's tribute to Marky in the end is moving in its simple realism. Marky was a philosopher. Not all his 'life theories' held water but he had a clear-eyed view of the world. He told the truth and got beaten up for it daily. In the end, his honesty and spontaneity get him killed. Dig acknowledges that Marky's theories 'might be bollocks' but Dig's summing up is this: 'He told the truth, not all the time, but more than anybody else I know.'

Production Notes

Although the plot of this piece is straightforward, the story underneath is complex. The media's response to the tragedy is distasteful. Andrew Payne's view is that the media can be lazy and take the first angle that is presented to them as fact. And it is that first angle that sticks. The Gawpers represent the adult world and seem so removed from the reality of the children. Scenes where they feature demonstrate the way that the public has become so familiar with TV news coverage that they tend to talk to camera in banal soundbites. This represents another form of mugging, a 'mugging of the truth'.

Marky is a kind of playground philosopher, who is either very attractive or repulsive to kids of this age. He goes from being 'a pikey little knobhead' at the beginning to being 'a lovely young lad' at the end. The play therefore exposes the flimsiness of our morality. The character who is least influenced is Dig, who manages to retain his sense of what is right and is not seduced by peer pressure or the media. His journey through the play is the toughest because his best friend Marky becomes everyone's property.

You'll need to explore how the characters react differently to the same events. The play asks the question: should you go straight for a problem and confront it? Or minimise risk and skirt round it?

Andrew is also interested in the thin line between fighting and flirting, one where a situation that starts out as playful can suddenly turn genuinely violent.

434

THE OPENING SCENE

The school referred to in *Mugged* doesn't appear to enforce its rules very effectively. The schoolkids seem to be from an estate, probably in London somewhere.

The police siren at the beginning is so common in London it is easily and quickly dismissed. But in this case it adds a danger and also shows from the first, a remote adult world of troubles far removed from the lives of the children.

A lot of the action is anchored to the benches. Find ways of making the action around them dynamic. The benches almost become characters in themselves. The use of the stage might be more stylised in the second half of the play but the acting should be naturalistic throughout.

The appearance of Marky and Dig at the beginning is intended to be comedic, Marky outdoing the dishevelled Dig with his spectacular scruffiness, the boys weighed down by an outsize bag of crisps and a giant milkshake respectively – the milkshakes carried by Marky at the start of the play and Dig at the end should be as large as possible and plain white, free of any colour or logo).

It's important that we never see the knife that Dig has stolen. It ceases to be an issue, and we forget about it until much later on in the play.

The kids don't much want to go to school, but Dig is worried about Marky getting into trouble. They are eating and jumping around on the bench, they are very relaxed on it when they are alone. It feels safe. There are areas of territory for each group and year at most schools, and they change regularly, often depending on how the oldest or biggest kids feel on a day-to-day basis.

When you reach the line, 'I dunno I thought I saw something,' there is a change. Dig and Marky lose all status. The focus shifts to the relationships within the whole group and each individual relationship onstage. The idea of 'cool' changes: Dig and Marky had their own cool which is lost when the others come on.

The girls are bitchy, arrogant and vain, in the way that is particular to teenage girls. Soph has higher status than Mel as she can stand up to her. We don't really know how close they are as friends, since they seem rather tense around each other. Taylor is learning to manipulate and play people, which is why he says, 'It's politics.'

The kids put themselves through this every day because it has become a habit – an elaborate game and a way in which to waste time before school. It is not as bad in the mornings as it is in the afternoons, because generally the 'worst' ones aren't out of bed in the morning. If Dig and Marky go to the bench, there is a chance they might see the girls who they fancy. For some of the kids it's just a chance to show off, as when Leon takes the crisps and asserts his power. But this isn't a dangerous or scary situation.

Leon can't handle Marky's talk so he reacts in a violent way to hide his confusion, but his behaviour means that everyone has to take sides. Make sure the reactions of the rest of the group are true to the mood at any moment and reflect the shift from playfulness to threat. Leon's use of the word 'bitch' is a term of possession and very negative, more offensive in this case than the rather casual way kids often use the word.

Soph lets Leon treat her in this derogatory way because he's the guy to go out with at school. Who you're going out with makes a big statement about status or lack of it. He probably treats her much better when they are alone.

The fun in bullying someone like Marky – who not only doesn't fight back, but almost encourages Leon to hit him – is that it makes Leon feel he looks good in front of the girls. Taylor completely avoids getting involved, so appears as a bit of a coward. Once the girls leave, Leon and Taylor don't have such an important audience to play to, but they still need to play to each other.

Leon's line 'I'll kill you, you thieving slag,' is for show; the muggers can't hear him, but the group can. The whole group becomes united in the face of a common enemy at this point in the play. But Leon is all talk: he is not prepared to act on his threats.

Marky is an observer who takes things in and then adds them to his theories. He has been forced to think for himself because of his home situation. But now he has the information the others had, and so now they need to talk to him. He lacks the fear that the others have, and he is the one in a position to make decisions. He has an impulsive honesty and is not out to impress the others, rather he just gets bored by their circular conversation. He believes he can talk himself out of any situation.

After Marky leaves, and during the scene where he is murdered, Dig becomes the spokesperson for the group. It is the first time he has been properly addressed by any of them during the play. They all have a common interest to protect Marky. Leon seems to care about what has happened. The territory of the benches is completely forgotten.

You might find it useful to introduce the convention where the kids can't see the muggers unless they are on the benches. If the benches are quite chunky, you could have some of the cast standing on the back of them creating different levels of height.

We assume, with the physical presence of the reporters, that they are on TV. But you don't necessarily need to introduce cameras and crew. It is also important that, although it would be easy to send them up, it is *what* they are saying, not *how* they are saying it, that is important, and it should be played very straight. Avoid using projection or pre-recorded sound because it might detract from the importance of what is being said. It is possible to have as few as two newsreaders here or as many as five or six. The most important thing is that they are delivering bland facts as they find them, and trying to find a culprit and motive. But the reality is that the *only* facts they have are that Marky was fourteen and that he was murdered.

The true facts are: there was only one gang and it wasn't the group we saw; there was no gang warfare. The group and gang have become one and the same thing. As soon as you slip out of these known facts into the half-truth, the half-truths become the realities. The facts are not the facts as we recall them. The media don't make any differentiation between fact and opinion.

THE GAWPERS

The Gawpers are the locals trying to get their two minutes of fame or just locals wanting to get on their soapbox and sort out their own issues – they all have their own agendas.

Start to toy with the audience, in that we can show them how they might react, while showing a number of people who are trying to put the blame elsewhere rather than looking to themselves. The blame ripples out to school management, the parents and the environment.

The irony is that the Gawpers talk about how something should be done, but when the police come and offer them the chance to do something, they don't want to know. They seem to be scared of repercussions. It is not only the children who are afraid of the muggers, but the adults as well. Nobody is willing to take any responsibility for fear of bringing trouble on themselves. None of them has the facts, but they are all willing to give their opinions. This part of the play should be simply done, and briskly paced.

By now Leon has started to lose his lead. The group are anxious and in unfamiliar territory. Before they were a (dysfunctional) unit, but now they are powerless and throwing guilt about to try and ease their individual pain. All kids feel guilty around the police, and all their immediate reactions will be to question how they were involved and how they could be implicated in what happened. The important thing to remember at this point is that *none* of the characters has all the facts. Everyone has forgotten about the knife. Even Dig, possibly.

Everyone has a different agenda. Taylor adds Clive to the mix of names to muddy the water – he is playing the politician. Leon knows the law of the streets and doesn't want to grass on anyone because of the likely reper-cussions. Dig only cares about truth and justice because he wants the truth about his best mate to come out.

The fear of repercussions is used to dissuade Dig from telling the truth. The fact that Soph 'borrowed' her mother's phone is another reason for not telling the police the truth. Andrew said that they all think of themselves as complicit and therefore have reasons not to talk to the police.

If you look at each character's role in the events leading up to Marky's murder, all could be responsible to some extent. Taylor has been concerned about his status and reputation. He uses his skill at manipulation to play on the others' fear and to get his own way.

Dig loses his temper because they are saying things that aren't true, and making out that they were mates with Marky when they weren't. He can't stand the way that Marky has become public property. His grief comes out in the form of aggression. The agenda moves away from the murder and on to different issues. They are sidelining what's important and turning opinion into fact again.

It has been announced on the news that Marky was carrying a knife at the time of his murder. The turning point in the play is when the group make the connection between Dig and the knife. Dig's complicity is revealed for the first time.

Taylor becomes aggressive. He now has Dig as a scapegoat. For the same reason, Dig is badly beaten by Leon. This is real, shocking violence, not horseplay. Soph finally takes a stand against Leon. Marky has stopped being the issue and is replaced by Dig. Soph and Dig are united in their dissatisfaction.

It is more effective if the Gawpers in Scene Five are the same people as before but it's not essential if you want to have a bigger cast.

The group's response to the TV Reporter's questions is not genuine. Taylor's in particular is practised. They have turned Marky into a martyr. They almost seem to 'out' newsread the Newsreader'. Leon and Taylor get more and more outrageous and elevated in what they are saying about Marky.

The Gawpers must be very genuine, to make the audience understand that what is being said is a polar opposite to what was said before.

Dig's realises that Marky's 'life theories' were ambiguous at best, something he used as a coping mechanism. Finally, Marky has now been turned into a religious icon as well. The religious community has hijacked Marky and is using him for its own agenda.

Workshop facilitated by Lawrene Till
with notes taken by Ellie Cary

SAMURAI

Geoffrey Case

Characters

Yuki

Sharaku
the ploughman

Buncho
the metalworker

Nishimura
the office worker

Utamaro
the builder

The Empress

Kung
the bandit

The Golden Samurai Warrior

The Proclamation Reader

Guards at the Palace

From blackout, a pin-spot lights the golden Samurai Sword, suspended in mid-air in the horizontal position. It slowly moves into the vertical. Suspended about eight feet in the air, with steps for people to stand on in order to touch it, the Sword has the feeling of being in a shrine.

A very fat man (Sharaku) enters. He wears a huge, expensive kimono, encrusted with jewels, and huge diamond rings on his fingers.

Sharaku (*bows his head to the sword*) Golden Sword of Tenshan. As a good citizen of the city of Utagowa, I bow before you.

He climbs up to touch the Sword.
Nishimura enters. He is even fatter than Sharaku, his clothes even finer, his rings even larger.

Morning, citizen.

Nishimura Mid-morning. What an unholy hour to get up. (*yawning*) And what shall I ask for today, I wonder.

Sharaku Psst.

Nishimura What?

Sharaku You haven't bowed to the Sword.

Nishimura You're absolutely right.

Sharaku Well, do so.

Nishimura Do I have to? Bowing, reciting silly chants. It is the tenth century after all, we are supposed to be civilised.

Sharaku takes Nishimura aside.

Sharaku Ritual is ritual and custom is custom. That Sword has been in this city for one year.

447

Nishimura I know.

Sharaku And during that time it has become the custom to observe this ritual every single day.

Sharaku bows his head to the Sword and touches it.

Nishimura I'm sure the Sword would grant our wishes whether we bowed to it or not.

Sharaku I don't want to take that chance.

Nishimura It's so boring, bowing to a Sword.

Sharaku It provides all our needs. Bowing is the very least we can do. We must observe the ritual and so keep the gods who watch over our city happy.

Nishimura Oh, don't start about the gods again.

Sharaku How dare you. The gods . . .

Nishimura I'm bowing, I'm smiling at the Sword. I'm chanting my chant. Golden Samurai Sword of Tenshan, as a citizen of Utagowa I bow before you. Can I now have my breakfast, please!

He touches the Sword and his breakfast appears.

Thank you.

He eats.

Nishimura Happy?

Sharaku There was very little respect in your voice.

Nishimura This Sword is here to serve us. It is our servant.

Sharaku But the gods . . .

Nishimura Oh not the gods again. Look, I've never seen any of our gods. Have they ever done anything for me? No.

Sharaku Was it not the gods who saved our city from starvation?

Nishimura No. When we were hungry . . .

Sharaku Starving.

Nishimura Oh, come on . . .

Sharaku There was no food in the city, people were dying in the streets.

Nishimura My brain must be going soft. I find it hard to remember how things were then.

Sharaku Then I'll remind you. Please, Sword, a demonstration.

Enter one wretch or several. Grey, starved and moaning, with a crumbling city wall fastened round him/them.

Nishimura This is what we all looked like in those dark days before the Sword came. We were poor, wretched people. The city walls were crumbling . . .

Sharaku Oh, get rid of it. Sword, have it disappear.

Exit the Wretch.

Sharaku That was how we were one year ago . . .

Nishimura Is it really only a year? Good heavens.

Sharaku The gods saved us.

Nishimura The Sword saved us.

Sharaku It was sent by the gods . . .

Nishimura Sent? It didn't walk here.

Sharaku Brought by a messenger from the gods.

Nishimura No, by some fellow who used to live on the east side of the city.

Sharaku Moved to find the Sword by the gods.

Nishimura Moved to find the Sword by his empty stomach. I really do think you take this gods business a little far.

Sharaku He was directed to find the Sword by the gods and that is my last word on this subject. Breakfast please, Sword.

His breakfast appears.

Thank you.

*Buncho the metalworker enters. He is very fat and
dressed in fine clothes. He touches the Sword.*

Buncho Good day, good day. (*He pulls out a list.*) One
bowl of stewed ox. One platter of venison sides . . . the
meat was rather tough yesterday, Sword. Two bowls
of steaming-hot bean soup, and four golden necklaces.
I have guests for lunch.

All he ordered appears.

Sharaku You didn't bow to the Sword.
Buncho Oh, just a touch with one hand is all you need.
Sharaku You must show some respect.
Buncho Why? I got everything I asked for, didn't I?
Nishimura Precisely.
Sharaku We must observe the ritual.
Buncho It wastes time.
Nishimura Of course it does.
Sharaku There is a distinct change in attitude towards
things sacred in this city.
Nishimura Nonsense. We're just being more practical
about things.

Utamaro enters. Fat, rich, etc., etc.

Sharaku Good morning, Utamaro.
Utamaro Good day, Citizen Sharaku. Citizen Nishimura,
Citizen Buncho.
Nishimura Utamaro the Builder, my house needs a new
roof, and the door needs widening. I can't seem to get
through it these days.
Sharaku You've put on weight.
Nishimura I'm not fat. Who says I'm fat?
Sharaku I just said you'd put on a little weight.
Nishimura Weight? No. I've known poverty in my life.
I know what it means to be hungry.
Sharaku I merely made a comment . . .

Nishimura I'm not fat . . . all my family are big. Big . . .
not fat. All my family have had their house doors
widened . . . for years. Nothing wrong with that.

Sharaku Fine. I'm sorry. You're right.

Nishimura Well . . . don't say I'm fat. First you say I
must bow to the Sword, now you say I'm fat. What's
this all leading to, eh?

Sharaku You're not . . . you're thin.

Nishimura Thank you. Utamaro, will you do the building
work for me?

Utamaro I'll certainly undertake to do the work, but
costs have risen. I shall have to charge you a dozen
diamonds, and a gold sword-buckle.

Nishimura You already have a gold sword-buckle.

Utamaro Oh, so I do. Very well . . . make it a silver
sword-buckle and I'll just wear it for work.

Nishimura Agreed.

Utamaro I'll do the job straightaway if you like.

Nishimura Wonderful.

Utamaro Sword, put a new roof on this citizen's house,
and widen the door.

*They look towards Nishimura's house as the work is
done.*

Nishimura There it goes now. Excellent.

Utamaro I am a professional. It is a beautiful job.

Nishimura Sword, pay Utamaro.

A dozen diamonds and a silver sword-buckle appear.

Utamaro Thank you. Any building work you require,
always come to me.

They all applaud him.
*The citizens sit down and eat. Food keeps
appearing. Utamaro orders breakfast.*

Utamaro You know, I was thinking only this morning about the dark days of our poverty.

Sharaku Whatever for?

Utamaro I find it strangely comforting. You know, the same feeling as standing on the high bridge over the river and watching the swirling torrent below. No danger of falling in but a stimulating experience.

Buncho (*cleaning a diamond*) The poverty of those days was terrible.

Utamaro But good days for all that.

Sharaku Oh yes. We shouldn't forget them. They're good to look back on.

Buncho From a distance.

There is a contented silence.

Sharaku Yes.

Pause.

Buncho Yes.

Pause.

Utamaro Hmm.

Pause.

Nishimura Perhaps I'll go and sit under my new roof (*Pause.*) Perhaps I'll do it later.

They all yawn.
    There is a sudden loud crash of thunder and the sound of heavy rain.

Utamaro Oh, not rain.

Sharaku It won't last more than a few minutes.

Buncho But we're getting wet out here.

Utamaro Someone do something.

Nishimura Sword, please build a canopy over us. We're getting wet.

A canopy appears over them.

Sharaku Thanks, Sword.
Utamaro Another crisis over.

The rain begins to fade.

Nishimura The storm is passing. But in case it returns,
Sword, I had better have a waterproof cloak . . . with
just a simple gold motif around the edge.

A golden cloak appears.

Sharaku Are you sleeping, Utamaro?
Utamaro No, but I should be. Putting a new roof on a
house and widening the door is exhausting work.

They settle down to sleep.

Buncho I'm bored.
Sharaku Well, ask the Sword to un-bore you.
Buncho Sword . . . un-bore me.

Pause.

Nothing has happened.
Utamaro What? You mean the Sword has failed to
answer a request?
Sharaku Is the Sword losing its power?

General panic.

Sharaku Wait, wait. Be quiet. (*Pause.*) Oh. Most
wonderful Sword, sword of plenty, sword of life . . .
please give me a diamond as big as an eagle's egg.

A large diamond appears. They all laugh, relieved.

Buncho That was an exciting moment. Broke my
boredom. Clever old Sword.

They all sit down. Silence

I think I'm still bored.

Utamaro Well, why don't you go away somewhere?

Buncho I couldn't do that. Besides, where is better than here? Oh no . . . I couldn't go away.

Utamaro Ask the Sword to provide you with an adventure.

Buncho Adventure? That could be dangerous.

Nishimura Ask for a nice safe adventure.

Buncho Yes, an adventure that goes on around me but doesn't require me to take part or move from this spot.

Nishimura But something exciting all the same.

Sharaku A nice armchair adventure.

Buncho But what? Utamaro, what do you think?

Utamaro Oh, go to sleep. Have a dream. That's a nice way to have adventures.

Buncho Go to sleep. Right.

Sharaku Sleep, sleep. Day in, day out. Do you think the Sword can stop us getting old?

Silence. They all look at Sharaku.

Buncho We could ask. Of course, it would take rather a long time to find out whether it could or could not. I mean to say, I look at myself in the mirror today and I seem exactly as old as I did yesterday.

Utamaro The only way to tell would be to look in the mirror and see if you look as old today as you will tomorrow.

Nishimura Impossible.

Utamaro Not if we ask the Sword to let us see into the future.

Sharaku Yes, into the future.

Buncho Sword . . . let us see into the future.

Sharaku I'm sure I'll be distinguished and wise.

They all look into mirrors.

Buncho See anything?

Nishimura No.

Sharaku No.

Buncho No.

Utamaro Nothing.

Nishimura This Sword is getting lazy.

> *Yuki appears. He is a young boy of about sixteen.*
> *He is not as fat as they are, or dressed in expensive*
> *clothes.*

Yuki Good day, citizens of Utagowa.

Utamaro Who are you?

Yuki My name is Yuki.

Utamaro Yuki. I've heard that name before. You're Yuki, the eastern-side ploughman's son?

Yuki No.

Sharaku He dresses shabbily like you.

Buncho Your face is somehow familiar. Have you appeared with the travelling players around these parts?

Yuki No.

Nishimura We know the name, and the face, but the deed escapes us. Are you famous for something?

Yuki Obviously not.

Sharaku The name Yuki does mean something to me, but I can't think.

Yuki It was I who found the Golden Samurai Sword and brought it to the city.

Utamaro Yes, of course. The boy who saved our city.

Buncho Who saved us all from starvation?

Utamaro That's right.

Buncho Well, well.

Sharaku I said that name was familiar. Well, well. And how have things been going for you, young man, since you saved the city?

Yuki Very well, thank you. I've travelled a great deal.

Sharaku That's . . . nice.

455

Nishimura By the way, did the gods order you to find the Golden Sword for us?

Yuki Not as far as I know.

Nishimura See, what did I tell you!

Utamaro I am Utamaro the builder. Why are you dressed so shabbily?

Buncho A hero should be dressed like a king.

Yuki Am I a hero?

Buncho Well, I imagine you are. Isn't he?

They all agree: 'Suppose so,' etc., etc.

Yuki I don't think I'm dressed shabbily. I could ask why you are dressed so lavishly?

Utamaro This is not lavish. These are our ordinary weekday clothes. You must dress well, Yuki, or you will be thought a beggar, and there are no beggars in our city. You have to keep up appearances. You don't want to stand out, do you – seem odd?

Yuki The Sword seems to have brought great wealth to the city.

Nishimura It fulfils our humble needs. Our lives are much the same as ever they were.

Utamaro For one who worked so hard to save this city you seem sadly out of touch with its habits and customs.

Yuki I left the city a year ago. In fact on the very day I handed the Golden Sword to our Empress. I have travelled the world since then. The habits and customs seem to have changed a great deal in my absence.

Sharaku Not really. Our clothes may be a little finer, but underneath we are the same people as ever.

Nishimura Warm, honest folk, troubling no one.

Buncho Tell me, why did you travel? I mean, everything you could possibly want is here. Travel is so exhausting.

Yuki Travel is exciting.

Utamaro Well, you might think so, but we could travel
without moving outside the city walls. I'm sure if we
asked the Sword it would bring India to us. . . instead
of us having to go to it.

Buncho Or Africa.

Nishimura Or anywhere.

Yuki But you would miss the adventures of the journey,
of meeting new people.

Sharaku I don't think he quite grasps what a wonderful
life we have here .

Nishimura If he enjoys travel so much, why, I wonder,
has he returned?

Sharaku I'll ask. Tell me, Yuki . . . do you intend to stay
in the city long?

Yuki Oh no.

Sharaku Why did you return?

Yuki To fulfil the promise I made to the Golden Samurai
Warrior.

Nishimura Warrior?

Utamaro Promise?

Yuki That after one year I would take the Golden Sword
back to the forest it comes from so that other . . .

Utamaro *What?* Wait!!

Sharaku I knew it. The gods are angry with us.

Buncho Our Sword!

Utamaro Returned.

Nishimura Never! It's our Sword now.

Utamaro Are you mad? Are you insane? Do you realise
what you are saying?

Yuki But I promised the Sword would be returned. It
saved the city . . .

Sharaku We never promised. It's our Sword. We all bow
to it. Really we do, gods! We're good people, gods! Let
us keep the Sword.

Buncho It stays with us.

Sharaku We must pray hard to the gods.

Yuki But. . .

Utamaro No buts.

Yuki But. . .

Utamaro Tut-tut.

Yuki But. . .

Utamaro Tut.

Yuki If you break the promise I made you will incur the wrath of the gods.

Sharaku Oh, no, he's their messenger.

Utamaro A moment, young man.

The citizens go into a huddle. Then they turn and smile.

Sharaku Yuki, we were hasty.

Buncho Of course we must return the Sword.

Nishimura We were foolish to think we could keep it for ever.

Utamaro Forgive us, Yuki. This great wealth is but a small thing compared to the promise given by the one who saved our city. Our lives have changed, and so it seems have we. We show only the ugly side of our character. The Sword must be returned. We will meet you outside the city walls tonight, and there we will hand over the Sword.

Yuki Thank you. You are wise.

Yuki exits.

Sharaku What are we going to do?

Utamaro Become wise. We must think.

Buncho Think? I haven't thought for so long, I don't think I can think.

Nishimura We could ask the Sword what to do.

Utamaro The Sword would hardly take our side against Yuki and the gods. Besides, the Sword might want to go back to the forest. We have worked it rather hard over the last year.

Nishimura Perhaps if we gave it a rest.
Sharaku Let's not ask for anything for a few minutes.
Utamaro No, no. We must think.
Buncho I'm trying to think but I don't seem able to.
Utamaro Try harder.

They all try to think.

Sharaku No, we'll have to ask the Sword to help.
Utamaro It won't help, not in this.
Buncho Well, what are we going to do?
Sharaku We must seek the advice of our Empress. We are
her subjects . . . if anything happens to us it's her fault,
not ours.
Utamaro At last we are thinking.
Sharaku What do you mean 'we'? I thought of it.
Utamaro Sssh! We are united in a common cause. *We*,
therefore, are *we*. It is important we see the Empress
alone. We need to impress upon her the importance
of keeping the Sword in the city. We don't want her
ministers or her guards interrupting. Sword, put all the
ministers and all the Imperial Guard to sleep . . . for
about an hour!

Sharaku looks offstage.

Sharaku The guards on the palace gates have fallen
down.
Utamaro The rest will do them good.
Utamaro Sword, take us into the presence of our
Empress Tiasharn.

They find themselves in the presence of the Empress.

Voice Bow, humble subject, before your Empress.

The citizens try to bow but it isn't easy.

Buncho I find the bow such a difficult manoeuvre these
days.

Nishimura I think we should do away with everything difficult.

Sharaku Another ritual to go, eh?

Voice Silence.

Empress My subjects, it has been many months since you came to seek my advice.

Buncho How does she know we need advice?

Empress I sit here in the Imperial Palace, surrounded by the Imperial Guard, and I do nothing. I rule over a kingdom that appears to rule itself. You do not call to pay your respects, or visit to enquire after my health.

Utamaro You have been ill, Majesty?

Empress No . . . but that is not the point.

Sharaku We haven't called, Majesty, because things have been going rather well on the outside.

Empress But you are here now. Does that mean that things are no longer going well?

Nishimura (*aside*) She has insight.

Utamaro A slight setback, Majesty. Nothing more.

Empress Setback?

Sharaku A slight one. But nothing the gods in their great wisdom can't help with.

Buncho Sssh. Nothing to worry about, Majesty.

Empress Then why are you here?

They all look at Utamaro.

What kind of setback?

Nishimura We can't think.

Empress You have lost the power of thought?

Buncho We think so.

Pause.

Empress Rubbish.

Utamaro No, it's true.

Sharaku We need a plan and we can't think of one.

Empress Why do you need a plan?

Utamaro Sssh. Majesty, one year ago our city was
crumbling, your subjects were dying of starvation. We
were brought the Golden Samurai Sword of Tenshan.

Empress By the boy, Yuki, from the Northern Forests.

Buncho Assisted by you, Majesty. You travelled to the
Northern Forests, Majesty. A brave thing to do.
Something . . .

Utamaro Majesty, you will agree that the Sword has
brought great wealth and happiness to the city.

Sharaku Thanks to the gods!

Buncho *And* to Her Majesty.

Empress The Sword made the crops grow, the rain fall.

Sharaku Made us rich.

Empress Money doesn't interest me. I've always been
wealthy.

Utamaro I'm sure you will agree, Majesty, that it would
be a tragedy if the Sword were to be . . . taken away
from us.

Empress As I remember, Utamaro the builder, it was
agreed that we should keep the Sword for one year
only. When we were starving we readily agreed to that
arrangement.

Utamaro Someone came to that arrangement on our
behalf, Majesty.

Empress Yes . . . the young boy, Yuki.

Sharaku Life is so much nicer with the Sword than
without it, Majesty. For a whole year we've had food
to eat and all the money we need . . . well not quite
all . . .

Utamaro Majesty, the Sword is now ours, and it must
stay with us.

Empress Must!

Pause.

Utamaro Must.

Buncho A certain person has returned to the city.

Empress Who has returned?

Sharaku The boy Yuki, to take the Sword away.

Empress (*excitedly*) Yuki is here in the city?

Utamaro I don't like the way she said that.

Sharaku Do you think she likes him?

Utamaro Could be. We must tread carefully. We thought
. . . hoped you would share our opinion that the
Sword should stay in our city.

Empress The Sword should stay in our city . . . until the
agreed time is up. Then it should be returned to the
Forbidden Forests of the North.

Utamaro No!

Pause.

Please . . . no.

Empress How dare you disagree? I am your Empress.

Utamaro Well, actually, with the power of the Sword
we can all be emperors, empresses, knights, warriors
or wealthy merchants. We can be anything we want
to be.

Empress Where is your allegiance to me?

Utamaro Fading.

Sharaku Oh, do be careful, Utamaro, we don't want to
do anything controversial.

Utamaro Do you want the Sword to go or stay?

All Stay.

Utamaro There, the will of your people.

Empress And I say, the Sword is returned. Guards, arrest
these people.

Nothing happens.

Where are my guards?

Utamaro We asked the Sword to put them to sleep. A
precaution we thought wise to take before coming here.

Empress By plotting to keep the Sword you are working for an evil purpose. The Sword will not help you in this.

Utamaro Then we will make the Sword believe our purpose is good.

Sharaku How, Utamaro, how?

Utamaro Well, I don't know! Must I think of everything?

Empress You will have to think very hard and be extremely cunning to fool the Sword. For people who have not thought for themselves for so long it will not be an easy task.

Utamaro Then we will find someone cunning.

Sharaku Who, Utamaro, who?

Utamaro The one person who has never been able to ask the Sword for anything. Who has been in the palace dungeon for a year?

Buncho Who?

Utamaro The Royal Proclamation Reader. Citizen, release him and bring him here immediately.

The citizen dashes off.

Empress Are you fools? Don't you remember when you were all starving how the Proclamation Reader hid sacks of grain in his home?

Utamaro A wise precaution. We should learn from such a man.

Empress He would have let you starve to death. Do you not remember how he plotted to seize power from me?

Utamaro So he's ambitious. A powerful force, ambition.

Empress He would have ruled you as a tyrant.

Utamaro That is only your opinion. He is cunning, crafty and ruthless. Just the man we need in this time of crisis.

Empress No.

Utamaro Majesty, you would hand the Sword back. We wish to keep it, and our wealth. We need a hawk not a dove. Sword, free the Royal Proclamation Reader from the palace dungeon. Sword, prison is an evil place.

Sharaku Have we taken command of the palace?

Utamaro Well . . . yes, I believe we have. There has been a coup.

Sharaku Oh, I see.

The Royal Proclamation Reader appears in chains.

Proclamation Reader So, the good people of Utagowa have a problem. I knew you would need to call on me one day.

Utamaro Royal Proclamation Reader . . .

Proclamation Reader *Ex*-Royal Proclamation Reader. Someone here had me stripped of my title and thrown into a dungeon. Didn't they, Majesty!

Empress A fitting place for a scoundrel.

Proclamation Reader But now the people want me.

Utamaro Proclamation Reader, you must help us.

Proclamation Reader What if I choose not to?

Utamaro Then the Golden Sword will be taken by the boy Yuki and returned to the Forbidden Forests of the North.

Sharaku And we'll lose everything.

Utamaro And we can't let that happen.

Proclamation Reader What are you willing to do to prevent this happening?

Sharaku Oh, anything . . . aren't we?

All Oh yes.

Proclamation Reader Excellent.

Empress Don't be so stupid. Don't you realise what will happen if you follow this man?

Buncho Yes, we'll keep our lovely homes and jewels, and be happy.

Proclamation Reader Bind her hands.

They tie up the Empress.

Proclamation Reader You should have thought of that straight away. She could have run to the shrine and asked the Sword to put you all to sleep for a week, and then where would you have been?

Buncho Well, if we were asleep we wouldn't really know where we were. One really has to be awake to know where one is exactly.

Proclamation Reader What you have to say is not worth listening to. I advise silence.

Buncho Sorry.

Proclamation Reader When is the boy Yuki coming to take the Sword from you?

Utamaro Tonight. We arranged to meet him outside the city walls.

Sharaku A good place for an ambush, eh?

Proclamation Reader We are not going to adopt the cudgel tactics of the common herd, citizen. To outwit Yuki and the Golden Sword we need cunning. Is there a metalworker among you?

Buncho I was a metalworker.

Proclamation Reader I shall require all your skills. First, remove these chains, and then . . .

Buncho Oh . . . we . . . you see . . . I haven't actually worked for a year. My metalwork may be a bit rusty. See, since we've had the Sword we haven't needed to work. If anyone wants anything in metal they ask me and I ask the Sword. Labour-saving . . . so to speak.

Proclamation Reader So you are a metalworker in name only. Your skill has gone.

Buncho It wasn't my fault. I mean, the Sword did everything. What would you have done?

Proclamation Reader Something different. We shall have to do the best we can in the time we have left. Meet me tonight outside the city walls.

Utamaro But we must know . . .

Proclamation Reader Do not ask me questions.

The Proclamation Reader exits.

Sharaku Well . . . I suppose we do need his help.

Buncho Oh, why did Yuki have to come back? I wish the boy no harm, but why couldn't he have been eaten by some wild animal in one of those countries he visited. This is all his fault.

Sharaku Well, I know what I'm going to do. If the Sword does have to be returned, I'm going to ask for as much as I can before it goes.

Buncho That's a good idea. We can stock up.

Nishimura Utamaro, what shall we do with the Empress?

Utamaro We shall . . . er . . . we shall . . . we shall ask the Proclamation Reader. Come.

As they exit:

Nishimura We don't really want to do this, Majesty, but we have no choice. You understand?

Exit.
Evening, outside the city walls. Yuki enters. The great city bell chimes the hour: eight o'clock.

Yuki Where are they? I wanted to be on my journey by now.

Suddenly a voice speaks to him in a ghostly echo.

Voice Yuki –

Yuki spins round but there is no one there.

Yuki Who's there?

Yuki goes to where he thought the voice came from.

Who called me?

The voice comes from behind him.

Voice Yuki.

Yuki Who's there?

Voice (*all around him*) Trust no one. Beware.

Yuki Who is that?

A light comes up and fades on a Golden Samurai Warrior.
   Yuki runs to the spot but no one is there.

Wait!

Music is heard. Utamaro leads the Citizens in a torch-lit procession.

Utamaro Yuki, there you are. We decided to hold a street procession to make the farewell to our golden benefactor a joyous occasion. After all, when the Golden Sword has been returned to the Forbidden Forests of the North others less fortunate than ourselves will seek its help.

Yuki I must say you are taking this very well.

Utamaro That's the kind of people we are. This morning we were blinded by greed. We have seen our mistakes and are big enough to admit them. We were fools this morning.

Nishimura But we aren't fools now.

Sharaku That's true.

Utamaro Yuki, the Golden Sword of Tenshan.

Utamaro steps back and the hooded Proclamation Reader enters, holding ths Sword. It is covered in a golden cloth.
   Yuki takes the Sword. the hooded Proclamation Reader exits. Yuki watches him go.

Utamaro Carry it safely. Off you go. Goodbye. Good luck.

They all wave at Yuki. He stares at them.

Yuki Yes, but . . .

They stop waving.

Utamaro Yes?

Yuki Well, I mean . . . is that it? Just 'Here you are, goodbye.'

Utamaro Do you want a reward for returning the Sword?

Yuki Oh no. You don't seem very concerned about it leaving.

Utamaro Yuki, as you get older you will realise that one has to be philosophical about such things. Today a Golden Sword, tomorrow rusty scissors. Goodbye. Good luck. Go.

They all wave at him.

Yuki Well . . . goodbye.

He exits. They watch him go.

Utamaro He's going.

Sharaku He's going.

Buncho He's going.

Nishimura He's going.

All He's going.

They all laugh. The Proclamation Reader enters.

Utamaro You were right. We fooled him.

Proclamation Reader Of course. By the time he realises what we have done he will be back in the Forbidden Forests. The Keepers of the Sword will naturally assume he is trying to keep the real Sword for himself. Let us hope their vengeance will be final.

Utamaro How can we ever thank you, Proclamation Reader? You are of course a free man now, and you may stay with us to enjoy the freedom of the city.

Proclamation Reader Oh, I intend to enjoy the freedom of the city, Utamaro. I intend to do a great many things. I have already begun. For security reasons I have removed the Sword from the shrine you had built and put it in a safer place.

Utamaro Where?

Proclamation Reader A safer place.

Utamaro But we need to know where it is.

Proclamation Reader You no longer have the bother of walking all the way to the shrine in order to ask the Sword for help. Walk to me and I shall ask the Sword for you. This will save you time, and trouble.

Buncho You mean you are the Sword's representative?

Proclamation Reader Precisely. And for our protection I plan to raise an army.

Nishimura But the Sword will not help us with weapons of war.

Proclamation Reader My army will make peace . . . everywhere!

Sharaku But we have peace.

Proclamation Reader All the more reason for having an army. Make sure we keep it. We are a wealthy city. Who knows how many vagabonds are at this moment plotting to steal all we have?

Utamaro I'd never thought of it like that.

Proclamation Reader We must be prepared. Our security is paramount. Be alert, be afraid. Trust me, I'll take care of you. If you need me I shall be at the Imperial Palace.

He exits.

Utamaro The Imperial Palace?

Buncho Is he our Emperor now?

Utamaro I have no idea.

Sharaku What a confusing day. This morning everything was wonderful. Now, cunning plots, counter-cunning plots. He has the Sword, he's living in the Imperial

Palace, and the Empress is in a dungeon. Can that be right, Utamaro?

Utamaro He kept the Sword in the city. We haven't lost our wealth. That's all you need remember.

Buncho True. Well, I'm tired. Anything worth doing today can always wait until tomorrow . . . as the new saying goes. I wish the Sword were still here. I'd ask it to lift me home and straight into my bed.

Buncho is looking at the now empty shrine.

Sharaku He's removed the Sword! It won't work for us any more. I knew we should have organised our own plot.

Nishimura We couldn't think of one . . . remember?

Sharaku We should have tried harder. Oh, this is a fine state of affairs when you can't get lifted to your own bed any more. Right! That's it! There's only one thing to do now! That is it!

Utamaro What?

Sharaku We walk home.

Buncho Walk? Walk? But . . . it's half a mile.

Sharaku We'll take a rest halfway. Come on.

They all mumble their discontent as the lights change.

A forest. A curtain of vines and large spiders' webs, thick as tree trunks, appears. Strange bird calls are heard.

Yuki enters. He looks at the obstacle before him. He tries to break through with his bare hands but fails.
He takes out the Golden Sword.

Yuki Golden Sword, work your magic.

He swings at the vines with the Sword but fails to get through. He can't believe it. He stares at the Sword.
He tries again but fails to cut a way through.
He tries again and again, nothing happens.

The Sword has failed. I don't understand. Wait . . . the gold is peeling from the blade.

He touches the blade and gets gold paint on the palm of one hand. He takes a half-hearted swipe at the vine and more paint comes off the blade.

Yuki So, you thought to fool me with a useless sword, did you? Well, good citizens, now you must beware. You will not enjoy your new power for long. I shall shake the foundations of your imperial city! The guardians of the Golden Sword shall have their revenge.

As he runs off, a golden light comes up on the Golden Warrior. The light fades quickly to blackout.

Palace dungeon.
     There is the sound of something scuttling in the darkness.
     A single spot hits the Golden Sword. It is fixed on its point to a pedestal. The pedestal stands about eight feet high.
     A door slides open and a shaft of light floods in.
     Standing in silhouette are the Proclamation Reader and the Empress. He fixes a candle in a sling near the door.

Proclamation Reader There, Majesty. My Golden Sword, the source of my power. I shall be the greatest emperor the world has ever known. You are silent. I take that to mean you have no objection to my seizing power. This will be your home. You threw me into this dungeon. It would be impolite of me not to return the kindness. I do hope you will try to reach the Sword.

Empress I shall try . . . fool.

Proclamation Reader Good. The creature I have set to guard my Sword will be pleased.

Empress Creature?

Proclamation Reader If you listen you will hear it moving around in the darkness.

They listen to the Creature scuttling around.

Empress What is it?

Proclamation Reader I will leave you to imagine what it might be. A leopard, perhaps? A thing that is half-man, half-beast? Or an enormous deadly spider hanging from the roof . . . ready to spring on you at any moment? Think about it . . . Majesty.

The Creature scuttles around again. The Empress reacts.

There it is again. It will watch you day and night. You are safe so long as the flame burns. But when the flame dies . . . it will leap upon you. Goodbye, Majesty. Gaze upon my power and envy me.

He exits and slams the door closed.
The Creature moves in the darkness. The Empress stands near the burning torch.

Empress A spider.

She feels it could be anywhere.

The nightmare.
Sharaku wakes, screaming. He is covered in a diamond-encrusted bed sheet. The only light comes from the jewels.

Sharaku It's not my fault. It wasn't me! Are you awake next door? Buncho?

Buncho Yes. I can't sleep.

Nishimura Normal life has become absurd.

Utamaro (*waking*) Noisy neighbours.

They get up, pulling jewel-encrusted bed sheets around them. Like slow-moving cones they meet in the town square.

Sharaku I dreamed the boy returned to take revenge.
Utamaro Dreaming? Well, at least you are doing something for yourself for once. He will not return.
Nishimura I heard the Watch ride out.
Utamaro Then they will find him and finish him. What can a boy do against the Watch?

The Proclamation Reader's face, white, ghostly, seeming detached from his body, suddenly appears.

Proclamation Reader He has entered the city. Join the guards, the Watch, and search for him.

Pandemonium breaks out – shouting. Torches and lanterns lit as the Watch and citizens search for Yuki.

The palace dungeon.
   The Creature is heard in the darkness. The burning torch is almost out, but the Empress prods the darkness with it.
   The Creature hisses as she tries to move towards the Sword. The hissing gets louder. She keeps moving forward.
   Suddenly the cell door is thrown open and Yuki stands framed in the doorway.

Yuki Majesty.
Empress Yuki! You returned! The Proclamation Reader has seized power. Stay back. There is a deadly creature guarding the Sword. Stay back I say.
Yuki Run to safety, Majesty.
Empress I must reach the Sword. I cannot allow that evil man to rule my city.
Yuki But the Creature . . .

Empress Silence. If I can just touch the Sword it will be unable to harm us.

She moves forward.

Yuki It's there above you!

The Empress jumps back.

It is crawling down the wall of the cell. Run, Majesty.
Empress No.

She moves forward. The Proclamation Reader is heard.

Proclamation Reader Guards, the boy Yuki has been seen in the palace. Seek him out.
Yuki The Proclamation Reader is coming this way.
Empress So the choice is between a spider and a rat.

She leaps for the Sword and grabs it.

Sword, defend us against evil.

There is a silence.

It worked. The Creature seems to sleep. It cannot fight the power of the Sword.

They move away from the cell door.

We are safe now.

The Proclamation Reader stands in the doorway, Sword in hand. He creeps towards them.
　The Empress spins round and points the Samurai Sword at him.

Empress Do not move or try to call for help.
Proclamation Reader What are you going to do?
Empress Climb.
Proclamation Reader But the Creature is up there.

Empress It is powerless against the Sword. Climb.
Proclamation Reader But if you take the Sword away
I will have no protection against it.
Empress You trained the beast!
Yuki Reason with it.

*She points the Sword at him. He climbs onto the
pedestal.*

Proclamation Reader You can't leave me like this.
Empress Why not? You wanted to be Emperor. Surely
being put on a pedestal is the fulfilment of all your
dreams.
Proclamation Reader It will kill me.

*Yuki and the Empress exit. They close the door.
The Creature hisses and moves.*

Help!

*The lights come up on the town square. The Citizens
enter in a state of nervous excitement.*

Sharaku He's sitting on top of a pillar, I tell you. I peeped
through the spy-hole in the door. There he was, calling
for help.
Buncho And did you help him?
Sharaku I didn't have the key to his cell.
Nishimura Was the Sword in the cell with him?
Sharaku No.
Utamaro It is obvious where the Sword is. Yuki and the
Empress were seen leaving the city. They are returning
our Sword to the Forests of the North.
Buncho It's all the Proclamation Reader's fault. He
thought he was so clever.
Sharaku Should we release him from the cell, Utamaro?
Utamaro No, let him rot. We have no further use for
him.

Nishimura Who else can we ask to help us? The people in the north of the city are blaming us for losing the Sword. They say we must get it back . . . or else.

Utamaro Or else what?

Nishimura Or else there won't be an east side to the city. They threaten to burn our homes and drive us into the mountains.

Buncho They can't do that. They're our friends.

Nishimura Not any more. It's a bad business.

Buncho So what are we to do?

Utamaro enters.

Utamaro We must pursue Yuki and the Empress and try to rescue our Sword.

Sharaku You mean . . . go outside the city walls?

Utamaro Yes.

Sharaku I don't know, it sounds dangerous.

Buncho Couldn't we send someone to do it for us? Pay someone . . . a champion. (*Pause.*) Someone we all respect . . . Utamaro . . . dear friend.

Nishimura Of course. Someone who is a natural leader. Utamaro?

Sharaku Someone we admire . . . Utamaro . . . brave Utamaro.

They stand before him, smiling, humble.

Utamaro Do you have anyone in mind?

All Well . . .

Pause.

Utamaro No! No, no, no! I refuse to go alone.

Sharaku You're being very unreasonable.

Utamaro How dare you! Who thought of releasing the Proclamation Reader for you?

Buncho Yes, and look where that got us.

Utamaro Did you have any better ideas?

476

Buncho Might have done . . . given time.

Utamaro We didn't have time. Besides, you said you couldn't think.

Buncho I never did. That wasn't me. Someone else . . .

Utamaro It was you . . . and you . . . and you . . . all of you.

They break into a big general argument.

Stop! Silence! We are wasting time. Our Sword is being carried back to the Forbidden Forests. Once there we will never see it again. Let's stop arguing and do something.

Sharaku What?

Utamaro Got to the Forests of the North!

Buncho Oh . . . it shouldn't happen to civilised folk.

He leads them off.

The foothills leading to the Forests of the North.
A cold wind howls. Yuki and the Empress enter.

Empress The wind of the Northland.

They listen to the moan of the wind.

Yuki Legend tells how an angry god, displeased with the wind, banished it to these mountains. The sad wail is the wind crying to be released from this desolate place.

Empress I think that highly unlikely. Poetic but unlikely. Do you suppose there are bandits lurking in these hills?

Yuki We have the Sword to protect us if there are.

Empress Should we go on? It is almost dark. The mountain paths will be dangerous at night. Perhaps we should camp here.

Yuki Very well. There seems a good place. Perhaps I can hunt for our supper.

Empress Why hunt? We have the Sword.

Yuki Of course. Sword . . . supper for two.

Food appears.

It works. I've never actually seen it in action.

The Empress tucks in.

Empress My subjects have been stuffing themselves from
the moment it arrived in the city. They are all so huge
they have to build larger houses all the time. Some are
now almost as large as my Imperial Palace. Do they
think endless wealth and a life of ease will make them
happy?

Yuki After the poverty they have known, I think it's safe
to assume they'd answer yes.

She looks at him for a moment.

Empress These people, my subjects, are pursuing us with
ill intent. Don't forget that. Goodnight.

Yuki Goodnight.

*The Empress goes to sleep. Yuki checks there are no
beasts or bandits around, and then goes to sleep.*
   *Kung the bandit appears. He is old, tired, and sick
of being a bandit. He carries a lantern and mumbles,
dejectedly.*

Kung I am the once mighty Kung, bandit and thief. But
I'm not so mighty any more. You can't make a decent
living as a bandit in a desolate place like this. I suppose
it's berries for supper again. Hello.

He spots Yuki and the Empress.

Asleep. A young man and a rich-looking lady. I'll make a
fortune. A quick kill, steal their purses. Where's my
club?

He fumbles for his club. He moves towards them, club

478

raised. In his other hand is a lantern.
Just as Kung is about to hit Yuki, he turns over.

Yuki Aahh!!
Kung Aahh!!

The Empress leaps up and grabs the Sword.

You!
Yuki Who are you?
Kung Who am I? You don't remember?
Yuki Should I?
Kung Should you? Should you?
Empress Are you a bandit? What do you want?
Kung What about my head?
Empress Your head?
Kung My head. I can't do my work properly because of
my head.
Empress Oh . . . dear. Step back, Yuki, I think he's mad.
Kung And it's your fault.
Empress As an Empress one is of course blamed for
many things that have nothing to do with one.
Kung One year ago you were in these mountains. Am I
correct? I am. You were going to the Northern Forests.
Am I right? Oh yes.
Yuki How do you know?
Kung A certain hard-working bandit tried to rob you.
Am I right? You know I am. He was a daring bandit.
He had great fighting skills.
He knew all the tricks he did. You fought with him
and the bandit had the upper hand . . .
Yuki I remember fighting, but I wouldn't say he had the
upper hand . . .
Kung Yes he did! Oh, I just wish . . . (*He emphasises his
point by tapping the Sword Yuki is holding.*) I could
show you that fight. Then we'd see who had the upper
hand.

479

A year-younger Kung and a year-younger Yuki appear, fighting. Kung has the upper hand.

Younger Kung I have the upper hand.

Kung He had the upper hand. Until a heavy object . . . a boulder, in fact, rendered the bandit unconscious and gave the young man something of an advantage . . . as you can imagine it might. (*realising he's just seen a fight from a year ago*) How did that happen?

Empress We didn't see anything.

Kung I think I just had a vision.

Yuki But how do you know all this?

Kung Know what?

Yuki The fight, the boulder.

Kung Because I've still got the lump on my head. I am that bandit!

Yuki You? But you've changed so.

Kung I've fallen on hard times.

Empress We must beware, Yuki.

The Empress threatens Kung with the Sword.

Kung There's no need for that. I'm retired as a bandit. After that lump on my head things went from bad to worse. Well, now it's visions. I couldn't seem to co-ordinate my Sword swings and the knife-thrust properly, and the chops and kicks . . . well . . . desperate, they were. I'd stop the odd traveller, but they'd always get away. If I'd worked in your city I would have got money for my injury.

Empress But as an outlaw you must have expected some injury in the course of your career.

Kung Not permanent damage. I can't work now.

Empress Then go the city and find other employment.

Kung I tried. I went to your city of Utagowa. Are you really the Empress?

Empress Actually, yes.

Kung Right, well, I'll tell you about your citizens. They asked me where I was from, who I was, what I wanted to do. 'You must answer all our questions truthfully.' So I did. I said I'd been a bandit but had to give it up for health reasons, and I quite fancied something in trade.

Yuki And what did they say?

Kung 'Get out and don't come back or we'll chop off your head.' So much for telling the truth.

Empress But that's a terrible thing. You told them the truth as they asked. They should have respected that.

Kung That may work in the circles you move in, but clearly not in mine. I don't suppose you'd have a piece of food I could borrow?

Empress Borrow? No, I'm afraid . . . oh . . . Yuki could you trap something, and cook it for our friend here?

Yuki Oh yes, Majesty. You look as though you could do with a good meal.

Kung I certainly could. I've been living on berries for the last few months, and that's not all it's cracked up to be.

Yuki I'll see what I can do for you.

Yuki runs off.

Kung Anything will do . . . so long as it's not berries again. Funny, meeting you two up here.

Empress Yes.

Kung Come here every year, does he?

Yuki appears with a platter of food.

Aahh. How . . . I mean . . . how . . .

Yuki It's for you.

Kung How did you . . . ? You didn't trap and cook that. You've only been gone a second. I'm dreaming. Not another vision, is it?

Empress Yuki is a fine hunter.

Kung Fast, too.

Yuki Eat.

Kung This is very nice of you. What are you doing up here in the mountains?

Empress We are making our way to the Forbidden Forests.

Kung Strange area, eerie. Why are you going there?

Yuki Oh, just to return something.

Empress What will you do now that you can no longer work as a bandit?

Kung I don't know. I'm not trained for anything else. I'd be fine if I could come across someone travelling alone . . . someone weak – little old lady, say. But the chance of finding someone like that up here is very remote.

Yuki Yes, it must be difficult.

Empress Yuki!

Yuki Oh, I don't mean that I agree with stealing from people, Majesty, it's just that . . . well we are sort of responsible for his dilemma.

Empress The man is a common thief. He should not be encouraged in his life of crime.

Yuki Oh, I wasn't encouraging him, Majesty.

Kung He couldn't encourage me. I'm sick of crime.

Empress Then why do you wish to find some little old lady to steal from?

Kung Old habits die hard. Once you've seen action . . .

Yuki Majesty, I'm sure he could help us. He knows these mountains. He may know a more direct route to the Forests.

Kung I do. I'll guide you, if you like.

Empress You will be rewarded.

Kung Really? Well, honesty may not be such a bad thing after all . . . but time will tell.

Empress I think we should go now. If they are following us they won't see us at night.

Kung Someone after you?

Yuki Well, yes.

Kung How many?

Empress We're not sure. Maybe one . . . maybe six . . . maybe a hundred.

Kung A hundred? Yes, well, I'll tell you what, I'll just point you in the right direction and slip back to my cave.

Yuki No, wait. We really need you to guide us. The mountain paths are dangerous. One false step and we could plunge a thousand feet into a canyon. We could die.

Kung Very possibly. Now, take this path until you come to . . .

Empress If you help us, I promise you a free pardon.

Kung Pardon?

Empress I said if you . . .

Kung Yes, I heard you. Pardon, you say? Pardon me?

Empress You have my word on that.

Kung Another chance? I'll be able to go to the city and get a good, honest, highly paid job?

Empress Of course, provided suitable employment can be found for you. After living this kind of life you can hardly expect to slip cosily into the ways of the city.

Kung Why not?

Empress Because the ways of the city are different to the ways of the mountains. What I'm trying to say is that you must not expect too much from the city. It is not a city paved with gold. Well, as a matter of fact it is paved with gold at the moment, since we've had the Sword, but things won't be all that easy for you. You'll have to adjust to city life. But you will be free – so long as you obey the laws and do as you're told.

He stares at them.

Kung Yes, well, if you follow this path until . . .

483

Empress No, no, please help us, and we'll help you in the city.

Yuki It's a matter of life and death.

Empress Only you can help us.

Kung Only me? You need me?

Empress Yes.

Kung No one's ever needed me before. I'm necessary. Follow me.

They all exit.

Another area of the same forest.
The citizens enter. They are tired and have lost weight, their clothes hang on them like dirty wash-rags.

Sharaku Oh, this is too much. I can't go on. Look at me. I've lost pounds in weight already. My clothes hang on me like dirty wash-rags.

Utamaro We must keep going. They can't be far ahead.

Buncho That's what you said four hours ago. And how do we get through there?

Utamaro Climb through. We must catch them and rescue our Sword. Come on.

They try climbing through the vine.

Nishimura I'm so hungry. Did anyone bring any food? I can't get through here.

Buncho Even something simple to eat would do. A pheasant, a bottle or two of wine. Nothing elaborate.

Utamaro We can't eat because we don't have the Sword to provide us with food. So we must go hungry. Can't you understand that? Oh, there's no way through.

Nishimura Why don't we try hunting for food?

They all freeze in different parts of the vine.

Utamaro I beg your pardon?

Nishimura Why don't we try hunting for food?

Utamaro Have you ever hunted for food?

Nishimura Many years ago, when I was young.

Utamaro Very well, if you think you can catch our
  supper, by all means go and do it. We will wait here.

Nishimura It will be much easier if we all help.

Sharaku We're not hunters.

Nishimura How hungry are you?

Sharaku Extremely.

Nishimura And do you want to eat?

Sharaku Of course.

Nishimura Then hunt with me. Let us all hunt together.
  Think of the feast we could enjoy.

Buncho He does have a point.

Utamaro Very well, we'll all go.

Nishimura Good. First take your clothes off.

Utamaro I beg your pardon?

Nishimura I don't mean all your clothes. We can't hunt
  for food if we're wearing heavy city clothes.

Utamaro But this coat is made from the finest silk.

Nishimura You can always get another coat, Utamaro . . .
  but not another stomach.

Utamaro I accept that, but all the same . . .

Nishimura Do you want to eat or not?

Utamaro I'll leave the coat here. I can collect it on the
  way back.

Nishimura Come on, take off everything that isn't
  absolutely necessary.

They remove their fine clothes.

And our jewels.

All Oh, come now.

Nishimura We will need to use our hands. How can we
  if they are weighed down by heavy jewellery?

Reluctantly they remove their jewellery.

Utamaro And now what?

Nishimura We go into the woods and try to catch our supper. Utamaro, Sharaku, that way; Buncho and I, this. We will return to this spot the moment we catch something.

Utamaro Oh, very well.

Utamaro and Sharaku exit.

(*off*) There's a rabbit.

They rush across the stage.

(*off*) Stop that rabbit.

They exit.

Buncho This is all getting out of hand. Wait for me.

Another part of the forest.
  Yuki, the Empress and Kung enter. They are very tired.

Yuki Oh no! More undergrowth to cut through.

Empress Yuki I must rest for a moment.

Kung Now you know why I don't come to the Forbidden Forests very often. It's like this all the way. Nice berries up here, though.

He eats the berries he has found.

Empress Do we have to go very far?

Kung About two more hours. Over that ridge, down into the valley, and then we'll see the Forest on the skyline. Berry?

Empress No. No one can catch us before we enter the Forbidden Forests.

Yuki Just what I was thinking, Majesty. We can afford a long rest here. The forest is dark and the undergrowth difficult to cut through. We will need all our strength to cut our way through to the Golden Statue.

Kung Golden what?

Empress Yuki!

Yuki Er . . . oh, nothing.

Kung You said something about gold.

Yuki No. Cut through to the . . . olden statue.

Kung Olden statue?

Yuki From the olden days.

Kung That doesn't make any sense. You did say gold.
Come on, admit it. You said gold, didn't you? Come
on, play fair.

Yuki looks at the Empress.

Empress Yes . . . he said gold.

Kung I knew he did. What Golden Statue?

Yuki The Golden Statue that stands at the very centre of
the Forbidden Forests. The Golden Statue that has for
five hundred years held and guarded the Golden
Samurai Sword of Tenshan.

Kung The Golden Samurai. I've heard of that. It's a
magical sword.

Empress Correct.

Kung And whoever has the Sword can have whatever he
wants?

Yuki Yes.

Kung And you're going to find this Sword?

Yuki No, we're taking it back.

Kung Are you out of your mind!

They hear voices.

Empress The citizens!

Kung Quick, climb.

They climb into the vines.
*Nishimura and Buncho rush across the stage with a
rabbit.*

Buncho We've got one! We must show the others.

They rush off.
Kung, Yuki and the Empress hang on to the vines.

Kung You're taking it back! Are you mad!

Empress How dare you.

Kung Well, I mean . . . the Golden Samurai. You can't take it back.

Yuki We can and we are.

Kung But you . . . And who were those two?

Empress Citizens from my city. They are trying to prevent us returning the Sword.

Yuki The Sword was only ours for one year. The year is up and so it must be returned.

Kung Say you forgot the date.

Empress No.

Kung Look, if you've finished with it, I don't mind taking it off your hands . . .

Empress No

Kung Why not? I could put it to good use.

Yuki No.

They hear the citizens call to each other.

Buncho Utamaro. Hello?

Utamaro Where are you?

Nishimura We've caught a rabbit.

Yuki If we don't move, they'll stumble upon us. Come on.

They jump down and Yuki cuts a way through the vines. The Empress and Yuki lead off. Kung runs after them.

Kung No, don't go. What about the Sword . . .?

They exit just as Utamaro enters.
Nishimura and Buncho enter from the opposite side. They all hold rabbits.

Utamaro I have one. Did you not see how I leapt at this wild rabbit?

Nishimura Did you see me corner the first rabbit? It's the first time I've hunted for my own supper.

Buncho With my help.

Nishimura Well, you were there, but it was I . . .

Buncho And I.

Utamaro Oh, come along and help light a fire. Where is Sharaku?

Buncho Utamaro look!

They stare at the hole cut through the vine.

Utamaro They must've come this way. Where's that fool Sharaku? We can't go on without him.

Nishimura (*shouts*) Sharaku!

Utamaro Sssh. The Empress and the boy may be nearby. We don't want them to hear us. Whisper.

They exit calling for Sharaku in whispers.

Another part of the forest. Yuki and the Empress enter. They creep through the undergrowth. Kung enters.

Kung Look . . . what right do you have to stop me having the Sword? It's not yours now the year's up.

Yuki I promised to return the Sword. I think we've thrown them off our track, Majesty.

Kung If you gave me the Sword I wouldn't ask it for much. Just a nice warm cloak and some food. Nothing much.

A cloak and food appears behind Kung.

Yuki Look behind you.

Kung Aahh.

Yuki All you asked for. Now you're satisfied, we can go on our way. Do you think they'll follow us here, Majesty?

Empress It would be safer to move to higher ground.

Kung puts the cloak on and picks up the food.
  Yuki and the Empress move off.

Kung I've just thought of something else I really need.
Empress And so it goes on. More and more. Come, Yuki, let us find safer ground.

Kung draws his sword.

Kung No. I'm sorry to have to do this, but that's a prize I can't let go. I don't want to fight you, but . . . if I have to . . . I mean . . . really have to . . . I suppose . . . I'll have to.

Yuki draws his Samurai Sword.

Yuki This Sword contains all the fighting skills of the Samurai Army of old. It does not need my hand to guide it.

The Sword flashes through the air and leads Yuki along.
  A loud swishing sound is heard as the Sword cuts through the air

It is the Sword that will defeat you, not I.

Kung tries to defend himself but is no match for the Golden Sword.

Kung Surrender. I'm sorry. (*He throws his sword away.*) I'm unarmed, and I'd like to remain unharmed.

Yuki stands facing Kung.

Empress According to ancient law, Yuki may take your life.
Kung I've never really taken much notice of the law. I'm a bandit. I'm retired but set in my ways. Of course I'd try to take the Golden Sword. Social conditioning. I suppose you're going to kill me now.

They hear voices.

Utamaro But you didn't see how I cornered that rabbit.
Others (*off*) Oh no, we all helped.
Yuki They're still after us! They're eating as they march.
Empress Then we must hide until they have passed by.
Kung There, behind the rocks. I'll send them on a false
 trail.
Yuki How?
Kung I'll tell them you went another way.

Yuki and the Empress stare at Kung.

Don't you trust me?

They shake their heads.

Empress Betray us, and even if we die . . . our spirits will
 haunt you.

They hide.

Kung Believe in ghosts, do you?

Kung steps into the shadows: the citizens enter, eating.

Nishimura This is the finest meal I have ever eaten.
Utamaro What about the fire I built? Was it not the
 finest blaze you've ever seen?
Buncho Is that the first fire you've ever built, Utamaro?
Utamaro No. Oh no, no, no. I built one when I was
 eight years old. That was my second fire.
Buncho It was very good. You obviously have a talent
 for it.
Nishimura As I have a talent for catching rabbit . . .
Buncho With my help.

Sharaku follows behind, looking ill.

Utamaro Sharaku, you're not eating. Isn't the meal the
 finest you ever tasted?

Sharaku Well, no . . . not really.

Nishimura But it's delicious. It was cornered, cooked and consumed by us.

Sharaku Exactly. That's why I don't feel very well.

Utamaro How odd. I feel wonderfully exhilarated.

Sharaku I've always loved eating rabbit. Every week I would get it from the butcher.

Utamaro Then what is wrong?

Sharaku I never had to kill the rabbits I ate. Now I've killed one with my own hands . . . I can't eat it.

They stare at Sharaku. Kung steps forward.

Kung You should eat berries, then.

Utamaro Aah. Have a care, fellow. We are armed.

Kung Oh, have no fear, I mean you no harm. I am just a traveller, like yourselves.

Utamaro Ah. Coming perhaps from the direction of the Forbidden Forests?

Kung I have come from that way, yes, sir.

Utamaro (*aside*) He may know something. Tell me, fellow, have you seen a young couple passing this way?

Kung A young couple of what?

Utamaro Ha. Ha. (*aside*) This could take time. A couple of people. One male and the other female. You would probably spot them as one, the female, is dressed in the imperial robes of an Empress, and the other, the male, carries a Golden Samurai Sword under his arm. Seen them?

Kung An Empress and a boy with a Golden Sword. Now let me think.

Utamaro Not something you see every day, I'll be bound.

Kung Well . . . (*Pause.*) Is there a reward for the information concerning these two?

Yuki and the Empress peep from their hiding place.

Sharaku You mean you've seen them?

Kung I didn't say I had . . . and I didn't say I hadn't. Is there a reward?

Buncho Yes.

Nishimura Where are they?

Kung What do you want them for?

Utamaro Oh, just a chat . . . general conversation.

Kung Have they stolen anything?

Sharaku Yes.

Utamaro Nothing of value.

Kung You mentioned a Golden Sword.

Utamaro Plate. Gold-plated sword . . . one carat only. Purely sentimental value. Where are they?

Kung The Sword's not worth anything, then?

Utamaro No, no.

Kung Then why are you looking for it?

Utamaro We're very sentimental.

Buncho And pushed for time. Have you seen them?

Kung If I said yes . . . what would you give me?

Sharaku We would give you gold.

Utamaro We are very wealthy people.

Kung Then why are you dressed like that?

Buncho We had to catch our supper.

Kung If you're wealthy you'd have servants to catch your supper. There's more to you than meets the eye.

Sharaku Just our luck to run into an intellectual. For the last time, have you seen them?

Kung Well – (*Kung wanders towards where Yuki and the Empress are hiding*) Yes, I have.

Utamaro You will be rewarded. Where are they?

Kung They are . . . running down that path over there.

Kung points off in some wild general direction.

Utamaro Good fellow. Call at the city gate and collect your reward. We won't forget you. Come on.

They all exit.

Kung You can come out now. I've saved the day.

Empress You have indeed.

Kung They lied about the value of the Sword. I can't stand dishonesty. Gold-plated, indeed.

Yuki We will never be able to thank you enough.

Empress When we return to the city, you will receive a great reward.

Yuki And now for the last stage of our journey.

Empress The Forbidden Forests.

They all exit.
   As the lights begin to fade Utamaro reappears: he watches the threesome walk away.

Utamaro So you thought to fool Utamaro. You are on the last stage of your journey . . . and the last day of your lives.

The lights fade to blackout.

The Forbidden Forests – strange light and sounds.
Yuki, the Empress and Kung enter.

Empress There is a strange presence here.

Yuki The forest is not as I remember it. The great wall surrounding it is crumbling, and the animal that guarded the gate has gone.

Kung The place smells of decay.

An animal screeches.

Kung Couldn't we just leave the Sword on the ground, and go?

Yuki We must find the Golden Statue.

Kung Yuki . . . the forest wall . . . it hasn't crumbled from age. See the gaping hole. It is as though some great force has burst through and gone into the world outside.

Yuki What could be so powerful to burst through? Wait. When I was in your city, Majesty, a voice – well, I think it was a voice – spoke to me.

494

Kung If it spoke it would have been a voice.

Yuki But there was no one there. Yet when I turned round I seemed to think I saw a Samurai Warrior, in golden armour. Majesty, the Golden Warriors have broken out of the forest and are at this moment searching for the Sword.

Kung The Golden Warriors are looking for that . . . and we've got it?

Yuki They are angry that their Sword has not yet been returned to them. Their vengeance will be terrible.

Kung Well, let's hurry and return it to them.

They move off, but hear a rustle in the darkness.

Yuki Ssshh. Did you hear that?

Empress I heard nothing.

In the darkness shadows begin to move.

Yuki I think we are being watched.

The shadows slowly surround the threesome.

Kung There is an evil presence here.

Kung draws his sword. Yuki draws his sword.

Empress Give me a dagger to fight with.

Kung hands her a dagger. They stand back to back and wait.

Utamaro You cannot escape this time.

Empress Utamaro!

The shadows move with menace.

Utamaro The Sword will soon be ours again.

Yuki We will fight to the death, Utamaro.

Utamaro So be it, Yuki, so be it.

Sharaku So be it.

Buncho So be it.

Nishimura So be it.

Silence.

Utamaro Now!!

The citizens rush from the darkness, and fight the threesome. Yuki drops the Golden Samurai Sword.
Yuki, the Empress and Kung are hacked to death by the citizens. Utamaro grabs the Sword.

The Sword is ours. We shall be the most powerful city on earth. We have everything.

The citizens cheer. Then there is silence. Then there is birdsong. The citizens stare at the dead bodies.

Nishimura Are they really dead?

Utamaro Yes.

Nishimura I didn't want to kill them. Well, not really.

Buncho What else could we do? We had to get the Sword.

Sharaku We had no choice.

Utamaro They started the fight.

Nishimura I know, but . . . well . . . the Empress never did us any harm.

Utamaro No one said she did. We had to get the Sword away from her. Not even a magic sword can bring the dead to life again. Let's just forget about it.

Buncho Yes, we'll only get depressed. Let's ask the Sword to give us something to cheer us up.

Nishimura Why don't you go hunting? (*referring to the bodies*) You seem to be good at that.

Utamaro We? We? You had a sword in your hand as well as us. This is as much your fault as ours. I didn't want to kill them either, but it was the only way. I'm not full of false remorse. If you're not willing to see something through to the end you shouldn't join in.

Nishimura But they're dead, Utamaro!

Words fail Utamaro.
Silence.

Buncho What will happen to us?
Utamaro We have the Sword . . . the power is now ours.
Isn't that what we wanted? What we plotted for?
What we pursued?

Silence.
In the distance the sound of swords cutting through
the air.

Sharaku What's that?
Buncho Quickly, let's get away from here.

The noise gets louder, coming closer.

Utamaro What can it be?
Nishimura I don't know, but it's coming this way. Let us
go.

From the darkness huge Golden Samurai Warriors
appear carrying Golden Swords. In the centre stands
the Golden Samurai statue, its arm raised but holding
no sword.

Utamaro The Golden Warriors!

The Citizens cry and beg for mercy.
Blackout.

In the darkness, Golden Swords cut the air. The sound
of battle becomes deafening. Then there is silence.

The city square, Utagowa. The citizens, as at the
beginning, are fat again. They sit, talking and eating.

Sharaku But do you think the Sword can stop us getting
old?
Buncho We could ask the Sword, but it would take
rather a long time to find out whether it could or could

not. I mean, I look at myself in the mirror today and seem exactly as old as I did yesterday.

Utamaro The only way to tell would be to look in the mirror and see if you look as old today as you will tomorrow.

Nishimura Impossible.

Utamaro Possible if we ask the Sword to let us see into the future.

Sharaku Yes. Ask the Sword to let us . . . Just a minute. I have a strange feeling I've been here before.

Utamaro And said these things before.

Nishimura I seem to think I've been in the mountains.

Nishimura You too?

Sharaku And before that I seem to think we released the Proclamation Reader –

Buncho – from prison, and he stole our Sword.

Utamaro But the Empress and a boy called Yuki took it to the Forbidden Forests, and we followed, and we . . . we . . .

Buncho Murdered them.

Silence.

Utamaro Did we do those things? Could we do such things? We who are civilised?

Sharaku We asked the Sword to let us see into the future . . . and it did.

Yuki enters.

Yuki Good day, citizens of Utagowa.

They all sit there looking at their second chance.

End.

When Need Becomes Greed

Geoffrey Case interviewed by Jim Mulligan

The citizens of a mythical town in Japan are bored. For a year they have been granted every wish and whim by a magic sword and now they are lazy, grotesquely fat, laden with jewels and *bored*. They think about what it will be like to grow old, and decide the only way to find out is to ask the Sword to give them a glimpse into the future. At first nothing happens and then the boy Yuki appears. Probably the audience will not notice but, from this point onwards, they are looking at the future, and it will only be at the end of the play, when they hear dialogue from the start of the play being repeated, that they will fully understand what they have been watching.

> In the final scene the citizens are exactly where they started off, in their wonderful clothes and lavish jewels. They have seen the future and seen what they have become: killers who hacked people to death in order to preserve what they had. They see that they justified the killing in the name of a greater good and they ask, 'Did we do those things? Could we do such things? We who are civilised.' And the stage directions are, 'They all sit there, looking at their second chance.' But I am afraid you only get second chances in the theatre.

Samurai is a swash-and-buckle, sword-and-sorcery adventure yarn. It is a legend made up by Geoff Case. It is primarily for entertainment but there are issues in the play that must be understood by the young people taking part. The citizens are not so much characters as mouthpieces for different points of view. They represent the moral choices that people make. The Sword represents a dependency culture and we are asked to contemplate what happens when the technology we depend on is taken from us.

> In this play you have to think about questions such as: how much is enough? what am I prepared to do to get what I want? and when does need become greed? I wrote the play at a time when there was a debate about using calculators in maths lessons. Some people were saying it dumbs down children, others that, if you use calculators and know what you are looking for, it is perfectly acceptable. The question I am interested in is: if everyone relies on the press of a button, what happens when you take the button away? The Sword is that button and the play shows how the citizens have become so dependent on it that they lose all moral perspective when they fear it will be taken away.

One of the issues dealt with in *Samurai* is the place of religion in our lives. Sharaku is scared of antagonising the gods who may then punish the town by taking away its privileges. Nishimura, on the other hand is a sceptic. His attitude is, 'I've never seen any of our gods. Have they ever done anything for me?' But the Sword is a graven image and has become a kind of god, and Sharaku reminds Nishimuru that it has saved them from starvation. In fact, the citizens do not mind who they pray to, whether it is a god or a Sword, as long as they get what they want.

The other major theme in *Samurai* is the nature of authority. The Empress is sitting in a palace when the town does not need her, yet she has authority over life and death. She is a benign ruler and has used her power to throw the Proclamation Reader into jail for the very good reason that he tried to overthrow her. But what happens if a ruler is a despot? When The Proclamation Reader is released, he consigns the Empress to the dungeon and plans to raise an army. Why? In the crazy world of power-politics the answer is simple: 'To make peace.' Little good it does him, however. He finishes up locked in the dungeon again, albeit on a pedestal, waiting to be gnawed to death by the beast he created.

Samurai is an opportunity for young people to explore the notions of democracy and tyranny. I'm not saying I set out to teach a lesson in citizenship. In all writing, things come to you that you haven't consciously thought of. But if young people are putting on a play they have a vested interest in getting it right, so they will ask questions and discuss things and maybe they will look at the way different countries and governments use force.

By setting *Samurai* in a strange country and a former time it is possible to look at some constant aspects of life that transcend time and place. Power, greed, laziness and desire are all constants, and this play allows us, in a non-threatening way, to look at how the citizens respond to these things and how we, in our society, respond to them. It also allows us to look at the effect society has on individuals. Kung is a bandit who is incapable of doing his job because of injuries sustained in an industrial accident. His industry happens to have been highway robbery but, though he wants to reform and get a job in the city, he admits he is set in his ways. 'Social conditioning' is his excuse.

I'm sure the young people taking part in or watching *Samurai* will love the physical stuff and I hope they enjoy doing it. That's the object of the exercise. If you enjoy it you'll get something out of it. It seems to me that endless wealth and ease will not make people happy. But let's not forget, nor will poverty. Not having a drive to do something dries your soul up. It is a very bad thing when people use wealth and status to intimidate. If there is a moral to this tale it might be that we get one turn in this world. There are no second chances. So it is incumbent on all of us to make the best of our one and only chance.

Production Notes

Geoff Case wanted to explore the scenario: 'If everything could be done by the press of a button, what happens when the button is taken away?' *Samurai* can be done as Peking Opera, in contemporary Western clothes or anything in between. Feel free to borrow from Noh theatre or Kabuki or martial arts such as Kuk Soo, which uses anything, even umbrellas, to confuse the enemy.

Listen to *Pacific Overtures* by Stephen Sondheim and John Weidman (several recordings are available). Written in 1976 it chronicles the sacrifices the Japanese people had to make in their social order, customs and dress in order to achieve their current affluence, and strongly draws from Kabuki traditions. It is a good example of a fusion of a Western text and a Japanese style of theatre. The four citizens could have a different speech pace from the other characters in the play. The language is robust enough to take stylisation.

Fans can be used as extensions of the arms to make trees/forest. The forest could move to enclose and conceal characters. Fans could also be used to punctuate the dialogue and create sounds by waving or tapping. Parasols could be used in a similar way. Naturalism could be juxtaposed with expressionist techniques to mark important moments. An example of this could be a real-time tempo seguing with half-speed cued by a music sting at the moment when a location shift is imminent. A length of rope could create a circle of security and then be rearranged to indicate danger. Lighting could be used to denote location and swift transitions from one 'place' to another. Noh theatre does not use lighting effects, so if you choose to borrow from Noh theatre your production could be performed in natural light.

The scenes should flow/ooze into each other. The stage directions could be used in the performances to help drive the play along if used to cover scene changes, or they could be another character. If you decide to include some or all stage directions make sure they don't slow the action of the play: be sure to hit each direction with pace and energy. Think about shifting location to serve the storytelling rather than to make the stage look different.

Create music/sounds from things other than musical instruments. Stamping is effective; the shape of the noise is important, as is the tempo, since both can heighten the excitement of the chase. Imagination is fickle; it can take over when a suggestion is made. Listen to Japanese thrash-metal music for inspiration. Live music onstage is much more impressive than a CD, and less likely to cause technical problems. One sound could be used in many different ways – go for a simple approach rather than complex use of many instruments and sound systems. Use a simple underscore – it could be just the actors' breath. It is important to pick up the pace when necessary, especially during the chase. The fans used for the forest could be used for set, and sound.

Explore different rhythms with sounds: use vocals, stamping, clapping, etc., progressing to sentences using percussive and hard sounds and vowels imitating instruments. Devise a piece to create an image suggesting the play's atmosphere. Work with just a handful of sounds.

The costumes are described in the text as being very ostentatious. The actors don't necessarily need to look fat, though it would be fun to experiment with padding.

Their weight can be suggested through movement and lethargy or they could be symbolically weighed down by wealth and wear fake jewels, cash boxes, etc. To experience the feeling of being heavy, out of condition, large and lazy, the actors may want to carry some kind of weight around during rehearsals. Even bags of sugar hung around the neck or waist in plastic bags will help. The four 'lethargies' are more points of view than characters. Their costumes could be surreal, they could be so lazy that they have chairs growing out of them, or they could be more naturalistic.

Vocalise the names of the four main characters – Buncho, Sharaku, Nishimura and Utamaru – with equal weight given to each syllable, steering the group away from received Western intonation patterns. With the names again, use movement as a wave: move forward slowly and then be repelled suddenly and say the name as you retreat, keeping a level eye-line throughout. Stopping and starting of movement is very effective in larger groups. Simple solutions can have a dramatic effect. Split 'Utamaru' into syllables and push them from actor to actor, driving the sound around the room. Have the whole group join in the exercise crossing a circle, pushing a syllable to another person to make a whole name.

The convention is that the Sword has to be touched when a request is made, but when the Sword is not there to touch you could use a line of people touching hands to reach it.

When the action switches back to the present in the play, it must be made clear.

Try different approaches, such as pantomime, for the entrance of the Proclamation Reader. He knows who he is and is on top of the situation, he has strength from within. You might have him speak quietly and beat with a big stick. Take the same scene and experiment with different tempi. Beat a woodblock while the dialogue is read. Try using fast, slow and medium tempi. Vary the tempo according to who is speaking and what is being said.

Have the actors lie down on a sheet of cheap lining paper and draw their outline round each, adding the name of their character underneath. Ask the actors to write their perception of their innermost feelings inside the outline, making sure the observations come from the script – they could use words or symbols. Have the rest of the company suggest words to describe how the characters are perceived by others and how they perceive each other. Add these observations to the relevant character outline. The Empress might be perceived as being detached, unaware, ironic, haughty and unnecessary (but inside: proud, brave, caring determined); Kung as being vainglorious, untrustworthy, nonconformist, having low self-esteem (but inside: lonely, lost, trusting); Yuki as being a troublemaker, curious, an outsider, part of the young generation (but inside: unselfish, brave, with a sense of justice); Sharaku as misguided, well-meaning, respectful. (but inside: traditional, a bit dumb); etc.

Physicalise the characters as written on the paper outlines by having the actors wearing masks. Add music. Ask the actors to react to the most dreadful thing they can imagine in silence. It is useful to do this exercise in a room with a mirror so the actors can monitor their work.

In the relationship between Yuki and the Empress, the adventure of returning the Sword is probably the biggest thing to happen to either of them. These two are nearest in age and both naive: he's young, and she is isolated in the palace. Like all the aristocracy, she was born old, but is redundant when the Sword is present. Yuki and the Empress could be seen as symbols of hope and innocence.

There could be a united body within the four main characters, rather in the style of a Greek chorus. Introducing the characters and giving them a theme individually could get messy but, for example, the Empress/Palace could have different sounds from the countryside. If things sound right, they generally are; if not, don't use them.

Silence can also be useful and effective. Have the actors sit in a circle silently. After twenty seconds of silence, tell them to react as if the most delicious banquet has appeared in front of them. (We tend to underplay in our own private space, and to overreact when in a group.) The magic is achieved by what the actors *do*. The question of food could be resolved in this way rather than by appearing from a sleeve as if by 'magic'.

An exercise which seeks to attain the state of 'armed neutrality' can be explored. In pairs and blindfold, use rolled-up paper in place of swords. Now try and make contact with one another. Repeat the exercise as if still wearing the blindfold. Take the actions of one pair and add music. Surround the pair with the rest of the cast, have the cast respond to the action unfolding before them.

Workshop facilitated by Anthony Banks,
music sessions by Craig Vear,
with notes taken by Sally Naylor

SEVENTEEN

Michael Gow

Characters

Ella

Jinny
her best friend

Mum

Dad

Dan
a relative

Wal
a relative

Sal
a relative

Erica
a personal assistant

*A group is also needed to play other characters,
especially relatives. Probably at least three,
but it can be as large as you like.*

Ella You can tell a birthday's coming, it's like a flying saucer appearing on the radar, blip-blip-blip. Only the blips actually sound like this –

Dad Have you heard about this new pizza place just opened up, sounds wonderful?

Mum So, Ella, you like bowling now!

Dad So which kind of wild animals do you like the most?

Mum Ella, have you read the reviews for this new alien-invasion movie?

Ella It happens every year, and I know a birthday party's coming, more than I know that Christmas is coming when Mr Knowles in our street puts the cut-out Santa on his roof. And the parties come like spring after winter. This'll sound far-fetched but I think I can remember even the earliest ones.

Mum Oddgy woddgy widdle bubba.

Dad Widdle bubba's gunna be a big gwirl.

Mum Hapfly burfuffday Mummy's beggest widdle big girl.

Dad Lotsa widdle pwezzies for you hoo –

Ella Although it might be hard *not* to remember that kind of thing.

Dad How many fingers?

Mum Five!

Dad Five!

Ella That's right, five, I can count.

Mum Let's all run around the garden because Ella is five!

Everyone runs around the garden like fairies.

Come on Ella, you wanted a fairy party.
Dad Flying, everyone's flying.
Ella Bombs away!

She joins in.

Dad Seven candles and seven presents for a seventh
birthday.
Mum You'll never blow out so many candles.
Ella Wanna bet.

She does.

Mum Oh, well done.
Dad Now everyone run around like wild animals on the
veldt.
Ella Seven, that was the animal party.
Dad Come on, Ella the giraffe.

They all run around like animals.

Ella Roooooaaar! (*Eveyone's thrown by her.*) I changed
my mind, I'm a cheetah!
Mum Ten, who'd have thought?
Ella Yep, time flies.
Mum Come on, everyone, we're all travelling though
space.
Ella Yes, it's an intergalactic party.
Dad Earth to Ella, are we having fun yet?
Ella Ella to space patrol gamma phi: this is great.

*They all run around like they're flying through
interstellar space.*

And running around is great but it's even more fun
standing on the sidelines and watching everyone else –
all the guests, school friends, neighbours, Mum and
Dad's friends, but no relatives, because we don't have
relatives, except for an aunt who lives in Paraguay and
a second cousin who's been working in Dar-es-Salaam
for years.

Dad 'We're a very far-flung family.'

Mum Everyone's feeling alright?

Ella Yes, we're just fine.

Mum No one's feeling nervous?

Ella No, honestly.

Mum Are you all comfortable in there?

Ella Eleven was a kind of follow-on from seven and ten. The tent was for me to use when studying native animals in the wild and also for possible expeditions on the Martian surface.

Mum I can't believe you'll get any sleep.

Ella It's a birthday sleepover, you don't sleep, except we did and when Dad wanted us to run around the garden in the morning to get the blood flowing, we couldn't even walk properly, we'd been so crammed in.

Dad Quick run around the garden, get the blood flowing.

They stagger around, stiff and sore from being crammed in a little tent.

Okay now, everyone, you've got your teams, now into the lanes.

Ella Last year.

Mum Let's go bowling!

Ella Sixteen. We were all facing the same way, chucking balls down the lanes, but it was still basically running around. But this year, seventeen, a restaurant, that's what we settled on. Four of us, Mum, Dad, Jinny and me. No running around in groups, something a bit grown-up. I can't take the credit for the idea. It was Jinny.

She'd just arrived at my school. I didn't have much to do with her at first. I don't actually have much to do with anyone, actually. Mum and Dad invite lots of kids I'm at school with to my parties, but I'm not really close to any of them. Too busy thinking. Which was what led me to Jinny. At my school we're all very busy. Very productive. Very positive.

Teacher Now, everyone, we've been studying galaxy formation. Who wants to show us their results?

Pupil Galaxies are formed by matter being drawn together by gravity.

Teacher Good, next?

Pupil They can take a large range of structures. Spiral, cloud, disc.

Teacher Good. What else?

Pupil They are all moving apart from each other and have been since the Big Bang.

Teacher Very good. What about you Ella? Ella?

Ella Well . . . I started off with gravity, which led me to time and how it's relative to gravity. If you leave a body, time decreases along with gravity. Time can move slower. Isn't that amazing? A clock slows down as you leave the Earth. So time is not constant. And galaxies, because they're so far away, appear to us as they were billions of years ago. When we look at them we're looking back in time.

Teacher You haven't really stuck to the question, have you?

Ella No.

Teacher Now. Fairies as used by Shakespeare in *A Midsummer Night's Dream*. Ella, what have you found?

Ella Well, I read about fairies in lots of different places and they're not as cute as we think. They're spirits of chaos, they can be evil, destructive.

Teacher But Shakespeare?

Ella He must have known, he knew all about folklore. I read about another figure from folklore, called Tom o' Bedlam, he's in *King Lear*, so I read *that* and it's incredible, so –

Teacher Now who's got something that's relevant to the topic?

Pupil Fairies were specific to particular areas and they had specific jobs.

Teacher The discovery of new trade routes by the Portuguese – some facts. Ella?

Ella What about all the discoverers who didn't make it? Do you know how many thousands of shipwrecks there are, all over the world, ships that found nothing, discovered nothing but got lost in storms or ran aground. The seas are full of them. Isn't that an amazing idea?

Teacher Ella, your mind really does wander all over the place. I think you need to talk things over with our school counsellor.

Ella So I was sitting outside the counsellor's office and Jinny walks down the corridor and sits next to me and starts talking.

Jinny All I did was make a joke. And they think I need help. Maybe I do. All I do is make jokes, maybe that's a sign of some problem. But I can't help it, I just see the funny side. We were in science and Miss Elvsted was explaining entropy and said, 'The universe tends toward a state of uniform chaos,' and I said, 'Sounds like my bedroom,' and she got really angry, and here I am. It probably is annoying. Why you here?

Ella I'm fascinated by the wrong things.

Jinny Like what?

Ella Shipwrecks, the age of the Earth, the size of the universe, the relativity of time to gravity.

Jinny Big ideas.

Ella Yes, big and kind of terrifying, but really exciting at the same time, makes me giddy. We're living in this fantastic mess that we're lucky to survive in. And that's amazing, isn't it?

Jinny It is. I hope we both survive this counsellor. It's like waiting to go into Room 101.

Ella You've read it?

Jinny Yes.

Ella *Nineteen Eighty-Four* is the best book ever.

Jinny It's great, yeah.

Ella We were supposed to be reading *Emma*, but there it was on the shelf in the library and I'd always heard about it so I read it instead. And it's incredible. I mean, what if there was a room like Room 101 – they could make you face the thing you're most afraid of, and you'd do anything to avoid it.

Jinny There must be rooms like that everywhere, we just don't see them.

Ella Don't you think we might have Big Brother, but not know it yet? Everything here looks okay, but what if we are being watched?

Jinny Happening already.

Ella You think?

Jinny Every time you go on the net you're being watched, they know what you're looking at, who you're talking to. One day they'll start using all the information they've gathered to start controlling us and there'll be no going back, they'll know everything about us. It looks a lot cooler than in the book, but they're doing the same thing.

Ella And we haven't really stopped talking since, some of it, you know, garbage and some of it, well it's great to have someone to say it to. So. My seventeenth birthday.

Jinny A restaurant.

Ella You think?

Jinny Absolutely. Let's do Nepalese.

Ella Really?

Jinny Yes, be great to see your mum order goat.

Mum Well. A restaurant.

Dad We could book a room, all to ourselves, all your friends.

Ella No I was thinking just for four, you and me and Jinny.

Mum Just for four?

Ella Yes.

Mum Not all your friends?

Ella Not this year.

Mum Why not?

Ella Something different.

Mum But you've always had lots of your friends at your birthday parties, the more the merrier. Remember the fairy party and the space party and the wild-animal party?

Ella Maybe I'm too old for mass parties. This time just four people. Sitting down.

Mum Are you sure?

Ella Yes.

Dad That'll be very . . . civilised.

Mum But you've always had lots of people.

Ella Not this year. Four. What about Nepalese?

Dad Nepalese? Well . . .

Mum Nepal?

Dad You wouldn't prefer Pizza Hut?

Ella That's for big groups of ten-year-olds.

Mum You haven't mentioned Nepal before.

Ella They do great things with goat.

Dad Terrific.

Ella So the booking was made. And life went on as usual for Mum and Dad and me. Weekdays they go to work, I go to school. Weekends, I play tennis, they do a bit of work, they garden, we eat in, nutricious, balanced meals except for takeaway once a month, we see entertaining movies with a positive message.

Today, Monday, the Monday morning before my birthday, on the way out to school, at the corner of the street, didn't think anything much, but there's three people looking at our house. A kid my age (*Wal*), a guy maybe Dad's age (*Dan*) and an old-looking woman in a really crazy hat (*Sal*). Never seen them before, don't know them, are they going to break in, doesn't look like it, they don't seem to care who sees them, maybe they're just . . . looking at our house.

Dan, Sal and Wal stand and look at Ella's house.

On the way past I look back at my own house. And then I look at them. One of them finally speaks.

Dan Hello.

Ella Hello.

Dan You live there?

Ella Yes.

Sal Lovely house.

Ella Uh-huh. Do I know you?

Wal No.

Ella You from around here?

Dan No.

Ella So?

Dan This house, well, how long have you lived here?

Ella My whole life.

Dan Exactly, but before that it belonged to someone else, right?

Ella I suppose so.

Dan Well, actually, our mum lived here. A long time ago.

Ella Really?

Dan Really, yeah.

Ella Well . . . okay.

Dan And she's not well, okay?

Ella I'm sorry.

Sal Dan –

Dan And she's not well and she's been reminiscing a bit, recalling the old days and she's been talking about this house where she lived and how lovely it was and the lovely garden with the lovely trees and everything and how lovely the street was so we thought, well, she's not all that well, and we thought if we could take a few pictures for her it might cheer her up. Do you see?

Ella Yes. I'm sorry she's not well.

Dan Yeah, yeah, really sad, actually, so would that be
   alright? If we took a couple of pictures to show her?
   We've taken the street and everywhere around here.

Ella Mum and Dad changed a lot of this house, it's very
   different.

Dan Exactly – we could show her all the developments,
   she'll love to see that, won't she?

Sal Yes, yes she will.

Wal I don't –

Sal She will, won't she?

Wal Right, yes.

Ella Then go right ahead.

I suppose I believed them, maybe I was trying to, and
   that's what was strange, but all day, couldn't get them
   out of my head all day, every class – why were they
   standing there, outside the house? And that night,
   during dinner –

Dad Cheer up, Ella.

Ella I'm okay.

Dad You don't look it.

Ella There's always been a ban on looking down in our
   family. Cheer up, Ella, even if I'm trying to decide
   which DVD to rent.

Dad Cheer up, Ella.

Ella I'm okay. Except –

Mum Yes?

Ella Something weird did happen today. There were
   these people outside the house when I left for school.

Mum What were they doing?

Ella Just standing there.

Mum Did they scare you?

Ella Not scare, it was just strange, they said their mother
   used to live in this house. They said they wanted to
   take a photo to show her. She's not well, she's been
   talking about this place, about the garden, all the trees.

Mum There weren't any trees when we moved in. The whole place was cement from the front gate to the back fence. There wasn't a tree in the whole street.

Dad Whole suburb.

Ella I *knew* it was weird.

Mum You don't know who they were?

Ella No.

Mum Never seen them before?

Ella No. Do you know who they might be?

Mum No, why would I? Of course I don't know.

Dad But it's made you very anxious.

Mum I don't like the idea of strangers hanging around.

Dad Ella. If you see them again, come straight to us. Yes?

Ella Yes.

Ella Next morning, the same as any weekday morning, except it's the day before I turn seventeen, the old routine we know and love, homework done, I've analysed the way natural disasters are portrayed in the media, I've looked at solar flares and their possible effect on the Earth's weather and I've actually forgotten about them completely until now, when I open the front door to go to school.

Sal We were just about to knock.

Ella More of them this time, crowding around our front door.

Who are you?

Dan We've come to see you.

Ella That's obvious, standing around our front door so early in the morning.

Sal I'm so sorry, please don't be upset.

Ella I don't want you here.

Wal Really, it's alright.

Ella Why did you make all that up about your mother?

Dan Five minutes.

Ella Go away.

Sal So you told your parents?

Ella Of course I told them.

Dan What did they say?

Ella They said you were lying, that's what they said. And they said if I saw you again to tell them and that's what I'm going to do right now.

Dan Ella, don't go.

Ella You know my name.

Dan We're related, did you know that?

Ella Related?

Sal Yes. We're relatives. Of yours.

Ella I've never seen you before.

Wal Have you seen any of your relatives?

Ella Umm . . .

Dan Have you got any? Relatives?

Ella An aunt in Paraguay.

Dan Right.

Ella And Dad has a second cousin who lives in Dar-es-Salaam. Very far-flung family. And now I'm phoning my father.

Dan It's your birthday tomorrow, isn't it?

Ella Yes.

Wal Seventeen.

Relatives (*all at once*) Seventeen. Yes, that's right, you're turning seventeen. Tomorrow's your seventeenth birthday. You'll be seventeen tomorrow.

Ella Okay, yes, I turn seventeen tomorrow.

Sal But, you see, you won't just be turning seventeen tomorrow. There's something else that's going to happen that's a lot bigger than just changing numbers. Something happens in our family. Your family.

Ella I'm going inside.

Wal You got a party planned already?

Ella No.

Wal Why not?

523

Sal Wal, it doesn't matter.

Wal But it's her birthday. And if she does have a party there won't be any relatives.

Sal It's alright, Wal.

Wal Except she has some now.

Ella I'm going inside and I'm ringing my father and if you don't go immediately I'm calling the police.

Dan Well, here's an address.

Ella I don't want an address.

Dan But if you do, if you want to find us.

Ella I won't.

Dan Just in case.

Ella Go! And I slammed the door and stood in the hall, not moving, hardly breathing, listening. I just stood there in the hall for about . . . I don't . . . it was probably five minutes , but I thought a week had passed for sure. I could hear them talking, arguing. Finally they went. I stuffed the piece of paper he pushed through the door into my backpack. In slo-mo I headed for the station to get the train to school, like in a dream, with two voices yelling at me in my head, one yelling, 'Don't be ridiculous none of that is true,' and the other voice saying, 'You can't do anything until you find out what they meant.' And I got the bus to the railway but I got a train going in the other direction, into the city, stumbled two blocks to where Dad works, up to Level 24. There's Erica – hi, Erica.

Erica Ella. Your dad's on a conference call.

Ella Oh really? Well I'm going in and there he is, looking at me.

Dad Ella, conference call, I'll be another ten minutes.

Ella Why don't I have any relatives?

Dad What, sweetheart?

Ella Relatives. I've never met any relatives. You've always said they've all passed away or there's one working in

South America or Africa. A small family and we're all far-flung. But what if I just met some relatives?

Dad Gerry? Sorry, no sorry, you'll have to stop there, I'm going to have to call you back. Yes, I know.

Ella He's dialling my mother. It's like there's been an explosion a long way away.

Dad We have to meet now, it's not that, it's bigger, now, don't care, get here.

Ella So we sit there and we wait. He tries to fill in the gaps.

Dad We really should wait until you mother gets here. She won't be long. (*Pause.*) We can, er . . . talk then, then we can, the three of us. (*Pause*) Talk.

Ella And the more he talks the more I know it's true. There's something big they haven't told me.

Dad, you don't have to try so hard, we can just sit here, it's okay.

Dad You still set on that restaurant? Nepal? Haven't ventured that far, in terms of food.

Ella Well, go on, talk, it's making it a bit easier for you to just mumble like this.

Dad Have you told school where you are?

Ella Finally she's here and she's been crying on the way but she's stopped now and they're doing their best.

Mum So many times we've asked ourselves if we should tell you. And we should have, everyone says that, all the experts, it's best to tell children the truth and yes on paper, it probably is. But when you look at the child you love you can't.

Ella I've figured it out. I'm adopted, right?

Dad No, you're not adopted. There's something else involved here, Ella.

Ella Those people I told you about, looking at our house, is this something to do with them?

Dad I'd say so.

Ella One of them said something was going to happen. Is there something wrong with me?

Dad There's nothing wrong with you.

Ella So why don't I have any relatives?

Mum We cut ourselves off, a long time ago, from the rest of our family, my family – it's my side, you see. I left, I . . . yes, I changed my name, disappeared from them all. Started a new life, became someone else so I could leave that behind. Your father did the same more or less, kept his side at a distance, so no questions would be asked. And we gave you the most normal, happy environment we could both give you and we thought we'd just move through this time and you'd emerge – well, still you, the daughter we love very much.

Ella Why? Please.

Mum In our family, sometimes, something happens to certain family members at a particular time.

Ella Turning seventeen?

Mum Yes.

Ella Seventeen. Those people told me. What is it, what happens?

Mum It's so difficult to explain.

Ella I think you'd better try.

Mum In this family, sometimes, when people turn seventeen, sometimes, they suffer some kind of – I don't know what you'd call it.

Ella Call it something.

Mum It's such a meaningless word now, really, it doesn't –

Ella What?

Mum People sometimes, when they turn seventeen, sometimes they undergo certain mental, emotional changes, they perhaps have psychological . . . shifts . . . their behaviour changes.

Ella Mad?

Mum That's not really a word people use now, it doesn't really describe what happens –

Ella Mad.

Dad We've known about it for quite a while. Someone, a long time ago now, looked at the family history and realised that certain family members do suffer some kind of mental, emotional shift –

Ella Mad.

Mum I'm sorry we didn't tell you.

Ella Why didn't you?

Mum It's so . . . it's not something – well, perhaps by not naming it we could avoid it.

Ella So you didn't say anything. My whole life, my past, all those birthdays, the intergalactic party and the animal party and the bowling party. All that was to keep this secret away from me.

Mum Well, not actively, but –

Ella They found me anyway, what was the point?

Dad How did they find her, do you know?

Mum I think I might. Once, when Ella was born, I sent a card, just to say everything was alright. I missed them. My family. Sent it from the post box on our corner. Did they come to where that card was postmarked and start looking?

Dad We agreed we'd sever all ties.

Mum I missed them. That's all. I'm sorry.

Ella You could tell *them* you were okay, but you couldn't tell *me* what might happen to me?

Dad I think we should all go home. Where we can just be together.

Ella And then what?

Dad Talk if you want, do nothing if you want.

Ella I remember a wildlife documentary about the nervous system in animals. In the wild, when they're being hunted and killed, their bodies are flooded with this drug that seems to numb them, block out what's happening to them. That's all I could think of. I was like a zebra being chased by a lion. I didn't feel

527

anything. But this wasn't an animal party. So we're sitting in our lounge room. No talking. I'm going to bed. I left them sitting in the dark. Here I am in my room – where to now, what do I do? On the internet, surfing for madness. Popular misconceptions, history of mental illness, romanticism and madness, the effect of the moon. There's even a test you can do, online, to see if you're depressed. So many words, so many versions. What if they *are* watching where I go, keeping track of what I'm looking at, entering data on this girl who thinks she's crazy, then I'll never be able to prove I'm not, log off, shut down. It's half past three in the morning, they've been talking for hours. I just sit. Fall asleep, down into the dark.

The Relatives appear.

Relatives You're not who you thought you were.
You'll soon be someone else.
You won't recognise yourself.
No one will recognise you.
You will lose yourself and your place in the world.
Lost, for ever.
No, no, get out of my room, go away. I'm shaking. It's Thursday. My birthday. And after that? I don't want to sit here. Bring up Jinny's number, dial, please be on and it is. It's me. I'm going away.
Jinny Now?
Ella Now.
Jinny It's four o'clock.
Ella Yes.
Jinny Where?
Ella Never mind.
Jinny What?
Ella I have to go. I just want you to know. I'll be okay. I'll see you in a few days.
Jinny Wait wait wait wait. Tell me slowly what is going on.

Ella Can't.

Jinny I'm coming with you.

Ella No.

Jinny Yes, something's wrong and I'm coming with you. Where are we going?

Ella I have to do this on my own.

Jinny Fine, but I'll be there too. What do I need?

Ella Someone with me, not family, just my friend? Okay. Pack some stuff, warm stuff, meet me at the railway in, in an hour? Don't ask, be there, okay? No, don't tell your mother. You can't. I'm not telling where we're going, just be there, in front of the indicator. Will she be there? Please be there. But I have to go. Go now. Can't see anyone in the street. It's cold out there. So I take a coat and a jumper and thick socks, pack them all in slow motion so I don't make any noise. Down the stairs, zombie girl, through the lounge room, no sound, in the dark corners of the room, it's them.

Relatives We know who we are.

Do you?

Our minds are clear.

Is yours?

Where are you going now?

Will it make any difference?

Ella Keep going, out the door into the grey street. This'll really hurt them, when they find I'm gone, but I can't stay here. Those people'll wait for me, spy on me, looking for the first signs. Mad. It's four o'clock, no public transport. I'll walk there. There's no one else on Earth, just this girl in a spacesuit walking across the alien surface with no family to call her own, just a bunch of relatives waiting for me to go crazy. It's so quiet. And yes, it's cold. Are they following me? What if they're waiting on a corner now, what if they're there all the time? Keep going, just keep walking.

Relatives You think you can get away, sneak off without us knowing?

We'll follow wherever you go, no point hurrying, we'll still find you.

Ella Walk fast to keep warm. Don't look back, just keep going. To the railway. And she's there.

Jinny I was sound asleep.

Ella Good thing you left the phone on.

Jinny I felt like a thief creeping around my own house.

Ella I'm glad you came.

Jinny What is this about?

Ella We're going away.

Jinny We can't go away.

Ella We are. I have to leave.

Jinny What did you do?

Ella This is very big.

Jinny Does it involve the police?

Ella My parents. And my family.

Jinny What's happened to them?

Ella Later. We're getting the first train that leaves.

Jinny Where to?

Ella Doesn't matter, we're getting out of town, go somewhere no one will know us, find us.

Jinny What for? Ella, what's going on?

Ella I have to be away until after my birthday. Something's happened that is completely . . . it's . . . come on.

There's a train in ten minutes, get some hot chocolate, a sandwich, grab the tickets and just make it onto the train. Sit in a corner in an empty carriage and try to tell her. Why does the truth always sounds like you're making it up there on the spot? When we turn seventeen something happens. It's like a line is crossed. In our minds. Some of us . . . they've traced it back through the family.

Jinny You're actually royal, fantastic!

Ella No. This thing happens.

Jinny What happens?

Ella We go mad.

Pause.

Jinny Of course you do.

Ella It's what my mother said, it's her family, they turn seventeen and they, yeah, they go mad.

Jinny All of them?

Ella Well, no.

Jinny So your mother's not a nutter?

Ella No.

Jinny Well, you said they turn seventeen and they go mad.

Ella There's a pattern. It hasn't happened for a while and it might be me.

Jinny It might not be. Come on, you don't go mad on a birthday like that, you can't, families aren't like that – well, we all go a bit crazy with our families and growing up makes it –

Ella I looked it up last night. There's all sorts of reasons for people going mad but you can inherit it, it's genetic they think. It *is* true.

Jinny But what does it mean? I'm going mad, everyone says that, but all they really mean is, things seem too much, there's too much work, nothing's going right, your parents won't let you do something or there's too many assignments, but these people – were they foaming at the mouth, screaming and pulling their hair out, rolling around on the ground?

Ella No. But is that what mad is? That's just movies.

Jinny So what is it then?

Ella Seeing everything in a completely different way from most people, not being able to make sense of things the way most people do. And you make less and less sense until you're . . . way out there on your own.

Those things you said, feeling like there's too much
pressure, yes, that's true, but eventually things go back
to normal, you know that somehow it'll calm down.
But what if it never calms down, the pressure stays, you
forget what it ever felt like to be without the pressure,
you don't even know you're behaving like . . . like
you're on your own and lost to the rest of the world?
You're in one version and everyone else is in another.

Jinny Like they're all in *Cinderella* and you're Little Red
Riding Hood.

Ella Yes.

So we talked and talked, we got lost in ideas, we ate our
sandwiches, fell asleep for a while and the countryside
rolled past. Passengers got on.

Passengers We know where we're going but there's
someone here who doesn't.

She doesn't have a clue.

Where will she get off the train?

What will she do?

What will she find?

Ella Stop, stop.

Jinny What – what – what's happening?

Ella Sorry, didn't mean to wake you.

Jinny What are you looking at?

Ella The passengers.

Jinny What about them?

Ella Don't look at them.

Jinny What? What's the matter?

Ella Just don't look them. I'm staring out of the window
watching fields, cows, there's a house, there's a river.

Passengers All the things you've been thinking, the wild
animals, the lonely stars, the laws of time, *King Lear*.
Were they the first signs?

Ella We're getting off.

Jinny Here?

Ella Hurry.

Jinny My leg's gone to sleep.

Ella Come on.

They get off the train.

Jinny This isn't even a proper railway station, just a couple of planks.

Ella It's perfect. Listen.

Jinny There's just the train in the distance.

Ella And what else?

Jinny Nothing.

Ella Yes. Quiet. This is a good place to be.

Jinny I'm tired. I need to clean my teeth.

Ella We walked along an empty road, it was early but it was already hot. A car came over the hill. Don't look at them, keep looking at the ground.

Jinny Then we'll look totally suspicious.

Voice (*from the car*) Didn't you always know you didn't fit? Now you know why your mind has always wandered down the wrong path.

Ella Let's go across here.

Jinny We'll be attacked by cows.

Ella Across a field, up over a hill, down the other side, trees, thick trees as far as you can see.

Jinny And so what do we do now?

Ella I brought a tent.

Jinny A tent?

Ella We used it for a birthday sleepover, we're going to spend the night in it. We're gong to spend the night in it, no one will know where I am.

Jinny Do you think we should call your parents?

Ella No.

Jinny This forest is very dark. Just one call to let everyone know that we're okay at least, not where we are.

Ella No.

Jinny But they'll be going crazy. Sorry.

Ella If I can just hide out here, no one know where I am, my birthday will pass and nothing will happen, the whole thing'll pass by and I can go back home and start again. Without going mad.

Jinny But my mother –

Ella You wanted to come.

Jinny She'll be going mental. Sorry. And your parents will be . . . I was going to say out of their minds. There's nothing I can say that doesn't sound like a bad joke, losing it, going insane, round the bend, that's what our parents'll be doing.

Ella My parents . . .

Jinny Those adults you live with, who are bringing you up.

Ella The people who kept secrets from me. All those parties we had, them thinking as long as she's having fun nothing will go wrong, let's just keep having fun. Surround her with lots of happy normal kids playing idiotic games so she'll stay sane. And somewhere else the rest of my family, thinking 'Five years, two years, one year to go and she'll start to slide down towards . . .' what?

We're in the middle of this forest. Just the sound of wind in the trees. The tent's up, the sleeping bags are inside, the sun will be going down soon.

Jinny I'm starving.

Ella There's some doughnut left.

Jinny It's going to get cold.

Ella Get into your sleeping bag.

Jinny I'm going to phone. I have to.

Ella No.

Jinny No signal. Great. Just what you'd expect for somewhere no one can find us. Please let her be okay, please.

Ella She will be.

Jinny If we're not eaten by wild animals or chucked in a shallow grave. As long as an alien mother ship doesn't come for us. It's so cold. Can't we light a fire?

Ella Someone'll see the smoke. Thankyou for coming with me. I'm really glad you're here. Jinny?

Jinny I heard you. Goodnight.

Ella Now the sun's gone it's like we've been swallowed up by the dark. I wrap myself in my sleeping bag, stay out here, let Jinny sleep. The stars move slowly through the trees. Something comes out of the blackness. A bear?

Wal comes out of the darkness, very slowly. He's got a coat draped over him, looks like an animal at first. During the following he spreads out the coat on the floor in extreme slow motion. In the middle of the coat he places the birthday cake he's been carrying. Sal approaches the tent, wearing an old dress from another era, the fifties maybe. She speaks in an over-the-top, 'lovely old lady' voice.

Sal What a wonderful place. The light has gone, the shadows have filled up the world. An absolutely perfect spot for such a ceremony, don't you think, absolutely perfect spot. (*She collapses into convulsive sobbing.*)

Ella Jinny? You awake? Come out here. Please.

Sal stops weeping.

Sal And what's your name, dear?

Ella You know what my name is.

Sal Yes, we found it out, didn't we, without you even knowing?

Dan bursts out of the darkness, full of manic energy.

Dan Okay okay, let's get started, thought you'd never get here, but you're here so now we can get started.

He shouts into the darkness.

She's here now, come on, what are you waiting for? She's here we can get started. (*He turns back to her.*) You didn't tell anyone else you were coming here, did you? Of course you didn't, runaway girl.

Sal Oh, but we knew where you were. We've had our spies out.

Other relatives come in, including passengers and people in the street and the people in the car, all in varying states of theatrical madness; muttering, wailing, pulling their hair, singing, laughing.

Dan Come on, come on, I told you to be ready hours ago, get over here now.

He goes to hit some of the relatives, they cringe and shriek.

And shut up. Stop all that moaning, just sit there and shut up.

They sit around the tent.

And now. The card.

He produces a card and hands it to Ella. She stares at it in silence.

Well. What's it say?

Ella just keeps staring at the card. One of the relatives jumps up and goes to read it, but she pulls it away.

Ella 'Thinking of you now, more than ever.'

Pause.

Sal Very, very beautiful. From the heart. (*She starts weeping again.*)
Dan You know who it's from?

Ella Is it from –

Dan Your mother and father, who didn't want you to go through this. Very moving. And here's ours. From the whole family. Open it.

She's still lost in the first card. Dan opens the card and reads it himself.

'Sweet sixteen no more. Welcome to seventeen.' Now the cake.

Sal (*through her tears*) Now we light candles. How time passes. I was only seventeen once.

Wal Can I light them?

Dan Sure, Wal. Sure, light them up!

Sal Now the hour is upon us. We gather here to honour someone close to us, to share her first steps on the long path this family treads.

Wal Yeah, this is the really important bit, this is where it starts.

Dan That's right, that's right, that's it, this is where it starts.

Five. Ten. Fifteen. There. Seventeen.

Dan paces while Wal lights the candles really slowly.

Come on, come on, that's it, you're too slow.

He knocks Wal out of the way and finishes lighting the candles himself.

The moment you've all been waiting for. And now. Blow them out.

They watch the candles. Ella doesn't move. They finally look up at her.

Ella No.

Dan Come on.

Ella No.

Dan Okay, okay, you're going to drag it out because you're afraid or something, you're upset because of the card.

Ella No.

Dan Blow winds and crack your cheeks and blow out the candles. Come on. It's what we're here for, what we've all come for, what the whole family is waiting for, not just us lot who can get out of the house, but all of us, wherever we're being kept. Blow them out.

Ella No. Please.

Dan (*blows out the candles himself*) Okay, okay, okay, okay, we don't have to do it in order, no, no, we'll leave the candles for the time being, there's other things we can do if that's the way you want it, we can come back to the cake, okay, okay, okay, okay, save it for later –

Ella I don't want to, please.

Dan freezes, seems to be hanging suspended for a moment, then slumps to the ground. The others watch him.

Wal Get up. Dan. Please. We have to keep going. Come on.

Dan just lies there.

Ummm. Okay. We have to keep going with this, Ella's birthday, okay, let's do the next part, Dan'll be okay. Okay. Our family. Your family.

Wal slowly starts to set himself up for his part of the story.

The past.
A cave.
Young caveman, seventeen.
Digs a trap to catch his prey.

Sal (*grunts*) Mammoth.
Wal Pounding through – come on, you lot – pounding
through the forest.

*Sal and Wal and the other relatives play the woolly
mammoth and all the characters in the story with
appropriate noises. Dan has come to and is pounding
on the floor to make the sound of the approaching
mammoth.*

Caveman thinks –
Sal (*grunts*) 'I make trap. Trap good. My trap. I get into
trap.'
Dan 'Caveman leaps into trap –'
Wal 'I live in trap, trap my home.'
Caveman lives in trap.

Dan, Sal and Wal play the family in the trap.

We live in trap
Trap our home.
Dan And there they lived, mad.
All Mad!
Dan Through every generation.
Sal Mad.
All Mad.

*Dan, Sal and Wal dance a family group rejoicing in
their madness.*

Wal What's next in the party?
Sal Some family favourites, I believe.
Dan Sir Stephen –
Sal Who led an expedition to the New World. When the
coast of Virginia came in sight he ran the ship
aground.
All Onto the rocks, drive the ship onto the rocks.

The relatives stage a shipwreck.

Sal Derek, who turned seventeen and left home that very day and never stopped walking again. Yelling at the world, trying to make everyone understand why he has to keep walking.

Wal walks around shouting gibberish.

Dan Who knows, if you're really lucky you might end up like him, walking the streets for ever and ever.

Sal Great Aunt Dora, who ate the *Encyclopaedia Britannica* page by page so she would know everything including the most impossible mathematics and the secrets of time, who lay on a hill looking at the stars trying to understand what they were saying to her.

They become stars while Sal lies on the floor.

Relatives
Twinkle twinkle little star,
Speaking wisdom from afar.

Sal Keep talking, you stars, I will understand you, I just need to break the code.

Dan And then there's us. Wal seemed the same for days after his birthday, weeks passed. But then we saw that he was slowing down, slower and slower.

Wal (*really slowly*) No. Everything is getter faster. I haven't changed.

Dan Sal, who sees everything good just as the bad sucks her under.

Sal breaks down again.

Nothing happened to me for weeks. That made me really really really angry waiting waiting waiting.

Wal And he stayed angry, always, and he never stops talking. He's talked for weeks sometimes.

Dan We're all part of this family. The same thing happens to all of us. What happens?

Sal Mad.

All the relatives erupt in a violent demonstration of madness that lasts several seconds. Ella burrows into her sleeping bag.

Dan And now it's your turn.

Ella No –

Dan You can't escape. And if it's not tonight, then it will be tomorrow, or next week, or next month. But it will come. You'll feel the first shiver, you'll first feel you're falling, or that you can't move, or you can't stop crying, or the world is looking into you, or through you, or the voices first start talking. The candles are lit. We're waiting.

Ella No, I won't blow them out, I won't.

Jinny sticks her head out of the tent.

Jinny Hey, what's going on, Ella?

Dan She's not alone.

Sal Oh dear, oh dear.

Wal The cake.

Dan We're out of here.

The relatives all vanish into the dark, taking the cake with them.

Ella I won't –

Jinny You're seriously scaring me, what are you yelling for?

Ella Have they gone?

Jinny No one here.

Ella Have they gone?

Jinny There was no one here. Come out.

Ella No.

Jinny You can't stay in there.

Ella I'm never coming out.

Jinny You should try to relax.

Ella Wherever I am, they're there, waiting for me. I can't even fall asleep, they're waiting for me there. I'm on the edge of a cliff and I'm slipping and can't hold on. I'm going to fall.

Jinny Okay, let's keep talking, that's the best thing to do, keep talking and you won't think about them, okay, let's keep talking.

Ella Lying underneath the trees, with the stars above us when the wind moved the branches. And she kept talking, just to make me feel safe.

Jinny Maybe, maybe it's like the pink-elephant thing, yeah, you know – tell someone don't think of a pink elephant and they do. Tell people they'll go crazy when they turn seventeen and they will.

Ella Her voice is filling the night, keeping the darkness away.

Jinny So when Dad first left Mum was well I don't know I was really little, but she says she was devastated. She's always saying, 'Who says two is better then one?' but I don't know, sometimes I think it would be better to have two of them, to share the load, the nightmare.

Ella In the silence of the night her voice seems so big, filling the night.

Jinny At least if you lived at Summer Bay you'd be at the beach all the time and I have to say the guys at Summer Bay are generally better-looking than the ones in Ramsay Street but in Ramsay Street there's probably more to do in the winter –

Ella And at last the sun's coming up and she's talked all the way to dawn and kept me awake and now she's just talking junk but she's kept the dark away. I haven't moved. Is this it? Not screaming, not shouting. Not moving at all.

Jinny Are you awake?

Ella Yes.

Jinny The sun's up. My voice hurts. Still cold.

Ella Yes.

Jinny I'm hungry.

Ella I know.

Jinny Ella? We can't stay here. How will you ever know if you're crazy or not, sitting here in the middle of this forest? Who could say whether you were mad or not? I think you have to go back and find out. I came because I thought maybe I could help, but I reckon the only help I can give you is to help you back to station. I could drag you, I suppose, even in your sleeping bag. But we can't stay here.

Ella And no, she didn't drag me. I walked, we both walked back through the trees, along an empty road, to the little platform and finally this train came with two carriages and no one on it and we sat there and watched the same trip we made yesterday backwards. There's no one to stare at, no one to stare at me, no voices, she's asleep, on my shoulder. Is this what it will be like? Silence? Just staring at the world? If it happens at all. But now I'm going home. To what? Will they be angry, crushed, pretending to be angry but really just afraid?

Jinny Is there any more doughnut?

Ella Somewhere in here there's still a piece of stale chocolate doughnut. And this piece of paper. The address.

Jinny How much longer?

Ella Another hour.

Jinny I suppose I'm glad I saw this part of the world.

Ella I'll come and see your mother if you want, to explain.

Jinny You do your home, I'll do mine.

Ella I left her there under the big clock. Wandering towards her life. But I'm walking on another planet, the air is thinner, gravity weaker, everything is slower,

movement, time. Where is this place? What if it's miles
away? A man at the ticket office says I can get there on
a local train, half an hour at the most. I've got my school
pass, will it work? Another train, another journey,
watching suburbs pass. Another man in the ticket office
where I get off gives me directions. A long walk. It's
getting hot. Bare streets. Rows of flats, red brick.
There's no one following me, no one muttering stuff,
watching me. At least. And it's here. I'm standing outside
a block of flats that looks like all the other blocks
of flats in this long, hot street. Slowly up the stairs.
I could be climbing a mountain on Mars. Or stalking
rhinos. Here is a plain white door with the number six
on it. I'm thinking at least it's not seventeen, and the
door opens.

Sal You're here so soon. Is everything alright?

Ella Yes. I decided to come and see you, that's all.

Sal Happy birthday. Did you have a nice party?

Ella No. I mean I didn't have a party.

Sal Do you want to come in?

Ella Yes.

Dan (*calling*) Who is it?

Sal Ella. She's here.

Dan (*calling*) She coming in?

Sal Yes, she's come to see us.

Ella There's not much furniture. A bed in the first room.
A table, some chairs.

Sal I'm speaking softly because Wal's asleep. He sleeps a
lot just now. But he'll be fine. Here she is.

Dan So soon.

Ella Yes.

Sal She didn't have her party.

Dan Anything wrong?

Ella It didn't happen. I ran away.

Sal Do they know where you are?

Ella No. I'll go straight home after this.

Dan Where did you go?

Ella Just ran, tried to disappear.

Dan That's understandable. We're probably to blame. We just want to keep some kind of contact with everyone in this family. To let them know we're here. Just in case things happen.

Sal I suppose it's better to know we're connected, even if we don't see each other.

Dan But sometimes it doesn't happen the way it should. Probably never will.

Ella All that stuff about your mother living there?

Dan I know. You caught us out, made it up on the spot.

Sal It was pretty feeble.

Dan I know.

Sal And he hasn't had a mother for years. Lived here with me for the last six, other relatives before that. Haven't you?

Dan That's right.

Sal His poor mother, she had a rough time of it.

Dan She said it was like two invisible people yelling into her ears all the time.

Sal We did what we could. There were some good bits.

Dan Yes, there were.

Ella So is it true? Seventeen?

Sal None of us knows who it will happen to. But it does happen. Some of us turn seventeen and a change begins. Some do what your mother did, try to get away. Some have vanished. Some have run and come back years later, just to show us they're perfectly alright.

Dan At least you came. Did you have a bad night?

Ella It was long.

Sal You look tired.

Dan Were you alone?

Ella I had a friend with me.

Sal Good. You're lucky.

545

Ella I was afraid of this word, 'mad'. Because it happens in my family. So I ran away from it. But that's what my mother did. I was doing what someone did before me anyway. How are we related?

Sal Dan's mother and your mother were maybe some sort of second cousins, how many times removed? Not sure, the trail gets lost.

Ella They'll be so worried. I wasn't there.

Dan They will.

Wal comes in.

Sal Did we wake you?

Wal No. Time to get up. You're here.

Ella Hello.

Wal Good birthday?

Ella Well . . .

Wal Mine was crap. Two years ago. We had a party, but I slept through it. Do that. It's like I'm in this car that's out of control – sometimes it's terrifying, all I can see is the headlights in the dark, sometimes it's hilarious, sometimes I'm just cruising. But it's very tiring. You look pretty tired.

Ella I am. I should go.

Wal Good, you came. Know where we are.

Dan If you want, when you're ready, we can tell you where others are as well.

Wal We're not too terrifying, are we?

Ella You're not terrifying at all.

Wal You know what? Once, I had to see a doctor and I told her I was a bit touched and you know what she said? Really? Most of the time I wonder how anyone can tell the difference? That was good, wasn't it?

Ella Well . . .

Sal Dan'll run you home, won't you?

Ella I can get the train.

Sal No trouble.

Dan No trouble.

Sal And you know where we are. Whatever happens to you.

Ella And all the way home in the car we talked, about his mother, about my family, my life, school, Jinny. I told him about the night I turned seventeen. He didn't come in, just dropped me outside the house. They were there, waiting. They knew, of course, Jinny's mother'd found them and they knew I'd be back and they didn't say anything. I didn't say anything. Like it had been said already and saying it out loud made it mean less. So we're sitting and looking at each other. And back to saying nothing. There are things that don't get said because you haven't figured out the right words yet. If you try too soon it just sounds pathetic, like –

Dad It was something you needed to do.

Ella Silence was better than stuff like that, we all knew that. Try and get back to everyday stuff. Are we still going to have our dinner in the restaurant?

Dad If you want to, we're more than –

Ella Why not? It'll still be my birthday.

Mum Good, that's good.

Dad Terrific.

Ella And silence again. So I called Jinny. She confessed she'd told her mother before she left to meet me. Told her to give us twenty-four hours before doing anything. She said –

Jinny I think enough people have been avoiding the truth. One more lie isn't going to help anyone.

Ella So they'd tried to stay calm, hadn't reported us missing yet. And we came back. I booked a table for that night, and then. I slept. Falling into the black and stayed there all day. And now we've eaten. Mum tried the goat –

Mum Tastes a bit like lamb.

Dad Tender.

Ella And here in the restaurant there's just the sound of other people's conversation, knives and forks on plates, the piped music. And chit-chat.

Jinny So you've met some relatives?

Ella I have.

Jinny And?

Ella Well . . .

Jinny Right. Not the time, I can read the signal, very clear, and now I'm changing the subject.

Mum (*who's taken her cue from Jinny*) Ella, there are a lot of things that will need to be said.

Jinny's shaking her head. Mum's relieved.

But perhaps not yet.

Ella Great advice. We've made it to the restaurant, we're eating goat and I'm seventeen. Enough said.

If You Start Running, You Keep Running

Michael Gow interviewed by Jim Mulligan

Michael Gow originally conceived *Seventeen* as a play with characters that would have the same ages as the young actors playing the parts for *Shell Connections* productions. He also started by writing with a UK audience in mind. In later drafts, however, he introduced older characters such as the parents, teachers and secretaries, and wrote as if for an Australian audience. Once he had decided to write it entirely to be performed in his world he felt that he had somehow been freed from self-imposed restraints.

The central character, Ella, is about to celebrate her seventeenth birthday when momentous events take place. Why seventeen?

> We are all familiar with 'sweet sixteen' – that has connotations of innocence – and eighteen is a recognised milestone in growing up, but seventeen is neither one thing nor the other so I decided to look upon that age as a critical moment in Ella's rite of passage. As her seventeenth birthday approaches, she notices a group of people at the end of her street and she doesn't know who they are. Eventually they introduce themselves as her relatives and she is amazed and terrified.

One of the themes of *Seventeen* is facing up to reality and the truth, and not living a lie. In the opening scene, as Ella's past birthdays flash past, she is taking pictures 'that will come back to haunt everyone'. And she tells the audience she has no relatives except a second cousin in Dar-es-Salaam and an aunt in Paraguay. Later, her mother admits that when Ella was born she had cut all ties with her family because of the dark things that happen when members of the family turn seventeen. Then, a madness descends on them. So the mother had run away but the family has caught up with her.

There is a fairy-tale quality to this notion, as when the evil fairy warns the princess that if she pricks her finger disaster will follow. But we know that just as the fatal needle will prick the royal finger, so inevitably something dreadful will happen when Ella turns seventeen.

Ella has a dark streak that is shared somewhat by her best friend Jinny. Ella is impulsive whereas Jinny is sceptical and realistic. In a sense she looks after Ella and has the common sense to tell her mother what is happening when Ella decides to run away. Although Ella's family life seems secure and happy, when she hears that weird things happen in her family and that they go a bit mad on their seventeenth birthday she sees the dark possibilities and runs away in terror.

The reality is that when Ella faces her demons and goes to visit her family for the party they have arranged she finds them living in a block of flats like any other. They appear normal and greet her with slight regret that she has missed the party. But perhaps Ella's fears have some foundation: perhaps there is a genetic disposition to madness, because they assure her that no one knows who it will happen to but when some of them turn seventeen a change begins. Dan explains: 'Not long after, there's the first shiver, you feel you're falling, or you can't move, or you can't stop crying, or the world is looking into you or through you, or the voices first start talking.' It seems that Ella has good reason to be scared. There, is after all, something sinister in the way the family has doggedly tracked her down, not to warn her but to embrace her in their madness.

Michael Gow sees *Seventeen* as a reflection on the hidden terror in the lives of young people.

> One of the things that draws Ella and Ginny together is that they both secretly read Orwell's *Nineteen Eighty-Four*. They feel it reflects the way they see the world. The rest of the kids in their school are busy doing things but these two girls are obsessed with the notion that the world isn't bright and cheerful, and they see the internet as a manifestation of Big Brother. They also see that there are three forces in the world and at any time two of them are at war with each other. And there is the personal terror of Room 101. It certainly happened to me when I was at school. I thought *Nineteen Eighty-Four* showed me the truth at last. It was terrifying. I think a lot of young people view the world in this way.

Linked to the terror is the inability of people to talk about their fears. It seems, the greater the fears, the more locked in the mind they are. Ella and her family seem to talk incessantly, but how much do they communicate? At the end of the play Ella, as narrator, says she and Dan talked in the car on the way back home and then they were back to silence. 'There are things that don't get said because you haven't figured out the right words yet. If you try too soon it just sounds pathetic.' And her Mum says, 'There's going to be a lot that will need to be said. But perhaps not yet.' And Ella's final comment as she and her parents and Jinny eat a home-made sponge that says seventeen: 'Enough said.'

> At the end of the play Ella is probably better prepared for whatever the rest of her life is. She probably realises that the thing you run away from is the thing that gets you in the end. She has seen that if her mother

had told the truth in the first place things would have been a lot easier. She has learned that it's better not to run when life kicks in. It may be hard to stay and deal with it, but if you start running, you keep running. She stops, turns herself round and goes to the thing she is terrified of. She learns to find a place for it and her place in it.

Production Notes

Michael Gow avoids writing stage directions in order to leave you to come up with your own solutions. He wrote *Seventeen* in Brisbane, Australia, intending it to work anywhere – after all, we have to turn seventeen wherever we are.

Turning seventeen is a strange time and seemingly not celebrated as much as becoming sixteen or eighteen. It can be a time full of both mental and physical change as well as a growing sense of the passing of childhood and the approach of adulthood. It is a time of questioning one's own identity, which sometimes involves feeling isolated.

The central character in this gothic tale is Ella, who is on the cusp of her seventeenth birthday. As if there isn't enough going on already, Ella discovers, through the arrival of a group of strangers who claim to be her relatives, that in her family turning seventeen often marks the onset of madness. This alarming revelation leads Ella to attempt an escape from what feels to her to be the inevitability of her own mental decline. Her journey to the forest (real or imagined, you'll have to decide) and her struggle to make sense of the situation is rendered even stranger due to the presence of the chorus. The chorus first appear as a relatively normal group of relatives, but their form changes into something much more surreal so that by the time we reach the forest they have taken on qualities almost like those of the Addams Family.

Michael wrote *Seventeen* imagining that the size of the chorus could be expanded through the scene in the forest and then decrease as the crisis diminishes and normality is restored. He would like to encourage directors to use their creative imagination in staging this piece and for young actors to avoid using technology, instead creating their own music and soundscapes.

EXERCISES

It is worthwhile breaking the play into manageable units. The following represent such units as were worked out with Michael at the Bath retreat, though yours might vary slightly. Once you decide on a unit, give it a title (we called the first 'The History of Birthdays'). Also included are some of the comments and issues raised in the workshop.

UNIT I

from Ella's opening speech until halfway through her speech ending: 'It was Jinny'

All the cast should be on stage for Ella's first speech.

Ella's parents are probably quite suburban. Ella is an only child. There is a superficiality to their 'normalness'.

The opening section needs to be as normal as possible to highlight the change later. Stretch 'normal' to the limit (particularly with the mother).

The birthdays seem to be cartoon-like, stereotypical versions of birthdays. Ella's birthday reminiscences are ironic, but don't push her disparagement too far – she's amazed at what she was interested in at the age of five. When Dad refers to the 'far-flung family' it is his standard response to family references. One that he has definitely used before.

Don't let the introduction of props and bits of set break up the action. For instance, the tent could be invisible or it could be a sheet over two chairs: whatever you need to make a tent. Get the chorus to set things up quickly and efficiently.

UNIT 2

from Ella's speech: 'She'd just arrived at my school'

More characters are introduced in this section. It's as if they're all 'gifted' and 'talented' at this school. It's very busy since they all talk about their gifted and talented achievements, but Ella and Jinny look out of the window all the time. Jinny acts out; Ella opts out.

Some character names are borrowed from Ibsen: the science teacher Mrs Elvsted is from *Hedda Gabler*, for example.

UNIT 3

from Ella's speech: 'And we haven't really stopped talking since,' to: 'They make a plan'

UNIT 4

from Dad's speech: 'Well, a restaurant'

Dad always wants to make large groups of happy people. When he refers to the dinner date for only four people as 'very civilised', it should be in a disappointed and resigned way. Ella's party choices have always been quite strange, so he's surprised that she's changed her habits.

Whatever Ella chooses to do for her seventeenth birthday, her parents are bound to be nervous, because of what might happen when she turns seventeen. Maybe the party itself won't even happen. They dare not think about that possibility nor admit it to themselves.

Ella's parents could be worried that she's lost her friends when she insists she only wants a small gathering. They may also fear having to talk to one another in a more intimate setting.

UNIT 5

from Ella's speech: 'Mum and Dad and me'

Dan's objective for this scene is that they're about to go mad but trying not to reveal it. There could be an effective tension between being mad and not letting it show.

They want this first contact to go well. There should be a sense of being sprung – of them always having heard of Ella but never having seen her before. They are taken by surprise on Ella's entrance. She could stand with the group, looking at the house, waiting to be told why they are looking at it.

Dan obviously speaks from experience of being mad, but he fails to admit it to himself. The group is bonded by their joint knowledge that something will happen at the age of seventeen.

Ella didn't know or see her parents when they turned seventeen, so she will need to question whether they are mad or not.

UNIT 6

from the end of Ella's speech: 'Can't get them out of my head all day'

Ella's mother is extremely unsettled about the situation.

UNIT 7

from Ella's speech: 'Next morning, the same as any weekday morning'

When the relatives say 'seventeen' in unison, it shouldn't be sinister. It's a statement of fact and cheerful. Ella should keep closing the front door (we see her on the other side of it). They have to get it all out before Ella really closes the door. This scene should be well paced. It should become clear that they've come out of concern, though Ella interprets this as an assault.

UNIT 8

from Ella's speech: 'And they went and I just stood there'

When Ella's Mum reveals the truth, it is an emotional outpouring. There could be sobbing and crying. It's awful for the mother, she'd thought she could get away with keeping the secret but she's on the edge of collapse, trapped. She is conscious that she previously lied to her husband by sending a postcard to her relatives. She's walking a very thin line. She's probably done research on the subject, but she's pushing the fear below the surface and doesn't want to use the word 'mad': it's a problem for her. She was told about the madness at an early age. It's had a negative effect. When we get to this revelation it feels very real, which leads us to empathise with the parents even more.

UNIT 9

from Ella's speech: 'I remember a wildlife documentary about the nervous system in animals'

There's quite a leap when the relatives come in. Don't make it more spooky or let it become too melodramatic. Let the words speak for themselves and don't overdo it. Visually, though, it *can* be spooky. Don't deliver the lines as a chant.

UNIT 10

from part of the way through Ella's speech beginning: 'Go now. Can't see anyone in the street'

UNIT 11

from Jinny's speech: 'I was sound asleep'

UNIT 12

from Jinny's speech: 'Here?' and Ella's response: 'Hurry'

UNIT 13

from Ella's speech: 'We're in the middle of this, what, forest?'

UNIT 14

from Sal's speech: 'What a wonderful place'

Sal should be very posh in this unit. Sal isn't the same as earlier. She's become a different personality and gives the effect of being nuts. She's quite a lot older than Ella – in her thirties or even older. The fifties dress she wears is there because Michael is fond of that era – the design for *Seventeen* could be fifties retro if this appeals to you.

UNIT 15

from the end of Wal's speech: 'Our family'

Wal slowly starts to set himself up for the first part of the story.

Wal is totally mad, while Sal moves between affected cheerfulness and sobbing. The three characters should all be different because each is a cartoon of madness. One is a manic depressive; one is slowed down; and the other is out of touch with the world. These are all things that Ella has seen. They're all at their most extreme here: this is another apparition, more extreme than at the house.

After Ella says 'I won't blow them out,' Jinny needs to look out of the tent.

The characters might embody aspects of the following types of mental illness:

> *Paranoid schizophrenics* believe what they want to believe: they are in their own world. They are disconnected from their thoughts and actions and those of others.
>
> *Psychosis* is a derangement of the whole personality.
>
> *Chronic mental behaviour* is often associated with social disorder.
>
> *Schizophrenia* will see a deterioration of and indifference to personal hygiene and a hearing of voices.

A good exercise to create a sense of *schizophrenia* would be to wear headphones through which are played a recording of voices. At the same time, try and have a conversation. This gives the effect of hearing voices in one's head. Or, put a toilet-roll tube to each ear, with one person talking down one tube, saying bad things, another saying good things down the other, while at the same time having a conversation with someone in front of you.

Mental illnesses are generally not suddenly manifested, there's usually a period of deterioration. Most mentally ill people are not diagnosed until their late teens or early twenties.

There are chemical disorders that can sometimes be hereditary, but nowadays are more likely to be linked to drugs. Nervous breakdowns can also trigger deterioration into a more severe mental disorder.

UNIT 16

from Ella's speech: 'I won't, Jinny. You're seriously scaring me'

Ella's line 'I'm never coming out' refers to being in her sleeping bag. Show a time lapse in this scene, the moon crossing the sky. The audience could suspect that Ella is 'turning' in this scene because her anxiety is about as intense as it could be.

UNIT 17

from Jinny's speech: 'Are you awake?'

UNIT 18

from Ella's speech: 'And no, she didn't leave me there, and no, she didn't drag me back. I walked'

Ensure that full stops don't become pauses. From the beginning of rehearsals, keep the pace up: some of these scenes are speedy. This piece is heavily punctuated, so hit cues, pick them up and watch punctuation. It's not 'listen, think, speak'. It's 'listen, speak'.

UNIT 19

from Ella's speech: 'I left her there under the big clock'

UNIT 20

from Sal's speech: 'Well, you missed the party'

This is where the chorus is as normal as can be. Dan doesn't know that Ella has seen the apparition. His line 'caught out' refers to his lies earlier, at the house. These were a means to an end.

UNIT 21

from Ella's speech: 'And all the way home in the car we talked'

Ella's parents don't send out a search party when she goes out because they trust Ella to come back; in addition Jinny's mother assures them it will be okay. Michael read somewhere that seventy per cent of parental calls to their children's mobiles go unanswered, so it's not necessarily reliable that they could have just called her. Jinny plays a game, pretending to be worried about her mum, and wanting to call her. She's being deceptive when she says, 'Look, no signal.'

Jinny's line, 'I don't think lying's a great way to deal with anything,' sums up the play. She's being slightly hypocritical here. She did after all tell her own mother about leaving, but didn't admit this to Ella. Equally she hasn't told her mother the whole story about where she and Ella will go – she hasn't revealed the location.

UNIT 22

from Mum's speech: 'Tastes a bit like lamb'

Everybody who features in the play could end up being in the restaurant scene. The meal is an opportunity for the family to be together and to open up to each other. It is a very positive ending where, rather than weirdness, there is instead a discussion about the family in which Ella acknowledges she has other relations now. It's good that we don't see that whole scene played out because it leaves more to our imagination.

CHORUS WORK

Stand alone, imagine a ball in your belly – your irritant. It's the size of a golf ball and represents your nastiness, jealousy, hatred or persistence – you decide. It has a voice and speaks all the time, telling you to do something bad. You need to resist it. It has a face. You're holding it down. Let your guard down; the ball becomes a tennis ball with a bigger face. It builds to a sound. Move around the room. The irritant goes through 'Levels of Irritation' from one to five (five being the strongest), shown in your physicality. When the leader calls 'Go', you have to get a grip on it, cover it up. But it's still there. Make a sound with it. Keep controlling the emotion and take the volume levels up.

Make a group of four or more. Create a diamond configuration, facing in one direction. Nominate the leader, who stands at the front of the diamond. Everyone should be able to see the back of the leader. The leader should make spontaneous abstract movements, and the group follow the movements closely and in time. Keep it simple to start with so you are in time with each other and the leader isn't obvious to observers. Pass the leadership on by turning to the right. The person on the right picks it up. Make sure the leadership changes are clear. This can build very easily into a chorus, to which you can add character. Work like this for ten minutes. Find ways of getting out of tight spots. Once the group is comfortable, explore a different rhythm and dynamic.

Move away from abstract to naturalistic (scratching, folding arms, etc. – not constant movement). Leaders then give obvious stereotypes (teenagers, old people). Add sound. Build on this exercise so that when the leader initiates movement, the group doesn't have to repeat it exactly, but can do something similar. Do this for a few minutes. Return to the neutral diamond and your irritant character. From neutral, move around the space, not bumping into other groups. Take the ball to Level 1 – movement and physicality don't have to be the same for the whole group, but you still move together. Sense how the pack works. Think how others' rhythms affect you and your emotions.

Imagine you have an important engagement to get to – quickly. Take the ball up to Level 3; then Level 4. Add some sound. Your guard drops completely; go to Level 5. Then back down through the levels.

On 'Go', the group needs to disperse – move away from each other, but still work as a group. The leader can choose three states of emotion (terror, love, etc.), which the group can adopt at Level 2. Walk anywhere in the space, but remain in touch and connected with the group, and increase the levels of intensity. Shift the leaders on. Go through three more emotions. On 'Go', reform as a pack.

When the relatives first arrive they're quite aggressive and demonic. Make the evil more about Ella's perception of it than an objective reality. Her inability to understand is what leads her to perceive them as being mad. Are they an expression of her anxiety? They should be seen as disturbed, but with equilibrium. At the end, when Ella returns home, we see that running away is less effective than staying and dealing with the problem: in essence this is the moral of the story.

When given a role in the chorus you need to decide how to tell the story when there is little dialogue. In terms of demonstrating madness in the context, the best way to do it is through physicality. Therefore the madness needs to be physically manifested.

Form a group. The character of Dan will demonstrate a gesture or tic and move around the space to express it. The rest of the group needs to find a gesture. When Dan uses his gesture, the group must follow with their own gestures. Have the group move around using the intention of finding Ella.

Add numbers to the group, only performing the tic when Dan does. Make sure that the characters appear sane otherwise. Add sound if desired. Disperse for a while, until Dan gives a particular movement to bring the group together again (e.g., hand on head). Dan gives another action (e.g., hand on left shoulder) to disperse the group again. Repeat a few times.

This is a very useful exercise to adopt with the chorus. The intensity can increase to show the relatives being quite normal at first and then madder in the forest. You need to decide how that madness will be manifested. The passenger scene is Kafkaesque. Make it sharper, physically.

Dress the actors playing the chorus of relatives at their maddest. Take your inspiration from the Goths or the Addams family or wherever you deem appropriate. Now reveal them to the rest of the cast. Their reactions could be significant. Think of this idea for the moment in the forest.

SCENE WORK

Split into groups of five. Have the chorus explore the following:

1 The opening scene, as the partygoers
2 First appearance of the relatives in the bedroom
3 The passenger journey
4 The ancestors – cavemen to Sir Stephen

5 The rest of the mad family members (to 'light the candles')

Workshop facilitated by Suzy Graham-Adriani,
movement sessions by Lee Lyford,
with notes taken by Emma Thirlwell

THROUGH THE WIRE

Catherine Johnson

Characters

Dan
young offender, seventeen

Chris
Dan's brother, fifteen

Amy
Dan's girlfriend, eighteen

Rashid
young offender, eighteen

Jo
Rashid's girlfriend, seventeen

Becki
Jo's friend, eighteen
(wearing a round charity sticker on her top)

Max
young offender, seventeen

Dom
Max's best friend, eighteen

Scott
young offender, nineteen

Shelley
Scott's girlfriend (eight months pregnant),
seventeen

Philip
young offender, sixteen

Penny
Philip's mum, thirty-six

Andrew
Philip's dad, thirty-nine

Ant
young offender, sixteen

PO Bishop
male or female, early forties

PO Robinson
male or female, thirties

PO Scully
male or female, twenties

PO Greene
female, early forties

Teresa
snack-bar attendant, twenties

Setting

The action takes place in the Visiting Hall of a Young Offenders' Institution. It is a long room with barred windows and locked doors at either end. One door leads from the Visitors' Waiting Room. The other door leads to the Wings.

There are fixed plastic tables and chairs throughout the room. In a corner, there's a play area, with a few toys and paper and crayons. There are posters on the wall about bullying and drug offences.

A small snack bar sells crisps, chocolate, Pot Noodles, hot drinks and sodas. There is a large, overflowing bin next to the snack bar.

By the doors, there are two large desks, manned by Prison Officers. This is where security checks are carried out when the visitors arrive and leave.

The Young Offenders are all male and aged between fifteen and twenty-one. The under-eighteens wear a red sports-bib over their clothes and the over-eighteens wear a blue sports-bib. The younger ones wear green tracksuit bottoms, T-shirts or sweat-shirts and trainers. The older boys wear red tops and jeans or trainers.

The Prison Officers wear white shirts, navy-blue trousers, and black, well-polished shoes. They all have keys hanging from their belts. The number of Prison Officers can depend on the size of the company, but should be at least four.

The Visitors are dressed appropriately for their age and character – e.g., Jo will be revealing more flesh than Becki, Shelley will be in maternity wear, and Dom will be wearing urban sportswear. Hats aren't allowed. Visitors can bring up to ten pounds (note or coins) and a locker key into the Visiting Hall, but nothing else.

A larger company can provide extra Prison Officers, another snack-bar attendant, additional Young Offenders and Visitors, who can be worked into the action as appropriate.

All the action takes place in real time and should seem naturalistic, so that when we are focusing on specific characters the other characters silently continue their story.

Don't be put off by the songs. Enthusiasm, energy and the ability to hit the right notes are more important than West End performances.

. . . indicates where two lines overlap and the dialogue in brackets is to be spoken over by the next speaker.

*As the audience take their seats, 'Through the Wire' by
Kanye West plays.*
   Lights down.
   Music – intro to 'House of Fun' by Madness.

*Lights up on PO Bishop, behind the desk stage right.
PO Scully stands by the door to the Visitors' Waiting
Room, facing into the Visiting Hall. PO Robinson is
behind the desk stage left. PO Greene is in front of the
desk, facing the door to the wings.*
   *Throughout the first verse, the Young Offenders come
in, one by one, and hand their ID cards to PO Robinson.
The door opens and Philip comes in.*

PO Robinson (*sings*)
   Gawd, here they come –
   (*to Philip*) Stand up straight, you scum
   You'll tell your mum? You are that dumb?
   (*to audience*) Heard it all before, yeah, here's the score –
   It's not their fault if they break the law.

Scott comes through the door.

   This boy ain't bad, fucked up by Mum and Dad –

Dan is coming through.

   And he got into drugs –

Max comes on.

   Hangs around with thugs –

Rashid comes on.

   Always gets the blame, he's got a bad name.

Ant comes on.

The poverty-trap – (*out to audience*) it's bull-shit crap.
POs Robinson, Greene, Bishop *and* **Scully** (*sing*)
Welcome to the House of Fun
Now you've come of Age
Welcome to the House of Fun
Welcome to the lion's den
You'll be back again.
Welcome to the House of –
PO Scully (*unlocks door and calls*) Carter?

Amy and Chris come in and go up to PO Bishop – at the same time, PO Greene sends Dan to one of the tables.

PO Bishop (*sings – to Amy*)
Stick your left thumb here –
No, no, your thumb, my dear
I said your left, not right
(*aside*) She's not too bright –
Okay, that's fine – go to table nine.

As Amy turns away.

Young girls inside – I wouldn't let mine.
POs Bishop, Robinson, Greene *and* **Scully** (*sing*)
Welcome to the House of Fun
Now we've got 'em caged
Welcome to the House of Fun
Welcome to the lion's den
They come in boys, leave men
Welcome to the House of Fun.

And now all the Prison Officers do a dance together to the backing of 'House of Fun'. Maybe some nutty-boy choreography – see old Madness videos.

As PO Scully unlocks the door again and Jo and Becki come in –

PO Scully (*sings*)
    Don't worry, son
    It's not so grim
    You'll have some fun
    In the gym
    Ev'ry day there's school
    You'll learn by your mistake
    Even a thick fool
    Can bake a cake.

PO Greene sends Rashid to a table.
    During the next verse, Jo and Becki go through
security with PO Bishop and join Rashid.

PO Greene (*sings*)
    In his heart and mind – life's unkind
    The world's unfair, why should he care?
    He's left behind
    He's hurting, so he'll hurt, I'm here to convert
    He accepts the light, knows what's right
    Welcome to the House of Fun
    You are all god's son
    Welcome to the lion's den
    All Daniels born-again
    Welcome to the House of –
All Prison Officers
    Welcome to the House of Fun
    Now you've come of age
    Welcome to the House of Fun
    Welcome to the lion's den
    You'll be back again
    Welcome to the House of Fun. (*Repeat.*)

At the end of the song, the Prison Officers go back to
their places.
    Rashid and Jo are kissing as PO Bishop passes.

PO Bishop No touching.

Rashid and Jo separate.

Rashid (*to PO Bishop's back*) Jealous, boss?
Jo He'll hear.
Rashid So? Stop him perving.

He leans over and kisses Jo again.

I had a dream about you last night.
Jo A wet dream?
Rashid Come here . . .

Jo leans in and Rashid whispers in her ear. They laugh together.

Becki Don't mind me.
Rashid We won't.
Becki 'Cos I don't want to be here anyway.
Jo Bec, don't be like that.
Becki Well, the sooner I get out of here, the better.
Rashid Nice to see you, too.
Becki I'm sorry, but it's horrible. They take all your stuff off you, even your phone, and then you've got to go through a metal detector and take off your shoes.
Rashid They do that when you go on holiday.
Becki And you get trapped between two doors, waiting for someone to unlock them – there were loads of us, I could hardly breathe.
Rashid I should have said you'd like your own key.
Becki (*to Jo*) You should have said it would be like this. I wouldn't have come.
Jo (*to herself*) Exactly.
Becki It's like a prison!
Rashid Nothing gets past you, does it?
Jo Oh, leave her. She's just a bit nervous.
Becki I feel like a criminal.
Rashid Yeah? Well, take your pick, Bec – 'nuff criminals here.

Jo laughs. Becki looks away, crossly.
    She notices Max, looking over at her. She quickly looks away again.
    Jo is taking a fiver out of her pocket.

Jo (*to Becki*) Fancy something from the snack bar? (*to Rashid*) What's want, honey? Coke?
Rashid Get three cartons of Ribena.
Jo (*holding the note out to Becki*) Three Ribenas, Bec?
Becki Why do I have to go?
Rashid 'Cos I'm not allowed.
Jo And we'd like a bit of time alone?
Becki (*taking the note*) I don't even like Ribena.
Rashid (*to Jo*) Don't bring her again.
Becki I'm never coming again.
Jo Can't we stop this and just have a nice visit?

Becki gets up and goes to the snack bar.
    During the next section, she buys three cartons of Ribena and Jo and Rashid talk and laugh together.
    While this is going on –

Ant (*recites*)
    Buy me chicken Pot Noodles
    A packet of Rolos
    Barbecue Wotsits, a Mars Bar and Polos
    Wine me and dine me
    On Fanta and Crunchies
    These are a few of my favourite munchies.

Becki makes her way back to the table with the drinks.
Max is eyeing her up again.

Max (*to Scott*) Who is *that*?
Scott Rashid's slapper-girlfriend's slapper-mate – fancy it, do you?
Max She's got tits and a pulse . . . d'you think Rashid would put in a word?

Scott Yeah – 'cos that's every girl's dream innit – a prison romance. (*in a girly voice*) 'What's *your* boyfriend do?' 'Six months for burglary and ABH.' Still, on the plus side, it'll be ages before she finds out you're crap in bed.

Max Fuck you.

PO Greene looks over.

Scott Cheers, but I'm spoken for.

Max Fuck off.

PO Greene Max.

Max Sorry, miss.

PO Greene You're too bright to be using such a stupid word.

As she turns away, Scott smirks and nudges Max.
Over at Dan's table –

Amy Dan, I really need . . . (to talk to you).

Dan (*over her – to Chris*) How's it going then, little bruv?

Chris Yeah, you know – usual.

Dan Safe.

Amy Dan . . .

Chris (*at the same time*) . . . Oh, yeah – and Mum says did you get the postal order alright?

Amy (*over*) . . . Dan, can we have . . .

Dan (*over, to Chris*) Yeah, yeah – tell her I'll call her tonight, after 'Stenders.

Chris You know how she worries. (*He glances at Amy.*) Sorry, I interrupted you.

Dan No – I think she was interrupting us – (*to Amy*) Manners, yeah?

Amy You're just ignoring me.

Dan Ah, she's all pissy 'cos I asked her to bring our kid in.

Amy No, I'm not.

Dan You know he can't come in by himself, he's not old enough. (*grinning*) Only a lickle boy.

Amy It's got nothing to do with Chris. I want to talk to you and we haven't got much time.

Dan I got time. (*He laughs.*) Get it? I'm doing *my* time. Get it?

Amy (*sighs*) Yeah.

Dan If you can't do the time, don't do the crime. (*to Chris*) The good old family motto.

Chris I've never heard it.

Dan Well, your dad isn't a jailbird, is he? Your dad's Mr Nice Guy.

Pity Mum didn't meet your dad before my dad, she'd have a nice husband and a nice son and she wouldn't have me, the troublemaking little bastard.

Chris Oh shut it, Mum's never said that.

Amy What's up?

Dan Nothing. Is there?

Amy I don't know. Is there?

Dan I don't know. Is there?

Amy Dan!

Chris (*getting up*) Maybe I shouldn't be here.

Dan (*quickly*) No. (*Beat.*) No – sit down . . . it's just this place, sketching me out.

As Chris sits back down, Amy puts her hand on Dan's arm.

Amy Don't let it get on top.

Dan Yeah – it's that easy.

Amy I didn't say it's easy, just you have to cope . . . . with it.

Dan (*cutting her off*) . . . Don't say anything, 'cos you don't know what it's like.

Sings – to the tune of 'Fly by' by Blue.

'Lectric doors and barred windows
Number two crop and crappy clothes
Hard stares and gangsta pose

579

Gets up – does a boy-band style gangsta pose.

Shout out Stokeleigh YOs!

Max moves forward to join Dan – also throwing boy-band moves.

Max (*sings*)
ABB and TDA
Crazy night got me locked away with the
Tough stuff – rough stuff – yo, I miss muff ev'ry day.

Dan/Max (*together*)
What a life (life)
Inside ('side)
No drink, no drugs and no ride (no ride)
Living like (like)
A Girl Guide (guide)
Think I might just try suicide – suicide

Rashid, Scott, Philip and Ant join the chorus with a choreographed dance.

Young Offenders
Got my head getting block-bound
Got the wing on a lock-down
In bed and I cry – why?
Wish time here would fly by
Got my head getting block-bound
Got the wing on a lock-down
In bed and I cry – why?
Wish time here would fly by –
Fly by – fly by – fly by – fly by.

During Scott's verse, PO Scully opens the door to Shelley and she has her thumbprint checked by PO Bishop.

Scott
Two months' time I'll be a dad
Best news that I ever had

Got banged up – my girl went mad
Need to prove I'm not so bad.

Philip
I did a wicked thing
They stuck me on the muppets' wing
With the rough stuff – tough stuff – get called puff
(And ev'ry thing).

Now the girls sing the bracketed lyrics.

Young Offenders
What a life (life)
Inside ('side)
No drink, no drugs and no ride (no ride)
Living like (like)
A Girl Guide (guide)
Think I might just try suicide – suicide.

Young Offenders *and* **Girls**
Got my head getting block-bound
Got the wing on a lock-down
In bed and I cry – why?
Wish time here would fly by
Got my head getting block-bound
Got the wing on a lock-down
In bed and I cry – why?
Wish time here would fly by
Fly by – fly by – fly by – fly by.

Rashid (*raps*)
Alright, I'll tell you the score, score
I was here last year and now I'm back for more
No next time 'cos I'm through with crime
I said it before
But this is for sure
The last straw.

Ant (*solo*)
What a life

Inside
No drink, no drugs and no ride
Living like a Girl Guide
Think I might just try suicide – suicide.

Everyone
Got the wing on a lock-down
Got my head getting block-bound
In bed and I cry – why?
Wish time here would fly by
Got the wing on a lock-down
Got my head getting block-bound
In bed and I cry – why?
Wish time here would fly by
Got the wing on a lock-down
Got my head getting block-bound
In bed and I cry – why?
Wish time here would fly by
Got the wing on a lock-down
Got my head getting block-bound
In bed and I cry – why?
Wish time here would fly by
Fly by – fly by – fly by – fly by.

*During the last verse, the Young Offenders return to
their places.*
   Scott sits down at a table with Shelley.
   He goes to kiss her, she pulls back a bit.

PO Scully (*opening the door*) Michaels.

Ant starts forward hopefully as the door opens.
   PO Greene stops him.

PO Greene (*to Max*) Table two, Max.

*Dom comes through the door and does the security
thing as Max goes to table two.*

*On his way to the table, Max and Becki exchange a
lingering look.*
*Max sits down at the next table to wait for Dom.
Ant hunches back against the wall.*

Ant (*recites*)
Buy me ice-cream and Kit-Kats
Peanuts and Nik-Naks
Monster Munch, Dime Bar, Pastilles and Tik-Taks
Wine me and dine me
On Coke and Cheese Quavers
These are a few of my favourite flavours.

*During Ant's song, Dom joins Max at his table and
they high-five each other.*

Scott (*to Shelley*) Thought you weren't coming.
Shelley I've been trying to get here all morning – three
 bloody buses, you know?
Scott No – I came the easy way, in the back of a van.
Shelley You're hysterical. I was up at half-seven, you
 know?
Scott I was up at half-seven. Breakfast in bed.
Shelley Nice. You're getting breakfast in bed and I'm
 dragging myself halfway across the country, feeling
 like a sack of shit.
Scott You don't look like a sack of shit.
Shelley I said I *feel* like a sack of shit. Though I expect
 I look like one, too. (*Beat – she's waiting.*) Don't I?
Scott No. You look alright. (*Shelley waits.*) You look –
 great.
Shelley You're going to have to work on your chat-up
 lines.
Scott I don't get a lot of practice in here.
Shelley Glad to hear it.
Scott Don't need chat-up lines, anyway. I'm took.
Shelley You reckon?

Scott Looks like it, doesn't it?

Shelley Don't take me for granted, Scott. I've still got a lot of thinking to do.

Scott C'mon – how's that fair?

Shelley Oh, yes, *please* let's talk about what's fair.

Scott Look, another month and I'm out of here, I can look after you proper, it'll be alright.

Shelley What if you get in a fight and lose your remission?

Scott Why am I gonna get in a fight?

Shelley Because you just do, don't you?

Scott Well, I'm not.

Shelley But you're always 'I'm not gonna get in any trouble' and then you go and do it again. I can't trust you.

Scott No, you're wrong.

Shelley (*quickly*) And I don't like it you've got to be tagged.

Scott I won't get out without a tag.

Shelley It's . . . I don't like my baby's got a daddy with a tag. People might say something.

Scott Okay. Fine. I'll just fucking stay in here, shall I? I'll ask them to keep me locked up and out the way – is that what you want?

Shelley No – but . . . (*She stares down at her hands.*) Scott?

Scott Yeah?

Shelley Is this going to work out – you know, me and you and the baby?

Beat.

Scott Don't you want it to?

Shelley I don't know if you know how much I've changed.

Scott I don't know what you mean.

Shelley Well, before – when you got in trouble – I was
always on your side, you know? No one could say
anything against you . . .

Scott What are you getting at?

Shelley Just . . . now we're not together all the time, I can
sort of see it isn't right . . . it isn't what I really want.

Scott Yeah. (*He exhales.*)

Beat.

Shelley Is that all you got to say?

Scott Yeah.

They stare at each other.
    *Over at Max's table, Dom has been chatting non-
stop.*

Dom . . . Yeah, so Townsy, right, he's getting all feisty
with these kiddies in the kebab-queue, 'cos he knows
me and Robbo's coming round the corner? And we
hears him, yeah? – mouthing off like he was some hard
bastard, so we just walks right past him, like we don't
even know him? – His face, man! Funny as fuck. . .

He laughs at the memory.

Max Who's Robbo?

Dom *Robbo* – oh – that's right, you don't know him, he
only started hanging round with us after you got sent
down? He's funny as fuck.

Max Yeah . . .

Beat.

Seen that new PS2 game been on the TV? I'm going to
ask my old dear if she'll bring it in for me.

Dom Don't bother, man. JB got it, it's fucking crap,
we're all bored with it. Oh fuck, yeah – did I tell you
JB's got this bike?

Max Yeah.

Dom Fucking cool as fuck, he took me for a burn-up and
we nearly crashed the fucker – we was skidding all over
the road, sparks everywhere, yeah? Fucking funny.

Dom laughs at the memory.
    Max leans back in his chair and looks over at Becki.
She looks at him. He smiles.
    She smiles back.
    Opening bars – 'Fuck u Right Back' by Frankee.
    This is a song-and-dance number involving the
whole company. For extra comic effect – and why not
milk this all we can? – the 'fucks' can be bleeped out,
maybe by PO Greene.

Girls
    Oh ohoooh – no, no, no.

Becki (*speaks*) You know, it might not be so bad here
after all.

She sings.

See, I saw
You smile
Now I don't wanna go
Somethin' I
Got to know
Your eyes
Give me butterflies
But it really isn't fair
'Cos you're sat over there
I'd be on ya like a rash otherwise
Don't be too slow, you got nowt to prove
You want me, boy – go on, make the first move
Heart's beatin' too fast I'm in cardiac
Fancy a fuck? – Fuck ya right back
You're a bad boy, I like to break rules

Bonnie and Clyde trip, if you got the balls
You know I'm hot, oh yeah – I'll blow your stack
Fancy a fuck? – Fuck ya right back.

Max (*sings*)
See I saw
You smile
Don't mean to be crude
But I wanna do something rude
Stick me into solitude
I'll be thinkin' of your eyes
I wanna fantasise
When I'm crackin' one off with the guys
Know what – you give me a lob-on
So what if you get a cob-on
I got a load here I need to unpack
Fancy a fuck? – Fuck ya right back
I know this don't sound romantic
Believe you're drivin' me frantic
'Cos you're so hot, girl, I'm blowin' my stack
Fancy a fuck? – Fuck ya right back.

The Company
Whoa whoa, uh-uh yeah
Whoa whoa, uh-uh yeah
Whoa whoa, uh-uh yeah
Whoa whoa, uh-uh yeah.

Becki
Now don't think
I'm a loser
I could get fixed up
Down the club or down the boozer.

Max
I know I'd
Choose her
And I'm no kinda wussy
I had lotsa pussy
Here on the wing guys call me fussy.

Max/Becki (*together*)
So's ya know I'm a hard nut to crack
But you split my shell – I'm under attack
'Cos you're so hot, girl (boy) I'm blowing my stack
Fancy a fuck? – Fuck you right back?
The Company
Whoa, whoa, uh-uh yeah
Whoa, whoa, uh-uh yeah
Whoa, whoa, uh-uh yeah
Whoa, whoa, uh-uh yeah . . .

As everyone returns to their places, Max and Becki
freeze, staring at each other.
     Then they sit back down.
     At some point in the next section, Becki sticks her
badge onto her carton of Ribena.

PO Robinson (*to Philip*) Gatehouse just called, Prosser.
Been a message from your mum – they're stuck in
traffic.
Philip Does that mean they aren't coming, boss?
PO Robinson It means they're stuck in traffic. Whether
they get un-stuck and over here in the next forty
minutes before you go back to your cell, I couldn't tell
you, not being psychic.
Ant Has the gatehouse called about me?
PO Robinson No. (*to Philip*) Cheer up, Prosser. Pray
Until Something Happens.

He moves away, half-smiling to himself.
     PO Greene comes up to him.

PO Greene Why do I get the feeling you're picking on
Philip Prosser?
PO Robinson Paranoid. I'm just taking an interest in
your little band of God-botherers.
PO Greene It isn't that you feel threatened when some
boys don't conform to your prejudices?

PO Robinson Oh, but they do. They all do.

He doesn't wait for a reply – he is off to patrol the room.
Over at Dan's table –

Dan My solicitor thinks I got a chance for appeal.

Amy No, he said you didn't, Dan.

Dan Yeah? So you know more than me, is it?

Amy *You* told me that.

Chris Yeah, you said he rates your chances of getting out on appeal alongside Ian Huntley and Harold Shipman.

Dan Shipman's dead.

Chris Yeah.

Dan Alright, smart-arses, so maybe I'll be home next week.

Amy What?

Chris Nah. (*Beat.*) Is it?

Dan (*to Amy*) Bend over, baby, I'm coming aboard.

Chris Yeah, but – I don't get it. What's happened?

Dan What's it matter what's happened – I'm getting out of here, isn't that good?

Chris Yeah.

Dan Doesn't seem like it. (*to Amy*) What's the matter, babe, why aren't you happy?

Amy I *am* happy. Course I am.

Dan You're not pissed off I'm getting out too soon?

Amy No. What do you mean by that?

Dan Nothing. You're happy, I'm happy – it's all good.

Beat. Amy looks at Chris.

Amy Don't you want to go to the toilet, Chris?

Chris looks at her.

Chris (*guarded*) No.

Dan You don't have to tell him he needs the toilet – he's a big boy now.

Amy I want us to talk. (*She looks at Chris.*) Please?

As Chris, reluctantly, gets up –

Dan Make yourself useful over the snack bar. (*to Amy*) Did you bring any money in?

Amy I've got two pounds.

Dan That's going to go far. (*to Chris*) I'll have a Ribena – whatever the lady wants and get yourself a little treat for going.

Chris Don't suppose I can get a pint?

Dan Only moonshine, and it makes you puke.

Chris takes the money from Amy and goes over to the snack bar. While he's still in earshot –

He's alright, our Chris. I know you think he's a bit of a twat, but he's getting there.

Amy I never said that!

Dan Alright – keep your thong on.

He leans back to address Rashid at the next table.

Why do they come in and just argue with you?

Rashid Yeah – innit?

Dan points at Becki's carton of Ribena.

Dan Oi – what flavour's that?

Becki (*jumpy*) What? . . . (Nothing.)

Rashid (*over her*) . . . Oh, it's just normal, mate – she put a sticker on it. (*to Becki*) Didn't your mum ever tell you not to play with your food?

Becki (*pushing the carton away*) I don't even like it.

Rashid Ungrateful.

Dan I'll have it.

Becki No – you can't – uh . . . (*She looks at Rashid.*)

Rashid Don't be so tight – you're not drinking it.

Becki I know. But . . .

She gives Rashid a little kick under the table.

Rashid Oi – don't start getting feisty with me. I'll get my girlfriend to give you a slap. (*He passes the carton of Ribena to Dan.*) There you go, mate –

Dan (*raises the carton to Becki*) Cheers.

They all freeze in position.

Ant (*steps forward and recites*)
Buy me Hula Hoops, Fruit Loops
Snickers and Mingles
Prawn-flavoured Skips and a tube of plain Pringles
Wine me and dine me
On juice, snacks and sweeties
These are a few of my favourite treaties.

Ant steps back.
Everyone unfreezes and goes back to what they were doing.

Becki (*to Rashid*) D'you know what you've just done?

Rashid taps the side of his nose, smiling.
Jo shakes Becki's arm to distract her attention.

Jo Someone's got an admirer.

Becki looks over at Max, who is looking at her. They both look away.
Rashid laughs.

Rashid Want me to fix you up, Bec?

Becki No.

Jo She does.

Rashid Course she does. He's sound, Max, he's on my wing. He isn't one of the bed-wetters.

Becki Who's the bed-wetters?

PO Scully (*opening the door, calls*) Prosser.

Rashid Prosser. He's a fucking bed-wetter.

Intro – 'Creep' by Radiohead.
   Penny comes in the door, followed by Andrew.
While they are going through the security check,
Philip makes his way to a table.
   Everyone glances at him as he passes.

Philip (*sings*)
   I want to run away
   I want you to find me
   Whenever I was scared
   You were always behind me
   You shouldn't leave me here
   I don't belong in this world
   You said I was special
   So very special –
   But I'm a creep
   I'm a weirdo
   You told me to be strong here
   But it's all going wrong here –
Penny (*coming over*) Sorry we're late, darling – the
   traffic! I was going frantic! Dad had to stop me from
   getting out of the car and yelling at everyone –

She leans over and kisses him.

Oh, it's so good to see you. (*She sits down.*)
Philip Mum, I hate it here.
Penny I know you do, love, I know.
Philip Can't you do something?
Penny But what? You know I would, I'd do anything . . .
   (*Doesn't finish.*)
Philip Please, Mum, please.
Penny Oh, Philip –

She tries to take his hand. He pulls it away.

Philip You're only allowed to touch me at the beginning
   of the visit and the end of the visit.

Andrew (*joining them*) That's a bloody palaver that thumb-print check, isn't it? (*sitting down*) How are you, son?

Philip Alright.

Andrew (*to Penny*) I don't know that I'm happy about my details going into a computer like that. It only takes one cock-up and I'm being mistaken for some bloody criminal.

Penny They've got to do it, Andrew, it's security.

Andrew I know *that*. But no system's foolproof – and it always ends up impacting on law-abiding citizens like me.

Penny Andrew.

There's an uncomfortable silence.

Andrew Well, who'd like something from the cafeteria? I'd kill for a cuppa.

Penny Andrew. Don't be tactless.

Andrew What? It's a figure of speech! Anyway – (*looking around*) – there's not any murderers here, is there?

Philip No.

Andrew See?

Philip They're all at anger-management class this afternoon.

Andrew What?

Penny (*touching his arm*) Do you know, *I'd* like a Ribena. (*to Philip*) Do you want anything, darling?

Philip No thanks.

Penny You must have something. What do you fancy?

Philip Nothing.

Penny Coke? Fanta?

Andrew (*getting up*) He doesn't want anything.

As Andrew heads to the snack bar –

Penny But we must get you something.

Philip Can you get me out, Mum?

Penny looks across at him.

Penny (*sings*)
  I thought you were special
  So very special.
All Young Offenders (*turn towards Philip and sing*)
  You're a creep
  You're a weirdo
  What the hell are you doing here?
  You don't belong here.
Penny
  You've got to be strong, dear. Try and get along here.

  Chris goes back to Dan's table with a carton of Ribena and a packet of crisps.

Dan Oi – you took your time. Wasn't like there's a crush at the bar.
Chris (*with a look at Amy*) I thought you wanted left alone.
Amy You needn't have bothered. He spent all the time chatting to the next table.
Dan Yeah, give her that Ribena, 'cos I had hers.

  Chris holds the Ribena out to Becki.

Becki No ta.
Rashid Take it.
Dan Yeah, go on – take it. He'll get all offended if you refuse his gift.
Becki (*reluctantly taking the Ribena*) Thanks.

  On Max's table, Max is watching Becki and Chris while Dom rambles on.

Dom . . . Nick Smith's playing funny fuckers, going around . . . like he owns the place.
Max (*over, about Chris*) Oi – what's his game?
Dom Are you even listening to me?

Max Yeah . . .

Dom No you ain't – you're just gawking like a gay. She isn't even that fit.

Max She's alright.

Dom Ah – should've been down 'Sticky', Saturday night. 'Nuff sexy women, man.

Max Yeah, what was I thinking to miss that?

Dom You'll be out soon.

Max Won't be soon enough, will it? End of this visit, I'll be back on the wing and she'll be walking out with that wanker.

Dom looks over at Chris.

Dom Want me to twat him outside? He won't look too impressive when I've headbutted him.

Max Yeah, that'd be clever, nutting someone right outside a nick. You in that much hurry to be my pad-mate?

Dom Oh – that'd be funny as fuck.

Max No, it wouldn't, you mong, you don't want to end up in here.

Dom I'll fucking end up here anyway, every fucker's getting whacked with an ASBO. Just for being in the fucking park! Fuck that – we always hang out in the fucking park – they can stick their fucking ASBOs – what about human rights, yeah?

Music – intro. to 'YMCA' by the Village People, and into a big song-and-dance number, with the hand movements.

Dom (*sings*)
Young man
You can go anywhere
I said, young man
You can mouth-off and swear
I said, young man

Give the old 'uns a scare
Make 'em glare, it makes us happy.

Max (*sings*)
Young man
They won't leave you alone
I said, young man
They ain't just gonna moan
I said, young man
They'll get straight on the phone
Call the cops, now it gets crappy.

Everyone (*sings*)
Oh, here we go –
It's an ASBO
Oh, here we go –
It's an ASBO.

Prison Officers
You can't do anything a young man would enjoy
You can't hang out with all the boys.

Everyone
Oh, here we go –
It's an ASBO
Oh, here we go –
It's an ASBO.

Young Offenders
I can't be young and free, I can't do what I feel
Break a butterfly on the wheel.

PO Bishop
Young man
Stay away from the park
I said, young man
Don't go out after dark
I said, young man
Every neighbour's a nark
And they want to get their pay-back.

Dom
Fuck that –

We're enjoying ourselves
I said, fuck that
Weren't they young once themselves?
I said, fuck that –
Can't you look to yourselves
Are we worse than kids from way back?

Everyone (*sings*)
  Oh, here we go –
  It's an ASBO
  Oh, here we go –
  It's an ASBO.

Prison Officers
  You can't do anything a young man would enjoy
  You can't hang out with all the boys.

Everyone
  Oh, here we go –
  It's an ASBO
  Oh, here we go –
  It's an ASBO.

Young Offenders
  I can't be young and free, I can't do what I feel
  Break a butterfly on the wheel.

Everyone
  ASBO
  Oh, here we go –
  It's an ASBO
  Young man, young man, don't be a cunt
  You can't do whatever you want
  ASBO
  Oh, here we go –
  It's an ASBO
  Young man, young man, you think it's not fair
  Young man, young man, blame Tony Blair
  ASBO

Everyone returns to their places.

597

As Shelley sits down, she is saying –

Shelley I feel sick.
Scott I thought you'd got past that?
Shelley Yeah, I get a bit gassy and it makes me feel sick.
  I need a good burp.
Scott Get yourself a Coke or something.
Shelley Yeah, I will – do you want anything?
Scott Do you want to get me anything?

*Shelley gets up. She looks down at Scott, who is sitting
with his arms folded looking around the room.*

Shelley Are we going to talk about this?
Scott What's the point?
Shelley The point?
Scott 'Cos you know what I do in here? You know, at
  night? I think about every shit thing that could
  happen, play it over and over like a fucking video of
  my life . . . I've done this already. I know what it feels
  like.
Shelley Scott . . .
Scott Get me a Ribena, yeah?

*Beat – then Shelley heads off to the snack bar, upset.
She nearly bumps into Andrew, who is carrying a tea,
a carton of Ribena and a small packet of Jaffa Cakes.*

Andrew Whoopsie –
Shelley Sorry.

*She continues to the snack bar, but overhears Andrew,
who is setting the drinks down on his table.*

Andrew Isn't that a depressing sight?
Penny Shsh.

*Shelley glances back, but she doesn't say anything.
  At the snack bar –*

Teresa Hiya. How's it going?

Shelley Yeah – alright. Kicking all the time now.

Teresa Ahh – has your boyfriend felt it kicking?

Shelley Yeah . . . (*She sighs.*) I don't know . . . I'm having a really crap visit, actually.

Teresa No? What's wrong?

Shelley Scott thinks I want to finish with him, but I don't. It's the last thing I want to do.

Teresa Yeah – you really like him, don't you?

Shelley I do, I love him. But I don't want him to go on the way he was before, you know?

Teresa Well, no. You don't want him in and out of prison for the rest of his life, do you?

Shelley No, and I was just trying to say that, but – it's like he doesn't care if I finish with him or not?

Teresa Oh, he does.

Shelley I don't know – we never planned to have a baby, but I thought he was pleased, but maybe now he's been away for a bit he's changed his mind? Like, why should he want to get out of one prison and straight into another?

Teresa Did he say that?

Shelley No, but . . . he didn't not say it.

Teresa Well. If you don't get it sorted this visit, you're just going to go home all worried and that's not going to do you any good. Or the baby.

Shelley No . . . no, you're right – it's crap trying to talk on the phone, we only get a couple of minutes and everyone else is there, listening in and shouting for their turn.

Teresa Talk it out now.

Shelley Yeah. Ooh, can you quickly get me a Ribena and a Coke – I'm busting for the loo?

Teresa That's me, nattering on.

Shelley No, you've been really helpful. I'll miss our chats when Scott gets out.

Teresa gets the drinks and Shelley hurries back to the table.

(*putting the drinks down*) Here, I'm going to the loo, I'm wetting myself.

Scott Give us your pissy knickers – they'll go for a fortune on the wing.

Shelley (*walking off*) Get lost, Scott!

Scott (*after her*) I'm joking! Shell –

Shelley doesn't turn round.
  Shelley asks PO Bishop to unlock the door.
  He lets her out. At the same time PO Robinson speaks to Ant.

PO Robinson Who've you got your visit with, Carter?

Ant Mum.

PO Robinson She wants to get a move on. Can't stroll in whenever she feels like it.

He starts to move off.

Ant Boss?

PO Robinson Yes?

Ant Can you ring down the gatehouse, see if she's here yet?

PO Robinson Oi, you cheeky little fucker, I'm not your private secretary, am I? I know the lunatics are taking over the asylum, but that's a cake-take.

He goes to the desk and picks up the phone.

Ant (*recites*)
  Make me ham and cheese toasters
  Steak pie and roasters
  Mug of hot chocky for dipping my Boasters
  Stories at bedtime
  A bell on my bike
  Please can you make me a mum I would like?

PO Robinson (*putting down the phone*) No one's seen your old dear, Carter. Mind you, it isn't last orders yet, is it?

He walks away.
Over at Dan's table –

Dan Yeah – anyway. I was joking about that appeal.

Amy What?

Dan I'm not getting out, am I? Not till they send me to big boys' nick. (*laughing*) Just a bit of a wind-up, guys, something to liven up the visit.

Chris Twat.

Amy Do you really think that's funny, Dan?

Dan Don't you?

Amy I think you're being a fucking pain in the arse, to be honest.

Dan Yeah, now you're being honest.

Amy Oh, piss off. I've had enough of this. (*She gets up.*) We're finished.

Chris Hang on . . . (*Doesn't finish.*)

Amy (*at Chris*) Hang on for what? You know? I can't do this any more. (*to Dan*) I'm sorry, but I mean it.

PO Scully (*coming up*) Everything alright here?

Dan Yeah, boss – (*to Amy*) Everything's fine, isn't it?

Amy doesn't reply, but she sits back down.
No one speaks till PO Scully goes away, then Amy leans forward.

Amy I mean it, Dan. I'm sorry. I didn't want to do it like this. You made me.

Dan Are you dumping me?

Amy I can't do this any more.

Dan Do what? What's your problem? I'm the one banged up, not you –

Amy sings – to the tune of the Dido sample from 'Stan' by Eminem.

Amy

    All my days drift by the same into nights
    I spend alone
    I need to hear you say my name but you
    Don't even phone
    I did everything with you
    And I'm nothing on my own
    Now I can't go on
    No, I can't go on . . .

Dan (*raps – over 'Stan' backing track*)

    Hey, babe, meant to write you coupla days ago
    Got headed notepaper here and a leaky Biro –
    Its end all chewed to fuck by some other bored YO
    Fuck, am rambling on here, what d'you want to know?
    So – hello, miss you, love you, cheerio –
    I know you're wanting pages, but what is there to say?
    Got up, had my breakfast, just like any fucking day
    Don't wanna write shit about this place anyway
    I'm gonna do my nut – miss you like fucking crazy,
    Miss your scrut – so keep it shut
    Got to cross that out or you'll be giving me some earache
    Yeah, I do, I trust you, but you're not here, for fuck's
      sake
    And it's getting to me now, yeah it's keeping me awake
    I know you're a good girl, but even good girls make
      mistakes
    I know this isn't what you want to hear in a letter
    I'll chuck this one away and write again, but better
    Don't wanna upset yer, ah fuck it, what to say?
    Not today.

Amy (*sings, again to the Dido sample*)

    All my days drift by the same into nights
    I spend alone
    I need to hear you say my name but you
    Don't even phone
    I did everything with you

And I'm nothing on my own
Now I can't go on
No, I can't go on . . .

Scott (*shouts – cutting off the song*) Miss! Oi – miss!

PO Greene comes over as Scott gets up.

PO Greene Sit down, Scott – you know you're not allowed to wander around during visits.

Scott Yeah, but it's my missus, miss – I don't know where she's got to?

PO Scully (*wandering over*) Got a problem, Scott?

Scott No, boss – just my missus ain't back from the bog yet?

PO Scully Do you think she's done a runner?

Scott I don't know, boss.

PO Scully We'll let the dogs out, she won't get far.

PO Greene (*to Scott*) I'll just check the Ladies, she's probably powdering her nose.

PO Scully She'd better fucking not be!

PO Greene (*gives him a look*) Powder? Toot? Cocaine? . . . Come on, Rosemary, didn't the Good Lord bless you with a sense of humour?

PO Greene Oh, he *did* . . . but then he sent me to work with you bunch of comedians.

PO Greene walks over to the door to the Visitors' Waiting Room and unlocks it. She exits. When she is out of earshot.

PO Scully You don't have to be mad to work here, but it helps.

Scott (*sitting back down*) Think you'd have to be total barking to work here – no offence, boss, but you don't actually like this place, do you?

PO Scully (*laughs*) Well, I wouldn't mind Parkhurst or somewhere – somewhere they got proper bad lads, real crims – not you pathetic little mam's boys with your spray-cans and your bags of weed. Bet you hear some good stories in a place like Parkhurst.

Scott For real? You'd rather have them than us?

PO Scully Don't be a twat. They give some right nasty bastard his day in court and they lock him away – end of story. Only it isn't, is it? Who has still got to deal with the right nasty bastard?

Scott The screws.

PO Scully The *prison officers*, Scott – that dedicated bunch of men and women who every day throw in their lot with the dregs of society. Who are civil to the least civilised.

Scott I couldn't hack that. If I was a scr – *prison officer*, and I knew someone was a kiddy-raper or something, I'd have to give him a beating, it's only right.

PO Scully Well, if I did that, I'd get done. No. I'm better off with you guys – short, sharp shock and some of you might just turn out alright.

Scott What about Prosser?

PO Scully Don't start me on Prosser. I'll never understand the Prossers of this world and I don't want to . . .

PO Scully/Scott (*together, sing*)
He's a creep
He's a weirdo . . .

They laugh together.

Scott Well, I'm not coming back when I'm gone.

PO Scully I haven't heard *that* before.

Scott For real, boss. I don't know what's going on with me and Shelley, but I'm going to be there for the baby, I'm going to be a good dad . . .

He breaks off as PO Greene returns. She is looking anxious.
Scott gets up as she hurries over.

PO Greene It's okay, Scott, nothing to be alarmed about.

Scott What's happened?

PO Greene She's fine – Shelley's fine, Scott, don't worry – but it seems her waters have broken and we've had to call an ambulance.

Scott (*shaking his head*) No! No way. No – she's weeks off.

PO Greene Well, sometimes you can have a bit of an early – leakage – and really, then, the best thing to do is get straight to hospital . . . (for a check-up).

Scott (*heading for the door*) No. No way. She can't go to hospital.

PO Scully (*trying to grab him*) Scott –

PO Greene (*at the same time, going after them*) Scott, you know you can't leave this room!

PO Bishop is moving towards the door.
    Dan, Max and Rashid are getting up. Everyone shouts at once while Scott is trying to barge past PO Scully.

Dan What's going on?

Rashid Run, Scotty – run!

Scott Come on, let me out – I want to see her!

PO Scully Alright, Scott, calm down . . .

Scott No, I won't calm down. My girlfriend's fucking hurt out there.

PO Greene She's alright, Scott – she told me to tell you not to worry.

Scott I want to see her.

PO Greene We have called an ambulance and she'll be in very good hands, Scott.

Scott So are you going to let me see her?

PO Scully Not now, Scott.

Scott Fuck you!

He headbutts PO Scully, rushes for the door.

*PO Bishop, PO Greene and PO Robinson struggle
to restrain him – using the proper legal restraint
methods, of course.*

PO Scully Ow – you little bastard!

*As the Prison Officers try to bring Scott under control,
everyone has a comment to make.*
Teresa comes out of the snack bar.

Rashid Do 'em, Scott – do fucking Robbo, the prick!

Teresa Scott – stop it – you're only making it worse for
yourself!

Jo What's he done? What happened?

Andrew (*to Penny*) This is unacceptable – I'm getting
you out of here.

Penny But we can't just *go*.

Andrew (*getting up*) It's an issue of personal safety.

Philip No! Don't leave me!

Max (*punching the air and chanting*) Scott-y! Scott-y!
Scott-y!

Dan/Rashid (*joining in*) Scott-y! Scott-y! Scott – y . . .

PO Bishop (*rounding on them*) Sit down and shut your
traps! Or I'll have you back on the wings and all visits
cancelled for a month!

Scott has been brought under control.
Everyone starts to sit down, with mutterings.

Rashid They can't do that.

PO Bishop It's not a threat – it's a promise!

Andrew (*to Penny*) It's a shambles, if you ask me. They
should have stun-guns.

Rashid (*to Jo and Becki*) We got rights, they can't stop
our visits.

Penny (*to Andrew*) Honestly! They can't go around
shooting people.

If there are any non-speaking Prison Officers, they can take Scott off – back to the wings. If not, PO Scully and PO Bishop take him, as he is marched away –

PO Greene (*to PO Scully*) Are you alright, Joe? Better get a check-up.

PO Scully I'm good. It's this little twat needs checking out.

Scott (*his head held down*) Fuck the fucking lot of you.

Teresa (*calls after him*) Shut up, you idiot! Don't you care what you've done here?

Scott and his Prison Officers exit. As he passes Ant:

Ant Hey – Scotty? You showed 'em, man.

Scott Did I fuck.

Scott and the Prison Officers are gone.
    A buzz around the room.

Rashid (*rubbing his hands*) 'Nuff excitement for an afternoon. (*Calls across.*) Oi! Danny-Boy! Good visit!

Dan Yeah, man. Whatever.

Max (*across to Becki*) You alright?

Becki (*smiling at him*) Yeah.

Max Thought it might've freaked you out a bit?

Dom It was cool as fuck! You shoulda all piled in, fucking riot.

Max (*to Becki*) Ignore him, he's a thicko.

Becki I will.

They smile at each other.

Max/Becki (*sing together*)
Smile on your face, addictive as crack
It's cooler than base, it's nicer than smack
This is the deal, girl (boy) – there's no holding back
Fancy a fuck? – Fuck you right back.

*They are leaning towards each other. PO Robinson
steps between them.*

PO Robinson No canoodling between tables, Michaels.
You've got your own visitor to play with.
Max There's no rule against talking.
PO Robinson There is now. Or do you want to join your
pal down the block?

*As Max leans back, disgruntled, PO Robinson smiles
to himself.*

Didn't think so.

PO Greene is walking to the snack bar with Teresa.

Teresa She was getting all upset 'cos she thought he
didn't care about her.
PO Greene She's got no worries there – (*as they pass
Philip's table*) Ooh, I could murder a cup of tea.
Andrew (*to the table*) See, *they're* allowed to say the 'm'
word. (*to PO Greene*) Excuse me?

PO Greene and Teresa exchange a little look.

Teresa I'll dig out the Earl Grey.
PO Greene Bless you. (*She joins the table.*) Hello, Philip.
This must be your mum and dad.
Penny Hel . . . lo.
Andrew (*interrupting*) Look, what's going on here? I'm
worried about your security – that boy nearly escaped.
PO Greene He wasn't doing any escaping through
alarmed and electric doors, sir.
Andrew Well, shouldn't someone obviously so volatile
have his visits separate from the others?
PO Greene It was an unfortunate incident, it's very
unlikely to ever happen again. (*to Penny*) I found his
girlfriend in the Ladies, too frightened to move, poor
girl. She's expecting a baby and things have started
happening a bit too early.

Penny Oh dear – oh, how sad.

PO Greene It doesn't excuse Scott's violent outburst, of course. That's the problem with a lot of these lads, they just don't know how to control their emotions.

Andrew Well, they have to *learn*. What kind of society would we have if everyone started shouting and hitting out when they didn't get their own way?

Penny We've never had that problem with Philip, of course.

She covers his hand with hers and smiles across at him.

Andrew (*with an edge*) No, Philip's always been nice and quiet.

Philip pulls his hand away. PO Greene smiles at him.

PO Greene Well, he's not so quiet in church on Sundays – I can hear his lovely singing way over all the others.

Penny Church? Philip doesn't go to church.

Philip Yes, I do, Mum.

Penny But we don't . . . (*to PO Greene*) . . . we don't really approve of *church*.

Andrew Philip's never been in his life. Well, apart from his christening, of course.

PO Greene If Philip has been baptised into the House of God, he's welcome to come home any time he chooses.

Penny But I don't suppose this is a *choice*, is it? I expect it's something you make them do. And don't call it 'home'. His home isn't in the church, it's with us.

PO Greene I'm sorry if this upsets you. But I feel Philip's found some comfort through prayer and Bible readings.

Penny (*to Philip*) Have you?

Philip Yes.

Penny But – why didn't you talk to me about it first? (*to PO Greene*) I'm sorry, I just think this is a mistake, this is going to change him.

Philip I want to change, I hate myself.

Penny But darling, I've told you – it doesn't matter what you've done, you're still my Phil and I will always love you and support you.

Philip I don't want to be me any more – (*about PO Greene*) She says I can be different, I can be born again.

Penny No, you can't! (*to PO Greene*) He's been born, okay? I didn't go through a twenty-hour labour with no pain relief just to be scrubbed out of the picture sixteen years down the line.

PO Greene I think it would be very interesting if we made some time to discuss this together.

Penny Discuss what?

PO Greene Well . . . what it means to Philip, what you can do to help?

Penny Me? I can't do anything – I can't choose his meals, I can't sit down in the evening and watch TV with him, I can't give him a hug when he's feeling piggly . . . (I can't . . .)

PO Greene Don't worry about the hugs, Philip knows he can always come to me when he wants a bit of mothering.

Penny stares at PO Greene – her face thunderous.
Music – intro to 'Wannabe' by the Spice Girls.
Penny stands.

Penny
Shall I tell you what I want, what I really, really want?
PO Greene
Yes, tell me what you want, what you really, really want.
Penny
I'll tell you what I want, what I really, really want.
PO Greene
So tell me what you want, what you really, really want.
Penny (*sings*)
I wanna, I wanna, I wanna, I wanna
I wanna really, really, really wanna slap your face hard

Think you're taking over?
Well, hold that thought
I won't stand by and watch you try
I know your sort.

PO Greene (*sings*)
Now don't be hasty, I'm on your side –

Penny
I've heard that line before, Miss – Self-Satisfied
I'll tell you what I want, what I really, really want

Everyone
So tell us what you want, what you really, really want.

Penny (*sings*)
I wanna, I wanna, I wanna, I wanna
I wanna really, really, really wanna slap her face hard.

*Everyone joins in on the chorus – a choreographed
routine. The Prison Officers who left come back on.*

Everyone
If you wanna be a mother
You've got to give up your life
Loving like no other
Father, friends or wife
If you wanna be a mother
You are gonna hurt
When the whole world and his brother
Calls your kid 'pervert'.

Penny
What do you think about that?

PO Greene
Now you know how I feel
The Lord hears every prayer –

Penny (*in her face*)
Are you for real?

PO Greene
Don't give me eyeball
And screw your scorn

I've got him on the Bible
Off the kiddy-porn
Yo – I'll tell you what I want, what I really, really want.

Everyone
So tell us what you want, what you really, really want.

PO Greene
I wanna, I wanna, I wanna, I wanna
I wanna really, really, really wanna slap her face hard.

Everyone
If you wanna be a mother
You've got to give up your life
Loving like no other
Father, friends or wife
If you wanna be a mother
You are gonna hurt
When the whole world and his brother
Calls your kid 'pervert'.

Penny/PO Greene
I'll slam your body down and wind it all around.

Everyone
Slam your body down and wind it all around
Slam your body down and wind it all around.

Penny/PO Greene
Slam your body down and slap your face hard.

As the song plays out, everyone returns to their places. Penny and PO Greene are still standing, glaring at each other.

Penny
If you want to be a mother, Mother . . .

Andrew Penny – sit down, everyone's looking. (*to PO Greene*) I apologise – my wife's been under a lot of pressure since – you know . . . (*Doesn't finish.*)

PO Greene There's a law against threatening members of staff. Your visits may be stopped forthwith.

Penny But . . . please don't do that!

PO Greene (*laying a hand on Philip's shoulder, to him*)
I will have to report this. I'm sorry. (*to his parents*)
And it means a closed visit next time.

Andrew What's that?

PO Greene You'll be in a room on your own and
separated by glass.

Andrew Oh now, come on – there's no need for that.

PO Greene I wouldn't want you to think we don't take
security matters seriously, sir.

*Philip laughs. PO Greene squeezes his shoulder, starts
to walk away.*

Penny (*to Philip*) I'm losing you. I just know it.

Philip Mum . . .

Penny (*to Andrew*). . . I have to get out of here – if I stay
another moment, I'm going to cry.

She stands up. As she does, Ant steps forward.

Ant (*recites*)
When the screws shout
When it's lights out
When I'm feeling sad
I simply remember where
I stashed some snout
And then I don't feel so bad.

Penny (*staring at Ant*) Who is that boy waiting for?

Philip (*turns*) Oh. His mum. He sends her Visiting
Orders, but she always forgets. Or can't be arsed.
(*quickly*) That's what *he* said.

Penny God. How sad. (*After a moment she sits back
down.*) Some mothers.

*At Dan's table, Dan is fiddling with the sticker on the
Ribena carton and not looking at Amy or Chris.*

Amy This is well pointless, just sitting here, not saying
anything.

Dan What do you want me to say? Thanks for dumping me – it's alright, I understand?

Amy I didn't mean to hurt you, Dan.

Dan doesn't say anything.

Look, I'll just go now, shall I? And you have the end of your visit with your Chris.

Dan Just take him with you, he's not allowed to be here on his own. He's too young.

Amy No, we'll stay if you want?

Dan What's the use?

He holds his hand out to her.

No hard feelings, yeah?

Amy No, I . . . I hope we can stay friends.

As Amy takes Dan's hand –

Dan (*loudly*) What the fuck? (*Shouts.*) Boss! Boss! Over here, boss.

PO Bishop is hurrying over.

Amy What are you doing?

Amy drops something on the table. PO Bishop picks it up.

PO Bishop What's this?

Amy I don't know.

Dan She just tried to pass me these pills, boss.

Amy No, I didn't!

Dan (*to Amy*) I told you I didn't want anything brought in! I told you I don't do drugs – why are you trying to get me into trouble?

Amy What the hell are you talking about?

Becki Rashid –

Rashid Shut up.

Dan (*to PO Bishop*) Believe me, boss, I never asked her to do this.

PO Bishop Well, I don't suppose you'd be shouting around the room about it if you had.

Chris This is fucking ridiculous, we don't know anything about any pills.

Dan They're right here – on the table! I didn't put them there, did I?

PO Scully (*joining them*) Alright, let's get this sorted. You two had better come with me.

Amy But we haven't done nothing! He just put them in my hand.

Dan Oh what? I don't believe this – you're not going to try and stick this on me?

Becki But what's going on?

Rashid puts his finger to his lip.

Dan You know I couldn't have had those pills, boss – I got searched before I came in here.

Chris You bastard.

Dan No, you're the bastard, bro – did you think I was going to let you get away with this – (*to PO Scully*) – oy, boss – check their locker, I bet you'll find something in his wallet – pills, skunk . . . (ketamine).

Amy They won't find bloody *anything* in the locker!

Chris is staring at Dan.

Chris Prick.

Dan laughs.

Amy Chris? They won't find anything?

Dan Didn't you know what a little dealer your new boyfriend is, babe?

Amy and Chris look at each other, then quickly look away.

Never goes anywhere without his stash. (*to Chris*) Only not very cool to bring it in here. You'll get a few years for that.

Amy Dan –

Dan What? Have I spoilt your little surprise? Sorry, but did you really think I wouldn't hear? In here? Even your mates wrote me.

Becki This is crap.

Rashid It's got nothing to do with you.

Chris (*going for Dan*) You two-faced, lying, double-crossing prick!

Dan Takes one to know one.

PO Scully pulls Chris off. PO Bishop takes hold of Amy's arm.

Amy (*to Dan*) I didn't pass you those pills. Tell them. You know I didn't.

Dan I don't know how you can just stand there and lie.

Chris Listen – maybe I asked for this, but you can't do it to Amy. She hasn't done nothing wrong. You're just being selfish. If you cared about her you wouldn't expect her to live her life around one-hour-a-week visits.

Dan You got that arse backwards – *I'm* the one's got to live around hour-a-week visits and now you're both gonna find out what that's like.

Becki But this is wrong!

Jo They deserve it.

Dan (*to Prison Officers*) Bang to rights, or what?

PO Scully and PO Bishop start to lead Amy and Chris away.

Amy No! No – you can't do this, it's not fair – please, please, Dan.

Dan sits back down, smirks over at Rashid.

Becki (*getting up*) I did it.

Rashid Will you shut the fuck up?

Jo What are you doing?

Becki I'm the one brought the pills in. (*to Rashid and Jo*) Sorry.

Rashid I don't know what she's on about. She's fucking mental.

Max Oi!

Jo (*hisses*) Bec – if you dob us in, I will never, ever forgive you.

> *PO Bishop and PO Scully are bringing Amy and Chris back to the tables.*
> *PO Robinson and PO Greene are coming over.*

PO Scully (*to Becki*) Let's get this straight. You say *you* brought in these pills and passed them on to this young lady?

Amy I've never seen her before in my life.

Becki No, no – I didn't pass them on to anyone, they were mine – I had them on a sticker and – um – I sort of took the sticker off and put it on a Ribena carton, you know, um – just messing around?

Rashid (*catching on*) Yeah – yeah – and then Dan asks for a drink, right? And I gives him the Ribena? I didn't know nothing about any pills.

PO Bishop So how did the pills get from a sticker on a Ribena carton to being dropped on a table? *Somebody* was passing *something*.

Amy I told you – Dan put them in my hand – I didn't know what it was?

PO Robinson Right. Chuck the lot of 'em in a van and get them down the nearest nick. Let's get to the bottom of this bullshit.

Becki But it was just an accident, nobody meant to do anything wrong.

PO Robinson Nobody . . .? You are aware of the penalties for bringing drugs into a Young Offenders' Institution? You are looking at a prison sentence, no danger.

Max (*getting up*) Yeah, but boss, isn't that if you're bringing something in with intent to supply? I mean, if it was her – (*to Becki*) Sorry, I don't know your name?

Becki Becki.

Max Becki . . . yeah, if it was Becki's personals, well, fair play she shouldn't have brought them in here, but you could let her off with a warning, couldn't you?

PO Robinson Ah. How gallant. No.

Max Well, you're all wankers. I mean, someone makes a mistake – one mistake –

Jo (*getting up*) It isn't drugs, anyway.

Dan/Rashid (*together*) What?

Jo It's my mum's homeopathic pills for her stiff knee.

PO Robinson That's drugs.

PO Greene Under what classification?

Jo We were playing a trick – Dan wanted to wind up his girlfriend 'cos he'd heard she was knocking off his brother. So Rashid asked me to bring in some fake pills and I'd give them to Dan and then he'd say – well, you know . . . but we didn't think anyone'd get into trouble because it's not really drugs, is it?

Dan/Rashid (*together*) Yeah, that's right. That's it exactly.

Jo And I'm really sorry, Bec, for getting you involved.

Dan (*to himself*) Fakes.

Jo (*to the Prison Officers*) I made Becki put the knee-pills under her sticker because I thought if we got searched on the way in and I've got them, I wouldn't get this visit and I'd *die*.

Rashid I didn't know it meant that much to you.

Jo It's what I live for. I count every second of every minute of every day.

Rashid grabs Jo. They kiss.

PO Robinson Right. I am terminating this visit now. All
YOs will be up to see the governor and all visitors
looking at closed visits for a month.
Come on. Everyone out.
Rashid But we still got a few more minutes.
PO Robinson I said 'now'.
Rashid And I say, bollocks. You got us, boss – you got
us every hour of every day of every week and you
think that means you got us nailed, but this time –
these sixty minutes – I'm not in here, I'm back where
I should be – and I'm not giving up a second of that.

*The Young Offenders all cheer and whistle and stamp
their feet.*
     *Song – 'I'll Be Missing You' by Puff Daddy and
Faith Hines.*

Rashid
     Every day I wake up
     My pad-mate's groanin'
     Dreamin' 'bout his girl and
     Givin' her a bonin'
     Hearin' screws unlock the doors, shouts across the wing
     Ain't goin' down for breakfast
     I'll just lie here on my bed and think about something
     I'll think about givin' you a pearl necklace
     Make that two, I'm feelin' reckless
     But I got tears instead
     Thinkin' about you
     Got the cold shivers
     For all that we've been through
     I miss you, Jo
     Can't wait till that day, when I see your face again
     I can't wait till that day, when I see your face again . . .

Max moves over to Becki.

Throughout this verse, the Prison Officers should quietly withdraw to the back of the room.

Max

Know, never saw myself as a Romeo
Love at first sight and all that crow
Believe, I got no future, got no dough
But now I don't wanna let you go.
This ain't the way it'll always be
I'll be so good if you can trust me
I can handle this half-arsed regime
If you'll let me have this one dream
In the future, can't wait to see
If you'll be waitin' at the gates for me
You don't have to give an answer, I can't cope
Goin' back inside, knowin' there's no hope
Let me look forward to that release day
Got my own clothes back and my prison pay
Steppin' outside with alacrity
You and me together, forever free.

Becki (*sings*)

Every step I take, every move I make
Every single day, every time I pray
I'll be missing you.

Jo (*sings*)

Thinking of the day, when you went away
What a life to take, what a bond to break
I'll be missing you.

Dom

Hasn't been the same since you got done
Shit we used to do isn't so much fun
Catch myself walking round to your place
'Member you're gone like a slap in the face
Doin' things I want to share with you
Sometimes wish I was there with you.

Andrew

> Every night I stare at your photo
> The one on the TV – you know –
> At the holiday bungalow?
> Took it down, put in a drawer
> You look so happy, it's too raw
> Then I started staring at the blank space
> Remembered terror on your face
> It's back in place, that way I won't forget
> When this hadn't happened yet
> I don't wish you hadn't been born at all
> I still love you, but it's a close call.

All the Female Visitors

> Every step I take, every move I make
> Every single day, every time I pray
> I'll be missing you
> Thinking of the day, when you went away
> What a life to take, what a bond to break
> I'll be missing you.

During the next section the Prison Officers take up their positions by the doors.
> *The Visitors silently embrace the Young Offenders.*
> *The Visitors and the Young Offenders drift off to their separate sides of the hall.*

Everyone

> Every step I take, every move I make
> Every single day, every time I pray
> I'll be missing you
> Thinking of the day when you went away
> What a life to take, what a bond to break
> I'll be missing you.

Spotlight on Shelley stage right and Scott stage left. Scott is sitting on the floor, taking his laces out of his trainers.

Shelley

On that morning
When this life is over
I know
I'll see your face.

Scott stands. He has tied the laces together. He puts the laces round his neck and pulls tight.
Cut light on Scott.

Everyone

Every step I take, every move I make
Every single day, every time I pray
I'll be missing you
Thinking of the day, when you went away
What a life to take, what a bond to break
I'll be missing you.

Fade lights.

End.

I'll Be Missing You

Catherine Johnson interviewed by Jim Mulligan

In a long room with barred doors at either end, prison officers, young offenders and visitors meet for one hour. Anything could happen but probably the least expected thing would be that, at the end, most of the characters will understand themselves better than when the visit started. In *Through the Wire*, Catherine Johnson has blended songs and dialogue to create realistic characters who tell stories that we listen to with compassion.

> In *Through the Wire* I wanted to tell a story about what it is like when a member of your family or a loved one is in prison. I had this opening image of prison officers dancing to *Madness* – I took it from there and I was able to write the lyrics to fit the story. For me the songs have to drive the story as much as when the characters are speaking. The dramatic thrust should always be in the songs. They have to have a purpose: either the characters are telling the audience their innermost thoughts or they are revealing something to another member of the cast.

Embedded in the songs and raw, realistic dialogue there are the stories about each of the young offenders and their visitors. There is the battle between PO Greene and Philip's mother for Philip's soul. There is the story of the lonely sixteen-year-old Ant waiting once again for a visit from his mother. There is the story of the unrequited love of Max and Becki, whose eyes meet in the visiting room. There is the story of drugs entrapment when Dan conspires with Rashid to take a vicious revenge on his

girlfriend who is leaving him for his half-brother Chris.
And there is the story of Scott and Shelley who, we are
led to believe, are reconsidering what their future might
be when Shelley has her baby.

Catherine Johnston is non-judgemental about the way
society deals with young people who are seen by many
people as a menace. The prison officers are not monsters
and the visitors are being punished just as much as the
people they are visiting.

I really wanted to show the visitors' side of things.
I hope we see the difficulties of being in a relationship
with a young offender, whether you are a mother or a
father or a girlfriend or a close friend. The offenders
have a life that is regimented but those on the outside
are dealing with great difficulties just getting by or
catching three buses to make a visit. Their loneliness
is just as acute as it is for the offenders. I suppose the
bottom line is that the offenders will leave the prison
but the prison officers are stuck with the job, and the
visitors have to go back and cope.

Catherine Johnson does not flinch from the realities of
life for young offenders. She understands that their hard
front is often bravado, covering up hurt and bewilder-
ment, sometimes leading to suicide, and that they are not
good communicators. She has a keen ear for the speech
they use and inevitably her characters swear. She is aware
that this could lead to problems with schools and she has
prepared a version that will be more acceptable to head
teachers and governing bodies.

It annoys me when I am asked to change things for
television but I totally understand that schools might
have difficulty doing this piece, even though I know
that, when swearing is cut from lines, it breaks up the

rhythm of the piece. The play is, after all, about young offenders and swearing is very much part of the way they speak. However, I honour the fact that schools have chosen my play and I have done what I can to make it acceptable.

Despite the bleak context, *Through the Wire* is a hopeful play in the sense that, in the final song, the characters say what they really feel and come to a greater understanding of their relationships. Rashid can't wait for the day when he sees Jo's face again. For the first time in his life Max sees a future with a woman he loves, and Becki responds with her love. Dom feels the absence of his friend like a slap in the face. But the most poignant, because Philip's offence is the one that is hardest to understand and forgive, is the confession of his father, Andrew, that he still loves his son and has put his photograph back on the TV so that he won't forget him. It was an inspired choice of song that allows the play to end with everyone singing, 'Every step I take, every move I make, every single day, every time I pray, I'll be missing you.' The power of this affirmation is strong enough to help us accept the tragedy of Shelley, who can sing: 'When this life is over, I know, I'll see your face.'

A lot of the relationships come out of this visiting hour a little stronger. A new relationship has started and, despite the tragedy of the suicide, I think the tone of the song will leave the audience with a sense of hopefulness rather than despair. I didn't set out to write a warning about the horrors of a young offenders' institution. But I wanted to make it authentic. The experience of relating to something dramatically gives a greater understanding than, for example, a visit to a prison. In a drama you step into an imaginary world. As a member of the audience you are invited into a world and can live in it for an hour. If you are in the production, you are caring about your characters and you will come away from it thinking about them. You will have an insight into what it is like for them and for their families. You should be able to say, 'Those young people could be me or could be my children. Those visitors could be me or my girlfriend or my mother.'

Production Notes

THE PLAY

Catherine Johnson was inspired to write this play after visiting a Bristol Young Offenders' Institution. Her play is about what it's like having somebody close to you on the inside. It shows the perspectives of both the young offenders and the visitors. Visiting time is the one hour where the two meet, and it's where the most interesting things happen. A drama develops at each table and people get lost in their own world, even though the next table is only a foot away.

The play is not written to convey any overriding moral tone. The character development is the most important element of the script, and all sides in the story are of equal importance. The Prison Officers and the Young Offenders have their own story, and both sides are represented through the different songs. Because of this equal representation, the audience are able to make up their own minds and form their own opinions about what they see onstage. There is a sense of understanding and sympathy for the Prison Officers because they are doing a very difficult job. They are at opposite ends of the spectrum: Greene is biblical, and her singing could represent this by being in a gospel-choir style, while the strict and cynical Robinson abides by the rules and regulations, viewing the Young Offenders in a much more demeaning manner.

When the Young Offenders enter, they stay in a block until their visitors come in. They could stand against the wall until a Prison Officer calls their name, which would set up a sense of control between the Young Offenders and Prison Officers. The Young Offenders cannot move by themselves.

DESIGN AND STAGING

The audience will get a very clear idea about what the environment is like from the way it is lit and how the piece is set. Different techniques can be used to create a sense of claustrophobia: the tables could be set very close together, or the lighting could be structured so that it features in an intimidating way on the stage – spotlights, bright lights, shadows and low-hanging bulbs can all add to this.

The set could start by having either a positive or negative aesthetic. The opening statement is very important, as this is a piece that lends itself to atmosphere. Using a cracker (ten per cent smoke) would make the mood very theatrical, drawing attention to the beams of light and not just the effect of the light itself.

MUSIC

There is a website for karaoke tracks allowing you to download instrumental versions of the songs used in the play. The lyrics scan exactly with the backing tracks, so the performance can be done using pre-recorded music.

The process of selecting the music varied from knowing immediately what tracks were going to be used, due to the nature of the script, to listening to different tracks and getting a sense of the atmosphere that each might create and how this could enhance the play.

Different songs lend themselves to being performed in different ways and styles: a karaoke backing track for 'YMCA'; acapella/acoustic for 'Creep'; guitar/rock style. There are no rules, rather it is about working with the abilities and strengths of your cast. The music numbers can be big dance numbers or small introverted solo pieces.

Make the musical instruments a part of the action. If your production is going to take place in a community hall, then have the piano in the corner dusted off. A guitar could be lying around or could belong to one of the Young Offenders. The ways in which the instruments are used also affects the atmosphere in the room.

The audience will be very familiar with most of the songs and will expect to hear the lyrics they are used to. This means it is even more important to enunciate each and every word. Make sure the consonants are exaggerated in all of the songs: the cast might practise singing in very posh voices to get used to every word and sound.

MOVEMENT/CHOREOGRAPHY

Think of ways to get into the song, out of the song and into the next scene as smoothly as possible – moving from a naturalistic state to an over-the-top musical number that is distanced from reality, then returning to the naturalistic state. If the set needs to be moved it can be integrated as part of the dance piece.

As in all musicals, there is the possibility that the choreography is not real, but is happening in the head of the person singing. In that case, imagination is the only restriction there is.

Choreography can be a way of stopping movement rather than necessarily creating it.

Play with tables and height. By placing the tables on wheels you would be able to have more flexibility with movement, using the rest of the company to move them backwards and forwards.

STAGING THE PLAY

From the moment the play begins, we need to create a sense of confinement and imprisonment. Spatially the Young Offenders are confined, so the audience needs to get a sense of this as soon as they step onto the stage. Experiment with different entrances and what statement the characters are making when they enter.

Both the Prison Officers and the Young Offenders are entering at the same time, and their status needs to be established straight away. PO Robinson is the focus of 'House of Fun' at the beginning, and as the other Prison Officers sing we see their status and relationship with each other develop.

Why has Becki come with Jo to visit? The audience should be asking themselves this question. She is bringing drugs in, but she wasn't expecting the place to be like this. Security is high and she has been searched. Her description of the environment should inform the audience's perception.

What have the Young Offenders done? This the cast can decide, though in some cases it emerges from the lyrics: Max is guilty of ABH (actual bodily harm) and TDA (taking and driving away) – 'Crazy night got me locked away . . .' Max's back-story should ensure that the audience develops a sympathetic connection to him, and make it clear that he can and does want to reform. This is a first offence, whereas Rashid is a repeat offender.

Assign the offences to help form the background to the piece: look at a variety of offences from burglary to murder, and why they were committed. (A boy who breached an ASBO might be placed next to a boy who has murdered someone.)

And how did the girls meet the boys? Such back-stories help to establish the emotional state of the characters and inform the hour they will be spending together.

Why is Ant singing and to whom? He could be singing to whomever is at the snack bar, or to anyone who glances at him while he is standing alone waiting for his mum to turn up. His music should begin running underneath before he begins , and then carry on for a short time after he finishes to lead smoothly into the next scene.

As Becki makes her way back to the table with the Ribena and looks at Max, make sure that this moment is made clear. Take time over all the moments that Becki and Max share: it's as though nothing else exists around them.

What we see in the first encounter of Dan with Amy and Chris is supposedly just a family reunion, but the audience don't know at this point that Dan has a lot more information than he's letting on. The idea of subtext is very important in this scene and would be worth looking at with the cast. (If you're under eighteen you have to be accompanied by someone who is over eighteen. This is the first time that Chris has visited.)

In 'Fly By', the girls should sing an octave lower in order to be singing in the same pitch as the boys. When the girls are not singing they should distance themselves slightly from what is happening and observe from the chairs at the side. ('Got my head getting blockbound' – the block is the wing, and indicates a mental state of being stuck in the block and shut away.)

The dance could be stylised or have a naturalistic feel: this is up to the director and dependent on the resources and abilities of the group. It could be a continuation of the style that has already been set up, or a complete break. You could use the music as a break and change the lighting – snapping to a musical state with different colours and effects.

Think about what happens to the other characters while the song is going on. The characters singing could use the different levels of the tables to stand on and create a performance space. The sequence should tell the audience that we are no longer in a reality.

When the girls start singing there is an element of surprise. The audience do not expect the passive characters to join in. This could be a funny moment.

Philip is an outsider, so without saying anything you can set this up onstage when he sings, in the way the other characters react to him and what he sings about. ('They stuck me on the muppets' wing' – where vulnerable offenders such as sexual offenders are kept together.)

What is Shelley's motivation in her conversation with Scott? She has moved on while Scott is still regular as clockwork and stuck on repeat. She has managed to distance herself from her situation and her relationship with Scott, and to look at both more objectively.

Dom isn't bringing any good news for Max. Life is moving on outside the centre. Dom gives Max a reason not to go back to where he was. Dom is building his life up because he misses Max and he doesn't really know what his function is when he is visiting Max.

'Fuck You Right Back', which could be performed as a pastiche of the pop video, could be quite sexy with the characters singing at opposite ends of the room from each other. The tables could be set up in a row with the group at each table having their own conversations. The Prison Officers could be walking up and down providing the percussion or using their whistles to bleep out the swearing. The song has a feeling of a twenty-first-century Danny and Sandy (from the musical *Grease*).

Max and Becki walk towards each other across the tables on a journey during the song. This adds a fantasy element, developing the pop-video style. This song is a perfect example of blending reality and imagination. Becki and Max could be acting it out or imagining it in their heads. This is the beauty of musical theatre and why there are no limits to what you are able to do with each song. As for 'Fly By', play with different states during the musical numbers. Percussion could be created using the everyday props that are surrounding the characters, such as Ribena cartons or crisp packets. (This could also be a comical way of bleeping out the swearing – crunching on the crisps or slurping the Ribena.)

The introduction to the song needs to be loud, with the chorus acknowledging the switch into a musical number with a change of position or a turn of the head as the first note is sung. The song has a strong comic element to it, so use this in the choreography.

The chorus should remain still during the duet and solo moments but make clear movements at key points during the song.

In the next section between Dan, Chris and Amy, Dan is trying to push Chris and Amy towards admitting to their relationship, and the audience should begin to realise that there is more to this relationship than first appeared.

The sticker on the Ribena has been planned between Becki, Rashid and Jo. Becki is reluctant to give the Ribena to

Dan. She thinks the drugs are for Rashid, but it transpires that Rashid and Dan have planned this exchange to frame Amy and Chris.

The song 'Creep' confirms Philip's status as a loner. His parents arrive late, setting him even further apart from the others, and the fact that he is not being visited by friends or a girlfriend accentuates his awkwardness. The music could continue after Philip stops singing to heighten the atmosphere and underlying emotions in this scene.

What is the relationship between Philip and his parents? They are an aspiring middle-class family. Explore the physicality of the parents. Andrew (Dad) appears to be trying to cover up his shame at being in a place like this and is clearly uncomfortable. Both parents are ashamed, but Penny (Mum) has a very different perception of the visit.

The character of Philip is very complex. He was an amateur magician who performed tricks at children's parties and then took something too far. It was a one-off incident. Penny sees the incident as a teenage thing that Philip went through and will grow out of, but Andrew sees it as something much more serious. There are clearly issues between Andrew and Penny as they try and deal with what Philip has done.

'ASBO' could involve the whole company. The number happens about halfway through the play, to inject a higher level of energy. You can choose to tell the story as it is sung or you could do a big dance number, but be adventurous: the song is so familiar across generations that you can push it into a fantasy world. Busby Berleley elements would work in this context. ('Break a butterfly on the wheel' – when two members of the Rolling Stones were sent down for drug offences, *The Times* wrote an editorial with this title. It can be interpreted as an

634

overreaction to something – in the case of the Young Offenders, taking a young free spirit and breaking it.)

The Village People are making statements by the way they dress, and the song extends this statement. The melody makes the piece feel positive regardless of the words that are spoken/sung. The characters could remain in character as they sing, accentuating the difference between the Prison Officers and the Young Offenders, and helping to enunciate the words and tone. This song opens up possibilities for using the set: perhaps panels could be rotated to show the letters A-S-B-O.

It is a long number, so there are opportunities to explore different dynamics and relationships. There are also comical elements that can be developed – e.g., Shelley, a heavily pregnant girl, dancing, then going straight into a serious scene with Scott, when she says she feels sick.

Scott thinks from what Shelley is saying that he has been dumped. He thinks that this is the reason for her visit. The Young Offenders have lots of time on their hands to think about the past and re-run situations over and over in their heads. It is frustrating that they're stuck inside, and yet for everyone else on the outside time is passing and people are changing. With Shelley, her body is evolving, so it is a very noticeable change that Scott can see, but her mind is changing as well. Shelley is undergoing a physical transformation. (Tagging – attaching a band containing a chip that is attached round the ankle. A box is placed in the home and the tag must be in range of the box at the time of curfew, between seven in the evening and eight in the morning every day. The tag must stay on until the end of the sentence. It is only offered to those who are deemed not to be a risk to society.)

Shelley tries to articulate what she wants from Scott, but neither is capable of saying what they really want from the other. Because of this, the conversation gets more confusing between them, resulting in miscommunication.

Investigate and develop a back-story for Shelley. She appears to be alone and isolated. She came in by herself and, as she mentions, she had to come a long way to get to see Scott. The look of Shelley is very important: is she frail and vulnerable or strong and independent? This visual image loads the dice for the audience. She may have got stronger since Scott has been inside, since she has had to deal with certain situations and events alone. Even though she loves Scott, she may have to decide to tell him to go for her own sake and for the sake of her child. She is a torn but sympathetic character, and the audience should want her to make the right decision.

Everyone feels sorry for Ant. He is waiting for his mum, who never turns up. He sings to himself throughout the play, and the others pay little or no attention to him. There is a sense that the other characters all want his mum to turn up.

Dan is being provocative , pushing Amy into admitting what is going on. She has no choice but to tell him what we find out he already knows about her and Chris.

The rap in 'Stan' could be pre-recorded, allowing the Young Offenders to be writing and even more detached from the loved ones who have come to visit. (Each table could have a drawer from which its occupant pulls paper and a pen and begins to write.) What Amy is singing about and Dan is rapping about is representative of all the Young Offenders and their girlfriends.

Think about ways of staging this scenario. Amy and Dan could be singing to each other or to the audience. This choice will affect the meaning and interpretation of the song.

This song is about two people who are finding it difficult to communicate with each other because of their different circumstances. The irony of the song becomes apparent because if they were able to hear what the other was saying then things might be different. Dan is trying to articulate how he feels to Amy, and what the audience hears is his internal monologue and struggle with himself and his situation. When he is rapping, he is reflecting. This could be done as a voice-over, or be lit differently to draw attention to the change in atmosphere.

There is a lot of tension in the song. The lack of touch and the fact that all letters are read before they are sent out contributes to the feeling of isolation and guarded emotions. All the Young Offenders are very young, and haven't yet learnt how to communicate properly with each other; their lack of social skills may be partly why they have found themselves in trouble.

It becomes clear that the Prison Officers, like some of the boys, have complex relationships. These relationships should be explored to discover how the dynamics work in the Visiting Room and how people interact with each other.

Scott appears to be more mature than some of the other boys. He has responsibilities to deal with on the outside. His scene confronting the Prison Officers is quite difficult to direct. There is lots happening within the room, and each of the separate groupings has to react in its own way to the situation between Scott and POs Greene and Scully. There is a gradual descent into chaos, which can be achieved by creating a solid structure to begin with and then letting it break down step by step.

Scott obviously wants to be with Shelley when she gives birth. He is supposed to be out by that time, which until this point has been keeping him going. He believes that things will get better when he becomes a dad. Now, he believes that had he said something different to Shelley she might not be going into early labour. The last thing he said to her was almost insulting and this is what he remembers. He is frustrated with himself, and his violent reactions come out of a desire to care. This is even more upsetting because the audience know that he has good intentions and only wants to be with the one he loves.

Scott realises what he's done and that he will have lost his remission. He has gone against everything he said he was going to do, and in the process he has broken his promises to Shelley about not getting into any more fights. Within a period of about five minutes he has thrown everything away.

The incident demonstrates the impact of locked doors and being trapped. All of the Young Offenders have to have the door unlocked for them. They are unable just to turn the handle and walk out, which is something that we all take for granted.

PO Greene comes across as a missionary. She appears to be recruiting and Philip is her target. This could be portrayed in either a negative or positive light. It might be that Philip is moving from one kind of control to another – or that a figure like PO Greene will help him oversome his dislike of himself and what he did. PO Greene believes that Penny drove Philip to his sin, but this is not necessarily the case.

'Wannabe' is a very light and happy song with a very dark content. It could begin in the style of a light-hearted Spice Girls number and end up as something more sombre.

The Spice Girls often spoke and sang about their mothers and the relationship each one of them had with her mother. This song is about a battle for possession, and for this reason it is very important where Penny and PO Greene are placed on the stage and where Philip is positioned in relation to both of them. He might change position during the song to emphasise what is being said and what affect this has on him: is he freaking out, crying or becoming frustrated by what is being said? Philip's reaction is crucial to your interpretation of this scene.

There are points when PO Greene does appear to be a nasty piece of work, as when she announces the need for a closed visit next time. However, if she didn't follow the procedures, then one of the other officers would. Despite this, there is a sense that she enjoys the moment by restricting the contact Philip has with his mother and therefore being able to tighten her own grip.

Dan places the pill into Amy's hand and accuses her of smuggling it in. There will be consequences to deal with, though these are not discussed. Becki was asked by Jo to come with her to visit Rashid and put the pills under the sticker she was wearing on her top. Jo told Becki that Rashid wanted them. Becki doesn't know about the plan that has been concocted between Dan, Rashid and Jo. Dan and Rashid thought they were real pills.

Jo is the only one who knows everything. She gave Becki her mum's knee pills to bring in, knowing that Rashid was going to pass them to Dan so that Dan could frame Amy and Chris to get back at them both for cheating on him. This explains why Becki was so reluctant to let Rashid give her Ribena carton to Dan, but Rashid knew what he was doing. Chris is in trouble because he will have a stash of something with him and Dan knows this. Dan has framed him, knowing that he is a drug dealer and wanting Amy to realise that she has made a mistake. Amy will not be in any trouble.

'I'll Be Missing You', the closing song, is a poignant opportunity for *touching* – a key element within the choreography, since the beginning and end of a visit are the only times that touching is allowed between the offenders and their visitors. Touching is something that we take for granted when we make contact on a daily basis. If it is normally denied, as in prison, an opportunity to touch is even more dramatic and moving.

The final image of Scott pulling the laces round his neck and hanging himself could just be a snapshot to ensure that the audience know that Scott has committed suicide. As Shelley sings and we see her in her final image, she is holding the baby to show the audience that Scott missed out on the one thing that he wanted to live for.

Workshop facilitated by Wayne Harrison,
music sessions led by Nicolas Bloomfield
and movement sessions by Darren Royston,
with notes taken by Imogen Kinchen

Participating Schools and Companies

Participating Schools and Companies

Activate Youth Theatre, Cork
Ad Lib Theatre Company, Cheltenham
Albany Youth Theatre, London
Allerton Grange High School, Leeds
Allerton High School, Leeds
Arc Theatre's Arc Youth Company, Trowbridge
Arnold School, Blackpool
Artsdepot, London
Ashcroft High School, Luton
Astor College for the Arts, Dover

Bablake School, Coventry
Barking College, School of Performing Arts, Barking
Behind The Scenes Youth Theatre, Buckhaven
Belmont School, Durham
Berzerk Productions, Reading
Best Theatre Arts, St Albans
Bishop Perowne CE High School, Worcester
Bishop Thomas Grant School, London
Bishop's Stortford Youth Theatre, Bishop's Stortford
Blue Coat CE Comprehensive School, Walsall
Bodmin Community College, Bodmin
Boomerang Youth Theatre, Cork
Borderline Theatre, Ayr
Borders Youth Theatre (Scottish Borders), Darnick
Boston Spa Comprehensive School, Wetherby
Brewery Arts Centre, Kendal
Bridlington School, Bridlington
Broadland High School, Hoveton
Brune Park Community School, Gosport
Burton Borough School, Newport, Shropshire
Burton Youth Theatre, Burton-upon-Trent

Business Academy, Bexley
Bydales School, Redcar

CATS Youth Theatre, Blackfield
Cabinteely Youth Theatre, Dunlaughaire, Co. Dublin
CADA Performing Arts, Cork
Caister High School, Great Yarmouth
Callington Community College, Callington
Camborne Community College, Camborne
Cardinal Newman RC Secondary School, Luton
Castell Alun High School, Hope, Wales
Castleford High School Technology College, Castleford
Caterham High School, Ilford
Catteral Hall, Settle
Celbridge Youth Drama, Dublin
Chafford Hundred Campus, Grays
Cheadle and Marple Sixth Form College, Marple
Chester Gateway Theatre, Chester
Chichester Festival Youth Theatre, Chichester
Chorlton High School, Manchester
Churston Ferrers Grammar School, Brixham
City College, Norwich
Classworks Theatre, Cambridge
Clifton Comprehensive School, Rotherham
Coleg Sir Gar, Llanelli
College of West Anglia, King's Lynn
Company of Teens, St Albans
Coopers Technology College, Bromley
Coulsdon College, Old Coulsdon
Crawshaw School (Jigsaw), Leeds
CRE8, Yeovil
Crofton High School, Wakefield
CRYPT, Warehouse Youth Theatre, Croydon

Dolman Youth Theatre, Newport, Wales
Dumont High School Youth Theatre, New Jersey
Dunraven School, London

EO45 Theatre, West Suffolk College, Bury St Edmunds
Ealing Hammersmith and West London College

Eastleigh Borough Youth Theatre, Eastleigh
Ellesmere College, Ellesmere
Estover Community College, Plymouth

Far East Theatre Company, North Walsham
Flies On The Wall Youth Theatre, Stroud
Flintshire Youth Theatre, Mold
Forest School, Horsham
Fowey Community College, Fowey
Francis Combe School and Community College, Watford
Fresh Perspectives, Mansfield
Fusion Theatre Company, Stevenage

Glenthorne High School, Sutton
Gordonstoun School, Elgin
Grays School, Grays

Hall Green Little Theatre (Youth Section), Solihull
Harrogate Theatre HT2, Harrogate
Haydon School, Eastcote
Haywood High School, Stoke-on-Trent
Headington School, Oxford
Heaton Manor School, Newcastle-upon-Tyne
Hemsworth Arts and Community College, Pontefract
Heywood Community High School, Heywood
Hope Valley College, Hope, Derbyshire
Hove Park School, Hove
Hreod Parkway School, Swindon
Huddersfield Technical College, Huddersfield

Ian Ramsey Church Of England School, Stockton-on-Tees
Independent Youth Theatre, Dublin
Intrepid Theatre (in association with Sussex Downs College), Lewes
Invicta Grammar School, Maidstone
ITV Junior Workshop, Nottingham
Ivybridge Community College, Devon

Jigsaw Youth Theatre Company, Barnet

Kennet School, Thatcham
Kidbrooke School, London

Kildare Youth Theatre @ Crooked House, Newbridge
Kimbolton School, Huntingdon
King Edward VI Upper School, Bury St Edmunds

Lewes Priory School, Lewes
Leyton Sixth Form College, London
Longdean School, Hemel Hempstead
Longley Park Sixth Form College, Sheffield
Lyndon School, Solihull
Lytchett Minster Youth Drama Company, Poole

Maelor School, Wrexham
Manor College of Technology, Hartlepool
Marple Hall School, Stockport
Mayfield School and College, Dagenham
McEntee School, London
Melbourn Village College, Royston
Methwold High School, Thetford
Mold Players Youth Works, Mold
More House, London
Much Wenlock Youth Theatre, Much Wenlock
Myrtle Theatre Company, Bristol

National Youth Theatre, London
Nescot College, Epsom
New Bridge Integrated College and Twiglet Theatre Company,
    Banbridge, Co. Down
New Everyman Youth Theatre, Liverpool
New Venture Youth Theatre, Hassocks
Ninestiles Technology College, Birmingham
North Cumbria Technology College, Carlisle
North Nottinghamshire College, Worksop
Nunthorpe Secondary School, Nunthorpe

Oaklands Community School, Southampton
Out of Eden Youth Theatre (in the Highlands), Inverness
Oval House, London
Oxford University Dramatic Society (OUDS), Oxford

Palace Theatre Watford's Youth Theatre, Watford
Park High School, King's Lynn

Parson's Mead School, Ashtead
Patcham High School, Brighton
Performance Academy, Newcastle
Perse School for Girls, Cambridge
Pilot Youth Theatre, York
Players and Faces @ Barnwell, Stevenage
Polka Theatre, London
Portsmouth High School, Portsmouth
Preston Manor High School, Middlesex
Prior Pursglove Sixth Form College, Guisborough
Pump House Children and Youth Theatre, Watford

Queen Elizabeth's Community College, Crediton
Queen Elizabeth's Grammar School, Horncastle
Queen Mary's School, Thirsk

Redbridge Community School, Southampton
Redruth School, Redruth
Regent College, Leicester
Rickmansworth School, Rickmansworth
River Theatre Company, Stanford-le-Hope
Rodillian School, Wakefield
Rossholme School, Highbridge
Royal Lyceum Theatre, Edinburgh

SFLA Shenley Court, Birmingham
Shetland Youth Theatre, Sheltand Isles
Sir Frederic Osborn School, Welwyn Garden City
Skelmersdale College, Skelmersdale
Smestow School, Wolverhampton
South West Youth Theatre, London
Southwark College, London
Southwell Minster School, Southwell
Springwell Community School, Chesterfield
St Benedict's School, London
St Benet Biscop High School, Bedlington
St Clere's School, Stanford-le-Hope
St Hilda's CE High School, Liverpool
St John Fisher Catholic High School, Harrogate

St John's School, Episkopi, Cyrprus
St Julian's School, Newport, Wales
St Julie's School, Liverpool
St Martin in the Fields High School For Girls, London
St Mary's RC Comprehensive school, Newcastle-upon-Tyne
St Mary's Youth Theatre, Leeds
St Monica's High School, Manchester
St Peter's School, Bournemouth
Stage 65, Salisbury
Stephen Joseph Theatre, Scarborough
Stocksbridge High School, Stocksbridge
Stoke Sixth Form College, Stoke-on-Trent
Straight Up Theatre Company, Wellingborough
Stratford-upon-Avon College, Stratford

Tamarside Community College, Plymouth
Tarleton High School, Tarleton
The Abbey School, Reading
The Academy at Peckham, London
The Beacon School, Banstead
The Bolsover School, Chesterfield
The Castle Arts Centre, Wellingborough
The Croft Drama Group, Carshalton
The Elizabethan High School, Retford
The Folkestone School for Girls, Folkestone
The Freewheelers, Leatherhead
The King's School, Peterborough
The Lindsey School and Community Arts College, Cleethorpes
The Loft Theatre Group, Exeter
The Manor Theatre Company, London
The Northampton School For Girls, Northampton
The Park School, Corscombe
The Purbeck School, Wareham
The Ravenscroft School, London
The Swinton High School Arts College, Manchester
The Trinity Catholic Technology Centre, Leamington Spa
The Trinity School, Nottingham,
The Westgate School, Winchester
Theatre Antidote, Larnaca, Cyprus

PARTICIPATING SCHOOLS AND COMPANIES

Theatre Royal Winchester, Winchester
Theatre Royal Young Company, Plymouth
Thomas Lord Audley School and Language College, Colchester
Thurrock and Basildon College, Basildon
Thurrock Youth Theatre, Horndon-on-the-Hill
Toonspeak Young People's Theatre, Glasgow
Toynbee School, Eastleigh
Tremor Theatre Company, Worcester
Tron Skillshops, Glasgow
Twynham School, Christchurch

Valley Park Community School, Maidstone
Varndean School, Brighton
Vienna International School, Vienna

Walton Girls' High School, Grantham
Warneford Youth Theatre, Highworth
Washington School, Tyne and Wear
Westfield School, Gosforth
Whickham School, Newcastle-upon-Tyne
Whizz Kids Theatre Company, Ely, Cambridgeshire
Winterhill School, Rotherham
Wired Youth Theatre, Leicester
Wortley High School, Leeds
Wycliffe Youth Theatre, Stonehouse

Xpress Theatre, Camberley

Yarborough School, Lincoln
Yeovil College, Yeovil
Young Actors' Theatre Islington, London
Young Dramateers, Dublin
Ysgol Aberconwy, Conwy

REGIONAL PARTNERS

Brewery Arts Centre, Kendal
Brighton Dome
Castle Arts Centre, Wellingborough
Clwyd Theatr Cymru
Everyman Palace Theatre, Cork
Greenwich Theatre
The Lowry, Manchester
Nottingham Playhouse
The Playhouse and The Garage, Norwich
Old Vic Theatre, London
Royal Lyceum Theatre, Edinburgh
Stephen Joseph Theatre, Scarborough
Theatre Royal, Bath
Theatre Royal, Newcastle
Theatre Royal, Plymouth
Watford Palace Theatre